T0331991

Before Method and Models

OXFORD STUDIES IN THE HISTORY OF ECONOMICS

Series Editor:
Steven G. Medema, PhD, University Distinguished Professor of Economics,
University of Colorado Denver

This series publishes leading-edge scholarship by historians of economics and social science, drawing upon approaches from intellectual history, the history of ideas, and the history of the natural and social sciences. It embraces the history of economic thinking from ancient times to the present, the evolution of the discipline itself, the relationship of economics to other fields of inquiry, and the diffusion of economic ideas within the discipline and to the policy realm and broader publics. This enlarged scope affords the possibility of looking anew at the intellectual, social, and professional forces that have surrounded and conditioned economics' continued development.

Before Method
and Models

The Political Economy of Malthus and Ricardo

RYAN WALTER

OXFORD
UNIVERSITY PRESS

OXFORD
UNIVERSITY PRESS

Oxford University Press is a department of the University of Oxford. It furthers the University's objective of excellence in research, scholarship, and education by publishing worldwide. Oxford is a registered trade mark of Oxford University Press in the UK and certain other countries.

Published in the United States of America by Oxford University Press
198 Madison Avenue, New York, NY 10016, United States of America.

© Oxford University Press 2021

Library of Congress Cataloging-in-Publication Data
Names: Walter, Ryan, author.
Title: Before method and models : the political economy of
Malthus and Ricardo / Ryan Walter.
Description: New York, NY : Oxford University Press, [2021] |
Includes bibliographical references and index.
Identifiers: LCCN 2021011904 | ISBN 9780197603055 (hardback) |
ISBN 9780197603079 (epub)
Subjects: LCSH: Malthus, T. R. (Thomas Robert), 1766–1834. |
Ricardo, David, 1772–1823. | Classical school of economics. |
Economics—Great Britain—History. | Great Britain—Economic policy. |
Great Britain—Economic conditions—1760–1860.
Classification: LCC HB161 .W255 2021 | DDC 330.15/3—dc23
LC record available at https://lccn.loc.gov/2021011904

DOI: 10.1093/oso/9780197603055.001.0001

1 3 5 7 9 8 6 4 2

Printed by Integrated Books International, United States of America

Para Carolina: muchas gracias por compartir tu vida conmigo.

Acknowledgements

This book would not have been possible without the generous support of the Australian Research Council (DE130101505), which allowed me to commit to a long-term project of this type. I am also grateful to Terry Peach, who sponsored my stay as a Visiting Scholar at the University of Manchester, where he cured me of my residual attachment to the 'corn model' reading of Ricardo. Sergio Cremaschi was a perfect host in Bergamo, as were Dennis Grube and Jason Sharman in Cambridge, and Richard Whatmore in St Andrews. Special thanks are due to Alexandre Mendes Cunha for the chance to preview the casuistry chapter at his Center for European Studies in Belo Horizonte, and to Gilbert Faccarello, Masashi Izumo, and Hiromi Morishita, who kept their guests safe after the earthquake in Sapporo in 2018. The most important setting for the development of this book's argument, however, has been my own institution, the University of Queensland. For my university boasts a rare bird: a research institute dedicated to intellectual history, formerly the Centre for the History of European Discourses and now the Institute for Advanced Studies in the Humanities. The core of the argument that is presented here was rehearsed there during a Fellowship in 2017, and I thank all those who provided feedback of such quality during my seminars.

Many colleagues found time to read chapters and offer help along the way, some despite being sorely pressed by their own deadlines. I am obliged to Lorenzo Cello, Alex Cook, Knud Haakonssen, Nick Heron, Ian Hesketh, Ben Huf, Gary Ianziti, Amy Jelacic, Leigh Penman, Mark Philp, Anna Plassart, and Richard Van den Berg. David Kearns has seen all the chapters in various states in his invaluable roles of research assistant and friend. Sergio Cremaschi and Niall O'Flaherty were kind enough to share draft manuscripts with me.

The support of four friends has been indispensable to this project from the beginning. Ian Hunter has always been willing to discuss my work in detail, and I am conscious of what a privilege this represents. Keith Tribe has been unfailing in both offering support and exemplifying the scholarly attitude since my PhD days. Conal Condren has been instructing me on how to study language for more than a decade, patiently. Richard Devetak encouraged me to return to Brisbane to pursue intellectual history in the subtropics and then provided the camaraderie that I needed to stay the course when it became difficult.

I would like to tally a final debt due to Donald Winch who passed away in 2017, to his discipline's great loss. In 2015, he agreed to meet me at the White Hart in Sussex so that I could pitch him the idea for this book. After hearing how many traps I was planning to walk into, it took him two pints to set me straight. I am glad that he did.

Contents

Conventions

The texts under study in what follows belong to a pattern of thought that is patriarchal in the strict sense: the government of the polity by politicians and legislators was discussed using metaphors and presuppositions that drew on the old idea of a father's government of a household. This is most visible in the tendency for 'economy' to be written with the ligature, hence 'œconomy', disclosing that the term is cognate with the Greek *oikos* (household) and *oikonomia* (the art of house-holding). Accordingly, gendered language has been used throughout this book to convey the original meaning of the texts. This is most commonly done in relation to the figure of the 'statesman', who was projected (and then addressed) as the agent of governmental action. While it seems likely that British political economy played a leading role in the ultimate demise of this discursive figure, we do not know as much as we should about this process and its long-term effects. It is clear, however, that the statesman was alive and well in the period being examined here.

References to Adam Smith's works and letters follow the conventions established in *The Glasgow Edition of the Works and Correspondence of Adam Smith*, 6 volumes (Oxford, 1976–1987). Hence, in lieu of titles, the following abbreviations are used, and, where appropriate, the original divisions of the work are given (such as book, section, chapter) along with the paragraph in lieu of page numbers.

> *Corr = Correspondence*
> *EPS = Essays on Philosophical Subjects*
> *LJ(A) = Lectures on Jurisprudence*: Report of 1762–1763
> *LJ(B) = Lectures on Jurisprudence*: Report dated 1766
> *TMS = The Theory of Moral Sentiments*
> *WN = An Inquiry into the Nature and Causes of the Wealth of Nations*

All other multivolume works are referenced in full in the notes, excepting these titles, which are abbreviated as follows:

> *Works = The Works of Thomas Robert Malthus* (eds. E. A. Wrigley and David Souden, 8 vols.)
> *Works and Correspondence = The Works and Correspondence of David Ricardo* (ed. Piero Sraffa, 11 vols.)

Writings and Speeches = *The Writings and Speeches of Edmund Burke* (eds. Paul Langford and William B. Todd, 9 vols.)

In the editions just named, the base text for Ricardo's *Principles of Political Economy* is the third edition (1821), with short variants provided in editorial notes at the bottom of the page and long passages at the end of the relevant chapter. In the case of Malthus's *Principles of Political Economy*, the second edition (1836) is the base text, with short variants provided in editorial notes and long passages at the end of volume 6. Since Part III of this book focuses on the second edition (1819) of Ricardo's *Principles* and the first edition (1820) of Malthus's *Principles*, it has been necessary to use the editorial apparatuses to reconstruct the second and first editions, respectively. For the sake of simplicity, editorial notes are not referenced, only page numbers and, when necessary, the notes of Malthus and Ricardo.

The titles of primary sources in English have been shortened and their capitalization modernized. When quoting from primary sources, a lowercase initial letter has occasionally been changed to an uppercase, and vice versa. All pound signs are modernized.

Introduction

This book's key premise is that the notion that there was such a thing as 'classical political economy' is a distorting myth. The fact that this myth plays a central role in our histories of economic thought suggests that we have a poor understanding of the thought of the past and of the historical process by which economics came to assert itself so forcefully in the modern world. What follows, therefore, is an attempt at revision: to use contextual intellectual history to expose the short-comings in our existing knowledge and to then establish a more reliable account of what Malthus, Ricardo, and their peers thought they were doing when they wrote texts of political economy.

Malthus and Ricardo form the focus because they are central to all accounts of classical political economy and because they played leading roles in the long-term process by which economic reason came to assert itself in British political life. More specifically, Malthus and Ricardo were the first self-styled 'theorists' who explicitly attacked their 'practical' opponents for being untheoretical in matters of political economy. This strategy was tremendously successful. Above all, it spurred the emergence of Tory political economists who claimed theoret-ical equality with their Whig rivals, thus helping political economists in general to achieve the institutional traction that they needed to reform the British state, most visible in changes to the Poor Laws (1834), Bank of England (1819, 1844), and Corn Laws (1846). The presumption of political economists to prospect such reforms to their societies outside of any institutional office has been an aspect of our (Anglo-American) politics ever since. But it is nearly impossible to grasp this fact when the category 'classical political economy' organizes the historical materials, not least because it usually does so in service to a polemic regarding the competing merits of neoclassical, Marxist, and post-Keynesian economics in the present.

This book must therefore confront the enduring presence of anachronism in the history of economic thought. The primary cause is that practitioners are willing to approach the past through the categories and controversies of the pre-sent. Traditionally, this practice has been defended by specifying the proper aim of research as recovering the 'analytical system' of a past thinker,[1] or the 'history

---

[1] George J. Stigler, 'Does Economics Have a Useful Past?', *History of Political Economy* 1/2 (1969), 217–30, at 220.

Before Method and Models. Ryan Walter, Oxford University Press. © Oxford University Press 2021.
DOI: 10.1093/oso/9780197603055.003.0001

of economic analysis' as distinct from the 'history of economic thought',[2] or as providing a 'rational reconstruction' in contrast to a 'historical reconstruction',[3] often in conjunction with Imre Lakatos's distinction between 'internal' and 'external' history.[4] At times these justifications have been intended to facilitate the recovery of lost ideas that are serviceable in the present.[5] More generally, however, these justifications for anachronism have been driven by the need to secure a place for history in the economics curriculum, which explains the field's anxiety to demonstrate that studying the past might be good for an economist's intellectual formation.[6]

This anxiety has been exacerbated by historiographical competition as the history of economic thought has migrated outside of economics departments since the 1970s and been taken up by scholars of different stripes, including English scholars, historians of science, and, above all, by professional intellectual historians. Whatever private beliefs historians may hold regarding the edifying potential of history for economists, they do not typically do their teaching in economics departments.[7] Thus unburdened by the obligation to sell their wares, intellectual historians have been free to push the history of economic thought into genuinely historical directions, dispensing with the self-serving distinctions noted earlier that presume to sort wheat from chaff. Instead, once it is simply taken for granted that history is a worthwhile pursuit, the guiding distinction is not between rational and historical reconstruction but between 'myth-making and historiography'.[8] As this alternative opposition implies, some of the results

---

[2] Joseph A. Schumpeter, *History of Economic Analysis* (Oxford: Oxford University Press, 1994 [1954]), 38–43.

[3] See, for example, Mark Blaug, 'On the Historiography of Economics', *Journal of the History of Economic Thought* 12/1 (1990), 27–37.

[4] See, for example, A. M. C. Waterman 'Mathematical Modelling as an Exegetical Tool: Rational Reconstruction', in Warren J. Samuels, Jeff E. Biddle, and John B. Davis, eds., *A Companion to the History of Economic Thought* (Malden: Blackwell Publishing, 2003), 553–70.

[5] See, for example, the essays; Marcella Corsi, Jan Kregel, and Carlo D'Ippoliti, eds., *Classical Economics Today: Essays in Honor of Alessandro Roncaglia* (London: Anthem Press, 2018); and Steven Kates, *Classical Economic Theory and the Modern Economy* (Cheltenham: Edward Elgar, 2020).

[6] See, for example, Ivan Moscati's figuring of historians as commentators who tell the story of the 'game' of economics for the 'players'—economists who do not have either the time or interest to tell its story but who might benefit from a fair recounting nevertheless: Ivan Moscati, 'More Economics, Please: We're Historians of Economics', *Journal of the History of Economic Thought* 30/1 (2008), 85–92, at 88. A shopping list of reasons is provided by Steven Kates, who was moved to write when the European Research Council attempted to remove the history of economic thought from the list of subfields in economics: Steven Kates, *Defending the History of Economic Thought* (Cheltenham: Edward Elgar, 2013), 21.

[7] The late Donald Winch was a rare example of someone who was trained in economics but transitioned to being a professional intellectual historian. The specialist nature of intellectual history and the closure of economics to humanist scholarship now makes a trajectory such as Winch's difficult to follow. See Keith Tribe, 'Donald Winch 1935–2017', *The European Journal of the History of Economic Thought* 25/1 (2018), 196–201, at 196.

[8] Conal Condren, *Argument and Authority in Early Modern England: The Presupposition of Oaths and Offices* (Cambridge: Cambridge University Press, 2006), 229.

are destructive for received accounts since one of the routine effects of contextual intellectual history is to reveal the tendency for academic disciplines to project imaginary auto-histories onto the past.[9] In this respect, this book is indebted to the pioneering work of Keith Tribe and Donald Winch, who have led the attempt to produce genuinely historical accounts of economic thought.[10]

If intellectual history does not deal with phantoms, then the question becomes one of determining what can be identified as a valid object of historical analysis. For intellectual historians, the short answer is texts, understood to include written records of wide variety, including philosophical treatises, government reports, the popular press, and much else besides. Unlike the conjectural nature of an analytical system that silently moves an author's thoughts behind their back or an economic analysis existing independently of the texts and contexts from which it is divined, positing historical texts as a thing in the world does not need to be underwritten by either teleology or metaphysics. That is, one can point to texts as physical objects, examine their literal contents and organization, and often identify their publication histories, none of which can be done to an analytical system or other hypothetical objects. The intellectual historian's confidence regarding the existence of texts as their object of study comes at a cost, however, for the historiographical horizon must be lowered to allow the messy, contextual features of the composition and reception of texts in historical time to come into view.

While shifting to the study of texts allows historians to ground their work in textual evidence, it does create a set of issues regarding the tools that should be used to sift that evidence. Indeed, some of the best historians in the world have been working through this question for decades without reaching a consensus. It should therefore be acknowledged that the approach adopted here draws on the so-called Cambridge school of intellectual history, associated most closely with the names of J. G. A. Pocock and Quentin Skinner.[11] In terms of their technical approach, Pocock and Skinner have both emphasized the need to attend to linguistic evidence when attempting to determine what a text might have meant to the society or milieu in which it was produced.

---

[9] For a classic exposé of the 'mythologies' that typically underwrite rational reconstruction, see Quentin Skinner, 'Meaning and Understanding in the History of Ideas', *History and Theory* 8/1 (1969), 3–53. Reprinted as Quentin Skinner, *Visions of Politics*, 3 vols. (Cambridge: Cambridge University Press, 2002), 1: chapter 4.

[10] In particular, Keith Tribe, *Land, Labour and Economic Discourse* (London: Routledge and Kegan Paul, 1978) and Keith Tribe, *The Economy of the Word: Language, History, and Economics* (Oxford: Oxford University Press, 2015); Donald Winch, *Adam Smith's Politics: An Essay in Historiographic Revision* (Cambridge: Cambridge University Press, 1978) and Donald Winch, *Riches and Poverty: An Intellectual History of Political Economy in Britain, 1750–1834* (Cambridge: Cambridge University Press, 1996).

[11] For programmatic statements, see Skinner, *Visions of Politics*, vol. 1 and J. G. A. Pocock, *Political Thought and History: Essays on Theory and Method* (Cambridge: Cambridge University Press, 2009).

For Pocock, the key task has been to ascertain the political language or idiom that an author mobilized. From here it becomes possible to determine if the author altered this language and, if so, if the alteration endured. By contrast, Skinner has typically identified a smaller target than languages: key terms and the accepted conventions for deploying them in a given milieu. This allows specific instances of word use, or an author's 'speech acts', to be assessed in terms of their conventionality or originality. A great deal has been said regarding the relative appeal of these competing principles and how they should be mobilized in practice.[12] When the issue is reduced to its core claim, however, the injunction is clear enough: examine which words are used in a text, what they may have been intended to mean by the person who wrote them, and what they may have meant to the people who read them, with openness to the possibility that the answers to these questions may not be the same.

What does all this mean for the history of economic thought in general? It means that if historians of economic thought redescribe the texts under study with a present-day vocabulary then they doctor the (linguistic) evidence.[13] Or, to put the same point the other way around, such doctoring is essential to the project of *rational reconstruction*, or a history of economic analysis as it has also been called, since the historian only knows what counts as economic analysis from the point of view of their proficiency with a contemporary vocabulary. For contextual intellectual history, by contrast, contextualized linguistic evidence must lie at the core of any interpretation of what a text meant to its author and readers in a given time and place, and this requires that the language of a text must be handled with great care and clearly distinguished from the historian's present-day vocabulary. To be plain, this does not mean that today's historian must write like their dead subjects, but it does mean that they must acquire the languages of the dead as best they can, explain how they worked, and signal to the reader when they need to switch between the

---

[12] The most thoughtful (if challenging) commentary comes from Conal Condren, *The Status and Appraisal of Classic Texts* (Princeton: Princeton University Press, 1985); Conal Condren, *The Language of Politics in Seventeenth-Century England* (New York: Palgrave Macmillan, 1994). A great deal has also been written by those who refuse the discipline of identifying historical contexts before reading texts, and this rejection of context by philosophers and historians of rival persuasions has ghosted its career from the beginning. On this point, see the indispensable account in Ian Hunter, 'The Contest over Context in Intellectual History', *History & Theory* 58/2 (2019), 185–209.

[13] What has been termed the 'Piltdown effect'. See Condren, *The Language of Politics in Seventeenth-Century England*, 13. In short, our conceptual vocabulary is first dug into the evidence to be studied, such that when we then claim to have made a discovery, it is on the basis of doctored evidence; we have no ancestor with a human cranium and the jaw of an ape, but a fabricated skull of this type was dug into the Piltdown earth and then 'discovered' (Stephen Jay Gould, 'Piltdown Revisited', in *The Panda's Thumb: More Reflections in Natural History* (New York: W. W. Norton and Company, 1980), 108–24).

voices of past and present in the course of making texts intelligible in historical terms.[14]

What do these precepts mean for the study of Malthus and Ricardo in particular? They direct attention to the language that is used in their texts and to the language that is used by economists today, with a standing suspicion that when the latter is substituted for the former the consequence will be to compromise historical understanding in favour of transforming past texts into participants in today's debates. As anyone familiar with the history of economic thought will know, such substitution is routine. As regards the ambition at work in this book, to acquire historical knowledge of Malthus and Ricardo, the consequences of language substitution are greatest in relation to three linked terms: *classical political economy*, *model*, and *method*. This claim can be substantiated with reference to some influential examples of the history of economic thought in its reconstructive mode.

Let us begin with the term 'classical political economy'. It has been known for some time that this category tends to unify the authors who are grouped within its boundaries without historical warrant.[15] Its origins seem to lie in Karl Marx's jaundiced reading of political economy, with the term coined in the context of Marx making a polemical assessment of his predecessors. The closest that one comes to finding an explicit definition of classical political economy in Marx's corpus is two consecutive footnotes towards the end of chapter 1 of the first volume of *Capital* (1867), in Marx's discussion of commodity fetishism. Marx's general point was that although Smith and Ricardo deserved credit for making scientific advances in relation to the role of labour in creating value, their categories and modes of thought were bourgeois. This is said to appear most clearly in Ricardo's treatment of the commodity-form as natural when in fact it was reliant on the capitalist mode of production and thus specific to a particular historical stage. This is the context in which Marx wrote that value was 'the weak point of the classical school of Political Economy'.[16] A similar point is made regarding 'classical economy' in the second note, following which Marx clarified his usage:

> by classical Political Economy, I understand that economy which, since the time of W. Petty, has investigated real relations of production in bourgeois

---

[14] On the notion that the historian's procedure involves distinguishing their own 'historical standpoint' from that occupied by those about whom they write, see W. B. Gallie, *Philosophy and the Historical Understanding* (London: Chatto and Windus, 1964), 120.

[15] As observed in Winch, *Riches and Poverty*, 8–9, 15.

[16] Karl Marx, *Capital: A Critique of Political Economy*, ed. Frederick Engels, trans. from the Third German Edition, vol. 1 (Moscow: Progress Publishers, 1954), 84 n1. The quotation corresponds to note 27 on page 41 in the first German edition, and here, as in the other cases, Marx is using 'klassische politische Oekonomie': Karl Marx, *Das Kapital: Kritik der politischen Oekonomie* (Hamburg, 1867).

society, in contradistinction to vulgar economy, which deals with appearances only, ruminates without ceasing on the materials long since provided by scientific economy, and there seeks plausible explanations of the most obtrusive phenomena, for bourgeois daily use.[17]

So clarified, Marx's meaning is plain: classical political economy is whatever economic thinking has scientific value, as judged from the vantage point of Marxist political economy. It is this partisan character of the category that allowed Marx to group together figures as discrepant as William Petty and Ricardo. In doing so, Marx merged Petty's seventeenth-century counselling discourse premised on a physiological analogy between the body politic and natural bodies with Ricardo's idiosyncratic analysis of rent and value. Here historical difference is flattened by epistemological polemic.

More recent renditions of the term have been produced within the history of economic thought. In his famous paper of 1978, 'The Canonical Classical Model of Political Economy', Paul Samuelson roped together Smith, Ricardo, Malthus, and John Stuart Mill by identifying a common model of equilibrium growth and distribution. Samuelson constructed this model using contemporary mathematical economics, secure in the assumption that 'within every classical economist there is to be discerned a modern economist trying to be born'.[18] In this case, it is not polemic but teleology that makes a mess of the historical materials, allowing the actual contexts and concerns of Malthus, Ricardo, and their interlocutors to be ignored as they are placed in a context prepared in advance by an economic theorist from another century.

Equally symptomatic is the voluminous work of Samuel Hollander, which has been a lightning rod for debates over the character of the classical heritage.[19] Hollander is revealing for his resistance to the rise of historical approaches to economic thought, even attempting to defend the category 'classical political economy' against the charge that it is an anachronistic reification. The defence takes the form of specifying the '"core" of classical doctrine' as the appropriate unit of analysis, which might vary historically in the sense that it can be found stated in 'different language', but the historian can cut through this noise by accessing the 'pure analytics of classicism', which the historian can redescribe in

[17] Marx, *Capital*, 85 n1. The quotation corresponds to note 24 on pages 34–5 in the first German edition. I am grateful to Keith Tribe for his assistance on this point.

[18] Paul A. Samuelson, 'The Canonical Classical Model of Political Economy', *Journal of Economic Literature* 16/4 (1978), 1415–34, at 1415.

[19] See especially Samuel Hollander, *The Economics of David Ricardo* (London: Heinemann, 1979) and the review by Keith Tribe in *Economy and Society*: Keith Tribe, 'Ricardian Histories', *Economy and Society* 10/4 (1981), 451–66.

algebra without danger.[20] Having the 'pure analytics' in view, Hollander concludes that the 'classics inhabited a "Marshallian" not a "Marxian" universe'.[21] For any professional intellectual historian, this is textbook anachronism, since writings from *c.* 1770–1830 are redescribed using language dating from the twentieth century and then judged to belong to a universe dating from the 1870s! Yet Hollander is adamant that his historiography is not anachronistic: 'I have been engaged in "historical" not "rational reconstruction"'.[22] This defence by fiat gives a sense of the field's traditional closure to historical approaches and of its continuing preoccupation with the 'classics' as pointing towards either Marx or Marshall.

This question of political economy's true nature was complicated by Piero Sraffa, whose *Production of Commodities by Means of Commodities* (1960) has had disproportionate influence on historians of economic thought. Sraffa aligned his work with the 'old classical economists' who were supposedly 'submerged and forgotten' by marginal analysis.[23] This narrative also produces teleology by linking the past with the present, only here the standard is neither Marx nor Marshall but a composite Ricardo-Marx-Sraffa. Thus a Sraffa disciple could repeat Marx's claim regarding William Petty without hesitation: 'Petty also failed to develop a systematic analysis of the determination of wages', as if it were even possible that Petty could have formed this intention in the seventeenth century.[24] In this example, the category 'classical political economy' excuses the historian from investigating what an author was trying to do because it is taken for granted that inside Petty was a Sraffian trying to be born. As Terry Peach has shown, the evidence against Sraffa's reading of Ricardo in terms of a corn-model of distribution is overwhelming, and resistance to this fact seems to be driven by the quasi-spiritual nature of the Sraffian school's attachment to Ricardo as their illustrious founder.[25]

The reference to the so-called *corn-model* that is central to Sraffian political economy directs attention to the second term that drives anachronism in the history of economic thought, 'model'. The idea that scientists produce models

[20] Samuel Hollander, ' "Classical economics": A Reification Wrapped in an Anachronism?', in Evelyn L. Forget and Sandra Peart, eds., *Reflections on the Classical Canon in Economics: Essays in Honor of Samuel Hollander* (London: Routledge, 2000), 7–26, at 8, 18.

[21] Ibid., 23

[22] Ibid., 18.

[23] Piero Sraffa, *Production of Commodities by Means of Commodities: Prelude to a Critique of Economic Theory* (Cambridge: Cambridge University Press, 1960), v.

[24] Christian Gehrke, 'British Classical Political Economy', in Gilbert Faccarello and Heinz D. Kurz, eds., *Handbook on the History of Economic Analysis*, vol. 2 (Cheltenham: Edward Elgar Publishing, 2016), 125–49, at 128.

[25] Terry Peach, 'On *Interpreting Ricardo*: A Reply to Sraffians', *Cambridge Journal of Economics* 22/5 (1998), 597–616; Terry Peach, *Interpreting Ricardo* (Cambridge: Cambridge University Press, 1993). As noted in the Acknowledgements, I have also struggled to escape the 'corn model' view of Ricardo.

is a phenomenon of the twentieth century, and for economists the start of the shift has been dated to the 1930s, in relation to Jan Tinbergen's work on business cycles.[26] Hence it is no surprise that Tinbergen's contemporary, John Maynard Keynes, appears not to have thought in terms of models, subtitling the two volumes of his *A Treatise on Money* (1930) as *The Pure Theory of Money* and *The Applied Theory of Money*.[27] Furthermore, he identified the polemical target of the first chapter of *The General Theory of Employment, Interest and Money* (1936) not as the 'models' of the classics but instead their 'economic thought, both practical and theoretical', especially its disconnection from 'the facts of experience'.[28] In short, model-talk is of recent vintage, and the assumption that even as modern a thinker as Keynes was producing models is highly suspect.[29]

It follows that to redescribe the texts of Malthus and Ricardo as if they contained models is to dig our vocabulary into the historical evidence, corrupting it in consequence. The leading example of this pathology is found in the endless readings of Ricardo's *Essay on Profits* (1815) in relation to Sraffa's construction of a corn-model. (That Sraffa tended not to use the term 'model', preferring instead to use 'theory' in both his own *Production of Commodities* and in his editorial introduction to Ricardo's *Principles of Political Economy, and Taxation* (1817), is evidence of semantic drift created by the rise of modelling in economics since the mid-twentieth century.) But Malthus has also been subjected to this treatment, with Hollander reading Malthus as implicitly developing an agricultural growth model.[30] More startling is A. M. C. Waterman's redescription of diverse texts in terms of an underlying model, as per Samuelson's 'canonical model' noted earlier. Malthus is one of the authors to receive this treatment from Waterman, being retrospectively endowed with a 'model of stationary equilibrium' as part of Waterman's 'rational reconstruction'.[31] At times these reconstructions of past thinkers in terms of models completely obliterate the historical point of their work. Consider Waterman's treatment of Burke in the following statement:

---

[26] Marcel Boumans, *How Economists Model the World into Numbers* (London: Routledge, 2004), chapter 2. Despite being aware of these issues, Mary Morgan adopts a contemporary definition of modelling as a style of reasoning and then projects it backwards in time, finding Ricardo to be a 'pioneer': Mary Morgan, *The World in the Model: How Economists Work and Think* (Cambridge, 2012), chapter 2.

[27] John Maynard Keynes, *The Collected Writings of John Maynard Keynes*, eds. Elizabeth Johnson and Donald Moggridge, 30 vols. (Cambridge: Cambridge University Press, 1978), vol. 5 and vol. 6.

[28] Keynes, *The Collected Writings of John Maynard Keynes*, 7: 3.

[29] More helpful is Victoria Chick's comment that economists who are accustomed to think in terms of models struggle to understand Keynes's method in the *General Theory*, which does not fit into the categories of either partial or general equilibrium: Victoria Chick, *Macroeconomics After Keynes: A Reconsideration of the General Theory* (Cambridge, Mass.: MIT Press, 1983), 14.

[30] Samuel Hollander, *The Economics of Thomas Robert Malthus* (Toronto: University of Toronto Press, 1997), chapter 3.

[31] A. M. C. Waterman, *Revolution, Economics and Religion: Christian Political Economy, 1798–1833* (Cambridge: Cambridge University Press, 1991), 40, 264–73.

both Burke's and Godwin's arguments are defective in exactly the same way. For by postulating a stable equilibrium at some different state from the status quo, and by treating the latter as unstable unless constrained by institutional bonds, they leave altogether unexplained the way in which society comes to be what it actually is.[32]

'Exactly so!' Burke might have replied, for such rational theory that presumed to 'explain' in mechanistic terms the formation of an entire way of life was viewed by Burke as a cause of social unrest, and he often aimed to foreclose such speculations.[33] This aspect of Burke's thinking is impossible to recover when he is transformed into a failed model builder.

To now turn to the final term that is central to the production of anachronism—'method'—it should be noted that this term (in today's sense) is less of a latecomer than either 'model' or 'classical political economy'. The discussion of scientific method in the sense of pursuing a general epistemological strategy, such as induction or deduction, emerged shortly after Ricardo's death, driven especially by William Whewell and John Herschel.[34] During Ricardo's lifetime, however, 'method' was used sparingly and primarily to refer to the need to proceed in an orderly fashion—in today's sense of being 'methodical'—and to conduct the intellect with ethical surety.[35] It should be emphasized that Whewell

[32] Ibid., 27.

[33] See, for example, Burke's distinction between a new society such as revolutionary France, the origins of which ought to be examined, and 'an old structure which you have found as it is, and are not to dispute of the original end and design with which it had been so fashioned': Edmund Burke, 'First Letter on a Regicide Peace', in *Writings and Speeches*, eds. Paul Langford and William B. Todd, 9 vols. (Oxford: Oxford University Press, 1981–2015), 9: 187–264, at 252. For the general tendency to translate Burke's distinctive common law approach to markets into an analytical form of political economy, see Ryan Walter, 'Conservative Politics and Laissez Faire Economics? The Burke-Smith Problem Revisited', *Critical Historical Studies* 7/2 (2020), 271–95. Of course, Burke was not opposed to *historiography* as a mode of understanding origins, and in this respect his debts to the Scots are deep. See Daniel I. O'Neill, *The Burke-Wollstonecraft Debate: Savagery, Civilization, and Democracy* (University Park: Pennsylvania State University Press, 2007), chapter 2.

[34] Richard R. Yeo, 'Scientific Method and the Rhetoric of Science in Britain, 1830–1917', in John A. Schuster and Richard R. Yeo, eds., *The Politics and Rhetoric of Scientific Method: Historical Studies* (Dordrecht: D. Reidel, 1986), 259–97; Richard R. Yeo, 'William Whewell's Philosophy of Knowledge and Its Reception', in Menachem Fisch and Simon Schaffer, eds., *William Whewell: A Composite Portrait* (Oxford: Oxford University Press, 1991), 175–99.

[35] On those few occasions when Ricardo used the word 'method', he used it in this sense: see, for example, David Ricardo, 'Ricardo to Maria Edgeworth', in *Works and Correspondence*, ed. Piero Sraffa, 11 vols. (Cambridge: Cambridge University Press, 1951), 9: 257–62, at 259; Ricardo, 'Ricardo to Mill', *Works and Correspondence*, 7: 376–83, at 378. As for the word 'method' in the early modern period in general, it has frequently been imbued with unhistorical meanings. Descartes, for example, is routinely misread on this point—note the title of his famous 1637 text: *Discourse on the Method for Rightly Directing One's Reason and Searching for Truth in the Sciences*. See the translator's comments, by Paul J. Olscamp, regarding the way the *Discourse* has typically been read in isolation of the three works that it was intended to introduce and his claim that 'Method consists in a set of rules or procedures for using the natural capacities and operations of the mind correctly': Paul J. Olscamp, 'Introduction', in René Descartes, *Discourse on the Method. Optics, Geometry, and Meteorology*, trans. Paul J. Olscamp, revised edition (Indianapolis: Hackett Publishing, 2001), ix–xxxvi, at xiv. Even more

and his political-economist ally, Richard Jones, were driven by their hostility to Ricardian political economy. This means that when we discuss Ricardo in relation to method and do so using Whewell's opposition between induction and deduction, we are not only using language that Malthus and Ricardo almost never used, but we are also unknowingly adopting language that was developed by Ricardo's enemies after his death for the purpose of attacking his work.[36]

All three terms—'classical political economy', 'model', and 'method'—are typically found in combined use in the scholarly literature. In fact, it is commonly claimed that model building first flourished as an explicit method in classical political economy, intertwining the three concepts. Here is a revealing example from Denis O'Brien's influential text, *The Classical Economists Revisited* (2004):

> Ricardo's deductive method, his model building, was to be of the greatest importance. Ricardo essentially invented these techniques. His procedure not only contrasts strongly with Adam Smith's basically inductive approach, but, as a process of heroic abstraction, it not only neglects the frictions in the economic system, but also habitually reasons in terms of the immediate relevance of the long run. Both these characteristics were to be of far greater importance for economics after the end of the Classical era: that they left their scars on Classical economics there can, however, be no doubt.[37]

Equally common is to find talk of the 'methodology of classical political economy'[38] or 'the classical method in the theory of value and distribution'.[39] If methodology and models postdate Malthus and Ricardo, and if 'classical political economy' was a label invented by Karl Marx for polemical purposes, then we need to ask: What were they doing? Answering this question requires returning to the actual vocabulary of Malthus and Ricardo and then using this evidence to reconstruct their intellectual context.

---

revealing is the study from Matthew L. Jones, 'Descartes's Geometry as Spiritual Exercise', *Critical Inquiry* 28/1 (2001), 40–71. Going further back to before Descartes, 'method' was a term of art in post-Renaissance scholarship, with Ramus a source of controversy, but its meanings were still linked to the idea of rule-of-thumb procedures. See Walter Ong's pithy comments on this: Walter J. Ong, 'Ramist Method and the Commercial Mind', *Studies in the Renaissance* 8 (1961), 155–72, at 163–4.

[36] See N. B. de Marchi and R. P. Sturges, 'Malthus and Ricardo's Inductivist Critics: Four Letters to William Whewell', *Economica* 40/160 (1973), 379–93.

[37] D. P. O'Brien, *The Classical Economists Revisited* (Princeton: Princeton University Press, 2004), 49.

[38] A. M. C. Waterman, *Political Economy and Christian Theology Since the Enlightenment: Essays in Intellectual History* (Basingstoke: Palgrave Macmillan, 2004), chapter 8.

[39] Heinz D. Kurz, 'The Surplus Interpretation of the Classical Economists', in Warren J. Samuels, Jeff E. Biddle, John B. Davis, eds., *A Companion to the History of Economic Thought* (Malden: Blackwell Publishing, 2003), 167–83, at 169.

Vocabulary and the Recovery of Context

As indicated in this book's title, one of the leading results to be reported is that, in the period under study (*c.* 1790–1823), neither model nor method played a major role in the conceptual vocabulary of British political economists or their critics. Indeed, it is hard to find these words being used at all by political economists, and, when they were, they were not used in today's senses. The vocabulary of political economists did, however, include 'theory', 'practice', 'experience', and 'enthusiasm'. Not only were these words used, but their meaning and range of reference was intensely contested in the leading disputes of the period. As anyone familiar with this period of British history will know, these terms had been extensively used in seventeenth-century England, amounting to commonplaces even, but they were energized in a lasting way by Edmund Burke's hostile response to the French Revolution in his *Reflections on the Revolution in France* (1790). Burke's essential point was that recent and erroneous notions of the rights of man had filled the people with 'passionate enthusiasm' and corrupted the reasoning of 'modern legislators'.[40] The tragic consequence was that this blinded the people to the benefits that their existing form of government actually produced because they fixated on a better, future society.

To be plain, one of this book's major findings is that this vocabulary was central to political economy in the time of Malthus and Ricardo and that political economy did not have a vocabulary of its own. Given the precepts articulated earlier regarding attentiveness to language, the importance of this fact is hard to overstate. Above all, it signals that the tendency to study political economy as if it were an autonomous discipline in the manner of economics today is anachronistic. Instead of enjoying intellectual autonomy, political economists operated in a context where the standing of theory was not something that they could determine for themselves, and they were thus participating in a larger set of debates and intellectual cultures than historians of economic thought have normally studied.

After Burke, theory aroused suspicion while practice and experience reassured. This is why political economists who understood themselves as theorists went to elaborate lengths to move their intellectual labours under the cover of the privileged terms by rhetorically aligning their work with notions of practice and experience. Political economists also attempted to deny each other the protection of these terms, often painting their opponents as enthusiasts. Here, then, is a rival starting point for historical inquiry that rejects the path of rational reconstruction: Malthus and Ricardo were neither doing macroeconomics nor building models, but they were attempting to balance theoretical speculation

---

[40] Burke, 'Reflections on the Revolution in France', *Writings and Speeches*, 8: 53–293, at 108, 232.

with the intense demand after the French Revolution that one also attend to practice and experience. This fact explains why Malthus and Ricardo can never be found to reflect on the nature of a good model but are found to have routinely reflected on the relationship between theory, practice, and experience and to have used these ideas to defend their own work and to attack the work of others.

This feature of the context can be illustrated by noting Jeremy Bentham's overview of this vocabulary in *The Book of Fallacies* (1824), with the relevant chapter bearing the title 'Anti-rational Fallacies'. Bentham, as a confirmed reformer, was attacking the vocabulary that had been used so successfully to keep back the tide of change. The key strategy, according to Bentham, had been to disparage 'reason' and 'thought' by qualifying them with the adjectives 'speculative', 'theoretical', 'visionary', 'chimerical', 'romantic', and 'utopian'.[41] Bentham's claim was that such attacks on theory concealed the fact that all argumentation involved some theory, even if its role went unperceived.[42] (This claim that theory is omnipresent has been a commonplace in the defence of theoretical argument ever since.) Bentham's other defence of theory was to concede that the 'fear of theory' was justified because of the tendency for theorists to ignore the complications raised by the 'particular case' that required an exception.[43] But such blindness to the need for exceptions was an affront to reason and utility, or bad theory, and not an invalidation of theory per se.[44]

Bentham could do more than defend: he developed several lines of attack against the anti-rational position. His campaign was at its fiercest when he claimed that the rejection of theory was typically motivated by the desire to protect private interests that were served by the existing system, interests that would be compromised if the science of utility were allowed to program the architecture of government.[45] Such interests were, according to Bentham, defended using the words 'experience', 'practice', and 'the wisdom of our ancestors' to urge legislators to trust in proven knowledge that usually dated to the sixteenth and seventeenth centuries.[46] Against this view, Bentham insisted that these centuries were barbaric, such that it was only from their mistakes that his age could hope to

---

[41] Jeremy Bentham, *The Book of Fallacies* (London, 1824), 295–6.

[42] Ibid., 299–300.

[43] Ibid., 299.

[44] For the cautionary and even casuistical character of Bentham's thought at times, see Jeremy Bentham, 'Place and Time', in *Selected Writings: Jeremy Bentham*, ed. Stephen G. Engelmann (New Haven, Conn.: Yale University Press, 2011), 152–219. I am grateful to Lorenzo Cello for bringing this text to my attention.

[45] Bentham, *The Book of Fallacies*, 80–1. In this regard, note the title to chapter 18 of Bentham's *Plan of Parliamentary Reform*, 'Interests adverse to adequate Reform — Support given by them to Moderate, to the Exclusion of Radical: Tories — Whigs — People's-men': Jeremy Bentham, *Plan of Parliamentary Reform, in the Form of a Catechism, with Reasons for each Article, with an Introduction, Shewing the Necessity of Radical, and the Inadequacy of Moderate, Reform* (London, 1817), 299.

[46] Bentham, *The Book of Fallacies*, 69–79.

learn. Bentham even braved an attack on the Ancient Constitution, overturning Burke's injunction not to examine the origins of a people's political inheritance.

> The constitution, why must it not be looked into? why is it that under pain of being *ipso facto* anarchist convict, we must never presume to look at it otherwise than with shut eyes? Because it was the work of our ancestors: — of ancestors, of legislators, few of whom could so much as read, and those few had nothing before them that was worth the reading. First theoretical supposition, *wisdom of barbarian ancestors*.[47]

With fallacies such as this in place, the anti-rationalists could conclude that acting without precedent or custom—as conveyed by the terms 'novelty' and 'innovation'—was harmful.[48] In fact, Bentham wrote, typically 'innovation' was used to mean 'bad change'.[49] The trouble with all this anti-rational language was that it obscured present evil and, simultaneously, directed attention to future evils that need never emerge when good theory was used to guide the way.[50]

Burke published his *Reflections* in 1790, while Bentham published his *Book of Fallacies* in 1824. There is thus *prima facie* evidence that, from before Ricardo's first publication in political economy (1809) until after his death (1823), the vocabulary of theory and practice was used to debate the relationship between abstract thought and the workings of the nation's political institutions. It is therefore no surprise that this vocabulary played a leading role in debates over the status and potential role of political economy in either emancipating or destroying society since the new science was deeply concerned with reforming the state. In other words, an existing vocabulary was used to discuss political economy. As this claim implies, political economy was perceived as a species of political speculation, or philosophy, or abstract thought, and it was therefore subject to the same standards of evaluation that were applied to these other activities.

To put this point in different words, by paying attention to vocabulary it has been possible to establish that the context in which political economy was pursued in Britain at the turn of the century was one in which political economy was neither an autonomous science nor a vocation. This finding marks as unhistorical the common conception of political economy as a science that developed via models of increasing sophistication and internal consistency. More positively, it also affirms and extends the classic study from Stefan Collini, Donald Winch, and John Burrow, in which the key context for Malthus and Ricardo was

---

[47] Ibid., 237.
[48] Ibid., 113–5, 384, 390.
[49] Ibid., 143–4.
[50] Ibid., 150.

found to be the 'science of politics'.[51] This science contained political economy as one of its subordinate elements, inhibiting intellectual specialization of the type that economists today enjoy. In short, one of the reasons that the political economist did not behave as a specialist was because they did not possess a specialized vocabulary.

Beyond Language: Ethics Not Epistemology

Studying vocabulary alone, however, is insufficient to come to terms with the history of political economy because the combative deployment of a shared vocabulary was only one of the activities in which political economists engaged. One might think, for example, of the annuity calculations that Ricardo used in his labour theory of value or of Malthus's reconstruction of God's laws for directing humans towards virtue and happiness in their earthly lives. These intellectual practices were sourced from distinct milieus: roughly, the London Stock Exchange and the rationalist wing of the Anglican Church as nurtured in latitudinarian Cambridge. It thus emerges that multiple phenomena need to be brought to view in order to study political economy in a historical manner: combative vocabularies and the history of their use, the choices that authors made when operating in contexts where these vocabularies were active, and the diverse milieus from which authors drew and adapted styles of argument to service political economy.

The tendency to fuse these phenomena in the pursuit of recovering a 'method' is thus resisted in this book. There are three reasons for doing so. The first has already been discussed: that this concept is anachronistic, only emerging after Ricardo's death and developed in large part by certain of his intellectual enemies. The other reason is that the assumption of methodological holism—that a thinker had a unified method that is expressed across their works—is in fact not a valid assumption but merely a hypothesis that the historian may test. For there is a competing hypothesis that is no less plausible: that a given thinker's work may possess no internal unity. With these competing hypotheses in view, it becomes possible to investigate whatever relation may have happened to exist between an author's legitimating vocabulary choices—which in this context will include theory, practice, and experience—and the way that they constructed their arguments across different texts. Here another of the book's leading findings can be reported: the texts of Malthus and Ricardo display high levels of sensitivity to argumentative context. More plainly, Malthus and Ricardo wrote texts that

---

[51] Stefan Collini, Donald Winch, and John Burrow, *That Noble Science of Politics: A Study in Nineteenth-Century Intellectual History* (Cambridge: Cambridge University Press, 1983), 37.

both obeyed the conventions of the genres in which they wrote and adapted and responded to arguments that others had made before they picked up their pens. Thus, the endless attempts to characterize Ricardo's method as deductive are not only marked by their anachronism but by their low explanatory power, too. There is a third and final reason for resisting the temptation to discuss thinkers in terms of their method: that in this period it was ethics-talk that did much of the work that today is performed under the headings 'method' and 'epistemology'.

'Ethics-talk' is used in this book to indicate written reflection on the varied styles of ethical self-cultivation that circulated in early modern Europe. Recent research has shown how restoring these arts to historical view can change the received image of Europe's intellectual life, most strikingly in relation to the history of political thought and the history of science.[52] To put the matter crudely, the concerns of early-modern philosophy were wholly different from today's focus on epistemology.[53] Instead, theology and philosophy provided templates for governing one's soul or mind. The idea of using the intellect to restrain the passions and our supposed duty to God to improve the mind's reasoning powers stood as two of the most common starting points. These injunctions were built into university curricula that were intended to train elite youths in how to be good citizen-subjects and, secondarily, enter careers in law, medicine, or divinity. 'Ethics-talk' is thus a shorthand for indicating this context and its leading implication for this book's overall argument: that scientific thinking was understood to be an ethical activity. As a result, one's very manner of thinking could be ethically sound or ethically flawed, not in the sense that it was morally right or wrong, but in the sense that the thinking might have been the product of a properly or improperly regulated mind. Engaging with abstract ideas, for example, could enchant the mind, studying a utopian theory could turn one into a fanatic, while private interest might imperceptibly skew intellectual inquiry.

To make these claims concrete, it is worth considering a brief example, that of Isaac Watts. He achieved wide acclaim for two instruction manuals in ethical self-cultivation, *Logick: or the Right Use of Reason in the Enquiry after Truth* (1725), and its companion, *The Improvement of the Mind, Or a Supplement to the Art of Logick* (1741). Watts's work was used at Oxford and Cambridge, in dissenting academies, and by private tutors.[54] The *Improvement* was republished

---

[52] See, in particular, Ian Hunter, *Rival Enlightenments: Civil and Metaphysical Philosophy in Early Modern Germany* (Cambridge: Cambridge University Press, 2001); Ian Hunter, *The Secularisation of the Confessional State: The Political Thought of Christian Thomasius* (Cambridge: Cambridge University Press, 2007); Stephen Gaukroger, *The Emergence of a Scientific Culture: Science and the Shaping of Modernity 1210–1685* (Oxford: Oxford University Press, 2006).

[53] Knud Haakonssen, 'The Idea of Early Modern Philosophy', in J. B. Schneewind, ed., *Teaching New Histories of Philosophy: Proceedings of a Conference* (Princeton: University Center for Human Values, 2004), 99–121.

[54] G. P. Brooks, 'Isaac Watts and the Uses of a Knowledge of Astronomy: "He Taught the Art of Reasoning and the Science of the Stars"', *Vistas in Astronomy* 36/3 (1993), 295–310, at 299; Lucia

consistently throughout the eighteenth century, and, in the 1780s and 1790s, it was reprinted almost every year.[55] Watts opened his work by describing its subject as 'the cultivation of the mind, and its improvement in knowledge', which was a necessary area of learning because all humans 'are under some obligation *to improve their own understanding*'.[56] Why? Because humans lived together, requiring the constant exercise of judgement regarding correct conduct, and because Christians were answerable to God in the next life regarding their deeds in this one.

Watts set out five means of improving the mind: observation, reading, instruction by lectures, conversation, and meditation or study.[57] Despite the lengthy treatment that Watts bestowed on these topics, it emerges that his primary concern was with the final item in his list—meditation or study—because it consolidated the knowledge gained through the other techniques and was central to the learned professions of medicine, law, and divinity. When studying, extreme caution was required before forming '*general and fundamental truths*', such as Newton's doctrine of gravitation, because such general notions had implications for practice and because they had the potential to overthrow the mind.[58] This danger was heightened when a person with a passion for abstract thought attempted to bring several topics under one master notion.[59] One could guard against this vice by illustrating abstract ideas using images and diagrams and by remembering that the limits of mortal knowledge would often oblige humans to accept probable arguments in lieu of proofs.[60]

It is hopefully clear that Watts was not articulating epistemological principles, such as induction and deduction or realism and instrumentalism. Instead, he was prescribing a series of techniques and disciplines, both practical and ethical, that would enable an individual to govern their thinking for ethical and professional purposes. What is perhaps most alien in these precepts for today's reader is the idea that thinking was a type of conduct that required internal discipline. Yet this presupposition was central to the period, expressed in its ceaseless ethics-talk.

Dacome, 'Noting the Mind: Commonplace Books and the Pursuit of the Self in the Eighteenth Century', *Journal of the History of Ideas* 65/4 (2004), 603–25, at 617–18; Graham Beynon, *Isaac Watts: Reason, Passion and the Revival of Religion* (London: Bloomsbury, 2016), 6.

[55] All references here are to the text of 1792. Note also that Ricardo's friend, Thomas Belsham, attempted to claim Watts for Unitarianism. See Isabel Rivers, 'Watts, Isaac (1674–1748), Independent Minister and Writer', *Oxford Dictionary of National Biography* (2004), https://www.oxforddnb.com/view/10.1093/ref:odnb/9780198614128.001.0001/odnb-9780198614128-e-28888.

[56] Isaac Watts, *The Improvement of the Mind, or a Supplement to the Art of Logic* (London, 1792), iii, 1.

[57] Ibid., chapters 3–13.

[58] Ibid., 126.

[59] Ibid., 129.

[60] Ibid., 131, 135, 136–7.

The recovery of the role of ethics-talk to political economy is perhaps this book's most important finding since it represents a historical alternative to accounts of method. Indeed, ethics-talk will emerge as essential for making sense of the patterns of attack and defence exhibited by Ricardo's critics and friends, with the former routinely accusing him of failing to subject his mind to any disciplines, especially when he came to make arguments for changing laws in the real world. In short, that Ricardo's intellectual failures were widely perceived by his peers to have been ethical in nature has gone unnoticed in the history of economic thought, largely because he has been discussed in terms of method.

In addition, ethics-talk also represents the major connection between political economy and the politics of the times. For, in 1790s Britain, even moderate reform could appear suspect.[61] To elaborate, the Whig party—the original agent and ally of political economy—split in 1794, as the core went over to preserve the current order of things, leaving Charles James Fox as leader of a tiny rump of Whigs supportive of the reform of Parliament. While Burke bemoaned this event for reducing politics to a contest between two men—Fox and William Pitt—Fox knew that his faction was too small to ever form an administration. This meant that the real contest was between the Court and the radicals, thus stacking the deck against change because both reform and political economy were exposed to being smeared as Jacobinical or enthusiastic.[62] (Malthus would have been acutely aware of this, having seen his former tutor, Gilbert Wakefield, sentenced to two years prison for seditious libel.[63]) To put it bluntly, to either think or appear to think like a Jacobin was to expose oneself to a maximal attack on one's argument, regardless of its propositional content, and political economists who made abstract arguments were exposed to this attack.

Ethics-talk was also central to how the link between political economy and lawmaking was understood, and this registers a further break between the intellectual world of Malthus and Ricardo and our own. In particular, macroeconomists today are perfectly within the conventions of their discipline if they produce a model and stay silent regarding its possible application to the real world since building models is a prestigious activity regardless of their relevance.

---

[61] Mark Philp, *Reforming Ideas in Britain: Politics and Language in the Shadow of the French Revolution, 1789–1815* (Cambridge: Cambridge University Press, 2014), 119–20; Anna Plassart, *The Scottish Enlightenment and the French Revolution* (Cambridge: Cambridge University Press, 2015), chapter 3. For the disrepute surrounding Adam Smith's name because of his association with reforming ideas, see Emma Rothschild, *Economic Sentiments: Adam Smith, Condorcet, and the Enlightenment* (Cambridge, MA: Harvard University Press, 2002), 55–61.

[62] Frank O'Gorman, *The Whig Party and the French Revolution* (New York: Macmillan, 1967), 233–4; L. G. Mitchell, *Charles James Fox* (Oxford: Oxford University Press, 1992), 152; more generally, see Gregory Claeys, *The French Revolution Debate in Britain: The Origins of Modern Politics* (Basingstoke: Palgrave Macmillan Education UK, 2007), chapter 6.

[63] F. K. Prochaska, 'English State Trials in the 1790s: A Case Study', *Journal of British Studies* 13/1 (1973), 63–82, at 70–2, 81.

For Malthus and Ricardo, however, much of the legitimacy of political economy derived from the presumption that its purpose was to produce counsel for legislators, a role that members of British letters had long assumed in the manner of something like an independent mandarinate that disseminated counsel via patronage and commercial publications.[64] That is, producing counsel could be treated as a duty, requiring that one quarantine one's private interest and pursue the public interest, conceived as good lawmaking. In such a context, producing elegant theories for their own sake did not enjoy status, as it does today.

It is primarily for this reason that the production of treatise-length texts in political economy was a minority pursuit, with the overwhelming majority of writing taking the form of pamphlets that were either prompted by parliamentary debate around specific issues or intended to influence the course of such debate. The enormous number of texts produced in this vein almost always mobilized the tropes and ethos of a counsellor, whether to parliament, the public, or the figure of the statesman or legislator.[65] Viewed from this angle, political economy emerges not as a scientific vocation in its own right but as an outgrowth of Britain's parliamentary politics. This point will emerge clearly in Chapters 2 and 3 and reinforce the difficulties of approaching the texts of Malthus and Ricardo in terms of a method that the historian imagines as operating independently of the argumentative context and its conventions.

At this point, it is worth noting that this account stands in tension with Mary Poovey's influential study of a similar terrain, *A History of the Modern Fact* (1998).[66] Poovey's focus is on the role of political economy in forging an 'epistemological unit' that is pervasive in today's social sciences: the modern fact, understood as a statistical datum that is supposedly free of interpretation, therefore enabling theory-building via the process of induction. As others have noted of Poovey's book, this notion of data postdates her historical materials by a century or more.[67] In place of Poovey's theory-data questions, in this book, Malthus and Ricardo are found to have worked with different terms: theory and practice, experience and enthusiasm.

These terms have complex histories. 'Practice' and 'experience' enjoyed a large degree of substitution, but 'practice' could also mean the realm in which 'experience' accumulated, something like lessons learned from history. 'Experience' was

---

[64] J. G. A. Pocock, 'Enlightenment and Counter-Enlightenment, Revolution and Counter-Revolution: A Eurosceptical Enquiry', *History of Political Thought* 20/1 (1999), 125–39, at 137.

[65] See the invaluable study by Julian Hoppit, *Britain's Political Economies: Parliament and Economic Life, 1660–1800* (Cambridge: Cambridge University Press, 2017).

[66] Mary Poovey, *A History of the Modern Fact: Problems of Knowledge in the Sciences of Wealth and Society* (Chicago: University of Chicago Press, 1998).

[67] Keith Tribe, 'The Modern Fact in Theory and in Practice', *History Workshop Journal* 52 (2001), 266–72, at 268. See how this affects Poovey's treatment of Malthus: Poovey, *A History of the Modern Fact*, 292–4.

semantically overdetermined, having emerged from theology,[68] common-law thought,[69] and from an opposition between 'speculative' and 'experimental' in seventeenth-century natural philosophy.[70] 'Experience', as used by Burke, produced not only knowledge but laws and institutions, while making 'experiments' in laws and institutions was reckless; here politics and natural science could diverge over the value of experiments, although Ricardo and his colleagues were prepared to propose 'experiments' in government and law. 'Theory' was a latecomer to political discourse, and 'political theorist' even later; 'theory' could even be used as a dysphemism in the seventeenth century by those committed to 'practice' and 'experience'.[71]

As for 'enthusiasm', accounts of this phenomenon proliferated in England after the Civil War (1642–1651). The term originally denoted an intellectual malady that led the afflicted to claim that they possessed divine inspiration, and it was wielded against the sectaries who were blamed for England's political troubles. For some decades now, enthusiasm in this sense has been recognized as the major target of Enlightenment thought. And, most importantly, this research has shown that the meaning of the word came to be expanded in the eighteenth century to take in nominally secular thought, such as speculation on political life and political economy.[72] The term therefore enjoyed a large measure of substitutability with terms such as 'love of theory' and 'phantom of the imagination', both of which Ricardo was supposed by his critics to have succumbed.[73] What was being suggested by these terms was not faulty epistemology but the failure to guard one's ethical person against the dangers inherent to abstract thought.

This explains why a piece of political economy articulated in abstract terms was vulnerable to being perceived as theoretical enthusiasm, which

---

[68] Peter Harrison, 'Experimental Religion and Experimental Science in Early Modern England', *Intellectual History Review* 21/4 (2011), 413–33.

[69] J. G. A. Pocock, *The Ancient Constitution and the Feudal Law: English Historical Thought in the Seventeenth Century* (Cambridge: Cambridge University Press, 1957).

[70] Peter R. Anstey, 'Experimental Versus Speculative Natural Philosophy', in Peter R. Anstey and John A. Schuster, eds., *The Science of Nature in the Seventeenth Century: Patterns of Change in Early Modern Natural Philosophy* (Dordrecht: Springer, 2005), 215–42.

[71] See David Kearns and Ryan Walter, 'Office, Political Theory, and the Political Theorist', *The Historical Journal* 63/2 (2020), 317–37.

[72] For an example of the polemic, see Meric Casaubon, *A Treatise Concerning Enthusiasme, As It is an Effect of Nature: but is Mistaken by Many for Either Divine Inspiration, or Diabolicall Possession, Second Edition: Revised, and Enlarged* (London, 1656). For enthusiasm as central to the Enlightenment in general, see J. G. A. Pocock, 'Enthusiasm: The Antiself of Enlightenment', *Huntington Library Quarterly* 60/1/2 (1997), 7–28; Michael Heyd, *'Be Sober and Reasonable': The Critique of Enthusiasm in the Seventeenth and Early Eighteenth Centuries* (Leiden: Brill, 1995).

[73] See, for example, Anonymous, 'Review of *Des Principes de L'Economie Politique et de L'Impôt*', *The British Critic* (December 1819), 561–78. Reprinted in Terry Peach, ed., *David Ricardo: Critical Responses*, vol. 1 (London: Routledge, 2003), 130–44, at 138. Anonymous, 'Article XV. Political Economy and Taxation', *British Review* (November 1817), 309–33, at 312.

compromised its ability to act as political counsel. This fact, in turn, explains why attempts to produce manuals in political economy were usually concerned with guarding against this danger. Consider Sir James Steuart's *Principles of Political Oeconomy* (1767), in which Steuart conceded that the production of abstract systems was a danger to the statesman's reasoning.[74] The more famous account of system as a danger to the statesman's reasoning comes from Adam Smith, set out at length in the sixth edition of *The Theory of Moral Sentiments* (1789). There the 'spirit of system' was treated as a malady because it compromised the statesman's officeholding, potentially inflaming his public spirit to 'the madness of fanaticism', at which point he would pursue aesthetic and political ideals regardless of either the degree of change involved or the people's ability to accept such change.[75] It is worth noting that Smith was judged to have failed to avoid exactly this vice in *Wealth of Nations* (1776) by his first and most acute critic, Thomas Pownall, the former Governor of Massachusetts, who identified 'metaphysicks' and 'theory' as key dangers in Smith's work, along with Smith's tendency for abstract thought, both of which disqualified *Wealth of Nations* from acting as a basis for counsel.[76]

As noted, this issue was inflamed after the French Revolution, making political economy even more exposed to the allegation that it represented abstract madness that endangered the reasoning of those who imbibed its lessons. This allegation was levied most colourfully by Robert Southey, an exemplar of High Toryism (after a youthful flirtation with the Revolution).[77] Southey's key target was Malthus, about whom he worried because of Malthus's potential influence with the 'metaphysical politician'—a legislator who suffered from philosophical pretensions.[78] Southey had particularly in mind the regulation of corn and bullion using political economy's metaphysics because he held that they diseased the legislator's mind in the same manner that scholastic philosophy had corrupted the reason of Europe. In this regard, it is worth quoting Southey's explicit attack on the idea of using Malthus's arguments as the basis for legislative action, for in it we can sense the force of his rejection of political economy as just another strand of metaphysical nonsense.

---

[74] James Steuart, *An Inquiry into the Principles of Political Oeconomy*, 2 vols. (London, 1767), 1: ix, 3.

[75] Adam Smith, *TMS* VI.ii.2.15.

[76] Thomas Pownall, *Corr* 337–76, at 338–40.

[77] Geoffrey Carnall, *Robert Southey and His Age: The Development of a Conservative Mind* (Oxford: Oxford University Press, 1960). For Southey on political economy, see especially Philip Connell, *Romanticism, Economics and the Question of 'Culture'* (Oxford: Oxford University Press, 2005), chapter 5.

[78] Robert Southey, 'Essay V. On the State of the Poor and the Means Pursued by the Society for Bettering their Condition. 1816', in *Essays, Moral and Political*, vol. 1 (London, 1832), 159–250, at 245.

To legislate upon theories of population would be as absurd as if a physician upon some theory of pneumatics were to set respiration to music, and order all his patients to regulate their breathings by the time. You might as well attempt to regulate the seasons, or to legislate for hunger and thirst.[79]

In sum, political economy was fighting for its place in the world of politics, with its champions treating it as a science of happiness, wealth, and reform, while its enemies perceived only new clothes for enthusiasm to wear. In this context, it is absolutely inappropriate for the historian to approach every thinker as if they had an analytical system since the construction of such systems was controversial in a society fearful of the linked threats of Jacobinism, revolution, and enthusiasm.

If political economy is to be connected with this historical context, then it will be necessary to study the ethics-talk of the day and abandon the method-talk of our own. Doing so will require investigating Ricardo's relationship to the general culture of ethical self-fashioning that was alive in this period. Ricardo certainly studied Bacon, Locke, and Stewart as guides to reasoning at the end of 1817. As James Mill advised Ricardo, the virtue of an author such as Locke was that he 'trains the mind into paths of right inquiry'.[80] Ricardo's other avenue to the culture of ethical government of the mind was through debates over religious belief, above all, the question of toleration, which he encountered as a Unitarian, the husband of a Quaker, and as a Member of Parliament.[81] Yet exposure to a culture and its active deployment are different things, and evidence for the latter must be investigated on a case-by-case basis. As noted, there is variation across the moments of Ricardo's work, which leads us to privilege the moment over both Ricardo the man and Mill the mentor, who failed to ever tell Ricardo that his arguments might contravene accepted protocols for good reasoning, something that Malthus and Hutches Trower did tell Ricardo. Of course, Mill might not have perceived the flaw, having been exposed to it himself on occasion.[82] The more general point is that, in the world inhabited by Malthus and Ricardo, the production of political economy by political economists and its uptake by statesman were regarded as *ethical* activities, a supposition visible in the vocabulary of theory, practice, and enthusiasm. This is a context different from our own,

---

[79] Ibid., 246.

[80] James Mill, 'Mill to Ricardo', *Works and Correspondence*, 7: 194–9, at 197.

[81] Sergio Cremaschi, 'Theological Themes in Ricardo's Papers and Correspondence', *The European Journal of the History of Economic Thought* 24/4 (2017), 784–808. We can look forward to Sergio Cremaschi's forthcoming monograph on this topic.

[82] See T. B. Macaulay's attack on Mill in these terms in the *Edinburgh Review* in 1829, reprinted as T. B. Macaulay, 'Mill's Essay on Government: Utilitarian Logic and Politics by T. B. Macaulay, *Edinburgh Review*, no. xcvii', in Jack Lively and John Rees, eds., *Utilitarian Logic and Politics: James Mill's 'Essay on Government', Macaulay's Critique and the Ensuing Debate* (Oxford: Clarendon Press, 1978), 97–129.

but we have largely been content to pretend that it was not by deploying the notions of method and model.

At this point it is worth being more precise and acknowledging that the specific contexts and intellectual traditions in which Malthus and Ricardo operated held points of attraction and repulsion towards one another and that each man was positioned differently regarding the great question of the day: reform. Ricardo's milieu can be described as one of utilitarianism and Unitarianism. James Mill has traditionally been seen as a key figure in Ricardo's intellectual formation, but this view needs to be revised.[83] It can, however, be said that Ricardo was encouraged by Mill to approach reform as if it were simply a question of translating the science of good government into legislation, at times requiring that society be given a 'shake' to precipitate the change.[84] The result would be progress and happiness, not only for Britain, but for the world. Sharing in this disposition, Ricardo had some blind spots when it came to politics as it was practised by his nation. For example, he scorned political parties in favour of the science of good government[85] and generally avoided the concept of the 'national interest' in favour of imagining what could be done to hasten the world's rational progress.[86]

This last feature of Ricardo's thought was bound with his Unitarianism and his relationship with Thomas Belsham, a leader of the Friends of Peace. For Ricardo was prepared to treat wars as driven by the pursuit of 'private advantage', the so-called war interest identified by the anti-war movement.[87] Ricardo's Unitarianism also manifested itself in his *ethos* of free inquiry after truth, a version of which Edmund Burke had identified as toxic for established institutions and the order that they provided for society.[88] It is at this point that Ricardo's flippancy towards the institutions of state power becomes intelligible not as mere recklessness, as it was portrayed by some of his intellectual opponents, but as an ethical commitment shaped by religious belief. He simply could not abide Burke's counsel to be grateful for the actual blessings delivered by an imperfect

[83] See especially Sergio Cremaschi, 'Ricardo and the Utilitarians', *The European Journal of the History of Economic Thought* 11/3 (2004), 377–403.

[84] Mill, 'Mill to Ricardo', 7: 198.

[85] See, for example, Ricardo, 'Ricardo to Trower', *Works and Correspondence*, 7: 258–61, at 260.

[86] For indicative examples, see Ricardo's Letters 103, 219, 234. For some of his rare uses of 'national interest', see Letters 27, 193 (Ricardo, *Works and Correspondence*, vols. 6 and 7).

[87] Ricardo, 'Observations on Parliamentary Reform', *Works and Correspondence*, 5: 495–503, at 498. J. E. Cookson, *The Friends of Peace: Anti-War Liberalism in England, 1793–1815* (Cambridge: Cambridge University Press, 1982), 3, 88, 163–6.

[88] For Ricardo's comments in Parliament in support of free discussion of religion, see Ricardo, 'Religious Opinions', *Works and Correspondence*, 5: 324–31, at 330. The Unitarian leader Thomas Belsham united free inquiry and Christianity in the manner that is characteristic of that faith. See, for example, Thomas Belsham, *Elements of the Philosophy of the Human Mind, and of Moral Philosophy* (London, 1801), i–vi. See further Sergio Cremaschi, 'Belsham, Thomas and Ricardo', in Heinz D. Kurz and Neri Salvadori, eds., *The Elgar Companion to David Ricardo* (Cheltenham: Edward Elgar, 2015), 14–17.

Constitution when rational reform could straighten the crooked timber: 'Whilst any evil can be removed, or any improvement adopted, we should listen to no suggestions so inconclusive as that we have been doing well'.[89]

As an Anglican divine, Malthus was obliged to mind a different set of ethical imperatives. Malthus developed his *Essay on the Principle of Population* (1798) using the materials of natural theology, and Mill rejected this genre as incapable of producing credible knowledge, even writing in correspondence to Ricardo of 'Poor Mr. Malthus . . . for a man to be *obliged* to believe a certain set of opinions'.[90] Where Mill's rejection of theology as a framework for political economy derived from apostasy, Ricardo seems to have arrived at his position through theology, something like a 'limited scepticism' regarding the powers of the human mind to know God's will.[91] In the place of this Unitarian stance, Malthus had a 'stern *paideia*', clearest in the first edition of his *Essay on the Principle of Population* (1798).[92] There a heterodox Anglican theodicy drove the argument: God created poverty to teach us how to govern our passions; the scientific reform of political institutions will align them with God's will as disclosed by natural theology. In other words, Malthus adopted precisely the program for knowing and reforming the world that Ricardo had rejected. This clash was clearest in their debates over the nature of rent, with Malthus deploying all the power of natural theology to construe rent as a gift from God. Rather like the rival natural law programs of the seventeenth century, here we have confession-specific programmes for reform, a fact that powerfully shaped their reception and (non-reception) by lawmakers in an intolerant Anglican state.[93]

---

[89] Ricardo, 'Observations on Parliamentary Reform', 499–500.

[90] Mill, 'Mill to Ricardo', *Works and Correspondence*, 7: 210–13, at 212. And note the contrast between Malthus's theodicy and Ricardo's intention to live in 'a state of doubt'. Ricardo, 'Ricardo to Mill', *Works and Correspondence*, 7: 204–7, at 206.

[91] Cremaschi, 'Theological Themes in Ricardo's Papers and Correspondence'.

[92] See J. G. A. Pocock, *Virtue, Commerce, and History: Essays on Political Thought and History, Chiefly in the Eighteenth Century* (Cambridge: Cambridge University Press, 1985), 293. For an account of the changes in Malthus's theology, see Sergio Cremaschi, *Utilitarianism and Malthus's Virtue Ethics: Respectable, Virtuous and Happy* (London: Routledge, 2014). But note John Pullen's review of Cremaschi for the difficulties in assessing the evidence: J. M. Pullen, 'Variables and Constants in the Theology of T. R. Malthus', *History of Economics Review* 63/1 (2016), 21–32. For the desire to secularize Malthus, see Donald Winch, 'Robert Malthus: Christian Moral Scientist, Arch-Demoralizer or Implicit Secular Utilitarian?', *Utilitas* 5/2 (1993), 239–53; Ryan Walter, 'Malthus's Sacred History: Outflanking Civil History in the Late Enlightenment', *Rethinking History* (forthcoming). Note also the excellent new study by Niall O'Flaherty, in which Malthus's connection with William Paley's theology is brought into clear view: Niall O'Flaherty, *Utilitarianism in the Age of Enlightenment: The Moral and Political Thought of William Paley* (Cambridge: Cambridge University Press, 2018), chapter 11.

[93] J. C. D. Clark, *English Society, 1660–1832: Religion, Ideology and Politics During the Ancien Regime* (Cambridge: Cambridge University Press, 2000). For the long-term process by which the theodicy was removed from the principle of population, see Ryan Walter, 'Malthus's Principle of Population in Britain: Restatement and Antiquation', in Gilbert Faccarello, Masashi Izumo, and Hiromi Morishita, eds., *Malthus Across Nations: The Reception of Thomas Robert Malthus in Europe, America and Japan* (Cheltenham: Edward Elgar, 2020), 18–52.

The differences between Malthus and Ricardo were also expressed in the divergent ways in which each sought to equip the figure of the statesman for rule. For Malthus, the legislator was to align human institutions with God's ordering of the world *and* to care for the state's interests in secular time. This task was not as bifocal as it may sound because of the central role of food in the world's divine order. More plainly, Malthus identified the food supply as a crucial component of the national interest that the statesman needed to keep in view. For Ricardo, by contrast, the statesman's key task was to root out private interests wherever they blocked the progress of good government. As for food, Ricardo had little to say regarding state prudence because he held to something far more rationalist: he simply trusted that free international markets would stabilize the food supply. These diverging outlooks even surfaced in relation to the very Constitution of the nation, which Ricardo wanted to reformat using a species of Mill's calculus of the few and the many. The result would have been the obliteration of the Constitution's balance (a consequence to which Ricardo appears to have been deaf), exactly the balance that a good country Whig such as Malthus was committed to protecting.[94] Thus, the doctrinal contest between Malthus and Ricardo was also a contest between ethical and intellectual cultures, something that is difficult to capture by pretending that this was all about method and models.

Preview of the Argument

This book is divided into three parts. In Part I, the new context for locating Malthus and Ricardo that has been sketched so far is embellished. This context is approached in terms of the vocabulary of theory, practice, and associated terms and this vocabulary's complex intersection with debates over the intellectual and ethical conduct of statesmen and political economists. That is, the vocabulary of theory and practice is taken to be a particular instance of the more general culture of ethics-talk. A debate over the relative merits of theory and practice was initiated by Burke, who attacked speculative theory in his *Reflections on the Revolution in France* (1790).[95] James Mackintosh confronted Burke's anti-theory claims in his *Vindiciae Gallicae* (1791); he then defended theory more prudently in later texts after having moderated his position on the French Revolution. As someone who was personally acquainted with both Malthus and Ricardo, and who held a Chair at the East India College before pursuing a parliamentary career,

---

[94] For Ricardo's deafness, see the last paragraph of Ricardo's letter to Trower: Ricardo, 'Ricardo to Trower', *Works and Correspondence*, 7: 365–70, at 366. For Malthus on balance, see Collini, Winch, and Burrow, *That Noble Science of Politics*, 75, 83.

[95] For the broader debate, see Gregory Claeys, ed., *Political Writings of the 1790s*, 8 vols. (London: Pickering & Chatto, 1995).

Mackintosh is a useful comparison for Professor Malthus and the Member for Portalington, Ricardo. Dugald Stewart also responded to Burke in the first two volumes of his *Elements of the Philosophy of the Human Mind* (1792 and 1814). There are known connections between Ricardo, Malthus, and Stewart's pupils.[96] Yet these personal connections are only noted in passing because the focus is rather on the way that the epistemological, ethical, and political were tied together in these texts via ethico-intellectual disciplines that came to be articulated with the vocabulary of theory and practice following the French Revolution. The aim, in other words, is to show how theory could be attacked and defended. Doing so will allow Malthus's *Essay* to emerge as a late intervention into this debate, taking the side of theory while expelling the dangerous speculations of Condorcet and William Godwin. This linguistic context then provides a new starting point for investigating the political economy of Malthus and Ricardo in Parts II and III.

Part II consists of Chapter 2 and Chapter 3, each examining a leading episode of the period: the Bullion Controversy and the Corn Laws debate, respectively. For those familiar with the debate over the nation's currency, it will be clear how it possessed precisely the elements at issue in this book since it concerned how a hallowed institution, the Bank of England, might be reformed in view of the precepts of the new speculative science. Ricardo distinguished himself in this setting as a champion of rational reform by identifying the Bank's interests as standing in opposition to the public's, and he treated the matter as a straightforward case of the application of scientific understanding to an archaic institution. His opponents accused him of theoretical enthusiasm and of encouraging a bold experiment—and at a most inopportune time, since Napoleon was still menacing Europe. Ricardo showed himself to be rhetorically adept by using the preferred vocabulary of his opponents against them. For his part, Malthus sided with Ricardo over the major issues but registered some reservations that, in hindsight, would seem to augur the future course of their confrontation over the nature of good theory and the ethical obligations facing the good theorist. In short, this chapter adduces the first piece of evidence for the central role of the vocabulary of theory and practice and the corresponding absence of our notions of method and model.

Chapter 3 examines the Corn Laws debate of 1813–1815 by focusing on the pamphlet literature published in anticipation of parliamentary debate in 1815. Ricardo's *Essay on Profits* (1815) was published in dialogue with—and using elements of—Malthus's *Observations on the Effects of the Corn Laws* (1814) and

---

[96] Collini, Winch, and Burrow, *That Noble Science of Politics*, chapter 1; Plassart, *The Scottish Enlightenment and the French Revolution*, 165–75. Pietro Corsi has shown how debate over the style of reasoning appropriate to political economy was mediated, in part, through a preexisting debate over Stewart's philosophy of mind. Pietro Corsi, 'The Heritage of Dugald Stewart: Oxford Philosophy and Method of Political Economy', *Nuncius* 2/2 (1987), 89–144.

Grounds of an Opinion (1815). All three texts are examined in relation to competing analyses of the issue from the parliamentarian Henry Parnell and from Robert Torrens, whose *An Essay on the External Corn Trade* (1815) shared key elements with the pamphlets of Malthus and Ricardo. The central claim advanced is that all four authors were engaged in *casuistry*, where the clash of rival principles was adjudicated in view of the circumstances of the case.

The general characteristics of casuistry have been described by Albert R. Jonsen and Stephen Toulmin in their classic study.[97] Above all, casuistry accepts that principles cannot fully determine conduct. This is because the circumstances of a given case are so difficult to determine or calculate in advance—given the complexity and vagaries of human conduct—that principles must be modified or made conditional on local factors in order to be applied. The other difficulty in moral and political reasoning that casuistry addresses is the indeterminacy that arises when there are rival principles operating in a given field. In such situations, casuistical reasoning steps in as a local means of ranking, suspending or modifying the competing principles. The purpose of casuistry is therefore not to produce universal proofs and deductions but to resolve particular cases by following maxims and adducing probabilistic arguments.[98] Casuistical reasoning still flourishes today in common law jurisprudence, international law, political decision-making, and medical ethics, but as an explicit genre of publication it entered into decline around the end of the seventeenth century. Before this occurred, however, casuistry had migrated into natural law and reason of state where it secured anchorage deep into the nineteenth century.[99] It is not, therefore, surprising that recent research has discovered casuistry in some interesting places in the late eighteenth century.[100]

By centring the casuistical character of the Corn Laws debate, Chapter 3 is intended to revise current understandings. Not only is the existing historiography ignorant of the existence of casuistry as a style of argument that was once central to Europe's intellectual life, but the current literature is organized around the supposed 'discovery' or proto-articulation of the concepts of comparative advantage and diminishing returns in this debate, with Malthus, Torrens, and

---

[97] Alfred R. Jonsen and Stephen Toulmin, *The Abuse of Casuistry: A History of Moral Reasoning* (Berkeley: University of California Press, 1988).

[98] Ibid., 250–65.

[99] Ibid., 276–88.

[100] Lorenzo Cello, 'The Legitimacy of International Interventions in Vattel's *The Law of Nations*', *Global Intellectual History* 2/2 (2017), 105–23; Ian Hunter, 'Kant and Vattel in Context: Cosmopolitan Philosophy and Diplomatic Casuistry', *History of European Ideas* 39/4 (2013), 477–502; Ian Hunter, 'Religious Freedom in Early Modern Germany: Theology, Philosophy, and Legal Casuistry', *South Atlantic Quarterly* 113/1 (2014), 37–62; Ryan Walter, 'Adam Smith's Free Trade Casuistry', *Global Intellectual History* 1/1 (2016), 61–82. More generally, see Carlo Ginzburg and Lucio Biasiori, eds., *A Historical Approach to Casuistry: Norms and Exceptions in a Comparative Perspective* (London: Bloomsbury, 2018).

Ricardo playing the lead roles in most accounts.[101] By revealing how the leading contributions were actually instances of casuistry, an old style of argument with its own history and logic, neither of which can be assimilated to contemporary economics, the entire debate takes on a new appearance. In particular, the usual complaints regarding Malthus's supposed vacillating on the issue of free trade appear as misunderstandings of the genre in which he was working, while Ricardo's famed theoretical rigor emerges as maladroitness in the same genre.

Part III shifts attention to the clash of doctrinal statements as found in the first and second editions of Ricardo's *Principles of Political Economy, and Taxation* (1817 and 1819) and Malthus's reply text, *Principles of Political Economy. Considered with a View to Their Practical Application* (1820). The contest is studied at length over the remaining three substantive chapters and takes the book into a technical domain. Yet Malthus's titular invocation of 'practical application' clearly signals that, in addition to being a counter-doctrine text, his book also attempted to demonstrate the correct manner of reasoning for political economists. Good reasoning in this case included the proper way of conceiving the links between doctrine and legislative action, and the ultimate aims of government. As a result, some of the differences between Malthus and Ricardo are best understood as a result of technical issues of a semi-autonomous nature, such as the question of an invariable standard of value, while other differences must be related to the fact that Malthus and Ricardo belonged to different intellectual milieus that were often at cross purposes in confessional and political terms, as discussed earlier.

In consequence, what has usually been studied primarily as a dry debate over doctrine was in fact a contest to define the role of Europe's newest intellectual, the political economist. Malthus and Ricardo managed to keep the debate civil in their correspondence, each giving the other ample warning of upcoming attacks and even opportunities to preview the criticisms.[102] Yet the stakes were high: the Constitution, the role of the landed aristocracy in the economic life of the nation, the relative merits of tradition and reason, and the confession that would underwrite political economy. Glancing ahead, Ricardo's move from political economy to constitutional design, undertaking the latter with the ethos of the former, has been mirrored in more recent times, above all in the so-called *public choice* approach to politics. This points to the overall significance of this book beyond revising claims in the history of economic thought: Ricardo's ambitions and successes were a shock to his society, but in ours they would barely make a ripple.

---

[101] See, again, John Pullen for the difficulties involved in making this claim regarding Ricardo and comparative advantage: J. M. Pullen, 'Did Ricardo Really Have a Law of Comparative Advantage? A Comparison of Ricardo's Version and the Modern Version', *History of Economics Review* 44/1 (2006), 59–75.

[102] Not always to perfect satisfaction. See, for example, Ricardo's complaint to Mill after Malthus had read to Ricardo sections of the draft of what would become Malthus's *Principles*: Ricardo, 'Ricardo to Mill', *Works and Correspondence*, 7: 371–3, at 372.

PART I

1

The Debate over Theory Before
Malthus and Ricardo

Burke, Mackintosh, and Stewart

This chapter establishes a new linguistic context for reading the works of Malthus and Ricardo, and it is intended to replace unhistorical talk of method and models. Nobody in Ricardo's lifetime thought or wrote in these terms as we do, but they often thought and wrote in terms of the correct relationship between theory and practice, and a minority was prepared to cautiously defend a new type of intellectual: the 'theorist'. Malthus and Ricardo would join this minority when they came to reflect on what they were doing when they wrote political economy, as we will see.

In attempting to establish a new context for Malthus and Ricardo, it is necessary to bring to view a major preoccupation of the period, which was to prescribe the qualities and attitudes that legislators needed to adopt if they were to make good laws. This advice often concerned the proper relationship between theory and practice and how to avoid being seduced by theory and thus succumbing to enthusiasm. That is, making good laws required that the politician govern their mind. The advice that a writer unfolded on these themes would usually bear a clear relationship with their political views, with those favouring immediate reforms tending to endorse theory, while the gradualist would prefer thinking that drew on practice and experience. Investigating this context thus requires revealing the complex links between the vocabulary of theory and practice, prescriptions for governing one's mind, and positions on reform.

This task is approached by discussing the debate between Edmund Burke, James Mackintosh, and Dugald Stewart over the role of theoretical knowledge in politics. In addition to their importance, these authors provide a useful benchmark against which to read the claims and tactics of Malthus and Ricardo. It should be stressed at this point that nothing like a spectrum of political identities is being assembled. Instead, the aim is to convey a sense of the possible vocabulary choices and rhetorical tactics that were available to theory sympathizers when they attempted to respond to Burke's attack on theory in a fraught political context. For Malthus and Ricardo also wrote in difficult political contexts in which theory was attacked from practice, thus, by being able to view their

Before Method and Models. Ryan Walter, Oxford University Press. © Oxford University Press 2021.
DOI: 10.1093/oso/9780197603055.003.0002

linguistic and strategic moves in the light of Mackintosh's and Stewart's, it will be possible to make sense of Malthus and Ricardo in historical terms and resist the temptation to invoke methods and models.

With this aim in mind, a few words should be said about Burke, Mackintosh, Stewart, and their texts before turning to examine their arguments in detail. Starting with Burke, the key to his attack on speculative theory was his claim that its teachings would lead to disaster, as they had in France. Above all, Burke targeted the notion that man possessed rights prior to his entry into society. Burke insisted that any statesman who thought in this way would be systematically misled when they came to ponder the Constitution: the correct stance was to instead trust in established institutions and traditions. In making this case, Burke made extensive use of the vocabulary of theory and practice. The key texts are *Reflections on the Revolution in France* (1790), and *Appeal from the New to the Old Whigs* (1791). Burkean principles were recognized at the time as having won tremendous intellectual ground, having been helped by the change in political climate that occurred once the Revolution began its ugly course in 1793.[1] In short, Burke's arguments popularized the rhetorical tactics that would be used against theory in the 1790s, and which were later used against political economy in general and Ricardo's brand in particular in the 1800s.

Burke's intellectual success was personally significant for the Scottish 'philosophic Whig' James Mackintosh.[2] Mackintosh was trained by Dugald Stewart in the broad intellectual culture of moral philosophy and natural law that had underwritten political economy's (now suspect) foundational text, Smith's *Wealth of Nations*.[3] Mackintosh's spirited defence of theory in his *Vindiciae Gallicae* (1791) helped his career with the Foxite faction of the Whig party, and it likely appealed to a Whig such as Malthus, too, because Mackintosh hit a middle position between Burke and Paine.[4] Alas, the turning of the tide that saw Burke's principles surge forward pushed the politically ambitious Mackintosh onto the back foot, signalled in his *Discourses on the Law of Nature and Nations* (1799).[5]

---

[1] Francis Plowden's assessment was that Burke's principles came to be widely adopted shortly after his *Reflections* appeared (Francis Plowden, *A Short History of the British Empire in the Last Twenty Months* (London, 1794), 19).

[2] Donald Winch, 'Introduction', in Donald Winch, ed., *Vindiciae Gallicae and Other Writings on the French Revolution* (Indianapolis: Liberty Fund, 2006), ix–xvii, at ix. For this notion more generally, see L. S. Jacyna, *Philosophic Whigs: Medicine, Science and Citizenship in Edinburgh, 1789–1848* (London: Routledge, 1994), chapter 1.

[3] Of course, Stewart and Smith diverged on some crucial issues. See, in particular, Stewart's 'Account of the Life of Adam Smith', where it is claimed that, at times, Smith was 'misled by too great a desire of generalizing his principles': Stewart, *EPS* II.41.

[4] Nobuhiko Nakazawa, 'Malthus's Political Views in 1798: A "Foxite" Whig?', *History of Economics Review* 56/1 (2012), 14–28; Seamus Deane, *The French Revolution and Enlightenment in England, 1789–1832* (Cambridge, Mass.: Harvard University Press, 1988), 48–9.

[5] The retreat is typically overstated. See the judicious handling of this issue in Knud Haakonssen, *Natural Law and Moral Philosophy: From Grotius to the Scottish Enlightenment* (Cambridge: Cambridge University Press, 1996), 265–93.

Mackintosh thus nicely illustrates the way that the debates of the time were cross-cutting, with one's position on the relationship between theory and practice correlated with one's political allegiances and position on reform. That is, it is taken for granted in this book that we are dealing with texts that had a combative character, which requires that we read them with an eye for the usual tactics of intellectual contest—above all, the strategic deployment of vocabulary, redefinition, and redescription.[6]

In contrast to his former pupil, Stewart was not buffeted by the winds of change, but he felt them nevertheless as Edinburgh followed the national mood and began to look unkindly on both French principles and any Scots who might sympathize with them.[7] Nevertheless, the fact was that Stewart enjoyed a university setting that had been shaped by those 'moderate literati' who had gained control of church and university around the middle of the eighteenth century.[8] In this context, *Professor* Stewart could suggest that it might be Burke who was on the wrong side of the debate regarding theory and politics. In examining how Stewart made this case for the role of theory in politics, it will become clear that he did not conduct his defence in the register of epistemology or philosophy of science, but in the idiom of ethics-talk. For Stewart provided detailed guidance on how to conduct the mental operations of abstraction and conception and how to safely apply their results, conceding that when this was poorly done the results could be enthusiasm and political turmoil. The key text is the first volume of *Elements of the Philosophy of the Human Mind* (1792), where Stewart was clearly responding to Burke in certain passages.[9] Stewart's concession that theory could go astray when conducted by the uninitiated created room for strategic manoeuvring: Stewart construed enthusiasm and the furious innovations of the Jacobins as false theory emerging from ethical failures. If Stewart were able to make the case that theory and abstraction were indispensable to the science of politics, then he might claim that the solution did not lay with spurning theory—the position of Burke—but in producing theory with ethico-technical

---

[6] This perspective is indebted to the invaluable study by Conal Condren, *Political Vocabularies: Word Change and the Nature of Politics* (Rochester: University of Rochester Press, 2017).

[7] See Collini, Winch, and Burrow, *That Noble Science of Politics*, 32–3.

[8] See Richard B. Sher, *Church and University in the Scottish Enlightenment: The Moderate Literati of Edinburgh* (Edinburgh: Edinburgh University Press, 1985); Nicholas Phillipson, 'The Scottish Enlightenment', in Roy Porter and Mikuláš Teich, eds., *The Enlightenment in National Context* (Cambridge: Cambridge University Press, 1981), 19–40; Nicholas Phillipson, 'The Pursuit of Virtue in Scottish University Education: Dugald Stewart and Scottish Moral Philosophy in the Enlightenment', in Nicholas Phillipson, ed., *Universities, Society, and the Future: A Conference Held on the 400th Anniversary of the University of Edinburgh* (Edinburgh: Edinburgh University Press, 1983), 82–101. Although Stewart paid a price for his respectful treatment of Condorcet; see Dugald Stewart, 'Memoir of Dugald Stewart', *The Collected Works of Dugald Stewart*, ed. William Hamilton, vol. 10 (Edinburgh: Thomas Constable and Co., 1858), i–cxv, at lxx–lxxv.

[9] See Ryan Walter, 'Defending Political Theory After Burke: Stewart's Intellectual Disciplines and the Demotion of Practice', *Journal of the History of Ideas* 80/3 (2019), 387–408, at 394–406.

proficiency of exactly the type that his text dispensed to a learned elite. We will see that this was Stewart's course.

Burke, Mackintosh, and Stewart on theory and practice: this is the terrain to be covered in what follows. Its importance for the overall argument of the book is hard to overstate because it will make it possible in future chapters to see that Malthus and Ricardo were doing the same thing—justifying a place for theorists in the science of politics—and not discussing method or building models. Discovering the similarity between the vocabulary and rhetorical strategies of Malthus and Ricardo and those of Burke, Mackintosh, and Stewart will also reveal that political economy did not possess its own set of terms for evaluating and defending its knowledge claims. Rather, the leading political economists of the day simply drew on ready-to-hand terms that were in active service in debates over the nature of theory and reform. There were not, in other words, 'economists' in the sense that we use that word today. Instead, there were freshly minted 'theorists' who had emerged unexpectedly as the science of politics processed the French Revolution.

Edmund Burke and the Attack on Theory

Burke's *Reflections on the Revolution in France* (1790) began by examining the claims and reasoning embodied in Richard Price's sermon 'On the Love of our Country.'[10] Price had delivered his sermon late in 1789, and Burke read the published version early the following year. According to Burke, Price misrepresented the Glorious Revolution of 1688 so that he could conflate it with the French Revolution of 1789. The nerve of Burke's factual rejection of Price's account is that what 1688 truly represented was an act of 'necessity'—a tolerable departure from the established principle of hereditary monarchy in order to preserve the Protestant Church and State. The crucial point of Burke's counter-narrative was that the Glorious Revolution did not establish popular sovereignty because the existing political nation did not 'dissolve' but merely 'regenerated.'[11] As a consequence, the monarchy that continued into Burke's time was not elective but hereditary.

Such was Burke's rejection of Price's facts. He also disqualified Price's reasoning because it represented a dangerous form of enthusiasm that exhibited disturbing similarities to the king-killing of the previous century. As might be expected, at this point of his attack Burke used the vocabulary of theory and practice. Burke

---

[10] See Richard Price, 'A Discourse on the Love of Our Country', in *Price: Political Writings*, ed. D. O. Thomas (Cambridge: Cambridge University Press, 1991), 176–96.
[11] Burke, 'Reflections on the Revolution in France', *Writings and Speeches*, 8: 53–293, at 72.

wrote, for example, that the claim that Britain's King was endowed with his office through popular election was an 'abstract principle', a 'theory', at variance with practice.[12] For a point of contrast, Burke nominated the *Petition of Right* (1628), a combat text produced by Parliament in their constitutional clashes with Charles I. In this text, Parliament did not invoke 'abstract principles' or 'general theories' or 'theoretic science' but referred to the 'practical wisdom' embodied in inherited and recorded freedoms.[13] The core of Burke's position was thus that real societies possessed institutions with histories and that the rights dispensed in such societies stood as the true boon of government, in opposition to speculative rights that were merely posited by theory and unanchored by existing institutions.

> Government is not made in virtue of natural rights, which may and do exist in total independence of it; and exist in much greater clearness, and in a much greater degree of abstract perfection: but their abstract perfection is their practical defect. By having a right to every thing they want every thing. Government is a contrivance of human wisdom to provide for human *wants*. Men have a right that these wants should be provided for by this wisdom ... as the liberties and the restrictions vary with times and circumstances, and admit of infinite modifications, they cannot be settled upon any abstract rule; and nothing is so foolish as to discuss them upon that principle.[14]

Burke's point, however, was that discussing rights in the abstract was exactly what the friends of French principles in England presumed to do. This made them dangerous because they were unable to draw on the intergenerational experience essential to the science of government. Such a time scale was necessary to political knowledge because the 'real effects of moral causes are not always immediate' but unfold over generations.[15] The implication was that those who planned better societies using a priori principles were ignorant of how human societies actually functioned.

More concerning was the fact that improvers were vulnerable to the intoxications of theory and utopia. Such intellectual intoxication was perceived to be a moral failing because it represented a lapse in the disciplines that defined the cultivated intellect. Undisciplined persons could become 'heated with their theories', while a 'spirit of innovation' was often linked to 'a selfish temper and confined views'.[16] Burke went further, however, and identified additional moral failings that accompanied a love of theory. For the argument here, the most

---

[12] Ibid., 64–5.
[13] Ibid., 82–3.
[14] Ibid., 110–11.
[15] Ibid., 111.
[16] Ibid., 108, 83.

important was that theorists allowed themselves to delight in 'sublime speculations' because 'never intending to go beyond speculation, it costs nothing to have it magnificent'.[17] In other words, theorists are not morally serious because they do not ponder the hard questions that arise from attempting to apply their knowledge to the world.

One of the theorist's closely related character flaws was indifference to the real benefits of settled government. This disposition arose because of the excessive value that theorists placed on imagined futures to be ushered in by revolution, in relation to which the good or bad administration of a government in the present was of small concern.[18] A final moral deficiency that made theorists and speculators ill-suited to the work of government was that their moral sentiments were deformed. Burke's leading example of this degradation was those representatives sent to France's Estates General early in 1789, who were only instructed to broach the topic of reforming the architecture of government; the idea of tearing down the existing arrangements for 'the erection of a theoretic experimental edifice in its place' was no part of their brief.[19] But the effect of wild politics was precisely to 'temper and harden the breast', enabling it to will violent action in the name of a new society, at the cost of corrupting 'all the well-placed sympathies of the human breast'.[20] For all these reasons, the heated theorist was a poor officer of reform and government.

This leads us to ask of Burke: What were the qualities and reasoning techniques that the good reformer was to possess? Much of his answer flowed from the premise that the work of government was primarily a technical and practical affair, not normative or theoretical: if you want to keep a person well-fed and healthy, you seek counsel from the farmer and the physician, not the metaphysician.[21] This did not mean that the good statesman was not a student of human nature. Rather, they were aware of the difference between first and second natures, the former given to humanity by God, the latter by education and habits.[22] That the citizen's second nature was so formed pointed the legislator to history for lessons and engendered a reverence for past examples, hence the legislator accepted the force of custom, prescription, and inheritance. All three concepts were tied together by Burke in his creative reworking of English common law for anti-revolutionary purposes.[23] The key point was to understand that political life

[17] Ibid., 114.
[18] Ibid.
[19] Ibid., 176.
[20] Ibid., 115.
[21] Ibid., 111.
[22] Ibid., 91.
[23] See Paul Lucas, 'II. On Edmund Burke's Doctrine of Prescription; Or, an Appeal from the New to the Old Lawyers', *The Historical Journal* 11/1 (1968), 35–63, at 57–8. Also see Paul Lucas, *Essays in the Margin of Blackstone's Commentaries* (unpublished PhD Thesis, Princeton University, Princeton, 1962).

mimicked the natural life of the human species in using time to transmit knowledge to ensure perpetuity. This precept yielded Burke's famous description of society as a partnership between the living, the dead, and those yet to be born.[24] A legislator who viewed society in these terms would not embrace purely theoretical plans for innovation: change ought to be natural and gradual.[25]

The fact that the government of a state was a practical task and constrained by history limited the materials with which the statesman could work. At this point it is crucial to underline what we might call the non-rationalist aspect of Burke's account. For the materials available to the legislator included the 'prejudices' of the people, understood in the older, non-pejorative sense of opinions.[26] Prejudices were a tremendous asset for the statesman because they could transmute duty into nature by making it a part of a community's non-reflective common sense. For example, an instinctive regard for the Constitution engendered protective obedience towards it, an asset for any legislator because of the stability that such obedience lent to a society. This boon was destroyed by the rage for theoretical reflection that not only encouraged citizens to explicitly reflect on something that ought to be taken for granted, but to look into its history with the aim of finding irrationality and imperfections as measured against a utopian standard.[27]

Perhaps the most important feature of the statesman's orientation as prescribed by Burke was caution. As the preceding discussion suggests, this caution was to be adopted in relation to the materials with which the statesman worked, namely, the existing interests and institutions of society, their established rights and privileges, and the prejudices that these phenomena generated. The greatest test for a cautionary statesman was those dramatic moments in the life of a state that saw a change in the architecture of power, as England witnessed in 1688. Even here, though, Burke was able to install prudence as the central value because he treated this moment as an act of preservation in which the existing structures were preserved as far as possible. The ideals were 'conservation and correction', and, to achieve them, 'We compensate, we reconcile, we balance'.[28] It

---

[24] Burke, 'Reflections on the Revolution in France', *Writings and Speeches*, 82–4, 147.

[25] Iain Hampsher-Monk has noted that Burke was drawing on Bacon's essay, 'Of Innovations' (Iain Hampsher-Monk in Edmund Burke, 'Reflections on the Revolution in France', in *Revolutionary Writings: Reflections on the Revolution in France and the First Letter on a Regicide Peace*, ed. Iain Hampsher-Monk (Cambridge: Cambridge University, 2014), 1–250, at 35 n72. For the passage of Bacon quoted by Hampsher-Monk, see Francis Bacon, 'Of Innovations', in *The Essays or Counsels, Civil and Moral of Francis Bacon*, ed. Henry Morley (London, 1883), 113–15, at 114. This is another example of how the defining event of the eighteenth century was processed through a seventeenth-century vocabulary.

[26] This claim is taken from Iain Hampsher-Monk's reading of this passage (Hampsher-Monk in Burke 'Reflections on the Revolution in France', in *Revolutionary Writings*, 90 n184).

[27] Burke, 'Reflections on the Revolution in France', *Writings and Speeches*, 142.

[28] Ibid., 72, 217.

followed that one of the statesman's key tasks was to calculate costs and benefits, as we would say today. In Burke's more casuistical phrasing: 'The rights of men in governments are their advantages; and these are often in balances between differences of good; in compromises sometimes between good and evil, and sometimes, between evil and evil. Political reason is a computing principle'.[29]

To bring these points together, and to anticipate the argument to come, these precepts are more than sufficient to indict every single text that Ricardo published. As stated in the Introduction, Ricardo rejected the idea that a society ought to be content with peace and prosperity when rational reforms could be identified, and if that meant trampling on established interests, then this posed no obstacle to his mind. The idea that compromise was needed to preserve the body politic appeared to Ricardo as mere apology for historically granted privileges, and history had no warrant in his analysis, which instead identified the public interest and then looked for its impairment by private interest. As will be seen in the following chapter, this was precisely how Ricardo portrayed the Bank of England: a private interest that obstructed good policy on currency. For others, however, the Bank was an august institution at the base of the Whig regime that had led England out of its troubles in the seventeenth century and into its preeminence on the world stage. For Burke the injunction was: preserve. For Ricardo it was rather: make rational.

Ricardo's attitude towards the issue of reforming the institutions of the state was driven by his Unitarianism and utilitarianism. It therefore had complex connections with the rationalist part of the Whig party, from which Burke had split in 1791. In this context of shifting party identities, Burke published *An Appeal from the New to the Old Whigs* (1791), a polemic on the true nature of Whig politics. Burke's key move was to redefine the meaning of 'reform' so that he might deny its use to his intellectual enemies. The pamphlet's key interest for the argument here is that, in the course of making his case, we find Burke issuing further precepts regarding the proper conduct of legislators. In particular, Burke insisted that reform ought to be neither violent nor destructive.

Once again, the experiment in France provided the negative example, representing an 'attempt to methodize anarchy; to perpetuate and fix disorder',[30] based on fraud and the 'madness of their declaration of the pretended rights of man'.[31] These actions did not constitute reform because they instead represented a design to overthrow the government. To be called reform, change must be proposed in good faith and by friends of the Constitution. The true 'spirit of reformation . . . refuses to be rendered the means of destruction'.[32] Statesmen

---

[29] Ibid., 112.
[30] Burke, 'Appeal from the New to the Old Whigs', *Writings and Speeches*, 4: 365–477, at 376.
[31] Ibid., 378.
[32] Ibid., 404.

therefore needed to guard against imbibing 'dogmas' that impugned an existing Constitution, even if these ideas were only championed in relation to 'moderate alterations' because 'Doctrines limited in their present application, and wide in their general principles, are never meant to be confined to what they at first pretend'.[33] In other words, reforms were often the Trojan horses of revolution. Rather than absorb dangerous doctrines, the true reformer would identify genuine grievances by viewing complaints in relation to a nation's traditions; where genuine grievances existed, the tradition would point out the means of remedy. In this way, the desire for change could be satisfied.[34]

Burke's related point was that destroying one government and replacing it with another could only be assessed as good if the lasting result were better government, as with the Revolution of 1688. Bias should always lie with the happiness of the present generation, who would likely pay for any revolution in blood, and so the statesman's mind must always lean to the existing frame of government and its capacity for improvement, to 'security', and away from the 'terror of a civil war'.[35] As we will see, Mackintosh would reject this premise in his projection of a bolder ethos for legislators.

In general, Burke's preferred style of thinking was to utilize the existing 'legislative record and practice' and aim to 'interpret one statute by another', amounting to a mode of political thought that was prudential and casuistical.[36] It followed that metaphysical speculation was completely inappropriate because

> Nothing universal can be rationally affirmed on any moral, or any political subject. Pure metaphysical abstraction does not belong to these matters. The lines of morality are not like the ideal lines of mathematics. They are broad and deep as well as long. They admit of exceptions; they demand modification. These exceptions and modifications are not made by the process of logic, but by the rules of prudence. Prudence is not only the first in rank of the virtues political and moral, but she is the director, the regulator, the standard of them all. Metaphysics cannot live without definition; but prudence is cautious how she defines.[37]

The point regarding definitions and metaphysics will recur, first in relation to Stewart's disciplines to be studied shortly, and then in relation to Ricardo, who was repeatedly attacked for his lack of definitional propriety. Indeed, Ricardo

---

[33] Ibid., 460.
[34] Ibid.
[35] Ibid., 382–4, 461–2, 461.
[36] Ibid., 420. For Burke's explicit discussion of casuistry see Ibid., 444–5.
[37] Ibid., 383.

imagined a political economy that operated like the ideal lines of mathematics, and definitional ambition was central to this project.

Returning to Burke, the *ethos* that he recommended for statesmen in relation to political change was one that eschewed 'extremes' and would always 'stop short of some hazardous and ambiguous excellence, which they will be taught to postpone to any reasonable degree of good they may actually possess'.[38] The essential insight was that government was too complex an art to be well effected by clumsy interventions.[39] Such an attitude is what Burke claimed he had mobilized in relation to American independence and what the French 'experimentors' now lacked, not least because the new philosophy of government was guided by 'the blaze of illumination' claimed by 'the enthusiasts of this time', just like their predecessors in the seventeenth century.[40] The issue was that 'theory concerning government may become as much a cause of fanaticism as a *dogma* in religion. There is a boundary to men's passions when they act from feeling; none when they are under the influence of imagination'.[41] A fanatic's disposition was extreme because their 'doctrines admit no limit, no qualification', linked to their building politics 'not on convenience but on truth'.[42] For critics of the new philosophy, such as Burke, the sectaries of the seventeenth century were rhetorically useful as a denigrating comparison because their *ethos* towards political change was acknowledged to have been untenable. More plainly, the allegation of enthusiasm was being fused with the memory of England's troubles in the seventeenth century for the purpose of attacking theory in the late eighteenth century.

Burke buttressed this argument from *ethos* with an argument from principle. According to Burke, the Whigs viewed the revolution of 1688 as a response to King James II's violations of the British Constitution; the Whigs were acting to restore the Ancient Constitution and preserve it into the future.[43] Burke claimed that his *Reflections* was consistent with these principles: government was founded on satisfying wants and enforcing duties; liberty played an indispensable role in achieving both but was ultimately subordinate to security and happiness.[44] By contrast, the 'new principles of Whiggism' differed dramatically, a reflection of the fact that they were not indigenous but imported from France and then spread from dissenting pulpits.[45] The leading principle that threatened so much destruction was that sovereignty lay unalienated in the people and that the people might therefore depose kings and establish new governments according to their

[38] Ibid., 470.
[39] Ibid., 472.
[40] Ibid., 384, 431.
[41] Ibid., 460.
[42] Ibid., 469–70.
[43] Ibid., 409–11.
[44] Ibid., 470.
[45] Ibid., 410.

will. The new philosophers used this notion of popular sovereignty to divorce the people from their attachment to the state, spurning the 'antient known policy of the laws of England' and the 'battery of laws, and usages, and positive conventions' that led the people to treat their nation as 'the ancient order into which we are born'.[46] Once again, it was a new principle conceived in abstract terms that allowed theorists to contemplate catastrophe.

The doctrine of popular sovereignty had two further negative consequences. The first was to unpick the indispensable work of duty, for the idea of popular sovereignty led people to examine and evade their obligations instead of allowing a sense of obligation to govern one's conduct while passing unexamined.[47] The second consequence of popular sovereignty was to contravene the experience of statesmen through the ages, who always located power where it might be restrained and never with the people, for there no judgement could be expected.[48] With these points made, Burke could then combine the arguments from *ethos* and principle:

> Amongst these nice, and therefore dangerous, points of casuistry may be reckoned the question so much agitated in the present hour—Whether, after the people have discharged themselves of their original power by an habitual delegation, no occasion can possibly occur which may justify their resumption of it? . . . if in general it be not easy to determine concerning the lawfulness of such devious proceedings, which must be ever on the edge of crimes, it is far from difficult to foresee the perilous consequences of the resuscitation of such a power in the people. The practical consequences of any political tenet go a great way in deciding upon its value. Political problems do not primarily concern truth or falsehood. They relate to good or evil. What in the result is likely to produce evil, is politically false: that which is productive of good, politically is true.[49]

What is most striking in these comments for the present-day reader is the explicit rejection of truth in favour of consequences: the statesman is not an inquirer after truth but, as Burke wrote, one who accepts that their task is to embrace the 'computing principle' in relation to costs and benefits.[50] It is now time to turn to James Mackintosh, for whom truth did function as the gold standard for political reason, which required theory to play a leading role in its discovery. As will be seen in future chapters, this is remarkably similar to the sentiment that would

---

[46] Ibid., 420, 440, 443.
[47] Ibid., 444.
[48] Ibid., 441.
[49] Ibid., 444–5.
[50] Burke, 'Reflections on the Revolution in France', *Writings and Speeches*, 112.

animate Ricardo's dive into topics such as value, while Malthus adopted his own version of the computing principle.

James Mackintosh and the Defence of Theory

In defending the revolution along with its English supporters, one of Mackintosh's key strategies was to align the French Revolution with the English experience of 1688. He did so by asserting that England's revolution had established 'the right of the people of England to revoke abused power, to frame the Government, and bestow the Crown'.[51] In making this claim, Mackintosh was both defending Richard Price and countering Burke's assault on exactly this point. Mackintosh's first move was to change the type of evidence that was relevant for reconstructing 1688, demoting in status legal language and statutes while promoting 'the un-restrained effusion of sentiment' during the Convention Parliament.[52] It was this phenomenon—the expression of enlightened sentiment—that Mackintosh wished to treat as crucial for understanding 1688. For it revealed the principle of election as the governing idea behind these events, despite its occlusion by sub-sequent legal trappings.

> Thus evidently has it appeared, from the conduct and language of the leaders of the Revolution, that it was a *deposition* and an *election*; and that all language of a contrary tendency, which is to be found in their acts, arose from the rem-nants of their own prejudice, or from concession to the prejudice of others, or from the superficial and presumptuous policy of imposing august illusions on mankind.[53]

Mackintosh's point was that Burke was simply continuing the elaborate con-spiracy to conceal the true nature of the revolution in order to preserve the prejudices of the day. The leading culprits here were Burke's cherished notions of 'precedent' and 'usage', which created reverence for the existing Constitution while aiding the campaign against natural rights.[54] We have seen that these were, indeed, two of Burke's key claims.

---

[51] James Mackintosh, 'Vindiciae Gallicae. Defence of the French Revolution and Its English Admirers, Against the Accusations of the Right Honourable Edmund Burke; Including Some Strictures on the Late Production of Mons De Calonne', in *Vindiciae Gallicae and Other Writings on the French Revolution*, 1–166, at 129. I am indebted to Anna Plassart's recent study of Mackintosh: Plassart, *The Scottish Enlightenment and the French Revolution*, chapter 4.

[52] Mackintosh, 'Vindiciae Gallicae', 138.

[53] Ibid., 140–1.

[54] Ibid., 92–4.

Mackintosh also aligned the revolution in France with England's revolution of 1688 in developmental terms. He did so by describing England's revolution as incomplete, a fact explained by the constraints of the times: seventeenth-century England was not ready for the grand political reorganization witnessed in the next century through the French and American revolutions.[55] As a consequence, the measures taken in 1688–1689 were merely remedies for urgent abuses and did not address their lasting sources, especially the fact that private interests had been engrafted onto the state's architecture.[56] The contemporary moment, however, offered the chance for a different type of revolution because Europe's condition had improved (in part due to England's example) and because Europe had become connected by mutual sympathy and enlightened knowledge.[57] The French Revolution was not, therefore, being carried on by disreputable lawyers of middling rank and the monied interest, as Burke had claimed. Instead, in France there was a 'REVOLUTION *without Leaders*. It was the effect of general causes operating on the people. It was the revolt of a nation enlightened from a common source'.[58]

As this fabulous image of enlightened knowledge causing a leaderless revolution indicates, Mackintosh was on the side of theory. This obliged him to confront Burke's leading arguments against theory and in favour of experience and practice. The first target was Burke's lament that French institutions might have been reformed instead of overturned. Burke's point here should be viewed alongside his claim in An Appeal from the New to the Old Whigs, noted earlier, that modest reform satisfied the demand for redress of grievances. Perceiving that France's military, judiciary, and church were all in their 'essence . . . irreconcilable with a free Government', Mackintosh rejected this idea.[59] In fact, history showed that, after modest reform that satisfied popular clamour of the type that Burke called for, corrupt institutions invariably returned to their original condition because the public mind resumed its tranquil condition, thereby losing the ability to demand deep reform. Mackintosh's claim was that 'radical reform' either had to be grasped in tumultuous moments whilst 'popular enthusiasm' was high, or it would not be grasped at all.[60]

Note how Mackintosh portrayed popular enthusiasm as playing an important role in reforming corrupt institutions. This analysis was affirmed later in the *Vindiciae* in the context of Mackintosh's attack on the notion of constitutional balance, which he treated as mere cover for a conspiracy of aristocrats,

---

[55] Ibid., 134, 144.
[56] Ibid., 147–9.
[57] Ibid., 54–5, 155–8.
[58] Ibid., 57.
[59] Ibid., 48.
[60] Ibid.

one that could only be conquered by 'the energy of popular opinion'.[61] The effect of this positive account of the role of popular passion in political change was to blunt the negative evaluative force of 'enthusiasm' as a leading anti-theory term. Mackintosh was even prepared to praise George Buchanan—who defended deposing bad kings—for carrying on 'from the ancients the noble flame of republican enthusiasm'.[62] Mackintosh similarly wrote that even though the circumstances of 1688 compelled the 'Tory interest' to support the revolution, the Tories still maintained their 'repugnance to every shadow of innovation'.[63] Anticipating Bentham's hostile review of the vocabulary that was used to block reform in his *Book of Fallacies* (1824), Mackintosh revealed that talk of innovation was an 'exhausted common-place', one of the 'sportive contests' intended for refining rhetoric since the time of Bacon but not capable of providing insight.[64] In other words, in these comments Mackintosh was attempting to blunt Burke's offensive vocabulary.

A further move in this linguistic contest was Mackintosh's affirmation of the need to uphold 'those *metaphysic* rights' that Burke had abhorred.[65] In Mackintosh's view, enforcing such rights was the only means for obliging governments to respect citizens. The important point to note is that this represented an attempt to lessen the negative connotations of 'metaphysics' that Burke had mobilized. This was a delicate task, however, for Mackintosh also sought to establish an account of bad metaphysics by endorsing Bacon's strictures against philosophy that was sophistical and seduced the intellect by being fanciful and poetical. In an attempt to turn Burke's own weapons against him, Mackintosh treated Burke's 'theory' of religious establishments as an example of just such bewitching sophistry.[66]

More interesting still is Mackintosh's redefinition of 'experience'. Mackintosh rejected Burke's emphasis on prescription and the accompanying *ethos* of gradual change, which together mandated a long time-scale for institutional change. By contrast, Mackintosh held that moments of unrest offered the only opportunity for meaningful reform, while he derided Burke's recommendations as amounting to the counsel that one surrender the formation of government to accident.[67] Following Machiavelli, Mackintosh viewed moments of public arousal as special

---

[61]   Ibid., 149.
[62]   Ibid., 135.
[63]   Ibid., 136–7.
[64]   Ibid., 31.
[65]   Ibid., 96.
[66]   Ibid., 64, at asterisked footnote. For the passage of Bacon cited by Mackintosh, see Francis Bacon, 'Novum Organum', in *The Works of Francis Bacon*, eds. James Spedding, Robert Ellis, and Dean Denon Heath, vol. 1 (London: Longman & Co., 1858), 70–366, at 175. For the English translation, see Francis Bacon, 'The New Organon', in *The Works of Francis Bacon*, eds. James Spedding, Robert Ellis, and Dean Denon Heath, vol. 4 (London: Longman & Co., 1858), 39–248, at 66.
[67]   Mackintosh, 'Vindiciae Gallicae', 49.

because they allowed government to be reshaped in view of first principles. But where Machiavelli had posited the *vir virtutis* as the key actor, Mackintosh instead addressed 'enlightened politicians'.[68] As this phrase suggests, Mackintosh claimed that there was a 'political science' available to legislators from 'the research of philosophy'.[69] He figured this science as geometry, as Ricardo would for political economy.

> Geometry, it may be justly said, bears nearly the same relation to mechanics that abstract reasoning does to politics. The *moral forces* which are employed in politics are the passions and interests of men, of which it is the province of metaphysics to teach the nature and calculate the strength, as mathematics do those of the mechanical powers.[70]

So far, we might suspect that this exactly fitted the account that Burke gave of abstract reasoning in relation to politics. Yet Mackintosh's crucial move was to acknowledge the prescriptive force of experience and then redefine it in such a way that it covered his political science.

Mackintosh did so by noting that the National Assembly had been accused of rejecting 'the guidance of experience, of having abandoned themselves to the illusion of theory, and of having sacrificed great and attainable good to the magnificent chimeras of ideal excellence'.[71] If such an accusation were true, then the National Assembly would indeed have been beyond defending. But the accusation could be shown to be false once the meaning of experience was clarified. For there were two meanings that the word 'experience' could be used to convey in relation to political life. In the first meaning, 'experience' provides models (in the sense of an ideal example to be imitated), as when an existing machine is reproduced. Not missing the chance to score a rhetorical point, Mackintosh wrote that 'The first visionary innovator was the savage who built a cabin, or covered himself with a rug'.[72] All improvements, in other words, progress past existing models. The second sense of 'experience' refers to the knowledge that one gains from learning principles, as one learns, for example, the principles by which a machine operates. 'Experience' in this sense allows the artist to build a superior machine. It was this second sense that Mackintosh used when he asserted that his political science was grounded in experience.

The key to understanding Mackintosh's argumentation in these passages is to see that he was exploiting the tight semantic relationship between 'experiment'

---

[68] Ibid., 48.
[69] Ibid., 52–3.
[70] Ibid., 53.
[71] Ibid., 50.
[72] Ibid.

and 'experience' that existed at the time. If history were 'an immense collection of experiments' that disclosed '*experimentally*' which institutions were good, which bad, and which both good and bad but susceptible of improvement, then the idea of copying an existing model that simply offered, as Burke put it, '*tolerably* to answer the common purposes of Government', was an irrational position because it neglected the chance to learn from experience's disclosure of principles.[73] Burke's approach surrendered political life to 'accidental circumstances'.[74] It followed that political science did not forsake experience but, in contradistinction, proposed to benefit from experience to the maximum degree. And the prospect that Mackintosh's science offered was not to achieve perfection but to pursue it using experience. Mackintosh was attempting, in short, to break down the special nexus that Burke had constructed between experience and counter-revolution.

Having considered Mackintosh's redefinition of experience, we are now in a position to understand his account of the appropriate way to combine experience and theory. Mackintosh had established that experience disclosed theoretical principles and that history could be treated as a succession of experiments. This authorized analogies between experimental philosophy and the science of politics. It followed that the task of this science was to sift history for the principles that governed the motion of peoples and governments. (It was in this regard that Mackintosh praised Machiavelli for his researches into the operation of ancient states.) Furthermore, given that Mackintosh took history to play a role akin to what we would call data, it could also serve the function of disproving false theory by acting as a collection of experiments that could be inspected to discover general principles.[75] The effect of these claims was to redefine experience—it no longer indicated Burke's grooves of custom and usage but now acted as a stock of experiments from which the theorist could derive general principles. Mackintosh had transformed a constraining discipline into an instrument of science. Even more liberating, however, was Mackintosh's belief that the 'modern times' of his life were different from all others. Above all, theory and practice had been fused together by the printing press because it allowed the wise to govern popular sentiment and thus the people.[76] Mackintosh had armed the legislator with tremendous prowess: the ability to extract principles from history and to govern the sentiments of humanity!

While observing the hubris of Mackintosh as a twenty-five-year-old in the metropolis is fascinating, the key aim of this discussion for the book's overall argument is to reveal the effort that Mackintosh directed (whether consciously or not) to redefining key combat terms. For these are the same terms that would be

---

[73] Ibid., 50–1.
[74] Ibid., 51.
[75] Ibid., 117.
[76] Ibid., 54–5. Here we might also detect the influence of Mackintosh's teacher, Dugald Stewart.

central to the debates that Malthus and Ricardo would enter, and they would also expend intellectual energy to manipulate their meaning. It is worth repeating that this attention to vocabulary is indispensable for the approach adopted in this work since it anchors attention to texts, thus inhibiting the inquiry from ascending to the level of 'analytical systems' and other hypothetical objects of the type discussed in the Introduction.

Returning to Mackintosh, what is the office and *ethos* that a politician would dispense when armed with Mackintosh's instrumentarium? The office was one of scientific reform in the interest of public happiness, and the *ethos* was one of a confident servant of progress. That this was a crucial point of difference with Burke was signalled on the first page of the text, where Burke was portrayed as someone whom history had left behind. Burke possessed an 'abhorrence for abstract politics, predilection for aristocracy, and a dread of innovation', which led him to misperceive the tremendous progress at hand as nothing more than 'transient madness'.[77] It followed that a crucial task for the enlightened politician was to understand that they were living in remarkable times and that old assumptions and prejudices were to be discarded. The three months that preceded the convocation of the States General in May 1789, for example, saw Paris advance to greater light and freedom than had been achieved in preceding *centuries*, and, in these circumstances, doctrines had been accepted that only a few months earlier would have been dismissed as 'the visions of a few deluded fanatics'.[78] In these comments we can see Mackintosh redescribing Burke's attack on theory as archaic, placing him on the wrong side of history.

For Mackintosh, the new statesman who was suited to the times would need to steel himself for replacing old institutions with those recommended by reason. To assist him in mustering the necessary courage, Mackintosh mounted a barely restrained exposé of Ancient Constitution thinking that removed the antiquarian reverence with which Burke had tried to cloak Britain's institutions. Mackintosh's only moment of restraint consisted in conceding that the 'illusion' of ancient liberty served a political function because it endeared freedom to the public mind.[79] But to govern rational men by illusion alone was an affront to human nature and represented a misunderstanding of the nature of rights. As Mackintosh insisted, 'It is not because we *have* been free, but because we have a right to be free, that we ought to demand freedom'.[80] With reason and natural sentiment in hand, a worthy politician could construct a stable system of enlightened rule. Here we can see Mackintosh's rejection of the particular and historical in favour of the universal and progressive.

[77] Ibid., 5.
[78] Ibid., 20.
[79] Ibid., 133.
[80] Ibid.

This point should not be taken to suggest that Mackintosh was an unhistorical thinker, which would be improbable given his Scottish training.[81] Rather, Mackintosh marshalled history to his attack on Burke's account of the Constitution in two ways. One was to identify a lingering barbarism: Mackintosh claimed that the 'Gothic Governments' of the day embodied the 'rude institutions and barbarous manners' that were established by those savages who had destroyed the Roman Empire.[82] The other historical claim that undercut the prestige of the Constitution related to the Tory interest that had resisted the march of reason in the seventeenth century, an interest grounded in a commitment to a system of military ranks, the divine right of kings, and landed aristocracy, all institutions that endured into the present.[83] The state's ornamentation that Burke so valued was portrayed by Mackintosh as regressive.

Such polemical redescriptions were to assist the legislator in turning away from precedent and usage. The imperative was to 'hazard a bolder navigation, and discover . . . the treasure of public felicity'.[84] The legislator's compass was to be 'the good of the governed', which authorized whatever 'fundamental' action was judged necessary for its realization.[85] This is the context in which Mackintosh undermined the power of 'innovation' as a standing accusation against political change by describing it as a mere debating commonplace, as noted earlier. For the legislator would need to innovate when pursuing 'public felicity' if they inherited a polity deformed by barbaric manners and entrenched interests, and we have seen that this was exactly Mackintosh's appraisal of the situation in France, where its leading institutions were irreconcilable with a free government. In short, the enlightened politician was obliged to perform greater deeds than cleaving to the accidents of history because rational institutions would only emerge from forceful change.

This meant that the enlightened politician might need to harden their heart, and here we see Mackintosh biting the bullet with respect to Burke's challenge that the costs of change were too high. Where Adam Smith counselled the statesman to revere existing interests as if they were parents, Mackintosh underlined the fact that change could be bloody, as was the case with the revolution of 1688, which led to civil war in Ireland, two rebellions in Scotland, and the deaths of thousands of citizens.[86] Similarly, American independence

---

[81] As per Plassart, Mackintosh drew on the progressive histories of Hume and Smith, but increased the ratio of Scottish republican thought and shaped his account for a Foxite narrative of progress in England and Europe. Hence Plassart concluded that 'There was in fact little, either in Mackintosh's philosophy of history or in his specific account of European institutions, that Hume or Smith would have recognised as theirs' (Plassart, *The Scottish Enlightenment and the French Revolution*, 87).

[82] Mackintosh, 'Vindiciae Gallicae', 159.

[83] Ibid., 136.

[84] Ibid., 52.

[85] Ibid., 30 at asterisked footnote.

[86] Ibid., 75.

was also bought with calamity and civil war, but, on the basis of Burke's arguments in relation to France, it should have been judged madness at the time to pay such a price for 'a speculative and ideal good'.[87] Mackintosh's point was not only that hindsight showed that American resistance was justified and noble in view of the nation's subsequent tranquillity and greatness, but that the American Constitution was a standing '*experimental answer*' to those who dreaded innovation more than they valued liberty.[88] It followed that the legislator had to be prepared to experiment with forms of government and to spend human life in doing so: 20 000 French lives would be a cheap price to pay for the benefits of American freedom or to buy even the lesser gains won by England in 1688.[89] In this example we see a stark illustration of how the arts of reasoning and *ethoi* recommended by Burke and Mackintosh led the politician in different directions. This is a key component of the context in which this book is attempting to locate Malthus and Ricardo: equipping legislators with an *ethos* was a part of the task of political writing, and political economy was a form of political writing.

Finally, it is worth focusing on the means of change that Mackintosh recommended. The legislator was imbued with a boldness that was justified by the historical moment that Mackintosh believed was at hand and by the perception that prudence of the type counselled by Burke was a leading obstacle to genuine progress.[90] Yet what must be underlined is that it was still the legislator who was to renovate society in view of Mackintosh's science. It was this fact that allowed Mackintosh to write that he was one of 'the most sincere friends of tranquil and stable Government' and that his desire was 'to avert revolution by reform'.[91] The ultimate message was that those in power should reform while they could still do so on their own terms, a point that Mackintosh quickly followed with the warning that the time might arrive when it would be necessary to pursue liberty by the sword. To offer a charitable interpretation, we might say that Mackintosh was adducing an additional prudential argument alongside the claims of his science of politics. To glance ahead, Ricardo's association with Mill and Bentham, in combination with his Unitarian links, would lead him to largely reject change by statesmen and to trust in the sheer force of science, reason, and progress, along with his own role as an MP in Parliament.

---

[87] Ibid., 76.
[88] Ibid.
[89] Ibid., 77.
[90] Mackintosh retreated from this position in James Mackintosh, *A Discourse on the Study of the Law of Nature and Nations* (London, 1799). See Winch, 'Introduction', x, xv–xvi.
[91] Mackintosh, 'Vindiciae Gallicae', 150.

Dugald Stewart and the Defence of Theory

If Burke is placed at the practice end of the theory–practice spectrum in terms of his rhetoric and vocabulary choices, and Mackintosh at the theory end, then in Stewart we encounter a middle position.[92] More confident in the skills and ethical acumen of the theorist than Burke, Stewart described procedures by which facts and experience could be sifted to produce theoretical knowledge of politics. Such knowledge included political economy. This last point is crucial, for Stewart was one of the few academics of the period who offered a course of lectures on political economy, and it was some of his students who founded the *Edinburgh Review*.[93] The Reviewers shared Stewart's belief that political economy was *the* science of reform and national happiness, hence new works of political economy that evinced poor reasoning represented a danger to the advancement of the master science and were reviewed severely, and in terms that reflected Stewart's precepts on good theory.[94] As was noted in the Introduction, these early issues of the *Review* played an important role in the development of political economy and in Ricardo's early formation, and they stand as a possible source of his vocabulary for describing good and bad political economy.[95]

Stewart's political economy was dependent on moral philosophy because of the prescriptions that he set out for governing one's mind. For only a well-ordered mind could produce scientific knowledge, whether in the field of physics, political economy, or any other. The point to emphasize is that precepts for good thinking played the role of what we think of as method. Furthermore, Stewart did not elaborate these precepts through philosophy of science, as we tend to do today, but through the moral philosophy that was his primary academic pursuit. A key aspect of this philosophy was that it served as a defence against enthusiasm by providing disciplines that the theorist was to apply to their mind. Stewart, in other words, represents a way of thinking about good and bad political economy that is inassimilable to any notion of method today.

The focus of Stewart's *Elements of the Philosophy of the Human Mind* (1792) is the conduct of the intellect, understood as the government of discrete faculties that ought to be cultivated to the maximum degree in the course of perfecting one's nature as a human. This ideal was held out as a prestigious form of

---

[92] See Walter, 'Defending Political Theory After Burke'.

[93] In the Hamilton edition, this is available as Dugald Stewart, 'Lectures on Political Economy', *The Collected Works of Dugald Stewart*, ed. William Hamilton, vols. 8 and 9 (Edinburgh: Thomas Constable and Co., 1855–1856).

[94] See, for example [Henry Brougham], 'Art. VIII. *An Essay on the Principles of Commercial Exchanges &c*', *Edinburgh Review* 9/17 (1807), 111–36; [Francis Horner], 'Art. III. *An Essay on the Theory of Money, and Principles of Commerce*', *Edinburgh Review* 10/20 (1807), 284–99. For the attribution of authorship see Frank W. Fetter, 'The Authorship of Economic Articles in the Edinburgh Review, 1802–47', *Journal of Political Economy* 61/3 (1953), 232–59.

[95] Ricardo, 'Ricardo to Trower', *Works and Correspondence*, 7: 245–9.

self-cultivation, one that was contrasted with merely being satisfied with developing those faculties that were called upon by whatever station one happened to hold in life. Stewart stipulated that a by-product of pursuing such perfection was happiness, which increased as the mind's powers approached the limit of their cultivation. Happiness and human perfection thus walked hand in hand, and keeping this point in view allows us to see that we are dealing with a peculiar pedagogical-ethical culture in which an inductee would be presented with the means and motivation for self-perfection.

Much of the motivation came from Stewart's repeated contrasts between, on the one hand, the abilities and perfection available to those who had mastered his philosophy of mind and, on the other hand, those whom Stewart referred to as the 'vulgar'. To the vulgar, for example, the philosopher's ability to conduct elaborate reasoning using terms that expressed complex notions could appear 'supernatural'.[96] Similarly, none of the powers of a vulgar mind would be lifted to their highest cultivation, while a metaphysician would likely have mastered the powers of abstraction and conception.[97] In a hierarchical society such as 1790s Edinburgh, these arts of reasoning were the philosophical counterpart to socio-economic distinction.

While the cultivated mind possessed reasoning powers that the ordinary mind did not, in Stewart's presentation it was also exposed to pathologies that did not afflict the uncultivated. The metaphysician who had developed the power of abstraction, for instance, might have neglected their mind's other faculties, and this lack of cognitive balance could endanger inner peace and good conduct. In these claims Stewart was reworking the trope of the unbalanced theorist or man of system—as we saw was deployed by Adam Smith[98] amongst others—using the terms of his own philosophy of mind. This fact points to one of the features of Stewart's response to Burke: his concession that theory or metaphysics could be poorly done, producing dangerous results for the theorist and for any nation that absorbed their ideas.

In the context of making this strategic concession to the Burkean charge, Stewart offered 'Platonists' as a (cheap) sacrifice to the anti-theory position:

> by withdrawing the attention from the distinguishing qualities of objects, and giving a common name to their resembling qualities . . . they conceived universals to be real existences, or (as they expressed it) to be the essences of

---

[96] Dugald Stewart, *Elements of the Philosophy of the Human Mind*, 2 vols. (London and Edinburgh, 1792 and 1814), 1: 210. The original editions of Stewart's *Elements* are used, not only to avoid imperfections in the Hamilton edition, but also because volume one is treated as participating in the debate sparked by Burke's *Reflections* (1790), requiring that the 1792 text forms the focus.

[97] Ibid., 1: 29.

[98] See Smith, *TMS* VI.ii.2.15.

individuals; and flattered themselves with the belief, that by directing their attention to these essences in the first instance, they might be enabled to pene-
trate the secrets of the universe, without submitting to the study of nature in
detail.[99]

Here was bad theory produced by undisciplined minds; the results were phant-
asms and absurdities. Similar results arose wherever fact and metaphysics were
mingled from want of properly specifying the true objects and methods of enquiry.[100] Such contamination could be hard to detect, Stewart claimed, because
metaphysical discourses tended to obscure the fact that the objects they purported to study were beyond human conception. Often, for example, speculators would attempt to disguise the absurdity of their theories by keeping the
metaphysical components concealed, focusing their discourses on the ob-
servable phenomena under which the metaphysical causes purportedly lay.[101]
These speculations were dangerous not only because they could dazzle and be-
wilder the understanding, but also because they obscured the limits of human
knowledge.[102]

Stewart conceded that a different type of visionary also existed, one who
claimed that a theory of politics or morality could be built after the manner of
mathematics. The desire was understandable enough: moral philosophy was be-
deviled by the ambiguity of language, a pathology from which mathematics was
free. This theme was developed at length in the second volume of the *Elements*,
published in 1814, and it holds added importance for the argument here given
that Ricardo announced exactly this ambition for political economy.[103] Stewart
explained that the work performed by 'principles' in most sciences was achieved
in mathematics by its definitions, which allowed axiomatic reasoning. Thus, in
geometry, the hypothetical definition of a circle was the basis for subsequent
demonstrations regarding its properties, in the manner of Euclid. The profound
consequence was that reasoning of this type did not produce truth claims concerning actual things in the world because it instead concerned the logical consequences of the initial definitions or axioms.[104]

If, however, the geometer were to claim that a general property of the hypothetical circle applied to a particular circle in the world, then they shifted from
demonstrative, mathematical knowledge to the world of the senses. The erroneous belief shared by Locke, Reid, Condillac, and Leibnitz was that if only the

---

[99] Stewart, *Elements of the Philosophy of the Human Mind*, 1: 216.
[100] Ibid., 1: 44–5.
[101] Ibid., 1: 65–6, 69.
[102] Ibid., 1: 91.
[103] Ricardo, 'Ricardo to Mill', *Works and Correspondence*, 8: 329–31, at 331.
[104] Stewart, *Elements of the Philosophy of the Human Mind*, 2: 39, 45–7, 151, 160.

definitions were rigorous enough then the ambiguity inherent to language could be removed and all sciences might aspire to the precision of mathematics. The issue, however, was not the precision of the definitions but the fact that it was only in mathematics that 'definitions can be attempted with propriety at the outset of our investigations', while in other branches it was first necessary to establish 'that the definitions which we lay down correspond with facts'.[105] In other words, outside of mathematics, there needed to be a connection between the facts of the world and the categories that attempted to capture them; the ambiguity of non-formal language was a separate, additional issue.

When mathematics was successfully applied to the world, as in theoretical mechanics, it was because there existed referents in the world that matched or closely resembled what was described in the definitions of mathematics. In some branches of geometry, Stewart claimed, instruments produced excellent data, making objects susceptible to '*mensurability*'.[106] The result was extremely accurate data against which practical applications could be tested, which, in turn, allowed the 'data' (in the sense of 'postulates' or 'premises') assumed in the theory to be tested.[107] If, for example, a circle were described on paper for which all the radii were exactly equal, then Euclid's theorems would hold, not in consequence of mathematical demonstration, but only in consequence of the confirming evidence that human sense organs could provide.[108]

What did all this mean for the possibility of a mathematical moral science? On the one hand, it was possible. As Stewart wrote, 'it might be possible, by devising a set of arbitrary definitions, to form a science which, although conversant about moral, political, or physical ideas, should yet be as certain as geometry'.[109] But, on the other hand, the science would not be one of true and false because the definitions that would form the 'principles' of the science would not relate to the facts of the world. In consequence, such a system 'could answer no other purpose than to display the ingenuity of the inventor'.[110] Stewart's position might be summarized as prescribing one set of rules for mathematics and another set of rules for all other sciences. The more important point for the argument here, however, is that Stewart held that a system of definitions in the moral sciences was only good for showcasing ingenuity. Ricardo's friends and critics alike would identify the ingenuous quality of his work, albeit to then apply divergent assessments of its worth.

[105] Ibid., 2: 158.
[106] Ibid., 2: 511.
[107] Ibid., 2: 206.
[108] Ibid., 2: 204.
[109] Ibid., 2: 153.
[110] Ibid., 2: 203.

Stewart's mix of facts and theory could only work for a science such as political economy if the theorist mastered the philosophy of mind, for only in this way could both facts and general principles be generated in a reliable manner. The crucial premise was that God had not made humans 'capable of reasoning concerning classes of objects, without the use of signs'.[111] In making this claim, Stewart was locating himself in a continuing debate between Nominalists and Realists.[112] It seems to have been Stewart's purpose to shift emphasis from reasoning in the sense of inspecting the relations between propositions—as when examining a syllogism—to inspecting the notions that propositions expressed. That is, attention was to be shifted from the logical connection between 'All humans are mortal' and 'All Irish are humans' to the categories 'humans' and 'Irish'. In this example, the categories are represented by words, but diagrams and formulae could serve in geometry and symbols in algebra.

In relation to this scrutiny of categories, Stewart described what he referred to as 'the other intellectual processes distinct from reasoning', and here we encounter the practical, instructional aspect of Stewart's philosophy.[113] The first of these other processes was 'application', a central theme in critical assessments of Ricardo. In algebra, for example, even the best exponents of calculus could fall into paradox and absurdity by failing to regard the conditions that a hypothesis involved: in a vacuum, a cannonball and feather would fall under gravity at the same speed, but we do not live in vacuums.[114] Geometry was largely protected against this danger because diagrams could act as a check on reasoning by revealing to the senses the relations that held between the quantities being investigated.[115] In the non-mathematical sciences, the role of diagrams was played by examples and illustrations.

The second non-logical process was signification. Its importance owed to the fact that ambiguity was an inherent risk when using words as an instrument of investigation. In algebra, the longest investigations could be carried on without any fear of a break in the chain of reasoning owing to the signs with which reasoning was conducted, while politics obliged one to pay constant attention to signification, placing great demands on the mind. The challenge could be met if the theorist cultivated a number of skills, and here the distance between Stewart's approach to knowledge and our own is at its maximal point. One skill was to make a habit of illustrating complex argumentation with cases or examples, thereby

---

[111] Ibid., 1: 190. See also 2: 119–31.

[112] Ibid., 1: 164–74, 182–8.

[113] Ibid., 1: 176.

[114] See Galileo Galilei, 'On Motion', in *On Motion and On Mechanics*, eds. I. E. Drabkin and Stillman Drake (Madison: University of Wisconsin Press, 1960), chapter 8.

[115] Stewart, *Elements of the Philosophy of the Human Mind*, 1: 176. See the valuable discussion in Richard S. Olson, *Scottish Philosophy and British Physics, 1740–1870: A Study in the Foundations of the Victorian Scientific Style* (Princeton: Princeton University Press, 2015), 71–83, 88–91.

meeting the need for application to check reasoning. Another skill was to reason using general terms, which allowed a person to avoid the danger of being distracted by their own particular experiences or by the arousal of their imagination.[116] Here one of the theorist's distinguishing features is on display, as the use of abstract and general terms not only protected the theorist from the ambiguity inherent in words, but it also made possible the discovery of 'comprehensive theorems' that augmented the power of reason.[117]

Despite their utility, abstract and general terms presented their own set of dangers. First and foremost, there was the potential for abstract thought to produce dazzling nonsense and enthusiasm because general terms often denoted abstractions, or things of a complicated nature, such as 'government' and 'religion'. At this point, Stewart again used his distinction between the cultivated mind of the philosopher, who could think about politics in an abstract manner with safety, in opposition to 'practical men' or the 'vulgar', who could not. Those with cultivated minds could use 'comprehensive terms' and 'abstraction' to access 'general truths' and 'general theorems', while practical men would not normally rise above 'particular truths'.[118] The philosopher's mastery was a result of abiding by certain disciplines. Most important was the capacity to focus the attention, typically requiring an early training in the habits of philosophical reflection.[119] Next in importance was the ability to ascend to abstract thought in the correct manner; namely, by beginning with individual objects, events, and facts, understood as both the groundwork for the act of classification and the unit into which a general principle ought to be reducible.[120]

At this point it is again worth looking ahead to the second volume of Stewart's *Elements*, where this topic is considered in greater detail. Stewart's assertion was that 'in proportion as the [abstract] objects of our reasoning are removed from the particular details with which our senses are conversant, the difficulty of these latent inductive processes must be increased'.[121] Some thinkers were so inattentive to this fact, Stewart claimed, that they fell into mysticism, Aristotelian logicians above all. The lesson was that observation and experiment were indispensable, not as ends in themselves, but as a means for resolving particular facts into other facts that were simpler and more comprehensive. The final result of this process was general facts, or laws of nature, that could yield 'synthetical explanation of particular phenomena'.[122] In summary, general laws might be

---

[116] Stewart, *Elements of the Philosophy of the Human Mind*, 1: 177–80.

[117] Ibid., 1: 212.

[118] Ibid., 1: 210, 224.

[119] Ibid., 1: 213.

[120] Ibid., 1: 215–18.

[121] Ibid., 2: 144.

[122] Ibid., 2: 327. It should be acknowledged that in this context one does find talk of 'method' and 'induction'. The context was Stewart's assertion that the role of circumstance must be clarified through repeated experiments. At this point, Stewart registered another of Bacon's failings: that he

discovered in this way. Yet a great complication was encountered in those cases where events were produced by multiple causes. A similar version of this claim would be used by Malthus to attack Ricardo's mode of stating general laws, as we will see.

In such cases of multiple causation, Stewart claimed, 'we must employ our reasoning powers in comparing a variety of instances together, in order to discover, by a sort of *analysis* or decomposition, the simple laws which are concerned in the phenomenon under consideration'.[123] Stewart asserted that this was the essential distinction between analysis and synthesis—between those approaches that began with a hypothesis springing from the imagination and those that began with general facts established by induction.[124]

Stewart's point was that a hypothetical theory ought to be derived from a knowledge of the phenomena that it was to explain. With such a theory in hand, the researcher could reason synthetically, comparing their deductions with observation and experiment, then moving to either correct the theory so that it was reconciled with the facts or abandon the theory as an unfounded conjecture.[125] Hypotheses had their place as long as they were subjected to the test of experience. If this test were passed, a hypothesis would graduate to become a principle. The danger arose when this stage was bypassed, such that a hypothesis became accepted as a principle, thus foreclosing inquiry at exactly the moment that it should have been stimulated. Stewart thus reproached 'those system-builders who, without any knowledge of facts, have presumed to form conclusions *a priori*'.[126] In Part III, it will be seen that Malthus developed an analogous account of Ricardo's failings, treating him as a system builder, while Malthus positioned himself as having correctly combined theory and practice.

To return to volume 1 of Stewart's *Elements*, the process of developing abstract hypotheses was said to expose the theorist to a number of ethical risks. Stewart was especially concerned to rebut the fears of Burke on this point—above all, Burke's polemical redescription of theoretical enquiry into the nature of political society as enthusiasm. As suggested earlier, Stewart's philosophy of mind provided a powerful source of concepts for countering Burke's attack on theory. In particular, Stewart redescribed enthusiasm as a by-product of the ill-government of the power of abstraction. This redescription is worth following in detail.

---

never formally specified the meaning of 'induction', which would need to wait for Reid and Turgot. Nevertheless, Bacon was clear enough, according to Stewart, when he claimed that comparing cases that agreed in some circumstances but not in all was the core of 'the method of induction'. Ibid., 2: 336.

[123] Ibid., 2: 333.
[124] Ibid., 2: 337.
[125] Ibid., 2: 406–7.
[126] Ibid., 2: 417.

Stewart held that abstraction performed an indispensable service for humans by allowing the mind to look past the distinguishing features of objects and focus on the attributes that they possessed in common, for this was a precondition for classification. However, the principle upon which any classification was organized represented a choice, and it was at this point that imagination entered the process. Stewart illustrated its role by explaining how a poet created.

> [T]he poet is supplied with all his materials by experience; and as his province is limited to combine and modify things which really exist, so as to produce new wholes of his own; so every exertion which he thus makes of his powers, presupposes the exercise of abstraction in decomposing and separating actual combinations.[127]

Because the poet's abstractions were subservient to their imagination, they would typically be able to state to themselves the objects on which they had brought abstraction to bear, at least as objects of conception, just like a painter who sketched a centaur could point to the conceptions of man and horse as the source objects from which they had abstracted. But this was not possible for many of the complex abstractions that were central to intellectual life. Length abstracted from breadth, for example, could not be conceived by the human mind. The failure to understand these limits to cognition had caused innumerable pathologies in Europe's intellectual culture. If it were widely recognized that Euclid's first definitions were not capable of human conception, for example, then they would only have been taught in passing. Instead, students all over Europe spent fruitless hours attempting to conceive of objects beyond their powers, with the result that Euclid's notions became mysterious.[128]

If the attempt to generate conceptions in relation to abstractions that were simply beyond the power of human conception was one source of mental derangement, then another was an excessive taste for the activity of abstraction. Such a taste was encouraged by the fact that one of the leading effects of civilization was to accustom the mind to using general propositions. Of course, the capacity was unevenly distributed, being more common amongst the educated, but, even within that class, some would be more disposed to the activity than others.[129] Yet those with a talent for producing abstractions were often found, according to Stewart, to neglect the quality of the observations and classifications from which they abstracted. Worse, this type of intellectual would often be

---

[127] Ibid., 1: 156.
[128] Ibid., 1: 157.
[129] Ibid., 1: 223–4.

careless when applying their principles to practice and not adjust their principles for the case at hand. Malthus would make both accusations against Ricardo.

The point to note regarding Stewart's riposte to Burke, however, is that this description of the dangers of abstraction had the effect of converting a phenomenon that functioned like a contagion in Burke's account into a far milder issue, something like poor intellectual technique. This is why Stewart could write that the solution lay in the mind's 'proper regulation', above all, the habit of treating general principles 'merely as approximations to the truth; the defects of which, must be supplied by habits acquired by personal experience'.[130] In these comments we see once again that ethics-talk included recommendations regarding something as banal as one's habits and in relation to something as personal as the conduct of one's mind.

With this remedial account in hand, Stewart could confront Burke on the issue of enthusiasm in politics. He did so by asserting the existence of 'the theory of politics', where the 'mere theorist' could struggle to apply their theories to lived experience if they lacked a certain 'practical or experimental skill'.[131] On the other hand, practical skill without theoretical knowledge limited one's horizon to known cases. To make this point, Stewart quoted from Burke's speech on American taxation, in which Burke claimed that, at times, statesmen would be obliged to rely on a general knowledge of humankind because there would not always be precedents on which to rely when facing the challenges of office.[132] The lesson that Stewart drew from Burke was that acting without the aid of general principles impoverished the legislator's mind. This was skilful rhetoric, for Stewart could claim that the fears around theory and speculation in politics that had so terrified Burke did not arise from some defect internal to political speculation. What Burke had referred to as 'enthusiasm'[133] and 'fanaticism',[134] Stewart was able to redescribe as merely the 'rash application of general principles'.[135] The dangers of theory were perfectly manageable.

Stewart's response was not purely defensive, for he also counter-attacked by portraying Burke's veneration for custom and usage as philosophically naïve. To this end, Stewart distinguished between two groups: those who cleaved to existing institutions (Burke), and those who were prepared to reason a priori from the principles of human nature (Stewart). Since 'the theory of legislation' used generalizations that were arrived at by abstracting from particulars, it could be

---

[130] Ibid., 1: 225.

[131] Ibid., 1: 226–7.

[132] Ibid. For the quotation from Burke, see Burke, 'Speech on American Taxation', *Writings and Speeches*, 2: 406–63, at 432.

[133] Burke, 'Reflections on the Revolution in France', *Writings and Speeches*, 108.

[134] Burke, 'Appeal from the New to the Old Whigs', 460.

[135] Stewart, *Elements of the Philosophy of the Human Mind*, 1: 233. For an extended version of this argument, see Walter, 'Defending Political Theory After Burke'.

just as grounded in experience as the claims of the 'political empiric', so long as one proceeded 'cautiously and philosophically'.[136] Burke, however, could not claim such intellectual virtues because his position amounted to 'an unenlightened veneration for maxims which are supposed to have the sanction of time in their favour, and a passive acquiescence in received opinions'.[137] This represented an abuse of general principles because the circumstances that generated the maxims were neglected, thereby foreclosing their universality. Only philosophy could remedy this weakness by revealing the correct method for generating general principles in politics—by examining the human constitution and the laws that regulated human affairs. This, Stewart claimed, would produce principles from 'a much more extensive induction, than any of the inferences that can be drawn from the history of actual establishments'.[138] Translating this argument into today's terms, the disciplines that Burke placed on the statesman's reasoning excluded too many data.

The final element of Stewart's attack was to undermine the supposed purity of facts. He did this by revealing the multitude of circumstances simultaneously operating in a society at a given moment, including ideas, manners, the character of the people, and the relations that held between the social orders. In consequence, simply tracking certain constitutional practices in the manner of Burke was an inadequate factual basis. Faced with the enormity of details and processes, the only remedy was to produce systematic descriptions of societies that worked rather like the rules of grammar in simplifying and organizing the materials to be studied. If such descriptions were to be called 'theory', then it was simply the case that 'every such description must necessarily be more or less theoretical' since every description was partial compared to the abundance of particulars.[139] (Of course, Stewart's gloss was unsatisfactory since Burke's history of constitutions was embedded in a history of manners of the type that Smith had deployed in Book III of *Wealth of Nations*.[140]) The lesson was that theory was inevitable, making an opposition between experience and theory in the manner of Burke philosophically untenable.

If we now turn to volume two of *Elements*, then we see a repetition of this move in relation to the category of 'experience' and with explicit reference to political economy. The context was another attack on the tendency for theory to be contrasted with experience in a philosophically unacceptable manner, this time in the field of medicine.

---

[136] Stewart, *Elements of the Philosophy of the Human Mind*, 1: 234–5.
[137] Ibid., 1: 236.
[138] Ibid.
[139] Ibid., 1: 239.
[140] Classically studied in Pocock, *Virtue, Commerce, and History*, chapter 10.

[I]t is by cautious theory alone, that experience can be rendered of any value. Nothing, indeed, can be more absurd than to contrast, as is commonly done, experience with theory, as if they stood in opposition to each other. Without theory, (or, in other words, without general principles, inferred from a sagacious comparison of a variety of phenomena), experience is a blind and useless guide; while, on the other hand, a legitimate theory . . . necessarily presupposes a knowledge of connected and well ascertained facts, more comprehensive, by far, than any mere empiric is likely to possess.[141]

A version of this struggle, Stewart claimed, was being carried on in 'the science of politics'—defined as consisting of the theory of government, and the general principles of legislation, with 'political economy' representing a subbranch of the latter. As with medicine, Stewart perceived a rift separating the discipline's practitioners—between political arithmeticians or *statistical collectors* and *political economists, or political philosophers*.[142] The political economists were routinely accused of being 'visionaries' and denied status in comparison with their rivals, the political arithmeticians, who invoked the prestige of Bacon.[143]

As might be expected, Stewart had little patience for these claims, and he demoted the knowledge produced by political arithmetic to little more than isolated particulars. By contrast, the political economist or political philosopher worked with facts available for inspection by all of humanity, by which Stewart seems to have meant the principles of human nature, such as the principle that self-love guided the allocation of capital. It followed that the pretended superiority of political arithmetic over political economy should be reversed: 'instead of appealing to political arithmetic as a check on the conclusions of political economy, it would often be more reasonable to have recourse to political economy as a check on the extravagancies of political arithmetic.'[144] (As we will see, this positioning of theory as a check on numerical claims is exactly what Ricardo did to Charles Bosanquet in their clash during the Bullion Controversy.) Stewart followed this claim with an explicit attack on Ancient Constitution thinking of the type central to Burke's account of good lawmaking: just like political arithmetic, the common lawyer's valorization of antiquated policy and their credulous regard for the monuments of the past was unscientific and pre-theoretical.[145]

Such was Stewart's case for the theoretical scrutiny of society: the vaunted rival of cleaving to experience was no rival at all. The point to underline is that

---

[141] Stewart, *Elements of the Philosophy of the Human Mind*, 2: 444.
[142] Ibid., 2: 447.
[143] Ibid. As did the pioneer William Petty, promising to scorn words and intellectual arguments dependent on the passions of men, reasoning instead 'in terms of *Number, Weight,* or *Measure*'; see William Petty, *Political Arithmetick* (London, 1690), Preface.
[144] Stewart, *Elements of the Philosophy of the Human Mind*, 2: 448–9.
[145] Ibid., 2: 452.

Stewart made his case in tandem with remedies for excessive abstraction and love of theory, understood as ethical failings. Above all, it was because theoretical schemas could exhibit beauty that the theorist with poor control of their faculties might overindulge in abstraction, leading, in turn, to inattention to the particular.[146] The love of theory also carried political dangers, hence the section title, 'Use and Abuse of General Principles in Politics'.[147] In particular, 'Utopian projectors' who had succumbed to theory's intoxications would sacrifice civic tranquillity for political change, even to the extent of embracing violence as a means for change.[148] Such passions could also be roused in a well-governed mind by encountering 'theoretical perfection' for the first time, as in the 'œconomical system' of the Physiocrats.[149]

The theorist's mind could be restrained, however, with the aid of the right ethical and intellectual disciplines. One was to keep in view the complicated structure of society since this would remind the theorist of the uncertain effects that would flow to the whole society from changes in just one institution. Another was to keep faith that the age of general progress was at hand, revealing that partial and violent change stemmed from impatience.[150] In other words, the defences against becoming a zealot for violent change amounted to cultivating some traditional virtues: prudence and temperance. Once more we are directed to notice that this argument is being carried on in the register of ethics-talk and that we have no equivalent form of self-cultivation today when it comes to governing the minds of theorists.

Imagination was another of the mind's powers that could lead to enthusiasm if it were misgoverned. Utopians were, by definition, engaged in the construction of imaginary objects. This fact, along with the social reclusiveness often inherent to abstract speculation and the corresponding decay in those faculties attuned to everyday occurrences could see the proper balance between the imaginative life and everyday life overthrown. More explicitly, 'the mind gradually loses that command . . . over the train of its ideas', and the ultimate result was that 'the most extravagant dreams of imagination acquire as powerful an influence in exciting all its passions, as if they were realities'.[151] Once a mind was so disturbed, exposure to everyday life could even exacerbate the situation because it stimulated further trains of thought in imaginative directions, even as the poor figure perceived himself to be acting with 'the most perfect wisdom and consistency' while others perceived only 'folly'.[152] Political speculators were exposed to madness,

[146] Ibid., 1: 216, 232.
[147] Ibid., 1: 233.
[148] Ibid., 1: 251.
[149] Ibid., 1: 258.
[150] Ibid., 1: 257–9.
[151] Ibid., 1: 508–9.
[152] Ibid., 1: 511.

and so Stewart's prudential disciplines related not only to the quality of their work but to their mental states, too. Talk of theoretical enthusiasm was not mere rhetoric but taken to be a serious ethical failing. This is a vital aspect of the context in which Malthus and Ricardo will be shown to have acted in future chapters.

Conclusion

Burke, Mackintosh, Stewart: three early salvos in a long debate over the role of theory and practice in political life. From today's point of view, what is so alien about these debates is that their ultimate import was self-conduct. That is, at issue was how to conduct one's mind and avoid the pathology of theoretical enthusiasm. Today we take theory for granted, with rival epistemological positions such as realism and instrumentalism presupposing equally that the theorist is a legitimate intellectual figure. We are not, in consequence, accustomed to thinking of 'love of theory' and similar phenomena as pathologies to be guarded against by cleaving to custom or to governing our imaginations with habits acquired at school. And because we tend not to project the figure of the statesman or legislator as the addressee of politico-economic discourse, we are comparatively relaxed about the pathologies that may enter their minds, which largely explains why we do not fret that our leaders may become intoxicated by 'system'. (Ideology is perhaps the closest equivalent concept, which is to say that we have different fears.) But Burke and his contemporaries were accustomed to thinking and talking in this way.

The rhetorical pattern that can be identified in the preceding discussion is one where fact-collecting, practice, and experience were allied with the Burkean preference for precedent, while political philosophy insisted on the need for theory to examine facts and precedent to determine if they were relevant, valid, or barbaric. It was noted that Stewart did write of 'induction' on occasion, but it did not represent an autonomous epistemological principle because he primarily used this notion to explain how a theorist could generate principles with ethical surety.

Identifying this argumentative pattern—that is, the vocabulary of theory and practice and some of its exemplary uses—provides two services for the book's overall argument. First, it shows how a vocabulary can be recovered from historical study in lieu of projecting today's vocabulary of method and model backwards in time. Second, it is possible to now test the hypothesis that Malthus and Ricardo also conducted their debates with the vocabulary of theory and practice. The remainder of this book reports the results of this test by treating the key debates between Malthus and Ricardo as the relevant evidence. Before taking up that task, however, something should be said about whether or not the evidence is available to claim that this vocabulary of theory and practice—and the style of thinking that went with it—was used by Malthus before the contests with Ricardo came to dominate his work.

The evidence does exist that Malthus used this vocabulary. In fact, Malthus devoted an entire chapter to the defence of theory in every edition of the *Essay* except the first, under the title 'Of the necessity of general principles on this subject', its place always being the penultimate chapter of the text and always followed by the anti-utopian final chapter, 'Of our rational expectations respecting the future improvement of society'. The cumulative message was this: theory was inevitable, but its role was not to usher in a new millennium but to point out the modest prospects for improvement that actually existed. His argument thus largely repeated what was stated in the first *Essay* in opposition to Condorcet and Godwin.[153] More specifically, Malthus's case for the inevitability of theory glossed Hume to the effect that, of all the sciences, it was in politics that appearances were most deceitful.[154] This allowed Malthus to frame the issue as one of determining what counted as judicious observation and experience, understood as prerequisites for drawing general inferences and producing just theory.

> We are continually hearing declamations against theory and theorists, by men who pride themselves upon the distinction of being practical. It must be acknowledged that bad theories are very bad things, and the authors of them useless and sometimes pernicious members of society. But these advocates of practice do not seem to be aware that they themselves very often come under this description, and that a great part of them may be classed among the most mischievous theorists of their time. When a man faithfully relates any facts, which have come within the scope of his own observation . . . he undoubtedly adds to the sum of general knowledge. . . . But when from this confined experience, from the management of his own little farm, or the details of the workhouse in his neighbourhood, he draws a general inference . . . he then at once erects himself into a theorist; and is the more dangerous, because, experience being the only just foundation for theory, people are often caught merely by the sound of the word, and do not stop to make the distinction between that partial experience which, on such subjects, is no foundation whatever for a just theory, and that general experience, on which alone a just theory can be founded.[155]

---

[153] Thomas Robert Malthus, 'An Essay on the Principle of Population (1798)', in *The Works of Thomas Robert Malthus*, eds. E. A. Wrigley and David Souden, 8 vols. (London: Routledge, 1986), 1: chapters 9–15.

[154] Malthus, 'An Essay on the Principle of Population (1826): Part II', *Works*, 3: 558. Malthus was referencing Hume's 'Of the Populousness of Ancient Nations' (David Hume, 'Of the Populousness of Ancient Nations', in *Essays Moral, Political, and Literary*, ed. Eugene F. Miller (Indianapolis: Liberty Fund, 1987), 377–464).

[155] Malthus, 'An Essay on the Principle of Population (1826): Part II', 558.

As with Stewart, discussed earlier, Malthus construed his rivals as theorists, which then made the issue one of distinguishing between good theorists and 'mischievous theorists'. Malthus arrogated the former status for himself in virtue of the fact that his work acceded to general experience—not least through some twenty-two chapters of conjectural-historical study—and identified the permanent effects that arose from the human constitution. In his own time, Malthus was a theorist.[156] Who, however, were Malthus's 'mischievous theorists' and 'advocates of practice'?

One target that Malthus had in mind was the Society for Bettering the Condition and Improving the Comforts of the Poor, whose reports he cited and whose intentions he applauded.[157] By targeting the Society, Malthus was also effectively replying to those critics who invoked practice, such as Robert Southey, discussed in the Introduction.[158] Southey had positioned the Society's 'experimental philosophy' in explicit opposition to Malthus's theories, especially the Society's presentation of evidence, which Southey judged to be accessible to the average person.[159] According to Southey, the Society 'collected facts' and 'tried such limited experiments as were in their power, and laid their observations before the public, as materials from which every man may draw the conclusion'.[160] The implication was that these were the methods by which legislation might be developed, not upon theories of population, which, we have seen, he considered 'as absurd as if a physician upon some theory of pneumatics were to set respiration to music'.[161] Malthus, however, detected in the Society's reasoning the danger of 'drawing general inferences from insufficient experience'.[162] In short, the relief for the poor that the Society delivered in their experiments had fulsome effects because it was partial and irregular, but if the relief were generalized and regular then it would be incorporated into the expectations of the poor, eroding their need for foresight and prudence. The failure of the Society to identify this danger was a failure of theoretical acumen: they focused on appearances. Contra Southey, neither the average person nor the average statesman were equal to the task of forming correct theory unless they submitted to the

[156] Hence there is no need to call him 'quantitative' or 'empirical', *pace* Robert J. Mayhew, *Malthus: The Life and Legacies of an Untimely Prophet* (Cambridge, Mass.: Harvard University Press, 2014), 67.

[157] Malthus, 'An Essay on the Principle of Population (1826): Part II', 560–1.

[158] For an account, see Winch, *Riches and Poverty*, 292–4, 336–48.

[159] Southey, 'Essay V', 192. For the statement of the Society's intended method that Southey quoted, see: The Society for Bettering the Condition and Increasing the Comforts of the Poor, 'Prefatory Introduction to the Second Volume', in *The Reports of the Society for Bettering the Condition and Increasing the Comforts of the Poor*, vol. 2, part 1 (London, 1800), 1–30, at 11.

[160] Southey, 'Essay V', 192.

[161] Ibid., 246.

[162] Malthus, 'An Essay on the Principle of Population (1826): Part II', 561.

appropriate disciplines. Malthus and Stewart aimed at different targets but they were shooting at the same enemy: critics of theory. More importantly, both authors were crafting the figure of the theorist as someone whose intellectual comportment was indispensable to effective legislation. The political economist was one of the theorist's faces, as we shall now see.

PART II

Introduction to Part II

Political Economy and Parliamentary Reasoning

The next two chapters concern what Arthur Young termed the 'two great political controversies' of the period: the Bullion Controversy (Chapter 2) and the Corn Laws debate (Chapter 3).[1] Both controversies developed around—and were resolved by—parliamentary debate. As indicated in the Introduction to this volume, Part II is intended to recognize this fact, resisting the temptation to treat political economy as if it were a scientific vocation with its own principles of development, as per the precepts of internal history. Instead, the contingencies of lawmaking and party politics form the context for some of the major statements of political economy in this period, at least as we have come to retrospectively construe the period in relation to the history of economic thought. Once this lawmaking context is brought into view, the expectation that counsel to Parliament would recommend a course of action by weighing the relevant factors emerges as decisively shaping the form and content of the texts that we are accustomed to celebrating. In other words, once restored to their historical contexts, Malthus and Ricardo appear less as pioneering economists and more as participants in preexisting debates that were carried on using established forms of argument.

By contrast, the traditional practice of sifting this terrain for conceptual breakthroughs has relied on reading these texts in relation to a different, unhistorical context: the concerns of academic economists since the twentieth century. In particular, monetary theory has provided much of the vocabulary with which the Bullion Controversy has been redescribed, while the concepts of comparative advantage and diminishing returns have structured discussion of the Corn Laws debate. Once again, the culprit is a relaxed attitude regarding substitution between, on the one hand, the vocabulary and forms of reasoning active in the historian's present and, on the other hand, the vocabulary and reasoning found in the texts under study.

Indicative of the tendency to read the Bullion Controversy in relation to contemporary monetary theory is the monumental new study from Ghislain

---

[1] Arthur Young, 'An Enquiry into the Rise of Prices in Europe', *Annals of Agriculture* 46/271 (1815), 144.

Before Method and Models. Ryan Walter, Oxford University Press. © Oxford University Press 2021.
DOI: 10.1093/oso/9780197603055.003.0003

Deleplace, *Ricardo on Money: A Reappraisal*.[2] One of Deleplace's leading aims was to establish Ricardo 'as a first-rank monetary theorist'.[3] This aim was primarily realized in Deleplace's idea of a 'Money-Standard Equation', central to his reconstruction of 'Ricardo's model of a monetary economy'.[4] In her sympathetic review of Deleplace, Maria Cristina Marcuzzo endorsed the motivation of recovering Ricardo's wisdom for the present but objected to the burdensome use of formulae, preferring a gentler form of translation.

> Inheriting Ricardo's wisdom means being able to translate his conceptual tools and forge them into our language and context so as to make them applicable to the present discussion. As in any translation, it is a delicate exercise that requires the ability to preserve the original meaning of a concept in rendering it into a different frame of language.[5]

The desire for theoretical relevance that Deleplace and Marcuzzo share stands as a useful contrast to the sensibility animating the discussion here. For the present argument is premised on the desirability of avoiding translation wherever possible since the aim is not to recover lost wisdom but to understand the past on its own terms as far as possible.

In relation to the Bullion Controversy, the leading fact to be brought to view is this: the debate focused on the behaviour of the Bank of England, an institution of the post-1688 Whig regime that enjoyed hallowed status among that regime's allies. It was a party bank, not a central bank. The Bank was attacked in a new way by the *Report of the Select Committee on the High Price of Gold Bullion* (1810), which adduced arguments purporting to demonstrate that the Bank was technically incompetent, or deliberately profiting at the public's expense, or both. The *Report* was rejected in Parliament as a dangerous form of metaphysics and thus unsuited to the task of guiding parliamentary reason. In other words, in the time and place of its composition, the *Report* was not perceived as a step forward in macroeconomics, this category being unavailable. What rather happened was that the enemies of the *Report* successfully deployed a version of Burke's rejection of theory in political life to disqualify political economy as a guide for legislators. As might be expected, in these events, the redescription of political economy as theoretical enthusiasm played a central role, as did the construal of the Bank's existing procedures as a form of tested practice on which the British state could rely. In this context, Malthus and Ricardo were obliged to defend the idea that both

---

[2]   Ghislain Deleplace, *Ricardo on Money: A Reappraisal* (London: Routledge, 2017).
[3]   Ibid., 3.
[4]   Ibid., 143–284, 389–94.
[5]   Maria Cristina Marcuzzo, 'Ghislain Deleplace, *Ricardo on Money. A Reappraisal*', *Oeconomia* 8/1 (2018), 119–24, at paragraph 18.

theory and political economists had a role to play in political life. Their work was not wholly defensive, however, for both writers launched powerful attacks on those 'practical writers' who stood as their intellectual opponents. Neither writer used the vocabulary of method and model, but both extensively deployed the vocabulary of theory and practice to provide rhetorical cover for their own intellectual conduct. None of this is easy to capture if our aim is to recommend Ricardo's 'model' for today, in the manner of Deleplace and so many others.

Chapter 3 considers the Corn Laws debate of 1813–1815. Once again, the central feature of the time to be brought to view is widespread hostility to the idea that Parliament adopt theoretical principles as a guide for its lawmaking activities—as seen in the rejection of the *Report* in the Bullion Controversy. But the pattern of argument differed to that produced in the Bullion Controversy in several respects. Perhaps the most important difference was that the equivalent Parliamentary Report—the *Report from the Select Committee of the House of Commons Appointed to Enquire into the Corn Trade of the United Kingdom* (1813)—was not judged by its critics to have been contaminated by metaphysics. Its lead advocate and author, Henry Parnell, was sympathetic to political economy and the principle of free trade, yet he insisted that the doctrinal truth of a claim was a separate issue from the expediency of its application in a given set of circumstances. This second task was a matter not of theoretical insight but of legislative acumen. More specifically, Parnell thought that his task was to use a style of argument in which free trade was a principle that had to find its place and application amongst rival principles of statecraft. We are thus dealing with a late appearance of casuistical reasoning, where Malthus, Ricardo, and Robert Torrens interleaved rival principles of government to resolve policy questions and did so as self-avowed theorists attempting to supervene on parliamentary reasoning.

Once again, the context is crucial for understanding the texts, and the context is remote from today's models of international trade. Perhaps the greatest intellectual distance for today's reader to cross is to come to terms with casuistry as a style of reasoning, but the entire debate is impossible to understand unless this is achieved. In brief, today's debates over free trade tend not to be casuistical in nature because free trade and protection do not stand as equally valid principles to choose between depending on the case at hand but as rival doctrines that are typically stated in isolation of circumstances, as if they could always and everywhere be valid. This is why textbooks present comparative advantage as a 'proof' of free trade, despite the fact that concessions must then be made for certain commodities such as nuclear weapons, oil, and humans. In short, to build a model is to abdicate the casuist's task of application to particular circumstances in favour of discovering a conclusion for all circumstances. Coming from a period when it was taken for granted that the circumstances mattered, the Corn Laws debate of 1813–1815 was conducted in relation to the task of stabilizing the supply of a special commodity: cereal grains, or 'corn', the staple food.

It is unhelpful to tell this story with the emergence of comparative advantage as the central theme for two reasons. First, comparative advantage had not become a standalone and prestigious defence of free trade. Second, as will be seen, even Ricardo was obliged by the context to address the arguments against free trade and weigh them in the scales of prudential judgement. Thus, the emergence of standalone free trade arguments—typically celebrated as conceptual breakthroughs in the literature[6]—really represents the decay and disappearance of the casuistical style of argumentation in which they first appeared. Whether or not this is something to bemoan or celebrate is not for historians to decide, but up until now only the celebratory narrative has been available because of the dominance of rational reconstruction and self-satisfied internal histories. In short, Part II represents a crucial step in this book's alternative account of this period by demonstrating that it was neither scientific progress nor a mystical internal reason that turned the wheels of political economy, for this was instead done by an old and distinctively British practice: parliamentary debate.

---

[6] See, for example, Roy J. Ruffin, 'David Ricardo's Discovery of Comparative Advantage', *History of Political Economy* 34/4 (2002), 727–48; John Aldrich, 'The Discovery of Comparative Advantage', *Journal of the History of Economic Thought* 26/3 (2004), 379–99; Christian Gehrke, 'Ricardo's Discovery of Comparative Advantage Revisited: A Critique of Ruffin's Account', *The European Journal of the History of Economic Thought* 22/5 (2015), 791–817.

2

The Vocabulary of Theory and Practice in the Bullion Controversy, 1797–1811

The aim of this chapter is to provide a historical account of the Bullion Controversy and the roles that Malthus and Ricardo played in its development. The results are treated as capable of supporting or undermining the hypothesis articulated at the close of the previous chapter: that Malthus, Ricardo, and their peers did not think in terms of method and models but rather deployed the vocabulary of theory and practice. The results reported in what follows support this claim. Those writers who defended the institution at the heart of the debate—the Bank of England—largely used the notions of practice and experience, while critics of the Bank, such as Malthus and Ricardo, typically avowed the need to use theory to appraise the Bank's actions. In sum, the vocabulary of theory and practice was central to the debate, while talk of method and models was absent.

While pairing the Bank's defenders with the notion of practice and the Bank's critics with theory indicates the general shape of the contest, some complications need to be brought to view. Their presence owes to the fact of Restriction: the government forbade the Bank of England from redeeming its paper in specie, and this created a paper pound note inconvertible into gold. The government's critics treated Restriction as an act of 'innovation' that exposed the nation to some long-held fears regarding the nexus of money and political power. In other words, Restriction was a contingency that, ironically, had placed the august Bank and its supporters on the *opposite* side to tradition and experience. The leading consequence of this circumstance was that those writers who typically revered practice above theory, and who clung to precedent while shunning innovation, were vulnerable to the very allegation that they normally made against their theory-purveying enemies. This opened the way for theorists such as Malthus and Ricardo to opportunistically draw on all the rhetorical force of practice and experience, which, we will see, they did, and with skill.

This rhetorical opportunism is most striking in the case of Ricardo, whom we find making statements regarding good and bad reasoning that read very much as if he were committed to accounting for facts and experience. Ricardo's statements can thus be shown to have been decisively influenced by the rhetorical needs and opportunities of the moment—by the context. This claim challenges much of the existing literature on this point because it implies that it is simply not

Before Method and Models. Ryan Walter, Oxford University Press. © Oxford University Press 2021.
DOI: 10.1093/oso/9780197603055.003.0004

feasible to treat Ricardo's scattered statements regarding the demands of good intellectual inquiry as if they provided insight into a method that preexisted the contingent contexts in which Ricardo produced these statements. Instead, Ricardo emerges in the Bullion Controversy as operating with a vocabulary that his enemies had used before him. His skill lay in reworking the terms of his opponents against them.

Regarding language, a subsidiary result is also reported in what follows: that the vocabulary of theory, practice, and enthusiasm played no important role in the earliest stage of the debate, in 1797, when Restriction was enacted, seemingly because an older vocabulary—normally studied by intellectual historians under the rubric of 'country' thought—was used instead to indict the Bank's actions. The vocabulary of theory and practice only began to be used in the period 1801–1804, and then came to dominate the debate following publication of the *Report from the Select Committee on the High Price of Bullion* (1810) and the extensive discussion of this document in Parliament. It was in this context that Ricardo elected to use this language, showing himself to be rhetorically astute, shifting his intellectual comportment under the cover of practice and experience while simultaneously portraying his intellectual rival, Charles Bosanquet, as an enthusiast.

As these results imply, the terms 'induction', 'deduction', 'method', and 'model' played no important role in this debate, while the vocabulary of theory and practice was central. The claims of Chapter 1 allow us to identify the source of this vocabulary as being Edmund Burke's widely disseminated attacks on Jacobinism and defence of the Ancient Constitution.[1] In other words, these results suggest that political economy did not possess its own vocabulary for discussing what we think of as method; rather, its intellectual operations were construed in relation to an established debate regarding the correct conduct of the minds of legislators and their counsellors when confronting questions of reform and tradition. The discussion begins with the Bank's imbrication with party politics and, in consequence, its history as an object of partisan admiration and hostility.

1797–1804: The Old Debate over the Bank, Restriction, and the Emergence of a New Debate

It is important to begin by emphasizing that the Bullion Controversy did not fall from heaven but grew out of an old debate over the Bank of England. For the Bank was at the centre of venerable discussions over the role of commerce and

---

[1] Which continued through to the beginning of this period. See, in particular, Edmund Burke, *Two Letters Addressed to a Member of the Present Parliament, on the Proposals for Peace with the Regicide Directory of France* (London, 1796); reprinted as Burke, 'First Letter on a Regicide Peace' and Burke, 'Second Letter on a Regicide Peace', *Writings and Speeches*, 9: 264–95.

corruption in the post-1688 regime. This 'Whig' regime was understood by its defenders as Protestant, commercial, and modern, while its so-called country critics construed the same regime as corrupt, warmongering, and constitutionally unbalanced. While the lines of country thought regarding the Bank are familiar to historians of political thought, historians of economic thought make little of this aspect of the Controversy.[2] Yet country thought and its complaints regarding credit and commerce should be important to the historian of economic thought because this strand of thinking provided the leading terms with which the Bank had been attacked, and they were combined with new terms of attack in the post-1800 period when Malthus and Ricardo made their marks.

The Bank was a target for country thought because it was identified with the post-1688 regime (being founded in 1694 as a Whig institution and resented by Tories from the beginning).[3] Indicative here is the figuring of 'Publick Credit' in the Whig paper *The Spectator* as a virgin seated in the Bank, surrounded by documents that defined the post-1688 regime, including the Act of Toleration and Act of Settlement.[4] By contrast, in the rival Tory publication *The Moderator*, public credit was figured as a woman whose health was tied to the fortunes of the Whig party.[5]

Despite its original and continuing character as a creature of party, the Bank managed to achieve a degree of indispensability in the eyes of many in the eighteenth century because of its role in Britain's fiscal-military state building.[6] The relationship between William Pitt and the Bank nicely illustrates the position that the Bank had come to acquire in the nation's political life at the beginning of the controversy: Britain was subsidizing its allies to fight wars against France, and, in this context, financial accommodation on the part of the Bank was reciprocated by Pitt with legislative favour regarding the Bank's Charter.[7] This

---

[2] J. G. A. Pocock, *The Machiavellian Moment: Florentine Political Thought and the Atlantic Republican Tradition* (Princeton: Princeton University Press, 1975), chapter 13; Pocock, *Virtue, Commerce, and History*, chapter 6; Boyd Hilton, *A Mad, Bad, and Dangerous People? England 1783–1846* (Oxford: Oxford University Press, 2006), 257–8, 309–10, 316, 323–4; Anna Gambles, *Protection and Politics: Conservative Economic Discourse, 1815–1852* (Woodbridge: Boydell, 1999), chapter 4; Hiroki Shin, 'Paper Money, the Nation, and the Suspension of Cash Payments in 1797', *The Historical Journal* 58/2 (2015), 415–42, at 435–9; H. T. Dickinson, *Liberty and Property: Political Ideology in Eighteenth-Century Britain* (London: Weidenfeld and Nicolson, 1977), 94, 170, 182.

[3] Steve Pincus, *1688: The First Modern Revolution* (New Haven, Conn: Yale University Press, 2009), 366–99, provides an account of the Bank of England as a Whig institution resented by Tories. Contemporary histories of the Bank also emphasized the political component of its existence. See, for example, the continuity established between Jacobite and Foxite critics in Thomas Fortune, *A Concise and Authentic History of the Bank of England*, third edition (London, 1802), 1–73.

[4] 'No. 3, Saturday, March 3, 1711', in Donald F. Bond, ed., *The Spectator*, vol. 1 (Oxford: Oxford University Press, 1987), 14–7, at 15. See Pocock's discussion in Pocock, *The Machiavellian Moment*, 455–6.

[5] *The Moderator*, no. 28 (25 August 1710).

[6] John Brewer, *The Sinews of Power: War, Money and the English State, 1688–1783* (Cambridge, Mass.: Harvard University Press, 1990).

[7] John Clapham, *The Bank of England: A History*, 2 vols. (Cambridge: Cambridge University Press, 1944), 1: 192–4.

intimate connection between government and Bank was viewed approvingly by those committed to the Whig regime but with alarm by those critics of commerce who feared that it was destroying the citizenry's political virtue. The most alarming prospect was that ministers might use the Bank's financial power to circumvent Parliament's control of war spending.

William Anderson's *The Iniquity of Banking* is a good example of this style of criticism. The text was published in two parts, both in 1797, but one part on either side of Restriction.[8] Anderson argued that the Bank had an 'interest in war' because it enjoyed the status of being the government's lender of choice and because war spending raised interest rates.[9] Furthermore, the Bank's paper increased prices in general but Bank notes did not represent a loan of actual currency because they were merely promissory paper. In short, the paper allowed the Bank and others to 'rob the public' by creating a *de facto* currency.[10] The shortest solution, in Anderson's view, was for the government to suppress non-government paper money.[11] Even more affronting to Whigs was Anderson's claim that the cherished Whig image of the Bank as a pillar of the state was merely a disguise for the 'war system'.[12] This was a smear term that denoted a monied interest composed of bankers and merchants who supported ministers in their wars. It followed that a national paper would simultaneously end the corruption of property and politics.

This fear that the Bank was compromised by its links with government was also apparent in Sir John Sinclair's *Letters Written to the Governor and Directors of the Bank of England* (1797), largely composed before Restriction, in September 1796.[13] Sinclair, a long-term MP whom we will meet again later in the story, repeated the usual nostrum that the Bank was a pillar of the nation, but he nevertheless worried about Restriction. Not only could Restriction cause an excess of paper, rather like the failure of France's 'state notes', but Restriction might also see the Bank become 'a mere political engine' under government control.[14]

The dangers that could arise if the government were to capture the Bank were acknowledged even in the apologetic text composed by Sir Francis Baring, *Observations on the Establishment of the Bank of England* (1797). Baring became

---

[8] Little remains of Anderson in the historical record. He also examined the Bank and the national currency in his *A Letter to the Right Honourable Lord Althorp* (London, 1832). J. M. Pullen has noted his anti-Pitt stance, see J. M. Pullen, 'William Anderson (fl. 1797–1832), on Banking, the Money Supply, and Public Expenditure: A Forgotten Interventionist', *History of Political Economy* 19/3 (1987), 359–85, at 360.

[9] William Anderson, *The Iniquity of Banking* (London, 1797), 43.

[10] William Anderson, *The Iniquity of Banking. Part II* (London, 1797), 11.

[11] Ibid., 39–43, 59–60.

[12] Ibid., 58.

[13] John Sinclair, *Letters Written to the Governor and Directors of the Bank of England* (London, 1797), 5.

[14] Ibid., 33, 35.

one of the largest loan contractors helping the government fund the nation's wars and thus, on the surface, might be a good fit for the finance-side of the supposed 'war interest'. His pamphlet, however, addressed key anxieties that surrounded the government–Bank nexus. The Bank was figured as the 'pivot' around which the nation's wealth turned, with money the lubricating oil.[15] That was the Bank's function, but what were its private interests? After all, the Bank's directors were only men, and Restriction might tempt them to service private motives ahead of the public good. In particular, an ambitious minister might extract loans to the government beyond what the general security and safety of the nation could justify.

The danger might be managed, according to Baring, if Bank paper were made legal tender for the duration of the war and a limit placed on the amount of paper that could be issued.[16] An additional point of concern was that the government might introduce its own paper, as France had done in the form of the *assignat*—the 'state notes' that Sinclair had disparaged. In France these state notes were issued to excess and deranged the circulation to the extent that not even Robespierre's terror could stop two prices from emerging—one for coins and one for *assignats*.[17]

Several rhetorical opportunities were created by comparing inconvertible Bank paper with France's *assignats*, and this is one of the contingent facts that made the task of defending Restriction so difficult since the fear that inconvertible paper would go the way of French paper was common and had been exploited in Parliament from the beginning of Restriction.[18] Charles James Fox, for example, had prophesied in 1797 that inconvertible Bank notes would fall victim to this fate.[19] Even earlier, Edmund Burke had provided a tremendous set of arguments for those opposed to Restriction when he had attacked France's *assignats* in his *Reflections* (1790) as another disastrous experiment with the state's institutions. In the first place, the currency was backed by property stolen from the Church; that is, the very currency was sacrilegious in Burke's eyes. Moreover, being backed by land, the *assignats* represented an attempt to establish something like the Tory land bank that had sought to rival the Whig Bank of England in the previous century and failed.[20] Ultimately, and worst of all, the *assignats* were designed to extract wealth from citizens so that the new state

---

[15] Francis Baring, *Observations on the Establishment of the Bank of England* (London, 1797), 1, 6, 34.

[16] Ibid., 72–3, 81.

[17] Ibid., 79.

[18] Jacob H. Hollander, 'The Development of the Theory of Money from Adam Smith to David Ricardo', *The Quarterly Journal of Economics* 25/3 (1911), 429–70, at 441.

[19] Edwin Cannan, 'Introduction', in Edwin Cannan, ed., *The Paper Pound of 1797–1821: A Reprint of the Bullion Report* (London: P. S. King and Son, 1919), vii–xlix, at xii.

[20] Burke, 'Reflections on the Revolution in France', *Writings and Speeches*, 280–1.

might survive: an instrument of fraud implemented by force.[21] What should be underlined here is that these arguments came from Edmund Burke, who was, as we saw in Chapter 1, the provider of the primary intellectual weapons that were used against reformers and theorists and now, by accident, against an action of the Whig regime: Restriction.

How was the Bank defended from such attacks? A leading strategy was to underline the political dangers faced by the nation. This is seen in *A Correct Detail of the Finances of this Country* (1797), by the otherwise-unknown Charles Hales. Hales's message was that Restriction was an act of prudence that conserved the nation's specie and, more importantly, prevented it from falling into French hands.[22] Given this precept, the only people who would refuse the Bank's notes were the ignorant and those corrupted by 'Jacobinical principles', who were properly seen as enemies of the state.[23] Hales thus used the maximal counterattack that was available to the Bank's defenders in 1797: those who criticized the Bank were being disloyal to Britain.

Hales's defence relied on the Bank's standing as a hallowed institution whose prosperity could be identified with the survival of the British state. In other words, the stakes were far higher than the inconvenience of rising prices. It can also be noted that this pattern of debate—alternately asserting the Bank's role in corrupting the political system and in ensuring its survival—had little use for the vocabulary of theory and practice. For these arguments tended not to contain theoretical accounts operating at high levels of abstraction. This leads us to ask the question: Did the vocabulary of theory and practice enter the Bullion Controversy?

The answer is yes. Debate over Restriction cooled for the next few years, returning to view in 1801, and, from this point onwards, the rhetorical contest between theory and practice came to predominate, along with rival characterizations of Restriction as a retrograde or progressive movement in the history of civilization. The proximate cause of the issue's resurgence was the publication of Walter Boyd's *A Letter to the Right Honourable William Pitt* (1801). Boyd had been a financier in Paris who had fled following the Revolution and then began contracting large loans to Britain and its allies.[24] Falling from favour, Pitt refused to allow Boyd to contract for the loan of 1799, and the next year Boyd was financially broken.[25] That Boyd wrote from bitterness is less important for the argument here than how he chose to attack Pitt and the Bank. Starting with Pitt, Boyd

---

[21]   Ibid., 286.

[22]   Charles Hales, *A Correct Detail of the Finances of this Country* (London, 1797), 39.

[23]   Ibid., 36.

[24]   S. R. Cope, *Walter Boyd: A Merchant Banker in the Age of Napoleon* (Gloucester: Alan Sutton, 1983), 48–9.

[25]   Clapham, *The Bank of England*, 2: 16–7.

accused him of innovation, exactly the pathology in politics that Burke and Pitt had been at such pains to avoid.

> *Innovation* has been the great danger against which your administration has laboured, and in many respects with success, to defend this country. But is there, in the annals of history, any innovation more remarkable or more dangerous than this was?[26]

For its part, the Bank was portrayed by Boyd as governed by self-interested directors who had deceived Pitt into passing Restriction in 1797 by starving the circulation in the preceding years.[27]

It is crucial to notice how Boyd developed his argument. He did not establish principles that linked the quantity of Bank paper with prices but merely invoked principles that he presented as either 'universally recognized' or indispensable: 'those principles of public œconomy, which no country ever abandoned with impunity'.[28] Boyd developed no discussion of his sources or authorities, and his claim to square his 'theory' of price rises with the 'symptoms' was similarly perfunctory.[29] Boyd merely posited circulation as a natural process, partly opaque to understanding, but one which the legislator should act on by attempting to gradually increase its quantity.[30] Once this quality of Boyd's thinking is understood, it is perfectly clear that he was not concerned to establish theoretical relationships but was content to casually equate an increase in prices with the depreciation of paper and to dismiss war and speculation as potential causes of the price rises without developing any substantial reasons.[31] In short, Boyd was not doing macroeconomics. Boyd's leading pieces of evidence, which were to be targeted by his critics, were a comparison of the quantity of banknotes in circulation between 1797 and 1800 (nearly 80 per cent higher on one measure), the exchange with Hamburg (14 per cent against London), and the price of gold bullion (around 10 per cent higher over the 1797–1800 period). As stated, however, Boyd's account primarily relied on describing Restriction with a negative vocabulary: it represented an 'innovation', and introduced a 'forced' paper on 'authority', like France's ruinous *assignat*.[32]

Boyd's association of Bank paper with *assignats* evidently angered the Bank's supporters. A good example of the reaction is Thomas Skinner Surr's reply, *Refutation of Certain Misrepresentations* (1801). Surr was an employee of the

---

[26] Walter Boyd, *A Letter to the Right Honourable William Pitt* (London, 1801), 74–5.
[27] Ibid., 1–4, 69–70.
[28] Ibid., 7–8.
[29] Ibid., 32.
[30] Ibid., 13, 17–18.
[31] Ibid., 35, 51–60.
[32] Ibid., 48, 74.

Bank and drew on his knowledge of its procedures in his defence: the analogy between Bank paper and the French *assignat* obscured the Bank's independence from government as expressed in the requirement that all loans to government be negotiated through the Court of Directors. The Court was responsible for guarding the Bank's interests, not the government's interests.[33] The other component of Surr's defence related to the Bank's discounting procedures, which drew on more than 100 years of 'experience' and were so effective, in fact, that Surr considered them to preclude even the possibility of over-issue.[34]

While Surr defended the Bank by pointing to its experience and tradition, another of the Bank's defenders portrayed Boyd's attack as an effusion of theoretical enthusiasm. In financial trouble, William Combe was attempting to be listed on the Treasury payroll once more through pro-government writings and in this spirit contributed to the debate.[35] He anonymously authored his *Brief Observation on a Late Letter Addressed to the Right Hon. W. Pitt* (1801), in which the leading worry was that the public were being seduced by 'delusive and dangerous theories' proffered by 'enthusiastic accountants' and 'financial theorists'.[36] The public was said to be susceptible to theories regarding public credit because of the topic's recondite nature. Thus, the dangers of theoretical enthusiasm related not only to the individual mind that could be overthrown, but to the public mind, too. In Combe's view, Boyd was nothing more than a political projector who was best dealt with by being ignored. The point to be noted in this defence of the Bank is that it focused not on the Bank's modernity and patriotism but on the fallacious, theoretical reasoning of its critics. For this represents a shift of *topos* that endured.

Boyd's pamphlet also drew forth the anonymous *A Twelve-Penny Answer to a Three Shillings and Six-Penny Pamphlet* (1801), and, following the second edition of Boyd's pamphlet, the critic took up their pen again to compose *A Second Twelve-Penny Answer* (1801).[37] We have already encountered the main points that the anonymous author made against Boyd. First, and as with Surr, it was denied that Bank notes could be issued to excess because of the Bank's procedures, by which the Bank 'issues no Notes but against the property of individuals

---

[33] T. S. Surr, *Refutation of Certain Misrepresentations Relative to the Nature and Influence of Bank Notes* (London, 1801), 27–30.

[34] Ibid., 10. See also 42–3.

[35] Vincent Carretta, 'Combe [formerly Combes], William (1742–1823), Writer and Literary Imitator', *Oxford Dictionary of National Biography* (2008), https://www.oxforddnb.com/view/10.1093/ref:odnb/9780198614128.001.0001/odnb-9780198614128-e-6022

[36] [William Combe], *Brief Observations on a Late Letter Addressed to the Right Hon. W. Pitt, by W. Boyd* (London, 1801), 5–6.

[37] Anonymous, *A Twelve-Penny Answer to a Three Shillings and Six-Penny Pamphlet* (London, 1801); Walter Boyd, *A Letter to the Right Honourable William Pitt*, second edition (London, 1801); Anonymous, *A Second Twelve-Penny Answer to a New (and Five Shillings) Edition of a Three Shillings and Six-Penny Pamphlet* (London, 1801).

convertible into Cash or Notes, or against Government Securities'.[38] In consequence, the increase in banknotes that took place was natural.[39] Second, Boyd's manner of reasoning was rejected, consisting in 'retrograding from effects to one principal cause of his own creation'; namely, the Bank's excessive issue of notes.[40] Boyd's flight from sound reasoning was further indicated by his having ignored the true causes that were apparent to all who would see: war and scarcity.[41] In the subsequent pamphlet, *A Second Twelve-Penny Answer*, this second line of attack was intensified. Boyd was accused of 'sophistry' and 'wild supposition', while the entire text was accounted for as 'chimerical speculations'.[42] The Bank's critics were being attacked for their theoretical style of reasoning.

Henry Boase's pamphlet of the following year, *Guineas an Unnecessary and Expensive Incumbrance on Commerce* (1802), pushed this strategy even further.[43] Boase declared that he would rely on 'experimental and demonstrative facts' in preference to 'preconceived speculative opinions, and all the tinsel of sophistical declamations'.[44] It is, therefore, not surprising to find that Boase deployed the more general set of vocabulary terms that we reviewed in the previous chapter: 'experience', 'facts', and 'practice' as against 'visionary schemes', 'abstract principles', and 'speculation'.[45] Boase's pamphlet is interesting, however, because of his intellectual honesty. For Boase conceded that Restriction did represent a legislative 'experiment', one that would have been considered 'the very climax of folly . . . even in speculation' were it not a 'necessity' called forth by the nation's needs of the moment; mercifully, the affair had yielded 'experimental proof' that the nation's circulation could, in fact, operate perfectly well without bullion.[46] This was a risky ploy for Boase to adopt because it conceded so much territory to the Bank's critics—admitting that Restriction was an experiment in statecraft and thus confirming the accusation that the government had innovated.

For the ploy to work, Boase needed to show that the experiment had proved a success, thus justifying the claim embodied in his pamphlet's title—that guineas were an unnecessary expense that hindered the nation's commercial life.[47] Boase admitted that his doctrine was novel, but that was no hindrance if it were supported by 'facts demonstrated by experience', which would allow the status of Restriction to shift from experiment to 'sound policy'.[48] Boase made his case by

---

[38] Anonymous, *A Twelve-Penny Answer*, 7.
[39] Ibid., 14, 16.
[40] Ibid., 8–9.
[41] Ibid., 21, 24.
[42] Anonymous, *A Second Twelve-Penny Answer*, 11, 32, 51.
[43] Henry Boase, *Guineas an Unnecessary and Expensive Encumbrance on Commerce* (London, 1802).
[44] Ibid., 122.
[45] Ibid., iv–ix, 58, 88, 91, 103, 122–3.
[46] Ibid., iv, 71–2, 75.
[47] Ibid., 33–5 39.
[48] Ibid., iv, 108.

treating the issue not as one of rising prices and the Bank's profiteering but as the health of public credit and the role of paper in its cheap and effective functioning.[49] It should be noted that the force of Boase's argument was limited by his decision to argue against a caricature, for nobody had argued, as Boase claimed, that 'the precious metals are the only true sign of prosperity; and the only legitimate medium, through which public credit can be advantageously circulated'.[50] As we have seen, the leading attack on the Bank was rather that the Bank had or would exploit the absence of the usual limits on its note issue.

Whatever the value of Boase's thinking for economists today, in his time, his text was novel because he attempted to neutralize the accusation that Restriction represented an innovation by accepting that it was, and then redescribed the results of that experiment as new, positive experience. Boase is also noteworthy for the way that he intensified the association between anti-Bank thinking, theoretical enthusiasm, and the question of reform in general. Regarding reform, Boase sarcastically referred to 'humane reformers', and remarked how pleasurable it was for a patriot to reflect on the growth of state power since Restriction, in contrast to the disaster predicted by 'theorists'.[51] Equally revealing was Boase's Burkean panegyric on the British Constitution as exceeding any other in perfection, with the full extent of the boon recently affirmed by the failure of France's political experiments. The abiding lesson was that reform must be specific to the issue, not general, and must be based on 'experience', not 'theories', whatever the object of reform, whether church and state or the Bank.[52]

For the larger argument being made in this book, this is a key moment. A debate regarding the Bank of England, which had been conducted in relation to concerns over political corruption, had come to be conducted using the vocabulary of theory and practice. The effect was to change what was at stake in the debate: from the polity's virtue and corruption to the status of theory as a Trojan horse for destructive enthusiasm. Crucially, the enemies of theory were unable to enjoy full recourse to the notions of practice and experience because Restriction seemed to be an innovation. This pattern of thinking is impossible to capture if it is translated into the terms of method and models. Of course, for rational reconstruction, this is all chaff to be winnowed away. But even the most unhistorical scholar will be obliged to pause when we see that Ricardo drew on these resources in his attacks on the Bank, such that if we want to understand the lead theorist of the debate, then we must recover the context. To finish this task,

---

[49] Ibid., 11–6, 22–5, 39, 43–5, 55, 60–2, 103–6.
[50] Ibid., iv. The anti-Bank position was also said to entail emphasis on the proportion of the total circulation that bullion represents (Ibid., 21, 26).
[51] Ibid., 89–90, 95, 103.
[52] Ibid., 104–6, 109–16.

attention now turns to two of the best-known authors from this stage of the debate, Henry Thornton and Lord King.

Thornton's *An Enquiry into the Nature and Effects of the Paper Credit of Great Britain* (1802) can also be seen as a response to Boyd's attack on the Bank, although its complexity guaranteed that it would be read in its own right. Thornton's text was no pamphlet, running to more than 300 pages and laying down 'some general principles' and 'doctrines' in relation to credit and paper currency while also correcting the 'theoretical' writings of authorities such as Smith, Hume, Locke, and Steuart.[53] That is, Thornton stands as one of those contributors to the controversy who self-consciously engaged in doctrinal criticism and correction; we tend to take this activity for granted when reconstructing the period's thought, but it was a minority pursuit. In setting this task for himself, Thornton was sure to underline his status as a well-known banker and MP, thus standing as a man 'much occupied in the practical business of life', lacking time but with access to information beyond the public's sources.[54] In relation to the rhetoric of theory and practice and the *ethoi* it could connote, Thornton was having it both ways.

The same point can be made in relation to Thornton's analysis. On the one hand, Thornton's first two chapters undermined so-called *real bills* thinking. This was seen in Surr's claim, mentioned earlier, that the Bank's procedures guaranteed that its note issue answered the needs of trade, and it was commonly deployed in contrast to the idea of 'bills of accommodation', by which one gentleman created a bill solely for the purpose of helping another gentleman in a time of financial need. According to Thornton, the key distinction was that a 'real bill' represented actual property, while bills of accommodation were largely imaginary. Thornton disputed the validity of making this distinction by developing an illustration: merchant A might sell 100 barrels of port to merchant B for £100, with B issuing a note in payment. But B might then sell the same barrels to C and receive a note, too, and C could do the same by selling to D. In this case, there would be £300 of new paper in circulation but only £100 of real goods—the 100 barrels of port sold three times. It followed that for bills to represent real property there would need to be some power given to the holder of the bill to restrict the property (the 100 barrels) from being used for any purpose other than being sold to discharge the bill. Of course, Thornton wrote, 'No such power exists'.[55]

On the other hand, Thornton neither blamed the Bank for engineering Restriction nor worried over its links with government.[56] Nor did he accept

[53] Henry Thornton, *An Enquiry into the Nature and Effects of the Paper Credit of Great Britain* (London, 1802), v, vii, viii.
[54] Ibid., viii.
[55] Ibid., 31.
[56] Ibid., 61–2, 68, 69n.

that an injustice had been committed against the nation by the Bank's note issue having arbitrarily changed the value of property through raising prices.[57] On this point, Thornton bit the bullet, claiming that the resources did not exist for all noteholders to demand payment; even attempting to do so would derange the system of public credit. In consequence, Restriction needed to be viewed as a re-action to national needs in novel circumstances, requiring that a literal interpret-ation of the contract be relaxed for the sake of the common good. Parliament's actions had protected the nation from the shock that such an 'extraordinary event' might have produced.[58] This was masterful redescription, and, for his *coup de grace*, Thornton reclaimed 'justice' from the critics of Restriction to enlist the term in its defence.

> The parliament, then, were led by the practical view which they took of the sub-ject, to disregard theory, as well as some popular prejudice, for the sake of more effectually guarding the public safety, and promoting real justice.[59]

So much for justice. What of the central issue of the supposed link between an excessive issue of Bank paper and rising prices? Thornton's analysis of the rela-tionship between paper and prices provided means for impugning the Bank, and he would later make this case as a member of the Bullion Committee and MP.[60] In *Paper Credit*, however, Thornton set out so many intervening complications that drawing a straight line of responsibility was difficult, and doing so does not emerge as one of the text's central themes.[61] Nevertheless, Thornton held that limiting the quantity of the Bank's paper was a means for preserving its value and that a permanent divergence between the mint and market prices of gold was proof of an excessive issue. His counsel was, consequently, that the Bank ought to extend its issue in prosperous times and gently contract the same when the exchange was continuously unfavourable.[62] Thornton's position, like his analysis, was complicated.

This phase of the debate was crowned by Lord King's *Thoughts on the Restriction of Payments in Specie* (1803), which extended his speech in Parliament.[63] Unlike

---

[57]   Ibid., 111.

[58]   Ibid., 113.

[59]   Ibid.

[60]   Ibid., 193–6, 202–3. See F. A. Hayek, 'Henry Thornton (1760–1815)', in *The Collected Works of F. A. Hayek*, eds. W. W. Bartley III and Stephen Kresge, vol. 3 (Indianapolis: Liberty Fund, 2009), 295–344, at 338–9.

[61]   For example, Thornton, *An Enquiry into the Nature and Effects of the Paper Credit of Great Britain*, 222–31, 240, 243.

[62]   Ibid., 236, 242, 295.

[63]   Peter King, *Thoughts on the Restriction of Payments in Specie* (London, 1803). A second edition appeared in 1804 entitled *Thoughts on the Effects of the Bank Restrictions* (London, 1804). For the speech, see Peter King, 'Bank of England Restriction Bill', in T. C. Hansard, ed., *The Parliamentary Debates from the Year 1803 to the Present Time*, vol. 1 (London, 1812), 1673–6.

the nostalgic hue of country thought and its anxiety that commerce might corrupt the state's institutions and citizenry, King accepted the modernity of paper currency. In fact, the invention of paper money was a crucial moment in the history of modern commerce, saving great expense in those nations that were able to regulate it appropriately. In other words, the direction of history mandated that paper money replace coin. However, the business could be poorly done. The convertibility of paper into specie upon demand would ensure that all worked well by keeping the circulation within due limits but, if this condition were lifted, then paper would take whatever value accorded with its quantity and the issuer's credit worthiness.[64] With this precept set down, King was in a position to explain the experiences of Ireland and England.

In relation to the Bank of Ireland, which also suspended payments in 1797, King found the directors to have exploited a public trust for private advantage.

An important trust, which upon mistaken principles of political necessity was committed to this corporate body by Parliament for the public benefit, appears to have been perverted to the private interest of the proprietors of their stock. An undue advantage has been obtained by the Bank, in the exact degree of the excess of their notes; but the loss and injury to the public, as in all cases of depreciated currency, has been in a much greater proportion. An indirect tax is thus imposed upon the community, not for the benefit of the public, but of individuals.[65]

King invoked Edmund Burke's authority on the need to curb men with laws lest they succumb to temptation.[66] In England, the removal of such laws had produced similar results: the directors of the Bank of England had also betrayed the public's trust.[67] In short, Restriction's leading flaw was that it exposed the public to the natural avarice of private individuals.

In this regard, the intensity of King's denunciation of Restriction should be noted. Recall that King believed in paper currency as a by-product of civilization that was advantageous to the nation.[68] What King found reprehensible about Restriction was that it violated one of the distinguishing features of a civilized nation: the limit that private property posed to political power.

[64] King, *Thoughts on the Restriction of Payments in Specie*, 1, 3–5.
[65] Ibid., 53.
[66] Ibid., 55. The full quotation reads: 'all men possessed of an uncontrouled discretionary power leading to the aggrandisement and profit of their own body have always abused it: and I see no particular sanctity in our times, that is at all likely, by a miraculous operation, to overrule the course of nature' (Burke, 'Thoughts on the Present Discontents', *Writings and Speeches*, 2: 242–323, at 302).
[67] King, *Thoughts on the Restriction of Payments in Specie*, 25.
[68] Ibid., 63–5.

A due regard to *general rules*, and especially to the great rules of property, forms a most important part of the duty of a legislator. They are the foundations of all private and political security; and the only means by which great principles can be effectually protected against rash speculation and hasty and inconsiderate judgments. A strict adherence to these rules, and a deep sense of their value and importance, is the great characteristic which distinguishes civilized nations, and which marks the progress of political knowledge and improvement. . . . Yet a more extraordinary deviation from all general rules has never occurred than in that change in the system of our paper currency, which commenced in the Act of Suspension of 1797 and is still continued. A law to suspend the performance of contracts has been suffered to remain in force upwards of six years. A power has been committed to the Directors of the Bank, which is not entrusted by the Constitution even to the Executive Government; a power of regulating, in a certain degree, the standard of the currency of the kingdom, and of varying this standard at their pleasure. A precedent has been established, by which, upon any suggestion of temporary expediency, the whole personal property and monied interests of the country may be committed to the discretion of a commercial body not responsible to the Legislature, and not known to the Constitution.[69]

Initially an ill-chosen remedy to a manageable emergency, Restriction had come to represent 'a revolution in the whole system of our paper currency'.[70] Its indefinite continuation owed to the fact that the Bank had not sought to free itself from a disreputable situation but had solicited further legislative interference for the benefit of its proprietors. Where Boase had conceded that the whole business was an experiment, with the hope that its results would give Restriction a retrospective sanction, King insisted that Restriction was no experiment but the gravest violation of property.

This was the core of King's attack on Restriction on constitutional grounds. Yet his text also advanced a rejection of the real-bills argument. King's essential move was to develop something like a concept of the demand for currency, using descriptions such as 'the actual demand of the public', 'the permanent demands of the public', 'general demand for currency', and 'effective demand'.[71] With these labels, King was attempting to differentiate this phenomenon from the desire that

---

[69] Ibid., 83–4.
[70] Ibid., 10.
[71] Ibid., 16, 19, 23.

merchants might have for the Bank to discount their securities. Under convertibility, the latter would be regulated by the former since the nation's demand for currency would act as a natural check on the Bank's issue (via the price of bullion and the exchange, as suggested by Boyd). In this way, the Bank's supply to merchants through its discounting facilities would be limited.[72] Under Restriction, however, the Bank was obliged to either guess accurately, a task beyond human reason, or surrender to the temptation to abuse its power and greatly expand its (now unlimited) note issue. Since the Bank's directors were merely men, and being unrestrained, they succumbed to the 'constant inducement' of their private interest, just as Burke had predicted.[73]

Our survey of this stage of the debate can be closed by noting the 1804 *Report* into Ireland's circulating paper. The *Report* was produced by a large Committee in which Henry Thornton seems to have played a leading role, and there was significant overlap in personnel between this Committee and the more famous Committee that produced the Bullion Report of 1810.[74] It is therefore no surprise that the diagnosis six years later was hardly changed from what we find in the 1804 *Report*.

> The great and effectual remedy to the high and fluctuating Rates of the Exchange, undoubtedly, would be the Repeal of the Restriction Act from whence all the evils have flowed; the common circulating medium being thereby restored, the rise of Exchange above Par would be limited to the expense of transporting Specie, and Paper being convertible into Gold its depreciation would be prevented.[75]

It is important to note, however, that the vocabulary of theory and practice was almost completely absent from this 1804 *Report*. To track the history of a combative vocabulary is to follow contingent events in historical time; it is not to assert the existence of a discursive straightjacket. More plainly, historical actors were able to choose whether or not to use the vocabulary of theory and practice. In the following section it will be seen how this vocabulary did play a role in the 1810 *Report* and that it shaped the subsequent debate, including the contributions of Malthus and Ricardo.

---

[72] Ibid., 13, 22, 26–9, 33.

[73] Ibid., 25.

[74] See F. W. Fetter, 'Introduction', in F. W. Fetter, ed., *The Irish Pound, 1797–1826: A Reprint of the Report of the Committee of 1804 of the British House of Commons on the Condition of the Irish Currency* (London: George Allen and Unwin, 1955), 9–62, at 30–1.

[75] 'Text of the Report of 1804', in *The Irish Pound, 1797–1826*, 63–87, at 77.

1809–1811: Ricardo, the 1810 *Report*, and
the Practical Critics

Ricardo's first foray into political writing was 'The Price of Gold', published in the Whig newspaper, the *Morning Chronicle*, late in August 1809. Further pieces appeared in September and November.[76] Ricardo's articles launched the next phase of the controversy, and this fact alone would likely have guaranteed him a place in retrospective histories of economics. Yet the foregoing suggests that we ought to invert the frame and emphasize that it was not the motor of scientific progress that drew Ricardo into public debate but an old struggle over a Whig institution.

The following quotation expresses the core of Ricardo's position, and it will allow us to locate him in relation to the preceding survey:

> When the Act restricting the Bank from paying in specie took place, all checks to the over issue of notes were removed, excepting that which the Bank voluntarily placed on itself, knowing that if they were not guided by moderation, the effects which would follow would be so notoriously imputable to their monopoly, that the Legislature would be obliged to repeal the Restriction Act.[77]

As can be seen, Ricardo had no patience for real-bills thinking and exhibited little caution when it came to suggesting base motives behind the Bank's conduct. His solution was for Parliament to oblige the Bank to withdraw 2 to 3 million of its notes from circulation, which would lead to a fall in the price of both gold and commodities in general. This experiment would then reveal that 'all the evils in our currency' owed to the Bank's having over-issued its notes, which was only possible because this group of private merchants had been given 'the dangerous power . . . of diminishing at its will, the value of every monied man's property'.[78] The cause, in short, was innovation from government and the normal operation of self-interest on the part of the Bank; Ricardo was perfectly at home in the contours of the existing debate.

Ricardo developed his thinking in *The High Price of Bullion* (1810), published approximately one month after the appearance of his November 1809 letter in the *Morning Chronicle*.[79] He invoked the 'admitted principles of political economy' as the proper basis for bringing the issue to a 'fair discussion', not claiming originality but rather to be building on existing writers who had already

---

[76] For Ricardo's further two articles and the private correspondence with Trower, who replied to Ricardo, see Ricardo, 'Second Reply to "A Friend to Bank Notes"', *Works and Correspondence*, 3: 28–46.

[77] Ricardo, 'The Price of Gold', *Works and Correspondence*, 3: 13–21, at 17.

[78] Ibid., 21.

[79] Piero Sraffa, 'Note on the Bullion Essays', *Works and Correspondence*, 3: 1–12, at 5.

'enlightened' the public, especially Lord King in his *Thoughts on the Restriction*.[80] Ricardo's argumentation was far more rigorous and conceptual in nature than what he had set out in the *Morning Chronicle* pieces, as one might expect given the shift from newspaper to pamphlet. Ricardo began by giving an account of the division of the world's precious metals according to their 'intrinsic value' as determined by scarcity, the quantity of labour required to produce them, and the value of the capital in those mines that produced the precious metals.[81] Each nation received the quantity of metal that corresponded with its share of the world's wealth, with each nation's imports and exports tending to equalize, allowing almost all international commerce to be carried on via bills of exchange, not the transportation of bullion. This, it hardly needs to be said, was a fabulous image of international trade in which Europe's nations essentially bartered their goods. How did the Bank of England feature in this image? It was analogous to the discovery of a gold mine: its note issue would increase Britain's share of the world's medium of exchange beyond its due level, causing the exportation of bullion. This was no bad thing because it represented the substitution of a worthless medium of exchange (paper) for a valuable one (bullion). So long as convertibility were in place, this substitution would remain within appropriate limits and have only beneficial effects.[82]

At this point of his argument, Ricardo came into disagreement with Thornton. Ricardo's basic claim was that, given convertibility, whenever the currency was excessive, or depreciated, Bank paper would be converted into coins, thence bullion, and then sent abroad, where its value was greater. If uninterrupted, this process would drain the Bank's coffers: if the Bank were to attempt to meet its obligations not by restricting its issue but by buying bullion to be coined into guineas, then private men would sell their melted guineas to the Bank. (Coin and bullion were taken by Ricardo to be the same thing because of the ineffectualness of the laws against melting coins.) The key to understanding these claims is that Ricardo's account examined the process from the point of view of a debtor needing to discharge a liability held in a foreign nation, and here we can imagine that his vocation gave his analysis its distinctive elements. The debtor faced the choice of becoming a merchant and sending goods in payment of the debt or of sending bullion, always choosing 'the cheapest exportable commodity'.[83] Ricardo could therefore claim that the exportation of coin was always

> caused by its cheapness, and is not the effect, but the cause of an unfavourable
> balance: we should not export it, if we did not send it to a better market, or if

---

[80] Ricardo, 'The High Price of Bullion', *Works and Correspondence*, 3: 47–127, at 51, 99.
[81] Ibid., 52.
[82] Ibid., 52–9.
[83] Ibid., 63.

we had any commodity which we could export more profitably. It is a salutary remedy for a redundant currency.[84]

The problem with Thornton's account, according to Ricardo, was that he was obliged to explain why any nation would refuse to receive Britain's goods in payment. As we will see, Malthus found this aspect of Ricardo's argument unsatisfactory because it seemed to ignore non-monetary factors, as we would say today.

Ricardo's analysis identified a remedy: the gradual contraction of the note issue over several years in order to eliminate the excess of circulating medium, as judged by parity of the market and mint prices of gold. At this point, Ricardo followed Thornton and acquitted the directors of the charge of having acted from self-interest, reversing the severe judgement of his *Morning Chronicle* piece. His argument was that, even if it were true that the price of Bank stock had nearly doubled since 1797, it was nevertheless the case that the directors of the Bank lost more by the depreciation of the currency (as monied men) than they gained from Bank stock (as proprietors of Bank stock).[85] If not from greed, then from error: the directors had unintentionally abused the power that they possessed to change the value of money.

In erring in this way, the directors had led the nation towards those 'dangerous experiments' that had produced the dire results of France's 'forced paper'.[86] Taking a broader view of the situation, Ricardo judged that the nation's 'system' was 'pregnant with so much disaster' because of the 'too intimate connection between the Bank and government'.[87] Lacking independence from government, the Bank might be coaxed by Ministers into making large loans, thereby weakening its ability to withstand a panic. In summary, while Ricardo moderated his rhetoric regarding the directors of the Bank, he still complained about the Bank–government nexus in a standard manner, even averting to French experience to make his case. And so the point made previously can be repeated: Ricardo pondered the relationship between the Bank, government, and debt not because it was a topic in macroeconomic theory but because it was a live topic of parliamentary and pamphlet debate, and he did so primarily using arguments that were already in circulation.

After Ricardo's publication, the issue once again attracted formal attention through a Committee led by some of political economy's brightest lights: Francis

---

[84] Ibid., 61.
[85] Ibid., 95.
[86] Ibid., 97–8.
[87] Ibid., 98.

Horner, William Huskisson, and Henry Thornton.[88] That the Committee's composition was not especially partisan is evidenced by the fact that, between the time when the *Report* was submitted to the Commons in June 1810 and its printing in August, the Tory press evidently perceived no party bias at work. This stance changed in September, and the government began targeting the *Report* in an organized campaign.[89] Charles Bosanquet's contribution, *Practical Observations on the Report of the Bullion Committee* (1810), has been recognized by contemporaries and modern commentators as the most impressive response to the *Report*.[90] Considering both documents will establish the context for Ricardo's further contributions to the debate.

To begin with the *Report*: as with King, paper currency was hailed as a progressive phenomenon, 'one of the greatest practical improvements which can be made in the political and domestic economy of any State', subject to the caveat that such a currency was convertible into specie upon demand.[91] We are not, accordingly, dealing with a specimen of the nostalgic country thought that was encountered at the beginning of this chapter. The *Report* also conceded the role of necessity in creating Restriction—'urgent reasons of State policy and public expediency'.[92] If it is remembered that Burke had justified departures from precedent for similar reasons, then we can see that this document was not unyieldingly rationalist. The *Report* was more focused than that, taking aim at two lead targets: the fact that Restriction had been continued far longer than was prudent and the Bank's profits during this period.

The *Report* began by establishing the leading facts of the matter as the high price of gold and the weak exchange. It was also noted that the Committee's commercial witnesses tended to ascribe the high price of gold to a scarcity arising from uncommon demand for gold from continental Europe.[93] The *Report*'s core position was then set out: a nonconvertible currency issued to excess will cause the price of gold to rise, the exchange to deteriorate, and prices in general to rise.[94] Next the *Report* addressed the issue of its own expert witnesses being at odds with its findings, describing their opinions as 'vague and unsatisfactory' regarding ultimate causes, even if it allowed that they were illuminating regarding

---

[88] F. W. Fetter, 'The Politics of the Bullion Report', *Economica* 26/102 (1959), 99–120, at 106. See also Biancamaria Fontana, *Rethinking the Politics of Commercial Society: The Edinburgh Review 1802–1832* (Cambridge: Cambridge University Press, 1985), 118–26.

[89] Fetter, 'The Politics of the Bullion Report', 106–13.

[90] See Ricardo's judgement (Ricardo, 'Reply to Bosanquet', *Works and Correspondence*, 3: 158–256, at 159). Sraffa also nominated Bosanquet as a serious opponent (Sraffa, 'Note on the Bullion Essays', 10).

[91] House of Commons Select Committee on the High Price of Gold Bullion, 'Report of the Select Committee on the High Price of Gold Bullion, 1810', in *The Paper Pound of 1797–1821*, 1–71, at 65.

[92] Ibid., 43.

[93] Ibid., 3–6.

[94] Ibid., 4–17.

certain particular details.[95] This fact would be seized on by the *Report*'s critics. The exchange was then examined and the conclusion reached that a portion of the fall in recent years could not be attributed to the state of trade and ought, in consequence, to be ascribed to the relative value of the domestic currency. Successive governors of the Bank had found no connection of the type claimed by the *Report*, and the Committee found, therefore, that the Bank was guilty of 'a great practical error' in thinking that the exchange and price of bullion were unaffected by the quantity of paper currency since this fact was demonstrated by the leading authorities on commerce and by the history of every state in modern times that had abused paper currency.[96]

As a further indication that the Bank was not so hallowed as to be unimpeachable, the *Report* noted that the Bank had been placed in a 'novel situation', making it understandable if the directors 'were not fully aware of the principles' that should have guided their conduct.[97] In other words, the directors might have lacked the relevant theoretical knowledge. This was a self-serving concession since the *Report* also maintained that, before Restriction, the Bank seemed to have monitored the exchange and price of gold as information relevant to determining the size of their note issue. The postulated mechanism was this: observing that its stock of gold was dwindling, the Bank would replace this gold by making purchases at a losing price, leading the Bank to contract its issue of paper instinctively, while the gold that the Bank paid out of its coffers was exported overseas by individuals and had the effect of restoring the exchange. Put differently, under the old system, precisely those principles that the *Report* identified as essential had been operating behind the Bank's back, regardless of the fact that they were not 'distinctly perceived by the Bank Directors'.[98]

In this description the august Bank of England is rather like an amoeba: it 'felt the inconvenience, and obeyed its impulse'.[99] Looking past its unkind implications for the Bank's intelligence, this description asserted that, before Restriction, a practical check had limited the Bank's paper. This description both removed a layer of gloss from the Bank's reputation and allowed the *Report* to shift the blame onto the legislature for failing to 'watch the operation of so new a law, and to provide against the injury which might result from it to the public interests'.[100] The Bank's reputation was subjected to further manhandling, however, for its acceptance of real-bills thinking. So long as the Bank's discounting was connected to 'real commercial transactions', so this view went, the issue would naturally

---

[95] Ibid., 21.
[96] Ibid., 36.
[97] Ibid., 43.
[98] Ibid., 44.
[99] Ibid., 45. Compare Fontana's characterization of the *Report* as perfectly respectful towards the Bank's directors: Fontana, *Rethinking the Politics of Commercial Society*, 120.
[100] 'Report of the Select Committee on the High Price of Gold Bullion, 1810', 49, and see also 53.

align 'the public interest' with the Bank's 'private interest'.[101] In the *Report*, this view was construed as a 'theory' and as a 'doctrine'—these words being used interchangeably—and then exposed as fallacious.[102] First, discounting bills augmented the quantity of circulating medium, which raised prices. Second, so long as mercantile profits greater than the Bank's 5 per cent lending rate were in prospect, merchants could be expected to make unlimited demands on the Bank.[103] Third, the Bank's version of real-bills thinking was not even a true principle for action because, as the directors had conceded in testimony, the Bank did not discount all genuine bills.

These points were tied together in the following attack: the Bank did not possess a 'distinct and certain rule to guide their discretion in controlling the amount of their circulation'.[104] Having reduced the Bank to a state of eminent ignorance, the final element of the *Report*'s attack was to place the task of correctly managing the quantity of circulation beyond human wisdom.

> The most detailed knowledge of the actual trade of the Country, combined with the profound science in all the principles of Money and Circulation, would not enable any man or set of men to adjust, and keep always adjusted, the right proportion of circulating medium in a country to the wants of trade . . . the natural process of commerce, by establishing Exchanges among all the different countries of the world, adjusts, in every particular country, the proportion of circulating medium to its actual occasions. . . . The proportion, which is thus adjusted and maintained by the natural operation of commerce, cannot be adjusted by any human wisdom or skill.[105]

In these comments the vaunted 'practice' and 'experience' that Bank defenders such as Surr had perceived in its discounting procedures were redescribed as hopelessly inadequate to the task of managing the nation's circulation. It followed that one of the pressing needs for the Bank's defenders was to deny the validity of the *Report*'s theoretical perspective that underlay these claims. The leading target of this counter-attack was the willingness of the *Report*'s authors to make general and abstract claims since this was vulnerable to being characterized as theoretical enthusiasm.

Indicative here was the attack that Sinclair mounted in his *Observations on the Report of the Bullion Committee* (1810), to which Ricardo responded, as we

---

[101] Ibid., 46, 48, 49.
[102] Ibid., 46, 50.
[103] Ibid., 46, 50–1.
[104] Ibid., 52.
[105] Ibid., 52–3. Ricardo objected to this claim (Ricardo, 'Notes on the Bullion Report and Evidence 1810', *Works and Correspondence*, 3: 343–78).

will see. Sinclair was noted earlier for his concern over Restriction, not least because it risked making the Bank 'a mere political engine' under the control of the government. The style of Sinclair's thought can be further gauged by noting his three-volume study, *The History of the Public Revenue of the British Empire* (1785–1790), which traced the operation of Britain's public revenue from the Romans to his own time and treated the Bank as part of the fabric of the state.[106] More important, however, was that Sinclair was a statist thinker in at least two senses. First, he elevated national strength as the overriding goal of state and treated the national circulation as its key manifestation, in roughly the same manner as that archetypal statist, Thomas Hobbes.[107] Second, Sinclair addressed the bullion question with a view to the geopolitics of the moment. Sinclair had in mind France's attempt to achieve 'universal dominion', which could only be resisted if all the strength of the British empire were directed against Napoleon.[108] As might be imagined, when the *Report* was seen against this backdrop it appeared as an alarming specimen of theoretical speculation disconnected from the state's needs in a desperate time.

One of the fascinating components of Sinclair's assault on the *Report* was a mini-history of the circumstances leading to the Committee being appointed. Sinclair admitted the disordered state of the circulation, along with the importance of rational enquiry into the topic by Parliament. The government, however, had failed to closely superintend the appointment of the Committee's members, with the result that, even though the persons appointed were capable, they were under the influence of 'prejudices' that had corrupted their reasoning to the extent that they championed 'the chimeras of political speculation . . . against the results of practical experience'.[109] Sinclair had primarily in mind the Committee's fantastic account of the low exchange, which he considered perfectly explicable in terms of the leading commercial and political factors: namely, Napoleon's commercial warfare, the payment of subsidies to foreign allies, and interest payments to foreign holders of national debt.[110]

The Committee might have developed a similar account merely by attending to the testimony of its expert witnesses, who also warned of the dire effects that

---

[106] John Sinclair, *The History of the Public Revenue of the British Empire*, 3 vols. (London, 1785–1790).

[107] Circulation understood in the old sense of the very matter of the commonwealth. Hence Sinclair's talk in his *Observations* of 'the abundance of our circulating medium, which operates like blood in the human frame, nourishing every part of the system, and enabling it to perform its functions' (John Sinclair, *Observations on the Report of the Bullion Committee* (London, 1810), 42). Compare this with Hobbes's comment on circulation in *Leviathan*: Thomas Hobbes, 'Leviathan', in *The Clarendon Edition of the Works of Thomas Hobbes*, ed. Noel Malcolm, vol. 4 (Oxford: Oxford University Press, 2012 [1651]), chapter 24.

[108] Sinclair, *Observations on the Report of the Bullion Committee*, 2.

[109] Ibid., 5.

[110] Ibid., 16–18.

resumption would likely have on the nation's power and prosperity. Sinclair explained the Committee's indifference to the potential harm of their policy in the way that we have seen was typical of attacks on theory.

> There is nothing, indeed, that speculative politicians, who entertain a peculiar prejudice in favour of any particular doctrine, will not approve of, if it has the effect of establishing the system they wish to recommend. All the immediate mischief is overlooked, from the expectation of future advantages which may never be realized.[111]

Throughout his text, Sinclair deployed this contrast between the calm, judicious reasoning that defined Parliament's duty and the Committee's failure to reach this standard, deploying the usual battery of negative terms and descriptions: 'zeal for inforcing certain speculative principles', 'new theory, unsanctioned by recent experience', 'fertile imaginations', 'rage for establishing speculative doctrines', and 'new experiments'.[112] In this way was the *Report* rejected as contaminated by theoretical enthusiasm and therefore unsuitable for guiding Parliament's deliberations.

A similar line of argument was followed by Randle Jackson, a skilled lawyer noted for his rhetorical powers, when he addressed the General Court of the Bank of England in late September 1810. This was no doubt a sympathetic audience for Jackson's message that the Bank was a bulwark of national strength. It followed that, if the Committee's recommendations were formed in error, then they might endanger the nation.[113] Jackson was led to suspect error by the Committee's contempt towards all of those 'whom they appeared to consider as mere "practical men"' who, like Jackson, preferred 'figures and facts' in contrast to the Committee's own 'elaborate and abstract reasoning'.[114] Worse, the Committee's attack likely reflected 'the spirit of party', given that the *Report*'s leading authors were opponents of the government.[115] In summary, Jackson's and Sinclair's attacks were two of the many attempts to delegitimize the *Report* by excluding the abstract theories of political economy as a useful type of knowledge for lawmakers. This hostility to theory represents a leading aspect of the context for Malthus and Ricardo that this book is attempting to reconstruct since so much contemporary historiography simply assumes that theory is the natural register for political economy, thereby unconsciously taking sides in the disputes

---

[111] Ibid., 48.

[112] Ibid., v, 13, 16, 50, 52.

[113] Randle Jackson, *The Speech of Randle Jackson, Esq. Delivered at the General Court of the Bank of England, Held on the 20th of September, 1810, Respecting the Report of the Bullion Committee of the House of Commons* (London, 1810), 5, 28–9, 33–5, 53.

[114] Ibid., 16, 24.

[115] Ibid., 5 at asterisked note.

of the past. Before turning to Malthus and Ricardo as the leading proponents of theory in the Bullion Controversy, one last anti-theorist must be considered since Ricardo explicitly took up his pen against him: Charles Bosanquet.

Bosanquet had written earlier in his career on behalf of the sugar trade of the British Caribbean, and he was the son of one of the Bank's former governors.[116] His intervention on behalf of the Bank was *Practical Observations on the Report of the Bullion Committee* (1810). He first disputed the propositions upon which the Committee rested its theory and its handling of evidence and then developed his own account of Britain's recent experience of price increases. Bosanquet prided himself on the fact that his rival account explained the rise in prices since 1793 using accepted principles of political economy.[117] What is central for the argument here is that, despite the fact that he was also engaging in political economy and using its arguments as the basis for evaluating legislation, Bosanquet understood his political economy as different from that of his enemies because his version mobilized a form of reasoning that relied on practice, facts, and experience, in opposition to the untested and enthusiastic theory of Ricardo and the Bullion Committee. Thus, in the place of notions of model and method, what the historical record yields is something completely different: the combative deployment of the vocabulary of theory and practice, which is what made it possible for so many writers to reject theory as a legitimate form for political economy to take. This is one of the major features of the period, but it is systematically screened out of history when the object of study is specified as economic theory, analytical systems, and so on.

To return to Bosanquet's text: he began by invoking political arithmetic and affirming its maxim that 'reasoning on things by figures' was a discipline essential to sound thinking.[118] Accordingly, he promised to reason in just this way, using the figures provided in the appendix of the *Report* along with the numbers in Robert Mushet's pamphlet, the latter being a popular source for figures relating to gold prices and the exchange.[119] By basing his claims on these 'facts', Bosanquet aimed to avoid the type of 'abstract reasoning' that he found in the

---

[116] Andrew J. O'Shaughnessy, 'Bosanquet, Charles (1769–1850), Merchant and Writer', *Oxford Dictionary of National Biography* (2008), http://www.oxforddnb.com/view/10.1093/ref:odnb/9780198614128.001.0001/odnb-9780198614128-e-2927; Grace Lawless Lee, *The Story of the Bosanquets* (Canterbury: Phillimore, 1966), 80–1.

[117] Charles Bosanquet, *Practical Observations on the Report of the Bullion Committee* (London, 1810), 92–100, 108.

[118] Ibid., 1. I have been unable to trace Bosanquet's exact quotation in either Sir William Davenant (to whom Bosanquet attributed his quotation) or Charles Davenant, but one imagines that he meant the latter, who did write in political arithmetic and made similar statements; for example, Charles Davenant, 'Of the Use of Political Arithmetic, in all Considerations about the Revenues and Trade', in *The Political and Commercial Works of that Celebrated Writer Charles D'Avenant*, ed. Charles Whitworth, vol. 1 (London, 1771), 127–49, at 128, 131.

[119] Robert Mushet, *An Enquiry into the Effect Produced on the National Currency and Rates of Exchange by the Bank Restriction Bill* (London, 1810).

'wholly theoretical' arguments of Ricardo.[120] In fact, according to Bosanquet, Ricardo had triggered the inquiry and shaped its conclusions before the first witness was even called.[121] The ability for theory to prejudice inquiry in this way pointed to the weakness of theoretical arguments: they were not 'brought to the test of experiment'.[122] In this regard, Bosanquet was like other critics in underlining a gap between the Committee's findings and the testimony of its own expert witnesses. What seems to have most galled Bosanquet, however, was the air of authority that the authors of the *Report* had assumed when pronouncing on 'the most speculative' topics, along with their dismissal of 'the results of practice and the dictates of experience'.[123] Bosanquet's task was to undermine this confidence by submitting the *Report*'s 'theories to the higher authority of fact'.[124]

Bosanquet targeted three propositions at the heart of the *Report*: that the unfavourable exchange was one of the symptoms of a depreciated paper currency, that the extent to which an exchange could be unfavourable was limited to transport costs, and that the price of gold bullion could not exceed the mint price of gold unless the currency were depreciated.[125] Consulting the tables that Robert Mushet produced in his pamphlet, Bosanquet noted that the exchange was in favour of Britain from 1802 to 1808, while the price of gold was 2.75 per cent above the mint price.[126] Furthermore, between 1797 and 1799, the exchange with Hamburg was favourable to Britain, at times by as much as 12 per cent—more than three times the value of transport costs.[127] Finally, between 1764 and 1768, before the recoinage that remedied the poor quality of the circulating coins, gold was 2 per cent to 3 per cent above the mint price, while the exchange with Paris was 8 per cent to 9 per cent against London and the exchange with Hamburg was 2 per cent to 6 per cent in favour. In principle, this implied that a merchant could make profits of 12 per cent to 14 per cent by simply paying debts in Paris with gold from Hamburg. In other words, even though the possibility of profiting to such a degree existed, the exchange was not rectified. Bosanquet claimed that this fact invalidated the 'intimacy of connexion which the Committee assumes to exist between the course of exchange and the price of gold'.[128] The *Report* was simply unable to account for the observed facts.

---

[120] Bosanquet, *Practical Observations on the Report of the Bullion Committee*, 1–2.
[121] This claim seems to be the start of the tradition of erroneously tracing paternity of the inquiry to Ricardo. On this tradition, see F. W. Fetter, 'The Bullion Report Reexamined', *The Quarterly Journal of Economics* 56/4 (1942), 655–65.
[122] Bosanquet, *Practical Observations on the Report of the Bullion Committee*, 2.
[123] Ibid., 3.
[124] Ibid.
[125] For a discussion of these theoretical issues in historical context, see F. W. Fetter, *Development of British Monetary Orthodoxy, 1797–1875* (Cambridge: Cambridge University Press, 1965), chapter 2.
[126] Bosanquet, *Practical Observations on the Report of the Bullion Committee*, 10.
[127] Ibid., 16.
[128] Ibid., 25.

With the core of the *Report* shown to be faulty, Bosanquet then developed his offensive in relation to the art of application. Bosanquet's point was that the abstract truth or falsity of a theory was one issue, but the dangers relating to its practical application were another altogether. It was seen in Chapter 1 that a version of this claim was at the heart of Burke's attack on talk of rights in relation to a nation's Constitution. Indeed, we saw that even Stewart's defence of theory had conceded that the art of application was an autonomous skill. We are describing a context that did not think in terms of method and models but had its own vocabulary that related to a different set of concerns.

The theory that Bosanquet had in his sights was that an ounce of gold bullion would not sell for more than the mint price for the same quantity in domestic currency unless the domestic currency were depreciated against gold. Bosanquet described this claim as representing an 'old, and in the abstract incontrovertible, theory'.[129] It was old in Bosanquet's eyes because it was the same theory that John Locke had used when recommending recoinage.[130] Locke premised that an ounce of silver must be of the same value regardless of whether it took the form of bullion or coin. It followed that once silver coin was returned to its full weight, silver bullion would no longer sell at a premium but fall to its mint price. Alas, what actually happened was that the price of silver bullion rose and the coins were melted down as quickly as they were milled, making a mockery of the recoinage and at great cost.[131] The issue was not the incontrovertible theory, but the mode of its *application* by one of the nation's great thinkers, John Locke.

Having reminded his readers of Locke's failure, Bosanquet was able to score a tremendous rhetorical point by noting that 'Men of less powers but more practical information foretold to Mr Locke the evils which would follow from the unlimited adoption of his theory'.[132] The advice went unheeded, rather like the advice of the Committee's practical witnesses. The general issue was that even if the *Report*'s theories were 'abstractedly [sic] true, they are not always applicable'.[133] Deploying an argument that Malthus would later use against Ricardo, Bosanquet explained that the trouble with the theory was that it worked perfectly well when it did not encounter 'external impediments', but

---

[129] Ibid., 23.

[130] See Peter Laslett, 'John Locke, the Great Recoinage, and the Origins of the Board of Trade: 1695–1698', in John W. Yolton, ed., *John Locke: Problems and Perspectives. A Collection of New Essays* (Cambridge: Cambridge University Press, 1969), 137–64.

[131] Bosanquet, *Practical Observations on the Report of the Bullion Committee*, 36. It was also noted in Locke's own time that he was relying on 'the Speculation and Theory of Foreign Coins': see Nicholas Barbon, *A Discourse Concerning Coining the New Money Lighter. In Answer to Mr. Lock's Considerations About Raising the Value of Money* (London, 1696), 19.

[132] Bosanquet, *Practical Observations on the Report of the Bullion Committee*, 36.

[133] Ibid., 47.

when applied to practice, it appears to me like the experiment in vacuo, where all friction, all obstruction, being removed, and the power of gravitation alone allowed to operate, the guinea and the feather descend with equal velocities. The fact is undeniably true under the circumstances of the experiment, but it is true only within the limits of an exhausted receiver, and is, therefore, wholly inapplicable to any of the common purposes of life.[134]

Abstract systems and theories were simply not applicable to the complexities of political life, at least not without great caution. And the *Report's* authors had not exercised such caution. The proximate reason for their abuse of good reasoning was that the Committee's conclusions were not developed on the basis of sober investigation but 'under the influence of a judgement very early formed'.[135] In this context, Bosanquet likened the bullionist position to the enthusiasm of the Physiocrats, 'who, not very attentive to facts, have established ingenious theories, and attempted to reduce every thing to a system, on which they reasoned till they became enthusiasts, incapable of appreciating anything that did not conform to the theories they had laid down'.[136] The bullionists, too, were in thrall to system. Once again, we encounter the accusation of enthusiasm, a standard claim in the ethics-talk of the period. It is now time to see how Ricardo and Malthus responded.

The Theorists in Reply: Ricardo and Malthus

Ricardo defended the *Report* and replied to Sinclair and Jackson in three letters published in the *Morning Chronicle* in September 1810, and then wrote a sustained answer to Bosanquet, *Reply to Bosanquet* (1811). In the first letter, Ricardo declared that the *Report* had been correct to identify 'ignorance of the principles' of currency among the Bank's directors as the leading cause of the depreciation and wondered if future generations would not be astonished at the 'delusion' involved in endowing a company of merchants with the power to regulate the value of the nation's property.[137] The whole affair stood as an example of the costs of government interference in commerce, and there was no way for the nation to exit the situation with perfect equity to all parties given the complex pattern of winners and losers that would follow the resumption of cash payments.[138]

---

[134] Ibid., 48.

[135] Ibid., 108.

[136] Ibid., 108–9.

[137] Ricardo, 'To the Editor of the Morning Chronicle', *Works and Correspondence*, 3: 131–9, at 131, 133.

[138] Accordingly, Ricardo did not project 'justice' as a leading virtue to be realized in the course of retuning to cash payments, but he did list 'ability, integrity, and firmness' as necessary attributes (Ibid., 132). However, since Ricardo did not address the figure of the statesman, it was not clear who

Against Sinclair's *Observations*, Ricardo enlisted Smith as an authority, especially to combat Sinclair's claim that the size of the nation's circulation was paramount, using for his counter-claim Smith's analysis of labour as the real source of wealth. Furthermore, Ricardo met Sinclair's prudential argument against contracting the national circulation by redescribing it as an instance of the 'mercantile system' that Smith had exploded. Thus Sinclair seemed to be advocating 'not only that money is exclusively wealth, but paper money depreciated to any possible extent'.[139]

Turning to Jackson's speech, Ricardo was dismayed by Jackson's attempt to construe the *Report* as an effusion of party sentiment since the issue was a matter of science. In this regard, Ricardo drew an analogy between the opinions of glass makers and the opinions of chemists: only the latter were 'qualified to give sound opinions on points of theory and science'.[140] In other words, the Committee had been right to treat its practical witnesses as the glass makers. What is striking in these comments is Ricardo's willingness to simply assert the supremacy of theoretical knowledge over practical understanding. If we now turn to Ricardo's response to Bosanquet, however, then a far more sophisticated rhetoric is encountered.

Bosanquet, it will be remembered, had levelled the accusation that Ricardo held a theory at variance with the evidence because he had succumbed to enthusiasm—of having been enchanted by his theory to the extent that he would expose the public to its dangerous practical application. As discussed in Chapter 1, the charge of enthusiasm was not primarily epistemological in nature because it rather alleged an ethical failing. That is, it was Ricardo's ethical person that had been impugned: Ricardo had failed to govern his intellectual passions. In response to this accusation, Ricardo agreed that theoretical systems needed to be tested. This allowed him to portray Bosanquet's accusation as merely an example of the 'vulgar charge' that 'theorists' only offered untested 'speculations'.[141] Ricardo, the theorist, was prepared to test his own speculations, at least on this occasion.

How did Ricardo test his theory? His creative act was to construe the history of the nation's currency as yielding 'principles' and 'laws' that could act as the test

---

would need to mobilize these qualities: the political nation, politicians, or political economists. In other words, virtues once had a clear bearer in Smith's statesman, but they could often appear free-floating in Ricardo's work. This might be understood as one of the consequences of the shift from addressing principles to the figure of the legislator to articulating correct doctrine. But more work is required on this topic.

[139] Ricardo, 'On Sir John Sinclair's "Observations"', *Works and Correspondence*, 3: 139–45, at 145.
[140] Ricardo, 'On Mr. Randle Jackson's Speech', *Works and Correspondence*, 3: 145–53, at 147.
[141] Ricardo, 'Reply to Bosanquet', 160.

when the principles of a currency, long established, are well understood; when the laws which regulate the variations of the rate of exchange between countries have been known and observed for centuries, can that system be called wholly theoretical which appeals to those principles, and is willing to submit to the test of those laws?[142]

From our perspective, this is a strange type of test. Today facts or data typically furnish the basis for formulating laws or principles, whereas Ricardo treated 'laws' as the data against which his 'system' could be tested. Ricardo's comments make sense when viewed in relation to the debate over the Constitution that was in the background of this entire period. For Ricardo was treating Britain's monetary history as yielding the 'principles' invoked in the preceding passage, mirroring the Burkean claim that Britain's Constitution yielded principles of government that meant it had no need to import French principles or notions of abstract rights and so on. Ricardo was attempting, in other words, to move his theory under the rhetorical cover of practice and experience. In fact, throughout his reply Ricardo's rhetorical choices constantly revealed the attempt to align theory with practice and experience. He wrote, for example, of 'a theory which rests on so firm a basis of experience', of 'a practical illustration of the truth of a most satisfactory theory', of 'opinions grounded on a just theory, sanctioned by practical men, and confirmed by experience', and of claims that contradict both 'theory and experience'.[143] Ricardo was engaged in sophisticated rhetoric that exploited the linguistic resources that were available at the time.

No mere ornament, Ricardo's rhetoric guided his argumentative strategy. In particular, his second chapter examined Bosanquet's alleged facts, beginning with his claim that the exchange had been known to vary by more than the cost of transporting bullion. Ricardo acknowledged that if these facts were true, then he would indeed have found them at odds with his theory. But the facts were not true: they were drawn from Mushet's table, which Mushet himself had acknowledged to be faulty because of a systematic error in his calculations.[144] Even the corrected figures from the second edition of Mushet's pamphlet were flawed. Nevertheless, Ricardo was willing to submit his principles to the test of these figures once they were corrected. They showed that the exchange had never been in favour of England by more than 7 per cent, excepting the year of suspension. In this year, Ricardo claimed, the quantity of circulating medium was low, which had caused bullion to be imported. Taken together, the event was 'entirely conformable with the principle of the Bullion Committee', not least

---

[142] Ibid.

[143] Ibid., 165, 172, 190, 218.

[144] Mushet had assumed an invariable par: that gold (the standard in England) and silver (the standard in Hamburg) had held a constant exchange ratio with one another as bullion.

because it affirmed the committee's suggested remedy of reducing the quantity of circulating notes to raise the exchange.[145] The manner in which Ricardo was open to what we would call empirical evidence should be marked, as this stance would not be carried through to the different context in which he composed his *Principles of Political Economy, and Taxation* (1817).

Of course, Ricardo's openness to an empirical 'test' did not obviate the need for decisions to be made regarding what would constitute a test and how it would be administered. This is seen in Ricardo's rebuttal of Bosanquet's claim that Bullionist theory was defective because imports of gold had no capacity to correct the exchange. Ricardo's crucial move was to respecify the theory's practical implications. He conceded the point that even when the figures were corrected they still showed that the exchange fluctuated between 5.6 per cent and 4.3 per cent in favour of England. But the principle did not exclude this range because a difference of up to 5 per cent was still within the bounds set by transport costs. Within this limit, a persistently favourable or unfavourable exchange did not invalidate the theory because it applied to the exchanges with all countries; for the theory to be invalidated, the exchange would need to be persistently unfavourable or favourable with all countries. Spain, for example, imported bullion from its colonies (hence the exchange favoured Spain) and exported bullion to the rest of the world (hence the exchange was against Spain). Returning to the case of England, Hamburg exported bullion to England in 1798 because bullion was in high demand in England owing to the low quantity of circulating material, and, once this demand was met, the exchange returned to its natural level.[146] A subsequent fall in the exchange then coincided with the increase of banknotes, more than 11 per cent against England as the price of gold bullion rose more than 10 per cent above the mint price, exactly the correlation that the Committee had affirmed.

This was a skilful piece of argumentation from Ricardo. He also deployed a version of the redescriptive tactic that Dugald Stewart was seen, in Chapter 1, to have used when he insisted that theory was present even in those arguments that were presented as practical. Hence, Ricardo wrote that 'theory Mr. B. has just as much as the Committee', but Bosanquet was unaware of his theory's structure and the proofs that it required.[147] Here we see Ricardo using the theorist's preferred counter-attack against those who invoked practice—to suggest that a lack of theoretical sophistication exposed the writer to being misled by first appearances. As we also saw in Chapter 1, Malthus made this tactic a central component

---

[145] Ricardo, 'Reply to Bosanquet', 169.
[146] Ibid., 170–2.
[147] Ibid., 173.

of his ripostes to practical critics in the *Essay*, and he would use it again in his bullion writings, considered shortly.

And so Ricardo lampooned Bosanquet for his theoretical naïvety, on display in the claim that enormous profits could be made by exporting gold to take advantage of movements in the exchange. For this revealed that Bosanquet was reasoning from figures without pausing to consider their accuracy or implications. Bosanquet was, Ricardo wrote, 'very like a man who is all for fact and nothing for theory. Such men can hardly ever sift their facts. They are credulous, and necessarily so, because they have no standard of reference', or, because they have no sound theory.[148] Such limited reasoning even precluded a writer from noticing that their facts were 'inconsistent, and disprove one another'.[149] Ricardo simultaneously adduced a further cause of Bosanquet's poor intellectual performance: political prejudice. This was why Bosanquet tested the theory not against the thousands of cases where it held, but only those two or three where it apparently did not.[150] Prejudice and vested interests corrupted reasoning by closing the mind to evidence.

Ricardo's greatest rhetorical win, however, was to reverse Bosanquet's charge of theoretical enthusiasm. It came in the context of Ricardo's response to Bosanquet's rival explanation of rising prices as driven by taxation and scarcity. Bosanquet had conscripted Smith's comment that a prince might issue paper money and demand that taxes be paid in this currency, and, if the face value of such paper were less than the nominal value of taxes to be paid, then the paper would yield a premium.[151] Bosanquet developed the vulnerable interpretation of Smith's passage that, so long as annual taxes exceeded the banknotes in value, over-issue was impossible.[152] As Ricardo pointed out, this was not quite Smith's idea.[153] In fact, Ricardo stated that if Bosanquet had inspected the years 1793 to 1797, then he would have discovered that although taxes had increased, the value of notes fell.[154] That is, taxes could rise without an increase in circulation.[155] That Bosanquet sought to link banknotes and taxation through his faulty appropriation of Smith was

---

[148] Ibid., 181.

[149] Ibid., 182.

[150] Ibid., 252.

[151] Smith, *WN* II.ii.104–6.

[152] Bosanquet, *Practical Observations on the Report of the Bullion Committee*, 86–91.

[153] Smith's point was that the price of money is determined by its supply and demand; payments of tax to the government were simply one factor influencing demand.

[154] Ricardo, 'Reply to Bosanquet', 238.

[155] Ricardo further claimed that the Committee was perfectly amenable to the idea that taxation accounted for part of the rising prices; only 18 per cent was to be attributed to the depreciation of the circulating medium because that was the extent of the divergence between the market and the mint price of gold (Ibid., 239).

a proof that even practical men are sometimes tempted to wander from the sober paths of practice and experience, to indulge in speculations the most wild, and dreams the most chimerical.[156]

Here we have Ricardo claiming that enthusiasm was not a pathology that only afflicted theorists, for the practical Bosanquet had also succumbed. This is strong evidence for the general argument of the book: far from being a model-builder ahead of his time, Ricardo was very much entangled in the concerns of his period, including its fears around abstract thought.

To conclude this chapter, it is time to consider Malthus's smaller role in the controversy and to investigate his vocabulary. Given that Malthus was shown in the previous chapter to have used the vocabulary of theory and practice in order to take the side of theory in his *Essay*, we can expect a similar finding here, and this is indeed the case. Malthus's contribution came in the form of twin reviews for the *Edinburgh Review*: *Depreciation of Paper Currency* (1811) and the follow-up *High Price of Bullion* (1811). Beginning with *Depreciation*, it covered texts by Mushet, Blake, Huskisson, Bosanquet, and Ricardo, including Ricardo's *Reply to Bosanquet*. Malthus began by praising the work of King and Thornton for combining 'extensive knowledge of detail with just principles'.[157] Ricardo was then praised for setting out doctrines and principles with skill, even if they were already known by those familiar with the subject; above all, that the circulating medium would be depreciated if issued to excess, a result derived from an 'application' of the 'general principles of supply and demand'.[158] Ricardo was faulted, however, for taking a 'partial view' of the causes that operated on the exchange.[159] Namely, Ricardo's focus on the excess or deficiency of the currency was only one cause, meaning that he had neglected the reciprocal demand between nations for goods and services.

Malthus's argument was that sudden changes in the pattern of trade could cause large balances of trade in favour of one nation over another. Such discrepancies required payments in bullion to discharge those imbalances and, in turn, restore the relative levels of currency. The two causes could exaggerate or offset one another, making some processes 'imperceptible' or 'concealed from view', as when the exchange was shown to improve at the same time as the note issue was increasing.[160] The intellectual task for the political economist was to keep both causes constantly in view, even if they operated on different time scales and with different intensities. By contrast, Ricardo had failed to maintain such analytical

---

[156] Ibid.
[157] Malthus, 'Depreciation of Paper Currency', *Works*, 7: 19–56, at 21.
[158] Ibid., 23.
[159] Ibid., 24.
[160] Ibid., 43.

openness to all the relevant causes affecting the phenomenon because he had allowed himself to take a confined view of the subject, thus ignoring the role of trade patterns.[161] Malthus construed this as hurting the reputation of theorists because merchants were active participants in the debate, and they were people intensely aware of the role of the balance of payments in commerce. In consequence, when merchants discovered that a theorist such as Ricardo was prepared to deny any role for the balance of payments they would be alienated from theory: 'A practical merchant must . . . be extremely surprised at such a denial, and feel more than ever confirmed in his preference of practice to theory'.[162]

Notice how the thinking of practical men was an object of concern for Malthus. As exemplified by Stewart's discussion of the 'vulgar' in Chapter 1, this was a distinguishing feature of the theoretical outlook. A similar point holds in relation to the Bank. Malthus was alarmed at the Bank's stated principles, above all, the belief that the note issue merely answered the needs of trade. Thankfully, Malthus averred, there was little evidence that the Bank actually acted on these principles—it was a case of rationalizing 'practice' by people who were not theorists and where the Bank's 'practical routine' was still anchored in pre-Restriction 'habits'.[163] Just as the *Report* had described, the Bank was a pre-theoretical institution that had nevertheless managed to respond to its environment in a manner that was *de facto* rational thanks to the role of its habits. The danger was that these habits were being reshaped under Restriction.[164]

Whatever corruption the Bank's routines may have suffered, Malthus's more important point was that practice was ineligible to serve as a guide for Parliament

---

[161] Ibid., 42. The unpublished fragment, 'An Essay on Foreign Trade', seems to suggest that this criticism of Ricardo was to be the focus of Malthus's second piece for the *Edinburgh Review*. It was likely rejected as unpublishable by Jeffrey because of this narrowness. (See the helpful introduction to the text by J. M. Pullen in Thomas Robert Malthus, 'An Essay on Foreign Trade', in *T. R. Malthus: The Unpublished Papers in the Collection of Kanto Gakuen University*, ed. J. M. Pullen, vol. 2 (Cambridge: Cambridge University Press, 1997), 141–58, at 141–3). Malthus's argument was that bullion was always in demand because it acted as the currency of the commercial world and hence could always be exported to discharge debts arising from an unfavorable balance of payments. From the point of view of the bullion merchant who examined the exchanges in different countries, it did seem to be a simple matter of price differentials. But from the point of view of those who 'studied the subject scientifically', it was necessary to get beyond the perceptions of the bullion merchant and examine the trade with respect to its 'real character' (Malthus, 'An Essay on Foreign Trade', 145, 158). Once again, Malthus treated the political economist as someone with the skills to see further. By contrast, he positioned Ricardo as failing in this office because he had cleaved to 'a very fanciful doctrine, supported neither by just theory, nor by facts' (Malthus, 'An Essay on Foreign Trade', 151).

[162] Malthus, 'Depreciation of Paper Currency', 44.

[163] Ibid., 53.

[164] Viewed in relation to the Bank's actual procedures, it is clear that the Bank's operations were subject to change, internal negotiation, and contest during this period, above all, between the Court and the Discount Committee, who mobilized rival notions of duty to the nation, on the one hand, and commercial prudence, on the other. See Ian P. H. Duffy, 'The Discount Policy of the Bank of England During the Suspension of Cash Payments, 1797–1821', *The Economic History Review* 35/1 (1982), 67–82.

on this issue. In the manner that we have come to expect of theorists, Malthus provided a general philosophical position on the limitations of practice.

> The habits of practical detail have a natural and almost necessary tendency to direct the view to particular, rather than to general consequences, and to identify the interests of the few, with the interests of the many. If, in addition to this almost unavoidable effect of constant habits of business, we take into our consideration, that the mercantile classes are greatly interested, both in the facility of obtaining paper loans, and in the progressive rise of prices which this facility occasions, it is quite impossible to affirm, with truth, that they are either the most capable, or the most impartial judges in the present question.[165]

This contrast between those people whose views were limited to particular consequences and those who could lift their analytical horizon to general consequences doubled as a contrast between merchants and the Committee members. The Committee emerged in Malthus's account as enjoying 'a more elevated seat of judgement . . . free from the possible influence of interested motives' and thereby achieved 'a more commanding and impartial view of the subject'.[166] This was a forceful assertion of the need to choose theory over practice, just as Malthus had insisted in his defence of general principles in the *Essay*.

In Malthus's second review, *High Price of Bullion*, also published in 1811, he set himself the task of tearing down the argument that the price of bullion had risen because the price of gold had risen. Malthus's leading exhibits were stationary bullion prices on the continent, the fact that commodities unaffected by the blockade had risen by around 17 per cent, and the Bank's having increased its issue by more than one-third of its 1808 level. Malthus also surveyed the whole period since Restriction, finding that the excess of the market price above the mint price of gold and the unfavourable foreign exchange both exceeded 'former experience'.[167] Malthus then portrayed the depreciation of the currency as an illegitimate form of taxation that primarily benefited the Bank at enormous cost to the nation.[168] Finally, Malthus predicted that this system, if it were to continue in its present manner, would end in just the manner that the forced paper of the French had ended.

> All that has yet happened is in exact conformity with the general principles which have been laid down on this subject by those who are called theorists; and the experience of the past enables us, with the utmost certainty, to predict,

---

[165] Malthus, 'Depreciation of Paper Currency', 55.
[166] Ibid., 56.
[167] Malthus, 'High Price of Bullion', *Works*, 7: 57–82, at 66.
[168] Ibid., 73.

that an excessive issue of paper in England will be accompanied with precisely the same results which have invariably attended it in other countries, with the same unavailing endeavours to prop the falling value of the paper, the same failure of confidence and check to all regular commercial dealings, and the same wide-wasting convulsion of private property.[169]

This passage reveals how unsatisfactory any account must be that treats Malthus as a conservative thinker or, less generously, as an apologist for the status quo. For, in relation to the Bank, Malthus was clearly on the side of rational theory as the appropriate guide to organizing the state's institutions, and this made him a critic of the government and its behaviour, and of the Bank, a cherished institution.

Conclusion: The Short-Term Victory of Practice, the Long-Term Victory of Theory

The lead tactic of Bosanquet, Sinclair, and Jackson essentially consisted in the Burkean move of rejecting the validity of theory as a guide for legislative action. The tactic was widely adopted by other opponents of bullionist thinking. Consider the following title: *A Replication to All the Theorists and Abstract Reasoners on Bullion* (1811). Equally revealing is the MP William Scott's *Some Observations Upon the Argument Drawn by Mister Huskisson on the Bullion Committee* (1811). Scott subjected Huskisson to extended description as an enthusiast. Above all, Huskisson had mistaken the subject as abstract and susceptible to mathematical demonstration when it was really dependent on shifting moral and practical circumstances that stood in complex relations; the consequence was that Huskisson's mind had acquired a 'fancied elevation' that had 'closed it against all further argument or information'.[170] Worse, Huskisson's theory was detected as sitting at the core of the *Report*. By contrast, Bosanquet was lauded for drawing on 'practical knowledge' to reveal the hollowness of 'unfounded Theories of unexperienced philosophy', above all, by 'applying the test of practice to their principles'.[171]

The same tactic and vocabulary was deployed in Parliament. George Rose was the most vocal high-Tory opponent of the *Report* in the House of Commons. When the *Report* was debated in May 1811, for example, one of Rose's central claims was that theory ought to be disqualified from parliamentary reasoning.

---

[169] Ibid., 80.
[170] William Scott, *Some Observations upon the Argument Drawn by Mr. Huskisson on the Bullion Committee* (London, 1811), 7, 14.
[171] Ibid., vii, 3.

For the 'theory of money' was not stable: 'Almost every writer since [Hume] has taken a separate line, agreeing only that formerly received opinions were mistaken'.[172] Rose's list ran from Locke to the present, running through Davenant, Hume, Smith, King, and Blake. Given this circumstance, Rose declared, it was hardly appropriate to enter into a contest of theory in the House, and instead he would subject the opinions of the Committee to 'the test of experience'.[173] By this Rose meant comparing the quantity of Bank notes in circulation with the market price of gold and the exchange with Hamburg, from 1710 to 1805, finding that these facts disproved the connection between the quantity of Bank paper and the price of gold as supposed by the Committee.

Francis Horner had spoken immediately before Rose, and it is revealing to note that he had tried to insulate his position against exactly the style of attack that Rose then launched despite Horner's defensive preparations. For Horner had framed the issue as a clash between modernity and tradition—on one side there stood those who held that a pure paper currency was 'the greatest of all modern discoveries in the improvements of commerce', while at the other end of the spectrum were those who insisted on 'reverting to ancient systems'.[174] Like Ricardo, Horner attempted to counter the hostile portrayal of 'mere theorists' as holding their 'theory against the conclusions of practice and experience' by aligning his position with the nation's 'long experience' of currency before the Restriction.[175]

Despite these and similar placatory efforts, Parliament was not won over to the reasoning of the *Report*, and Resumption would have to wait for 1819.[176] The effective mechanism for resumption was the 1819 Committee, of which Robert Peel was Chairman, producing the findings that underwrote the Resumption of Cash Payments Act 1819. Of this Committee, Boyd Hilton writes: 'Doctrinal truth, as promulgated in 1810, was taken for granted, and anti-bullionists were ignored'.[177] It is noteworthy that the key factor seems to have been the conversion of Peel to bullionist thinking.[178] Here the intellectual comportment of the real-world legislator was being shaped by the public–parliamentary debate; the ambitions of theorists and the fears of practical men were both being realized. (An

---

[172] George Rose, 'Report of the Bullion Committee – Mr Horner's Resolution', HC Deb 06 May 1811 Vol. 19 cc798–818, at 837.

[173] Ibid.

[174] Francis Horner, 'Report of the Bullion Committee – Mr Horner's Resolution', HC Deb 06 May 1811 Vol. 19 cc798–818, at 800.

[175] Ibid., 801.

[176] See William Smart, *Economic Annals of the Nineteenth Century, 1801–1820* (London: Macmillan and Co., 1910), chapter 16.

[177] Boyd Hilton, *Corn, Cash, Commerce: The Economic Policies of the Tory Governments 1815–1830* (Oxford: Oxford University Press, 1977), 43.

[178] Boyd Hilton, 'Peel: A Reappraisal', *The Historical Journal* 22/3 (1979), 585–614, at 589–92; Hilton, *Corn, Cash, Commerce*, 44.

enabling development may have been the rise of a new breed of Tory who was sympathetic to theory in politics generally and in political economy in particular, such as Edward Copleston, who influenced the thinking of Peel, his former student.[179]) For the overarching argument of this book, the significance of this episode is great: the rejection of theory as a guide for the conduct of legislators was successful in 1810–1811, as the arguments of Bosanquet, Sinclair, Jackson, and their allies held the day, but this defence was overwhelmed in 1819. Political economy was beginning to gain enough traction in Parliament to prescribe reform of the state's institutions, and the conversion of politicians to theory was a leading mechanism. This was a new development at the time, but we tend to take it for granted.

Ricardo, Malthus, and their allies clearly understood the nature and stakes of the contest—it is perhaps only necessary to note that in the political process of 1819 that saw the passage of the Act, Ricardo played a crucial role in Parliament by calming fears over the costs of resuming payments.[180] It is also worth noting that the Bank never again enjoyed the intellectual and political insulation that had protected it from its enemies before Restriction. To see this point, consider Ricardo's *Plan for the Establishment of a National Bank* (1824), published six months after his death.[181] When the Bank had been indicted as one element of a corrupt modernity that included patronage and war-mongering—as per William Anderson's *The Iniquity of Banking*—its defence could take the side of modernity, rallying the formidable intellectual allies of commercial society. After Restriction, however, the Bank faced a different type of opponent, one who also embraced modernity and was even prepared to legislate for its coming. Thus, in his *Plan* Ricardo was perfectly insouciant towards whatever historical claims that the Bank might have made regarding its role in helping the post-1688 state survive. He simply asked the question: 'Suppose the privilege of issuing paper money were taken away from the Bank, and were in future to be exercised by the State. . . . In what way would the national wealth be in the least impaired?'[182] Finding no objections that troubled him, Ricardo was good enough to draw up new articles for the Bank.[183]

We might suggest, therefore, that the Bank's status as a pillar of the nation was irreversibly damaged by its portrayal as a creature of ignorance and self-interest at the hands of theorists in the Bullion Controversy. If we glance ahead, then we

---

[179] Hilton, *A Mad, Bad, and Dangerous People?*, 324; Peter Mandler, 'Tories and Paupers: Christian Political Economy and the Making of the New Poor Law', *The Historical Journal* 33/1 (1990), 81–103, at 93.

[180] Hilton, *Corn, Cash, Commerce*, 46–8.

[181] Ricardo, 'Plan for the Establishment of a National Bank', *Works and Correspondence*, 4: 272–300, at 276.

[182] Ricardo 'Plan for the Establishment of a National Bank'.

[183] Ibid., 285–9.

see that the Bank was subjected to further manhandling. The Charter Act of 1833 nominally renewed the privileges of the Bank until 1854, but the Bank was held responsible for crises in the late 1830s, and this saw the 'break clause' in the 1833 Act applied.[184] In consequence, new legislation was written—the Bank Charter Act 1844—that separated the Bank's Issue and Banking Departments.[185] Such separation was a watered-down version of Ricardo's heady proposal. The Bank, a national institution since 1694, was now in the maw of theorists such as Ricardo, and they did not hesitate to reorganize its internal workings.

What does this mean for this book's argument regarding method and the study of texts in the history of economic thought? At the most general level, this case suggests the need to replace reconstructions of method with accounts of specific texts and contexts. Ricardo's arguments were not the product of a theorist above the fray but represented targeted attacks at particular intellectual enemies, deploying a vocabulary energized by the occasion; hence his efforts to move his theorizing under the rhetorical coverage of practice and experience, even to the extent of seeming to mimic Ancient Constitution talk. Looking ahead to the chapters of Part III, Ricardo adopted a starkly opposing style of defence when it came to his intellectual conduct, refusing to ally his work with experience and instead insisting on the free-floating nature of his demanding style of theoretical activity. That is, no consistent method can be found across Ricardo's works because his arguments varied with the argumentative context.

The other point to note is that Malthus had criticized Ricardo's intellectual conduct because he seemed to take a partial view of the issue, thereby missing the balance of payments as a factor affecting the exchange. Malthus treated this as a major failing because it disqualified Ricardo from realizing the political economist's goal of penetrating below surface effects to apprehend real causes in all their complexity. Malthus would make similar complaints against Ricardo's *Principles*. What was at issue was neither general epistemological principles— such as induction and deduction—nor the right model of monetary dynamics. At issue was the right conduct of the intellect for a political economist who wanted to guide Parliament's deliberations and win the support of practical men. This was the intense contest unfolding in issue-specific debates, but it has been occluded because we have been happy to talk of the methods and models of classical political economy instead.

---

[184] J. K. Horsefield, 'The Origins of the Bank Charter Act, 1844', *Economica* 11/44 (1944), 180–9.

[185] See clause I of the *Bank Charter Act 1844*: 'An Act to Regulate the Issue of Bank Notes, and for Giving to the Governor and Company of the Bank of England Certain Privileges for a Limited Period', in W. N. Welsby and Edward Beavan, *Chitty's Collection of Statutes, with Notes Thereon*, vol. 1 (London, 1865), 214–20, at 214. Ricardo's contribution is discussed in Horsefield, 'Origins of the Bank Charter Act', 184.

3

The Corn Laws and the Casuistry of Free Trade, 1813–1815

In his 1891 text, *The Scope and Method of Political Economy*, John Neville Keynes aimed to identify the parameters of a 'positive science'. In the course of his inquiries, he pondered but dismissed the idea an 'art of political economy' in which 'maxims for practical guidance are explicitly formulated'.[1] One of the reasons that Keynes set this idea aside was that it would require 'a body of doctrine' that covered all possible applications, which was impossible.[2] This objection would have been difficult to understand for the intellectual culture under study in this book, which had no need for Keynes's art because it was already possessed of a style of reasoning that took as its explicit purpose the resolution of those innumerable cases of everyday life that required the application of abstract principles. This style of reasoning was known as 'casuistry', as discussed in this book's Introduction. As the fact of Keynes's 1891 book suggests, however, as an explicit mode of reasoning, casuistry was falling into disuse by the close of the century thanks to the rise of 'positive science' and similar intellectual movements that were redrawing the maps of knowledge. But casuistry was very much alive in the time of Malthus and Ricardo.

This chapter shows how casuistry provided the argumentative structure for the most famous contributions from political economists to the policy debates over the 1815 Corn Laws. In doing so, the chapter builds on Donald Winch's invaluable yet neglected essay on 'higher maxims' in statecraft, which he identified as the major divergence between Malthus's and Ricardo's science of politics.[3] In what follows, Malthus's preparedness to treat the food supply as a paramount reason of state that could override lesser goals is identified as an instance of casuistry, and it is placed in the context of similar arguments from other participants in the debate. This finding undermines the view of Malthus as having abandoned his 'protectionism' later in life.[4] In contrast, the argument developed here is that Malthus was a state casuist, hence obliged to make assessments by weighing

---

[1] John Neville Keynes, *The Scope and Method of Political Economy* (London: Macmillan, 1891), 54.
[2] Ibid.
[3] Collini, Winch, and Burrow, *That Noble Science of Politics*, chapter 2.
[4] Samuel Hollander, 'Malthus's Abandonment of Agricultural Protectionism: A Discovery in the History of Economic Thought', *The American Economic Review* 82/3 (1992), 650–9, at 650.

Before Method and Models. Ryan Walter, Oxford University Press. © Oxford University Press 2021.
DOI: 10.1093/oso/9780197603055.003.0005

competing principles in view of the circumstances or case at hand. Ricardo is also shown to have mobilized casuistry, albeit maladroitly. For the general argument of the book, the implication is again that the context decisively shaped the style and content of Malthus's and Ricardo's arguments. On this occasion, it was not Restriction that dominated their rhetorical choices but the fact that Parliament treated the stability of the food supply as a goal of government. The issue was not, therefore, one of free trade versus protection, but the difficult task of balancing competing priorities for a nation facing an uncertain future. It follows that any attempt to reconstruct Malthus's and Ricardo's so-called methods as if they were a variable independent of the argumentative context will be misleading. This is why Parliament must be at the centre of the investigation into political economy in this period: its debates provided political economists with most of their topics and constrained their styles of argument.

The Shape and Substance of Parliamentary Debate: xHenry Parnell and Protection

The publications of Malthus, Torrens, and Ricardo represented interventions into a preexisting parliamentary debate, and registering this fact is a precondition for understanding the nature of their arguments. The general question to ask is thus not: What was their macroeconomic and international trade theory? But instead: How did they bring theoretical argument into contact with parliamentary argument? In the case of Malthus and Torrens, the answer is: in the manner of casuistry. As stated, this was a style of reasoning that was intended to produce an argument for a specific course of action by applying accepted principles of government in view of topical facts—above all, fluctuating grain prices. In the case of Ricardo, the sheer awkwardness of his presentation requires qualifying this answer. For Ricardo did balance free trade against security, but without attempting to ascertain the facts of the case. It was, in other words, a theoretical casuistry. The reason for Ricardo's disconnection from the case was that he had developed the core of his argument independently of the Corn Laws debate and in a theoretical register, only connecting his inquiries with the prudential and casuistical arguments circulated by Malthus and Torrens in order to join the parliamentary debate.

The argumentative context into which all three writers intervened can be established by bringing to view the claims of Henry Parnell. An Irish landlord who chaired the Select Committee appointed to examine the corn trade in 1813, Parnell may have allowed himself to be influenced by the agenda to increase Irish export markets.[5] Earlier, Parnell had sat on the Bullion Committee, and he seems

---

[5] Donald Grove Barnes, *A History of the English Corn Laws: From 1660–1846* (London: George Routledge & Sons, 1930), 117–18.

to have devoted some effort to mastering political economy, displaying famil-
iarity with Smith's *Wealth of Nations* (1776) along with subsequent contributions.[6] Parnell led the defence of the report that his Committee produced, *Report
from the Select Committee of the House of Commons Appointed to Enquire into
the Corn Trade of the United Kingdom* (1813). This was no easy task: the report
ran to just over five pages, excluding the evidence, which was equally truncated
and partial.[7] The *Report* was printed in May 1813 and debated in Parliament in
June. Its contents reflect the major concern of the time that Malthus and Ricardo
were also obliged to heed: that corn exhibit a steady supply and price. In hindsight, partial self-sufficiency in corn would remain the means by which Britain
would pursue this goal until mid-century, when the experiment in free trade was
launched.[8] We can thus think of this episode as analogous to the 1810 *Report*
from the Bullion Committee: an early and unsuccessful advance by theoretical
political economists in their long-run and ultimately successful campaign to
program legislative action.

The core of Parnell's *Report* consisted in a recapitulation of legislation back
to the middle of the seventeenth century, followed by a table of average wheat
prices, alongside the excess of exports over imports, for five-year periods from
1701 to 1794. The lesson drawn from this evidence was that 1765 represented
a turning point—the year in which the free importation of corn was permitted.
This amounted to a new 'system', under which imports exceeded exports while
prices continued to rise.[9] The remedy was clear: to return 'to the principles of
those laws which were so beneficial in practice from the time of their commence-
ment in 1670, till their abandonment in 1765'.[10] The practical mechanism was
to be a new system of duties on the importation of foreign corn, along with re-
scinding the bounty on corn exports.

The *Report* was ill-received initially, perhaps as much because of the scanty
evidence as because of the high prices that farmers were enjoying in 1813. But
by the time debate recommenced almost a year later, in May 1814, prices had
plummeted and Parnell suddenly had a warm audience.[11] In this context, Parnell
aired his case for protection again, this time as a pamphlet, which developed his

---

[6] G. F. R. Barker, 'Parnell, Henry Brooke, First Baron Congleton (1776–1842), Politician', *Oxford
Dictionary of National Biography* (2004), http://www.oxforddnb.com/view/10.1093/ref:odnb/
9780198614128.001.0001/odnb-9780198614128-e-21386.
[7] George Rose, for example, described the Report as 'such a one as I believe this House has never
yet acted upon'. See George Rose, *The Speech of the Right Hon. George Rose, in the House of Commons*
(London, 1814), 51.
[8] Hilton, *Corn, Cash, Commerce*, 19–22.
[9] 'Report from the Select Committee Appointed to Enquire into the Corn Trade of the United
Kingdom, May 11 1813', in *The Parliamentary Debates of the Year 1803 to the Present Time*, vol. 25
(London, 1813), lv–c, at lxi.
[10] Ibid.
[11] Barnes, *A History of the English Corn Laws From 1660–1846*, 118–22.

parliamentary speech of the year before and took note of Malthus's criticisms of Smith in his *Observations on the Effects of the Corn Laws* (1814).[12] Parnell's framing comments are interesting because they represented a gambit: he conceded enormous ground to the free trade position by installing the principles of political economy as the relevant basis for making a decision on how best to achieve a steady supply and price for corn. This is why Parnell insisted that, to enter the fray, one was obliged to be 'acquainted with the science of political economy'.[13] As Ricardo would demonstrate, however, the principles of political economy were susceptible to dramatic restatement, while Parnell's rider that they be 'exemplified and illustrated by experience'[14] was to be ignored in Ricardo's virtuoso performance of theory.

According to Parnell, the free trade position held that lifting restrictions would guarantee the lowest price for corn, which could be purchased by exporting British manufactured goods. Parnell acknowledged that this was valid reasoning consistent with the best principles of political economy. The justness of the principle, however, was a separate issue from the expediency of immediately applying it, which depended on 'the actual circumstances of the country'.[15] We are again meeting the insistence that the application of theory was a separate matter from its truth or falsity. The leading circumstance, according to Parnell, was artificially high prices created by more than twenty years of war, increased taxation, and a blockade of British commerce. Under these conditions, an immediate shift to free trade threatened the destruction of domestic agriculture because Polish corn would be brought to market for thirty-two shillings per quarter, a fraction of the current domestic price. This outstanding circumstance had been ignored by the advocates of free trade, along with the national danger that dependence on foreign supply represented.[16]

Parnell scored a further rhetorical point by invoking the authority of Adam Smith, and quite rightly, since Smith had only recommended free trade as the most useful means to increase the riches of the community. In consequence, free trade could be rejected if it did not serve other, higher objectives of state.

> Before, then, the principle of a free trade can be urged, as that principle which ought to govern us, when legislating on the corn trade, it ought to be made appear to be a trade, concerning which no other consideration should have weight, besides the limited consideration of what plan of dealing with it will,

---

[12] [Henry Parnell], *The Substance of the Speeches of Sir H. Parnell* (London, 1814).
[13] Ibid., 10. Note that in two places Parnell equated 'political principles' with the principles of political economy: we are once more directed to 'the science of politics' as the context (Ibid., 25, 27).
[14] Ibid., 8.
[15] Ibid., 11.
[16] Ibid., 15–19, 24.

in the end, give us the greatest amount of national wealth. But this has not been done; and, therefore, if any other great objects of public interest are involved in the question, those who urge the policy of a free corn trade, do so, subject to the charge of inadvertence, and of neglecting to attend to matters of still greater moment than the mere wealth of the state.[17]

The matter 'of still greater moment' that Parnell had in mind was the preservation of that quantity of capital and labour that was employed in agriculture. The preservation of so much wealth outweighed the desirability of having capital allocated in a natural manner. This argument was strengthened by the fact that the distribution of Britain's capital had been irrevocably distorted throughout the nation's history owing to endless legislative interventions, the Navigations Acts especially.[18] With these points in place, Parnell was ready to make his central claim. Preserving agricultural capital and employment through import restrictions was justified on the basis of Smith's explicit arguments in *Wealth of Nations*. As Parnell wrote, such action would 'fall under those rules, which he [Smith] lays down for making exceptions to the general rule of a complete freedom of trade'.[19] In particular, Smith had allowed that where a specific trade was necessary for national defence, it was to be regulated with that aim in view, not for the sake of wealth. Securing the nation with an independent supply of corn was always essential for security, and so the case could be left there. However, the present moment added further force to this conclusion: Napoleon had revealed his desire to conquer Russia (the disastrous Russian Campaign of 1812), presaging the larger threat that America might join with a confederacy of northern powers to humble Britain by strangling its food supply.

Parnell also underlined the fact that Smith had made an exception for taxation and for those industries that had grown up under protective duties—Smith's exception in the name of 'humanity'.[20] Taking all these points together, Smith's counsel was caution and circumspection. If the champions of free trade were to simply admit Smith's authority, then the dispute would be over: the 'theory' of free trade was not 'applicable to the existing and extraordinary circumstances of the country'.[21] This is textbook casuistry: the application of a principle is modified by circumstance and by the existence of rival, higher order principles. It is now time to see how Malthus, Torrens, and Ricardo approached the case of protection to agriculture.

---

[17] Ibid., 23.
[18] Ibid., 24, 26.
[19] Ibid., 53.
[20] Ibid., 54–5.
[21] Ibid., 33.

Malthus: The Casuistry of National Happiness

Malthus presented himself in his *Observations on the Effects of the Corn Laws* (1814) as addressing the legislature on the eve of its deliberations, with the purpose of providing the nation's legislators with a 'correct and enlightened view of the whole question' so that they might thereby reach 'a just and enlightened decision'.[22] This was public-counsel rhetoric, and Malthus played the role of counsellor by limiting himself to the task of providing the reasoning materials for the correct 'determination of the question, respecting the policy or impolicy of continuing the corn laws'.[23] What were these materials? They were the multiple and conflicting principles that needed to be balanced in view of the facts of the case. In setting out this account, Malthus was building on his earlier treatment of the issue in the second edition of his *Essay* (1803), where food was said to play a special role in the strength and prosperity of the state, requiring that an 'exception' be made to the 'objections against bounties in general' because of the current force of commercial jealousies and military animosities between the nations of Europe.[24]

In weighing this factor, Malthus diverged from Parnell by taking it for granted that Britain had permanently exited the league of corn-exporting nations.[25] The question to be determined, in other words, was whether it were wiser for Britain to continue to limit the importation of corn in order to secure a *measure* of self-sufficiency or to trust in cheaper sources of supply from foreign nations. Malthus then affirmed Parnell's claim that domestic industry would be destroyed under open competition, as neither British nor Irish agriculturalists could compete with their Polish counterparts in terms of price. This would not only cause the improvement of agricultural land and technique to cease, but it would also retrench much of the nation's existing cultivation.[26] These were the relevant circumstances for the legislature to keep in mind.

With the case stated in this way, the question became one of whether or not an independent supply of corn was a sufficiently desirable object to justify the legislature interfering in the nation's trade. For interference overturned political economy's 'general rule' that commodities should be bought from where they could be had cheapest, the rule to which the fewest 'justifiable exceptions can

---

[22] Malthus, 'The Corn Laws', *Works*, 7: 83–109, at 87, 88.

[23] Ibid., 94.

[24] Malthus, 'An Essay on the Principle of Population (1826): Part II', 686.

[25] Malthus, 'The Corn Laws', 94. It was a fair claim: since the 1780s, Britain's food exports were a fraction of its food imports. See External Trade, table 5, in B. R. Mitchell, *British Historical Statistics* (Cambridge: Cambridge University Press, 1988), 456.

[26] Malthus, 'The Corn Laws', 94–7. Malthus made this argument with reference to relative prices, drawing on *European Commerce* (London, 1805), attributed to William Playfair. That a datum as changeable as prices could form a crucial 'fact' of the case underlines the contextual nature of the assessment.

be found in practice'.[27] Once again, we have classic casuistry-talk, addressed to a legislature that must determine whether or not it ought to depart from a general rule under the force of circumstances. Malthus's casuistry was distinctive because the supreme criterion that was to guide legislative judgement was human happiness, as construed through Malthus's theological framework. That is, human happiness was normally served by following the general rule of noninterference in trade, but at times a departure from this rule was required.

In order to determine if noninterference were appropriate in the case of the Corn Laws, Malthus's next step was to understand how an independent supply of corn related to the nation's happiness, which can be seen as a further specification of the facts of the case. On the one hand, a regular free trade in corn would lead to stable prices, certainly more so than relying on domestic supplies, and steady prices played a significant role in the happiness of Britain because corn was the staple food.[28] In addition, restrictions also came with a long list of negatives: they represented a waste of national resources by diverting capital away from its natural course, they disadvantaged the nation in foreign commerce by raising the price of labour, and they required constant revision as the price difference between Britain's corn and the world's corn rose and fell.[29]

On the other hand, there was the issue of 'security': making a population dependent on a foreign supply of food was dangerous, especially given the recent tendency for nations to act from 'passion rather than interest'.[30] In this last comment, Malthus was signalling the danger that Britain might lose access to export markets for its manufactured commodities during an extended war, and, more seriously, it might also lose its supply of subsistence. If such an event were to happen, then the result would be an 'experiment' in distress never before observed.[31] Malthus was circling the point that, while the rule of free trade served happiness by augmenting wealth, the same principle might simultaneously threaten happiness by undermining what we call 'food security'.

Further happiness calculations also needed to be considered. First, removing protection would cause Britain to become an (almost) exclusively manufacturing nation. Such a departure from Britain's approximate balance between manufacturing and agriculture would detract from national happiness because wages in manufacturing were susceptible to fluctuations that caused discontent and because labour's real wages would fall with the price of corn. Second, and parsing Smith, Malthus held that departing from an existing system of regulation confronted the legislature with considerations of equity regarding workers,

[27] Malthus, 'The Corn Laws', 98.
[28] Ibid., 98–100.
[29] Ibid., 105–9.
[30] Ibid., 100.
[31] Ibid., 101.

landlords, and farmers.[32] Smith had discussed this issue under the rubrics of 'humanity' (for workers) and 'equity' (for manufacturers), treating both as precepts for the statesman to heed as components of justice.[33] While Malthus quoted Smith on the fate of workers who would lose their employment, his focus was on the 'impartial justice' that the legislature ought to dispense to landlords.[34] For impartial justice was wanting when one industry—agriculture—was subjected to free competition while all others continued to enjoy protection.

The whole question, in short, was one of 'contending advantages and disadvantages' that concerned the nation's 'interests': the security of the food supply and national wealth.[35] The nature of happiness as a composite good was a crucial feature of Malthus's casuistry. As with Smith and Parnell, Malthus allowed that security was of more importance than wealth. Yet Smith had used the hierarchy between the statesman's goals to settle the matter, while Malthus instead treated security and wealth as both contributing to the overarching goal of happiness. In consequence, Malthus was prepared to write that security and wealth were *only* valuable to the extent that they could 'improve, increase, and secure the mass of human virtue and happiness', a question belonging to 'morals and politics' and resembling 'problems *de maximis* and *minimis* in fluxions' because 'there is always a point where a certain effect is the greatest, while on either side of this point it gradually diminishes'.[36] The whole issue was complicated, however, by the prospect of a return to cash payments, as this would send a series of price adjustments through the body politic such that any final decision ought to be postponed.[37] Having registered this final point of caution, Malthus had discharged his counselling duty.

Malthus assumed a different office to public counsellor in his publication of the following year, *The Grounds of an Opinion on the Policy of Restricting the Importation of Foreign Corn* (1815). Where the *Observations* had aimed to provide an impartial account of the case alongside the relevant principles in order

---

[32] Ibid., 103.

[33] See Walter, 'Adam Smith's Free Trade Casuistry', 73–4.

[34] Malthus, 'The Corn Laws', 104.

[35] Ibid., 105.

[36] Ibid., 101, 102. This statement has often been taken to define Malthus's approach to political economy. See, for example, Winch, *Riches and* Poverty, 245. Yet it is simply a rhetorical gloss of casuistry, a style of reasoning that Malthus shared with parliamentarians such as Parnell and intellectual rivals such as Torrens. Winch's reading draws on John Pullen's influential article, where this statement is also treated as evidence of Malthus's 'doctrine of proportions', a doctrine that is then said to represent an early contribution to 'the introduction and development of the concept of the optimum in economics', before Pullen finally acknowledged that it involved 'exceptions to the general principles of political economy', a premise that is then translated into 'a general methodological principle'. As discussed in the Introduction, the idea of a general methodological principle belongs to a later period, while casuistry belongs to Malthus's time. J. M. Pullen, 'Malthus on the Doctrine of Proportions and the Concept of the Optimum', *Australian Economic Papers* 21/39 (1982), 270–85, at 271, 273.

[37] Malthus, 'The Corn Laws', 106–9.

to aid the legislature's reasoning, in this pamphlet Malthus set out his own assessment of the case, his 'opinion', using that word to denote a considered position. Ricardo noted the change of register, writing to Malthus that he had 'quite
thrown off the character of impartiality' displayed in the earlier text.[38] A similar
impression is registered today when the text is described as 'protectionist'.[39]
Nevertheless, Malthus had arrived at his position by continuing to adhere to
the reasoning protocols articulated in the previous publication, only taking into
account the new circumstances of the case. (In fact, the new pamphlet's extended
title signalled that it was an 'Appendix' to the earlier publication.) The matter
turned on the fact that the new circumstances altered the probability of some key
predictions.

Malthus brought forward three facts in order to bring his account of the case's
particulars up to date. First, rising corn prices had stimulated capital accumulation on the land in the form of high farming—intensive farming using the latest
techniques—but the subsequent price declines following the peace had seen
much of this capital evaporate. Malthus took this piece of evidence as confirm-
ation of his claim in *Observations* that a system of free trade would see British
agriculture more or less disappear, destroying a large portion of Britain's wealth.
Second, the exchange had strengthened as the value of paper money rose, which
threatened further price falls. Malthus's counsel was to allow these adjustments
to be processed by the nation's circulation before subjecting it to a further change
by shifting to a policy of free trade in corn. Third, the actions of France had
undermined the prospects that Britain might one day rely on foreign imports
of corn. For the French had again acted from the 'jealousies and fears of nations'
by legislating to ban exports of corn should even a mild scarcity be experienced
in that nation.[40] The issue was that the high quality and low price of France's
corn ensured that it would become the primary supplier to Britain. Hence, only
a moderate scarcity in France would be needed to see Britain's supply of subsistence seriously impaired.

Malthus took these facts to be fatal for the case to open the ports because they
altered the circumstances in which the principle of free trade was to be applied. It
is worth quoting Malthus at length on this issue.

> Such a species of commerce in grain shakes the foundations, and alters entirely
> the data on which the general principles of free trade are established. For what
> do these principles say? They say . . . that if every nation were to devote itself

---

[38] Ricardo, 'Ricardo to Malthus', *Works and Correspondence*, 6: 176–8, at 177.
[39] Hollander, *The Economics of Thomas Robert Malthus*, 810.
[40] Or, more accurately, to ban exports once the price exceeded a threshold price (49s per quarter)
set barely above the average (38–40s per quarter). Malthus, 'The Importation of Foreign Corn', *Works*,
7: 147–74, at 156.

particularly to those kinds of industry and produce, to which its soil, climate, situation, capital, and skill, were best suited; and were then *freely to exchange* these products with each other, it would be the most certain and efficacious mode, not only of advancing the wealth and prosperity of the whole body of the commercial republic with the quickest pace, but of giving to each individual nation of the body the full and perfect use of all its resources.

I am very far indeed from meaning to insinuate, that if we cannot have the most perfect freedom of trade, we should have none; or that a great nation must immediately alter its commercial policy, whenever any of the countries with which it deals passes laws inconsistent with the principles of freedom. But I protest most entirely against the doctrine, that we are to pursue our general principles without ever looking to see if they are applicable to the case before us; and that in politics and political economy, we are to go straight forward, as we certainly ought to do in morals, without any reference to the conduct and proceedings of others.[41]

When Malthus wrote that he protested 'against the doctrine, that we are to pursue our general principles without ever looking to see if they are applicable to the case before us' he was affirming the need for casuistry—for reasoning in relation to cases. In relation to political economy, Malthus's commitment to casuistry meant that general principles needed to be applied in a world of states whose behaviour was presumed to be driven by 'passions' and 'jealousies', along with interests. In other words, in Malthus's hands, political economy was a form of statecraft; as we will see, in Ricardo's hands, it was rather a form of rationalism.

Having specified the actual circumstances in which a free trade in corn would operate, in lieu of relying on a hypothetical account of its operation, Malthus was in a position to assess its relative merits. He did so by deploying a happiness calculus in which the effects of free trade on society's four major classes were estimated. Heaviest in the scale was the labouring class, whose numbers meant that it held 'the greatest weight, in any estimate of national happiness'.[42] Labour would not be served by the free importation of corn because the policy would throw agricultural labour out of employment, which would depress wages, as would cheap corn prices caused by free importation. Furthermore, the irregularity of supply—inevitable, given France's posture—would cause the price of corn to fluctuate more than it would under the existing laws, creating further distress for labour.[43] In short, the most important class would suffer under the new system.

---

[41] Ibid., 158.
[42] Ibid., 162.
[43] Ibid., 162–5.

The second most important class in society was those who lived off the profits of stock, or capital—approximately half were farmers, while the other half consisted of merchants and manufacturers. Perhaps only 12 to 13 per cent of all capital was tied to foreign trade. Given the certain destruction of most of the nation's agricultural capital, the question became one of whether or not the national gain could be expected to more than compensate for the loss. If the gains merely replaced the loss, leaving the overall level of wealth unchanged, then the policy was unjustifiable in this respect.[44] In forming his estimates, Malthus once again emphasized the role of jealousy among nations as a factor shaping their behaviour. In particular, the 'actual state of Europe and the prevailing jealousy of our manufactures' meant that rival nations desired to steal those markets to which Britain exported its manufactured goods.[45] It followed that the only section of the profit-taking class that would certainly benefit from free trade was that part engaged in foreign trade. But this was only perhaps one-eighth of the entire class. Malthus could therefore conclude that the happiness of the profit-taking class as a whole would also be harmed by a shift to free trade.

Landholders formed the third group whose fortunes Malthus predicted under a system of free trade. His key point was that even though this class could not claim to contribute to national wealth on the same scale as either workers or capitalists, it nevertheless deserved to weigh heavily in the calculation. At this point we might suspect, as his friend William Empson did, that Malthus still subscribed to the notion that the country gentleman played a special role in maintaining the British Constitution, and for this reason the landholder's material condition needed to be safeguarded to some minimal degree.[46] Whatever the role of that belief, in 1815 Malthus was prepared to write that there was 'no class in society whose interests are more nearly and intimately connected with the prosperity of the state': when landholders suffered, the state did, too.[47] And suffer the landlords would if the ports were opened to foreign corn because prices for agricultural produce would tumble, dragging rents down at the same time. At this point of his text, Malthus had shown that three classes would suffer under free trade.

Malthus then turned to the fourth and final class whose fortunes were to be weighed: stockholders and those who lived on fixed salaries. It was the class to

---

[44] Wealth understood as the quantity of goods at the disposal of the nation. In Malthus's phrasing, 'the quantity of produce permanently consumed at home' (Ibid., 166).

[45] Ibid., 165.

[46] William Empson, 'Art. IX. – *Principles of Political Economy Considered with a View to their Practical Application*. By the Rev. T. R. Malthus, F. R. S. Second Edition. To which is prefixed a Memoir of the Author's Life. 8vo. London: 1836', *Edinburgh Review* 64/130 (1837), 469–506, at 479–80. See also Winch's discussion of this point in *Riches and Poverty*, 356–8.

[47] Malthus, 'The Importation of Foreign Corn', 167. This line of argument was repeated in his *Principles*, see especially Section VIII of chapter 3 in the 1820 edition; Malthus, 'Principles of Political Economy: Part I', *Works*, 5: 158–68.

which he identified himself as belonging, seemingly to evidence his good ethos.[48] This class would benefit because open ports would force down the price of corn, causing the fixed payments that stockholders received to rise in value. In other words, Malthus was noting the way that price rises over the past two decades had helped the state by easing the effective burden of the national debt. If this trend were reversed, then who would pay the national debt? The labouring classes, capitalists, and landholders would all pay because their nominal incomes would fall while their nominal tax burdens would remain the same. The benefits accruing to this small class would be offset by the costs incurred by the other three classes of society.[49]

It should be clear that Malthus's policy assessment was unambiguous: the majority of the people would be injured by free trade in corn. In consequence, it was 'wise and politic, in the actual circumstances of the country, to restrain the free importation of foreign corn'.[50] Malthus buttressed this conclusion by referring to his *Inquiry Into the Nature and Progress of Rent* (1815), henceforth *Inquiry into Rent*, where rent was naturalized in moral terms as an accompaniment to progress.[51] Glossing this earlier argument, Malthus claimed to have shown that if any country were to reach prosperity ahead of its neighbours *without* possessing abundant land for agriculture, then it would need to either pay a high price for corn or be dependent on corn imports. The latter policy was undesirable given that an independent supply of corn was a higher object of government, while the former was no obstacle to a growing population, power, wealth, and happiness.[52] Malthus thus viewed import restrictions as a necessary departure from free trade because wealth was only one ingredient in national happiness.

Robert Torrens: Free Trade and Commercial Power

That Torrens adopted the same style of casuistical reasoning that Malthus deployed is evident in his text's full title: *An Essay on the External Corn Trade; Containing an Inquiry into the General Principles of that Important Branch of Traffic; an Examination of the Exceptions to which these Principles are Liable; and a Comparative Statement of the Effects which Restrictions on Importation and Free*

---

[48] Ibid., 168n. In some years Malthus's income from dividends exceeded his salary from the East India College. See J. M. Pullen, 'Further Details of the Life and Financial Affairs of T. R. Malthus', *History of Economics Review* 57/1 (2013), 16–31, at 16–19.

[49] Malthus, 'The Importation of Foreign Corn', 168–71.

[50] Ibid., 171.

[51] Malthus, 'The Nature and Progress of Rent', *Works*, 7: 111–45.

[52] Malthus, 'The Importation of Foreign Corn', 173–4. One might think of Malthus as recasting the so-called rich country–poor country debate, for which see Istvan Hont, *Jealousy of Trade: International Competition and the Nation-State in Historical Perspective* (Cambridge, Mass.: Harvard University Press, 2005), chapter 3.

Intercourse, are Calculated to Produce upon Subsistence, Agriculture, Commerce, and Revenue (1815).[53] This style of reasoning was affirmed in the preface: Torrens would identify the relevant principles to guide the statesman or legislature in relation to the corn trade and draw attention to the situations in which exceptions to these principles were required since the ability to identify exceptions was the test of the 'economist's' wisdom.

> [P]rinciples, incontestably true, may be practically inadmissible; and, conversely, what is practically beneficial, may be at variance with a theory generally correct. As he is the most skilful physician who, in complicated cases, cures one disease with the least possible aggravation of another, so he is the most sagacious economist, who, without deserting first principles as his general guides, so far restricts and modifies them, as to produce the greatest good, with the least possible evil, to the community. For there are few universal rules in any art or science; and, in all cases, he must be considered the wisest man, who follows the general principle, and yet avails himself of exceptions, as they occasionally occur.[54]

In fact, Torrens claimed that his ability to identify the 'limitations' to which his 'general principles' were subject represented his moment of originality and the point at which he might claim to have extended the limits of the science, presumably building on the account of the benefits from free trade that he had earlier developed in his *Economists Refuted* (1808).[55] That we have never taken Torrens at his word but instead tried to find his originality in light of our own fixation on the doctrine of comparative advantage is testimony to the distorting effects of anachronism.[56]

Torrens's desire to identify relevant principles *and* their exceptions structured his treatise. Part I lays out the principles of the corn trade, Part II identifies if exceptions are justified in relation to stylized cases, and Part III examines the effects of applying free trade or protection. Hence, for example, the title of Chapter II of Part II: 'On the Question, Are the Principles respecting a free external Trade in Corn liable to any Limitations in their Application to the particular Case of a

---

53 Robert Torrens, *An Essay on the External Corn Trade* (London: 1815).

54 Ibid., vi–vii.

55 Ibid., xiv.

56 It should be acknowledged that, in the third edition of his *Essay* (1826), Torrens claimed to have 'shewn' in the first edition of 1815 that 'comparative advantage' and 'comparative disadvantage' would still drive international trade despite price differences, representing 'principles' that Ricardo supposedly then adopted in his *Principles of Political Economy* of 1817. See Robert Torrens, *An Essay on the External Corn Trade* (London, 1826), vii. More plainly, Torrens was making a claim to precedence, and it spawned a dispute that continues today. Yet Parts II and III of the treatise were concerned with the 'exceptions' to free trade and with how to apply the principle to 'actual circumstances'. Hence, the third edition was still an extended piece of casuistry and not a work of pure theory.

Country, which is more heavily taxed than other growing Countries?' The style of reasoning is that of casuistry, while the domain of application is, as Torrens named it, 'political science'.

In returning to the structure and language of Torrens's text, one of the striking features that emerges is the manner in which Torrens combined a rationalist endorsement of international free trade, on the one hand, with an insistence on the paramount importance of the state securing a cheap and reliable food supply, on the other. If we begin with the rationalist side of Torrens's argument, the initial case for a free external corn trade was made through an analogy with the advantages of a free internal trade. His essential point was that although the quantity of agricultural produce in any given year was subject to variation, the degree of variation diminished as the extent of the territory increased. It followed that the greater the territory the more stable the supply, and, as the supply stabilized, so, too, did the price. This represented a standing rationale against placing any obstacles in the way of a perfectly free internal commerce because doing so would only cause variability in supply and price.[57] As a rule, free trade was good.

Torrens projected this analysis of internal commerce onto the corn trade of the world. The effect was to turn a blind eye to sovereign borders while centring growing prices and carriage costs. This made it possible for the political economist to determine which regions would export and which would import corn by comparing regions in terms of their 'growing price'—the price at which a region could bring its corn to market under usual conditions—and then adjusting these growing prices for carriage costs.[58] In effect, when one nation supplied another, the importing nation acquired new land under cultivation, thus decreasing the variability of both supply and price. This mechanism was exemplified by Holland's happy experience with a steady supply of corn by relying on the world's markets.[59]

Torrens supplemented this rationale for a free trade in corn—stable prices and supply—with a barter conception of international trade. This allowed Torrens to treat trade between nations as trade in which value was given for equivalent value (with the nature of value left unspecified). In reliance on Smith's claim that the statesman was simply unable to direct capital and labour more effectively than individuals, free trade between nations would ensure the greatest quantity of produce.[60] In this context, Torrens developed an intricate piece of argumentation that has come to be viewed in the secondary literature as an early statement of the doctrine of comparative advantage.

---

[57] Torrens, *An Essay on the External Corn Trade* (1815), 2–5, 13, 23.
[58] Ibid., 45.
[59] Ibid., 24–36.
[60] Ibid., 47–52, 86.

When a people exchange the produce of their soil, for the wrought goods of some neighbouring country, it has been supposed, that the raw materials and subsistence which they thus send abroad, might, to the great increase of the national opulence and prosperity, give employment to manufacturers at home. The slightest examination of the laws, which regulate the interchange of commodities between nations, is sufficient to show, that, for this supposition there is no foundation. When labour and capital are employed in cultivating the earth, and exchanging its produce for the manufactured goods of other countries, it is because these goods, thus obtained, are better, or more abundant, than those, which the same quantities of labour and capital could have fabricated at home. This interchange, therefore, of produce against manufactures, effects a clear addition to the wealth of the nation.[61]

Torrens's numerical example described a nation that exported corn in exchange for 1 000 yards of cloth, while, if the resources that produced the corn were repurposed at home to produce cloth, then only 900 yards would result; unfettered trade delivered a clear material gain of 100 yards of cloth.[62] It will be necessary to return to Torrens's supposed achievement later in the chapter.

Torrens combined this analysis of the output produced by different combinations of capital and labour with his account of nations in terms of growing prices and carriage costs to produce a spatial account of international trade. Torrens then added a temporal element by imagining progress as a process that operated in historical time. Again reworking Smith, the essential claim was that as a nation grew in opulence, the average level of profits fell, which allowed lands that were previously unprofitable to be brought under cultivation. In Torrens's hands, the argument was made by imagining the reallocation of capital between manufacturing and agriculture: whenever manufacturing profits sunk below the prevailing rate of return on the marginal unit of land, capital would be redirected to agriculture. The ultimate result was that 'At length cultivation ascends the hills and scales the mountains' because capital accumulates beyond the needs of foreign markets and so 'overflows, like fertilizing waters, on the soil'.[63] Taken together, these points amounted to a case for free trade as a means for deploying the world's capital and labour in a rational manner.

Torrens also deployed in parallel a negative argument for free trade that worked by revealing the costs to a nation of procuring its corn at greater expense than was necessary. To make this argument, Torrens used a technical vocabulary that drew on both Smith's *Wealth of Nations* and Malthus's *Essay on the Principle*

---

[61] Ibid., 41–2. See also the offhand statement at Ibid., 110.
[62] Ibid., 42.
[63] Ibid., 51, 53.

of Population. The leading terms were 'market price' and 'natural price', where the former was the price paid in the market as determined by the balance of supply and demand in the short term, while the latter price reflected the cost of production in terms of quantities of capital, labour, and land and exerted gravitational force over market prices. Torrens also developed conceptions of 'natural profit', 'natural wages', and 'natural rent'. Natural rent was a residual after deducting natural wages and natural profits, analogous to the treatment unfolded by Malthus and Ricardo in their essays on the Corn Laws; natural wages were a function of the habits of the country and stable over time, unlike market wages, which were subject to the mechanisms that Malthus had set out in his *Essay*.[64] Torrens's punchline was that wages were closely linked to the cost of corn. He used this claim to explain the consequences for a nation that paid high prices for its corn.

In brief, a high price of corn would be communicated to the price of labour and commodities. This was a serious national issue because the cost (in terms of labour and capital) of providing labour with its subsistence set a limit to the development of manufactures. In consequence, Torrens could conclude that 'an increase in the natural price of subsistence, diminishes the productive powers of all branches of industry'.[65] The crucial mechanism was Malthusian: corn represented perhaps a third of the wage bundle consumed by labour, and any increase in the cost of corn would be reflected in the level of wages. The cost of corn was thus a crucial determinant of natural wages, which, in turn, stood as a crucial index of a nation's ability to produce wealth.[66] The implication for the corn trade was straightforward: if a nation could import a part or all of the corn necessary to its food supply more cheaply than it could be grown at home, then restrictions on such imports would be harmful. To justify such restrictions would require arguments that were capable of justifying nothing less than the suppression of national wealth. Part II of the treatise concerned three arguments that could meet this threshold.

Torrens began Part II began by reiterating the validity of subjecting principles to the test of exceptions, a familiar refrain regarding the art of application.

> These are principles, the abstract truth of which, is as capable of as rigid a demonstration, as any political or physical proposition can admit.
>
> But, every general principle, however evident its abstract truth may be, is, in its application to particular circumstances, liable to exceptions and limitations.[67]

---

[64] Ibid., 55–9, 60–1, 63–6.
[65] Ibid., 72.
[66] Ibid., 77–81, 84, 89, 92.
[67] Ibid., 97

Each argument against free trade then received its own chapter: justice (Part II Chapter 1), higher levels of taxation (Part II Chapter 2), and high agricultural prices due to an established system of laws (Part II Chapter 3). The justice claim stemmed from the principle that the laws ought to deal with all members of the society fairly and equally. Given that Britain's manufacturing benefited from protection in the form of bounties and duties, it was only fair, so the argument went, that agriculture also received protection. Torrens was dismissive of this argument because it involved 'the absurdity of seeking to remove a disease, by increasing the cause which produces it'.[68] This argument perverted the notion of 'political justice', and it would not persuade an 'enlightened statesman' who would never attempt to remove one evil by inflicting another.[69]

Torrens then turned to the second basis for making an exception: the case where a nation was more heavily taxed than its neighbours. Torrens acknowledged the authority of Smith on this point, who had argued that an exception was valid when unequal taxation across nations 'destroyed the natural level of industry', requiring that the statesman impose 'a countervailing duty' to restore the 'equal intercourse between nations'.[70] While the grounds for an exception were strong in principle, they did not apply in practice to Britain because there was no direct tax on corn in Britain. More generally, the wage bundle determined the general level of prices, and prices within one nation could not permanently affect trade patterns because the balance of trade between nations would set price adjustments in motion through the export of specie.[71] In other words, price distortions from taxation would be corrected naturally by the normal workings of international trade.

The matter might be different, however, if there were a tax on agricultural production that raised costs for the domestic grower. Britain's tithes were a leading example of just such a tax.[72] Torrens bit the bullet here, acknowledging that the 'enlightened legislator' would recognize a valid claim on the grounds of equity and on the basis of public prosperity given the centrality of agriculture to the nation. But what to do? The simple solution would be to repeal the unequal taxation. If such a remedy were not politically possible, then the alternative solution was to lay countervailing duties that would coax capital back to domestic agriculture at the natural level. The hazard that arose here was that the remedy might be ineffectual because the amount collected through tithes was constantly

---

[68] Ibid., 99.
[69] Ibid., 101–2. Torrens identified the remunerating price (with profits of 10 per cent) as 70 shillings per quarter for wheat of middling quality, hence imports were to be prohibited if the price were below this level. Once this were done the legislature could introduce more enlightened principles into the commercial system; Ibid., 342–3, 345.
[70] Ibid., 121–2.
[71] Ibid., 124–33.
[72] Ibid., 134–5, 138–40.

shifting. As Torrens wrote: 'to determine with precision, the amount of the protecting duty which would be sufficient to indemnify the landed interest for unequal taxes, and to restore the equilibrium they disturb, must be impossible', and
this fact formed 'a sufficient objection to resorting to them [duties], as a means
of counteracting the operation of those imposts which fall exclusively, or with
disproportioned weight, upon cultivation'.[73]

This was a practical reason against making an exception, even though the
principle was valid. Torrens had another and more powerful reason to levy
against intervention: assuming that the right level of protective duties could be
determined by the statesman, the effect would be to bring infertile land under
cultivation. In other words, to restore the natural allocation of capital to British
agriculture was to restore capital to an inefficient use because Britain's lands were
relatively infertile.[74] Corn was so important a commodity that the ideal of a natural allocation of capital simply needed to be set aside.

The final possible ground for an exception to the principle of free trade was
the existence of laws that artificially raised prices. The existence of a class that
was accustomed to receiving protection from the state meant that this case raised
the difficult issue of introducing 'political change' and the associated risk that the
statesman might embark on a 'rash and injudicious attempt to introduce theoretic perfection', thereby violating the maxim in political science that 'sudden
change is evil'.[75] As we will see, Ricardo was also obliged to mind this precept.
Torrens acknowledged that the argument for departing from the rule of free
trade was aided by the ability to appeal to Smith's authority on this point, for
Smith was also in the business of exceptions.

> Our great political economist, Dr. Smith, in stating the limitations to which the
> general principle of complete freedom in trade is liable, seems to consider the
> actual existence of artificial encouragement as one. He urges, that when any
> commodity of our own production, has been encouraged for some time by high
> duties and protections, it would be injurious suddenly to restore a free import-
> ation of the same kind of article. 'Humanity, in this case', he contends, 'requires
> that freedom of trade should be restored only by slow gradations, and with cau-
> tion and circumspection'.[76]

Just like Parnell, Torrens treated Smith as an authority to invoke, not, as we do
today, in the name of free trade, but in the name of protection.

---

[73] Ibid., 150.
[74] Ibid., 157–66.
[75] Ibid., 174, 184, 341.
[76] Ibid., 174–5.

Torrens endorsed Smith's advice. War with France and the deliberate interruptions to British commerce caused by the Berlin and Milan decrees had diverted capital to agriculture and created an artificially high price for corn, presenting the 'statesman' with the dilemma of whether or not to protect investments made under this regime.[77] Torrens recommended enlightenment with prudence: 'enlightened principles' had to be followed because 'the general principles of a free external trade in corn, are strictly applicable', but, in order to obviate suffering, the statesman ought to apply them gradually and with circumspection, just as Smith had counselled.[78]

What should be noted here is how seriously Torrens took the danger of attempting to introduce what he termed 'theoretic perfection' into commercial relations. He predicted calamitous consequences if this were attempted in the case of agriculture: capital would be lost along with the skills of labour, producing distress and diminishing the nation's productive power. The harm could be minimized by opening trade slowly.[79] The context described in Chapter 1 is necessary to make sense of this advice: the French Revolution had raised the stakes attaching to the statesman's conduct, and the terms of this debate were used by political economists to construe their work, its dangers, and the necessary safeguards. Once again, we find that political economy was a branch of the science of politics that used the vocabulary of theory and practice.

With the exceptions set aside, Torrens had arrived at the final section of his treatise: the application of the principle of free trade to corn. The art of application required examining the effects of the principle given what he referred to as 'the actual circumstances' of the nation and comparing these effects with those that would emerge if the system of restriction were continued unaltered, thus making it possible for Torrens to make a recommendation regarding which principle it would be 'expedient for the legislature to adopt'.[80] The axes on which Torrens developed his comparison of free trade and restriction overlapped with those that Malthus had proffered, such that Torrens was brought into direct conflict with certain of Malthus's evaluations. What makes Torrens so interesting is that, like Ricardo, he advocated free trade but, like Malthus and unlike Ricardo, Torrens was perfectly prepared to confront the need for the state to triumph over

[77] For the context, see Katherine B. Aaslestad and Johan Joor, 'Introduction', in Katherine B. Aaslestad and Johan Joor, eds., *Revisiting Napoleon's Continental System: Local, Regional and European Experience* (New York: Palgrave Macmillan, 2014), 1–24. Torrens, *An Essay on the External Corn Trade* (1815), 174.

[78] Ibid., 201–2.

[79] Ibid., 176, 179, 192–7, 251.

[80] Ibid., 203–4. It is worth marking here the slide between the figure of the statesman, whose enlightenment and virtues acted as a test for the propriety of various lines of legislative action, and the legislature, which we might think of as the real-world agent that stood in for the fabulous legislator.

its rivals in commerce and power and to make recommendations on the assumption that that this objective was of supreme importance.

The first axis, in common with Malthus, was the effects of free trade on the food supply. Torrens accepted—in reliance on evidence from the Lords Committee[81]—that in the short term the domestic supply of corn would increase. Yet Torrens insisted, contra the mistaken notions of Parnell, that the ultimate effect of regulation would be to raise the natural price of corn. And we have seen that Torrens treated the natural price of corn as intimately connected with national prosperity. It followed that the ruinous effects of regulation would be to allow other nations to capture Britain's manufacturing markets.[82] Torrens's view of international trade as intensely rivalrous—his word was 'rivalship'—was explicit, and it made the task of winning export markets from rivals just as important as establishing a stable food supply.[83] This is Torrens's bifocal account of international trade: his rationalist view of international trade worked alongside his analysis of interstate rivalry. Applied to the case of British agriculture under a system of protection, it predicted the extension of cultivation to infertile lands that would raise rents ever higher, allowing agricultural interests to gain in the short run but at great cost to national wealth as foreign markets were lost.[84]

The opposite effects would flow from a system of free trade. In the context of observing how Torrens set out this claim, we will encounter another piece of argumentation that appears to represent an early statement of comparative advantage. Yet Torrens's statement represents one half of his comparative study of two courses of legislative action that were available to Britain given its postwar circumstances, with the need to outcompete rivals in manufactures firmly in view.

> If England should have acquired such a degree of skill in manufactures, that, with any given portion of her capital, she could prepare a quantity of cloth, for which the Polish cultivator would give a greater quantity of corn, than she could, with the same portion of capital, raise from her own soil, then, tracts of her territory, though they should be equal, nay, even though they should be superior, to the lands in Poland, will be neglected; and a part of her supply of corn will be imported from that country. For, though the capital employed in cultivating at home, might bring an excess of profit, over the capital employed in cultivating abroad, yet, under the supposition, the capital which should be

---

[81]   *First and Second Reports from the Committee of the House of Lords, Appointed to Inquire into the State of the Growth, Commerce and Consumption of Grain* (London, 1814).

[82]   Torrens, *An Essay on the External Corn Trade* (1815), 205, 207, 215, 208–17, 224–6, 238–42, 254, 256.

[83]   Ibid., 237, 249, 299, 330–5, 339, 254.

[84]   Ibid., 218–20, 257–8.

employed in manufacturing, would obtain a still greater excess of profit; and this greater excess of profit would determine the direction of our industry.[85]

The enduring lesson was that noninterference was best, an argument developed in relation to agriculture for a nation that had a limited supply of lands of the first-rate quality but had managed to acquire a lead in manufacturing. To be plain: Torrens's presentation was not of a generalized argument for all nations in all times and places, but a policy recommendation given the stylized facts of Britain's situation. In his historical context, Torrens was a skilled casuist; he can only be treated as a failed or successful theorist of comparative advantage by removing him from his context and relocating him in a teleological story determined in advance by the historian.[86]

In addition to Torrens's argument regarding the total level of wealth, he also favoured free trade because he predicted that it would stabilize the supply and price of corn as Britain came to act as a storehouse for Baltic grain.[87] At this point, Torrens targeted Malthus's idea that Napoleon's blockade might be repeated and hence ought to be guarded against. Torrens simply asserted that Napoleon's attempt to exclude Britain from the world's commerce had failed.[88] Another of Malthus's claims—that France's self-serving laws invalidated free trade as a strategy—was also contradicted by Torrens because he confidently predicted that this legislation would be self-defeating. In any case, Torrens maintained, if France's legislation did require remedial action then it was with respect to trade with that nation, not with respect to the trade of the world.[89] Malthus was also rebuffed regarding the likely fall in domestic tillage that could be expected following the introduction of free trade. As we saw, Malthus forecast that this collapse would be complete, while Torrens detected exaggeration in such claims.[90] In fact, Torrens adduced historical prices to show that only very inferior soils would be lost to cultivation under free trade because carriage costs afforded Britain a 'great natural protection', claiming in this regard that 'Providence has been our legislator'.[91]

The final set of claims to note moved Torrens even further away from Malthus. Where Malthus had held that an independent supply of food was essential to security, Torrens instead treated Britain's security as dependent on commerce.[92]

---

[85] Ibid., 264–5.

[86] Hence statements of this type: 'Torrens did not provide the further development needed to produce the doctrine [of comparative advantage]'. See Aldrich, 'The Discovery of Comparative Advantage', 396.

[87] Torrens, *An Essay on the External Corn Trade* (1815), 275–7.

[88] Ibid., 278–9.

[89] Ibid., 280–2. But, as noted earlier, this did not address Malthus's prediction that the quality and low price of French corn would see France become Britain's prime supplier.

[90] Ibid., 283.

[91] Ibid., 284, see also 291 at asterisked note, 286–8.

[92] Ibid., 330–40.

For an island nation was obliged to privilege commerce and manufacturing as the source of 'that justly cherished naval preponderance, without which an insular empire can take up no position among the nations of the world'.[93] This was a venerable line of argument that was stated with sophistication in seventeenth-century debates over England's 'foreign policy' vis-à-vis Dutch and French maritime power.[94] Torrens was novel because he accepted the maritime power argument but treated free trade as the appropriate strategy for its achievement, whereas Malthus nominated self-sufficiency as the appropriate strategy, not for maritime power, but for balancing the various factors that contributed to national happiness.

In summary, what should be noted about these points of difference between Malthus and Torrens is that they primarily concerned probabilistic judgements regarding relevant facts. This was not, in other words, theoretical contest but rather a classic example of casuistical argument leading to nuanced positions. Both authors enjoyed great freedom when it came to adducing and weighing relevant factors, and the facility with which they did this was the prized capacity. Free trade argument today is doctrinaire and irrelevant by comparison, and it is the retrospective projection of this quality onto earlier thinkers such as Malthus and Torrens that converts them into (failed) theorists of comparative advantage. But in a context of parliamentary debate in which casuistical counsel was the genre, not theoretical proofs, the performances of Malthus and Torrens appear accomplished. As we will now see, the same cannot be said for Ricardo.

Ricardo: The Discovery of Principles, and Policy

In his *Essay on Profits* (1815), Ricardo developed an intensely abstract argument for the first half or so of the text before then bringing it into contact with the practical issues of the day. In comparison with Malthus and Torrens, the process by which Ricardo brought theory into contact with legislative judgement lacked dexterity. The history of the text's composition provides a partial explanation for Ricardo's elephantine movement between advancing theory and pondering its application. Ricardo had been developing arguments on the nature of profits since the summer of 1813, as disclosed by his correspondence with Malthus.[95] Then Malthus published his *Inquiry into Rent*, in early February 1815, which seemingly spurred Ricardo, since only a few weeks later Ricardo's *Essay on Profits* appeared. Here Ricardo linked his new thinking with the definition

---

[93] Ibid., 335.
[94] Ryan Walter, 'Slingsby Bethel's Analysis of State Interests', *History of European Ideas* 41/4 (2015), 489–506.
[95] Also discussed in Peach, *Interpreting Ricardo*, 49–68.

of rent that Malthus had proffered in his *Observations*. In fact, Ricardo began his argument by quoting Malthus's definition, and it then provided a structure in which he could unfold the arguments he had been developing the previous year. This theoretical exegesis only comes to an end on page twenty-seven of fifty in the original edition. This fact largely explains the challenging nature of the text. As Malthus wrote to Ricardo in correspondence, the text might have been improved by more time and deliberation, but it was sufficiently intelligible to him because he was long familiar with the issues. Tellingly, the *Essay on Profits* struck James Mackintosh, then a Whig politician, as 'rather difficult, and not sufficiently practical' for the business of parliamentary reasoning.[96] But Mackintosh told Malthus that he might read Ricardo's pamphlet again if he were obliged to lecture on political economy. In other words, Ricardo's performance was judged to be unhelpful by a sitting politician committed to both reform and theory.

With his theory set out, Ricardo devoted the remaining pages of his pamphlet to questions of policy, responding to Malthus's 'comparison of the advantages and disadvantages attending an unrestricted trade in corn'.[97] This discussion seems to have similarly drawn on correspondence with Malthus, on this occasion, from around the time of Malthus's publication in February 1815. Ricardo addressed the injustices that would be suffered by the different classes under free importation and how to balance these particular harms against 'the general good', represented by national wealth.[98] In short, Ricardo's theory of distribution and his policy analysis were developed independently of each other and then collocated in the same pamphlet. Ricardo's improvised performance was therefore unlike Malthus's premeditated application of principles, and this fact explains the structure of the text. We are not observing the implacable development of economic analysis through history, but reading a text while noting how its composition was shaped by a series of contingencies, with Parliament's debate over corn foremost amongst them.

There is a final point to make regarding the structure of Ricardo's text. In the extract here Ricardo glossed the structure of the argument in Malthus's *Grounds of an Opinion*:

> From the general principle set forth in all Mr. Malthus's publications, I am persuaded that he holds the same opinion as far as profit and wealth are concerned with the question; —but, viewing, as he does, the danger as formidable of depending on foreign supply for a large portion of our food, he considers it wise, on the whole, to restrict importation. Not participating with him in those

---

[96] Malthus, 'Malthus to Ricardo', *Works and Correspondence*, 6: 181–3, at 182.

[97] Ricardo, 'An Essay on the Influence of a low Price of Corn on the Profits of Stock', *Works and Correspondence*, 4: 1–41, at 32. The transition page in Sraffa's edition is 26.

[98] Ricardo, 'Ricardo to Malthus', *Works and Correspondence*, 6: 176–8, at 178.

fears, and perhaps estimating the advantages of a cheap price of corn at a higher value, I have come to a different conclusion.[99]

As can be seen, Ricardo suggests that he followed Malthus's structure but made different assessments regarding the foreign danger and the benefits of cheap corn. This would lead us to expect that Ricardo was also making probabilistic judgements in order to reach a policy conclusion. But this was not the case, for we have already seen that Ricardo's position on free trade was connected to the account of profits that he had developed in 1813. Hence, when he wrote that it was 'The consideration of those principles' that led him to favour a policy of free importation, he meant consideration of the principles that governed rent and profits, not conflicting principles of statesmanship such as security and wealth.[100]

In fact, the principles set out in Ricardo's theory respecified the circumstances of the case so heavily in favour of free trade that the arguments for protection were always going to be underweight. Ricardo acknowledged as much.

> If, then, the power of purchasing cheap food be of such great importance, and if the importation of corn will tend to reduce its price, arguments almost un-answerable respecting the danger of dependence on foreign countries for a por-tion of our food, for in no other view will the question bear an argument, ought to be brought forward to induce us to restrict importation.[101]

How did Ricardo shift such weight onto the side of free trade? The core of the theory followed Malthus's treatment of ground rent as a residual that remained after paying the costs of production, where these costs included the ordinary rate of profits.[102] Hence, rent was determined by the size of the two other shares in a given produce: by the size of profit and wages combined. Ricardo illustrated the implications of this point by describing the effects on rent and profits of a declining input–output ratio. In a hypothetical original position—'the first set-tling of a country'—land ideally located was cultivated at a cost of two hundred quarters of wheat.[103] This unit of land yielded a total produce of three hundred quarters. Therefore, if rent were zero, profits would be one hundred quarters in wheat terms, or 50 per cent. As population and wealth increased and more food came to be needed, further cultivation would incur an additional cost of ten quarters. Profits on this second-rate land (when valued in wheat) would fall

---

[99] Ricardo, 'An Essay on the Influence of a low Price of Corn on the Profits of Stock', 9.
[100] Ibid., 9.
[101] Ibid., 26.
[102] Ibid., 10.
[103] Ibid. Heterogeneous input costs were estimated in terms of wheat. See Peach, *Interpreting Ricardo*, 69–70.

to ninety quarters, or 43 per cent. It was this extension of cultivation and the consequent reduction in the size of the profit share that gave rise to rent. That is, if the prevailing returns to capital were everywhere 43 per cent, the landlord of the first-rate land, where profits were 50 per cent, could extract rent of 7 per cent and leave the farmer in the same position as every other farmer. As Ricardo explained,

> [t]hus by bringing successively land of a worse quality, or less favourably situated into cultivation, rent would rise on the land previously cultivated, and precisely in the same degree would profits fall; and if the smallness of profits do not check accumulation, there are hardly any limits to the rise of rent, and the fall of profit.[104]

The effects of this argumentation were drastic. In the first place, the 'case' was now hypothetical. Commentators have often noted the apparent willingness of Ricardo to isolate what we think of today as variables, and it is true that Ricardo was obliged to bracket the other determinants of the rate of profits: the relative rates at which population and capital increased, improvements in the practice of agriculture, and the ability of foreign markets to supply cheap food. Ricardo's stated rationale for this simplification was so that 'we may know what peculiar effects are to be ascribed to the growth of capital, the increase of population, and the extension of cultivation'.[105] Yet neither Ricardo nor his contemporaries talked of variables when doing political economy, that being another retro-projection of later idioms. More important for the argument here is the fact that, unlike Parnell, Malthus, and Torrens, Ricardo developed his argument in relation to an imaginary nation. Hence his use of expressions such as 'this state of society' and 'all the fertile land in the immediate neighbourhood of the first settlers'.[106] There was no attunement to the actual circumstances of Britain, its security needs, and its commercial rivalries. Instead, there was the derivation of class interests in abstract terms.

These class interests represent the second modification of the case that Ricardo's mode of argument introduced. Critics immediately perceived this aspect of Ricardo's thought as dangerous to social cohesion. For landlords stood as Ricardo's parasitic class, enjoying a rent that was 'never a new creation of revenue, but always part of a revenue already created'.[107] Tenant farmers represented the class that sustained the landlords under increasingly unfavourable conditions, whereas labourers stood as the industrious poor. Although Ricardo

---

[104] Ricardo, 'An Essay on the Influence of a low Price of Corn on the Profits of Stock', 14.
[105] Ibid., 12.
[106] Ibid., 12, 13.
[107] Ibid., 18.

acknowledged that fluctuations in population would influence wages and therefore profits, this factor was suspended from the analysis at an early stage because 'nothing can be positively laid down' about the topic.[108] The interests of landlords were isolated as a minority interest due to these two links: between farmers and labourers, and between farmers and all capitalists via the role of food in wages. This perspective produced the claim that scandalized Ricardo's society while gaining the warm approval of the aristocracy-hating James Mill: 'the interest of the landlord is always opposed to the interest of every other class in the community'.[109]

Now it is possible to appreciate what Ricardo had earlier called his 'consideration' of the relevant principles for deciding the issue: in Britain profits were kept low by the march of progress reducing the input–output ratio. But if corn raised on good lands overseas could be imported, then the capital employed on poor British lands could be diverted elsewhere more productively, most likely to produce goods that could be exchanged for the imported corn. Accordingly, the importation of corn would enable the normal process of rising rents and falling profits to be reversed, to the benefit of two classes and at the expense of only one. This conclusion, it should be clear, was derived in relation to a hypothetical situation where classes were construed in relation to an abstract, imaginary process intended to reveal the general relationship between rent and profits. Yet this account had the effect of respecifying the British case from a real nation in historical time to a hypothetical nation existing in theoretical time. That is, for Parnell, Malthus, and Torrens, Britain was a nation returning to peace conditions after straining to meet its own food needs during wartime. In Ricardo's hands, by contrast, Britain was simply a particular instance of the general process by which food became harder to produce. Ricardo had also specified the stakes of the Corn Laws in a general form: a clash between those classes that did not receive rent and the class that did. With the case thus understood, Ricardo turned to matters of policy and concrete contextual factors that *were* particular to Britain, but he nevertheless construed them in relation to this hypothetical presentation.

The first contextual factor that Ricardo brought to view was the level of opulence that Britain had reached, which mandated that it would be a regular importer of corn under free trade. At this point in their arguments, Parnell, Malthus, and Torrens had all adduced price information to establish the likelihood that Britain would become an importing nation under free trade. Ricardo, by contrast, adduced no such evidence despite numerous sources being available.[110] He

---

[108] Ibid., 23.

[109] Ibid., 21.

[110] Torrens used the table that the Secretary of the Board of Agriculture laid before the Lords' Committee (Torrens, *An Essay on the External Corn Trade* [1815], 286). Parnell drew on his *Report*'s table, itself a composite of sources, including custom house returns to Parliament ([Parnell], *The Substance of the Speeches of Sir H. Parnell*, 5). As noted earlier, Malthus relied on Playfair's *European*

instead treated this point in relation to his general argument regarding the benefits that flowed from a lower price of food: a higher level of profits across all trades that would drive capital accumulation and a greater level of material abundance. Accordingly, when Ricardo wrote of 'the many advantages which, circumstanced as we are, would attend the importation of corn', the content of 'circumstanced' was limited to Britain's place in an abstract typology of nations.[111]

Having asserted this status for Britain, Ricardo could maintain that it was only the danger of depending on foreign countries for the national food supply that could tilt the question in favour of restrictions. This position was then subjected to sustained refutation, in the course of which Malthus's arguments regarding the effects of free trade on different classes were the leading targets. Ricardo began his attack by diminishing the seriousness of the dependence argument. The dangers arising from dependence did not 'admit of being very correctly estimated' because they were 'in some degree, matters of opinion'.[112] It is worth noting that Ricardo's dismissal ran directly counter to the premises of the analysis of interest, the presumption of which was precisely that such matters were a matter of science because the actions of states could be understood in relation to the objective interests of states and their inflection by the private interests of rulers.[113] Malthus, for example, was drawing on this style of analysis when he acknowledged that if a cabal of nations were to cut off Britain's food supply, then it would require a policy 'against the interest of those nations', but the risk was hardly diminished by that fact because the present moment was one of 'governments acting from passion rather than interest'.[114]

Having redescribed the dependency argument as resting on mere opinion, Ricardo's next step was to characterize it as presuming two dangers. The first was that a combination of continental powers, or a powerful enemy such as France that might one day control the continent, could halt the supply of corn to Britain. In response, Ricardo appealed to the manner in which markets operated and the patience of the people. The nerve of Ricardo's claim was that, if Britain were to

---

Commerce. Ricardo referred to no such sources of political arithmetic but to Malthus's theoretical principle that a nation that was advanced in capital and manufacturing skill would be obliged to import its corn from its less advanced neighbours. (Ricardo's reference is to page 42 of Malthus's *Inquiry Into the Nature and Progress of Rent* [London, 1815]), but it seems that he meant pages 42–4 in the original, or Malthus, 'The Nature and Progress of Rent', 136.

[111] Ricardo, 'An Essay on the Influence of a low Price of Corn on the Profits of Stock', 27.
[112] Ibid.
[113] A genre described by James Tully as amounting to 'pan-European sciences of comparative politics and international relations': James Tully, 'Editor's Introduction', in James Tully, ed., *Samuel Pufendorf, On the Duty of Man and Citizen According to Natural Law* (Cambridge: Cambridge University Press, 1991), xiv–xl, at xv.
[114] Malthus, 'The Corn Laws', 100. The analysis of interest was also a rival intellectual tradition for Adam Smith, who went to some efforts to defuse its claims in his *Wealth of Nations*. See Walter, 'Slingsby Bethel's Analysis of State Interests', 506.

become a regular importer of corn, then the exporting countries would expand their cultivation significantly and so hardly be able to halt their supply to Britain without suffering 'ruinous commercial distress' themselves.[115] Ricardo's wager was that no sovereign would be prepared to inflict this harm on their people, and, if such a sovereign did emerge, then the people would quickly throw off such a measure, as Napoleon had found when he attempted to halt the export of produce from Russia. Note that here Ricardo disregarded Malthus's warning that interest was only a weak guide to the actions of passionate states in the present moment. Instead, Ricardo simply posited a long-term mechanism—popular revolt—that would ensure the ultimate force of 'interest'. In other words, Ricardo's argument contained no calculative or prudential element but was simply an assertion regarding the power of the people to keep their rulers in check, independent of any analysis regarding the capacity and proclivities of the people in any particular nation.

Ricardo did concede, however, that Britain would suffer during a period in which exports were halted. His nation would nevertheless survive, he maintained, by drawing a supply from neutral nations and by relying on its stores of grain. At the same time, capital would be rapidly redirected to agriculture. Even given the availability of such contingencies, the situation would still represent an 'evil of considerable magnitude' and an 'afflicting change'.[116] Ricardo was nevertheless prepared to stare down the possibility of these events because he judged their probability to be so low: 'Would it be wise then to legislate with the view of preventing an evil which might never occur; and to ward off a most improbable danger, sacrifice annually a revenue of some millions?'[117] Despite the offhand nature of the comment, this is plainly probabilistic reasoning: weighing probabilities in relation to costs and benefits and setting one type of benefit (cheap food leading to higher profits and material abundance) against a cost (the evil of famine). It does not seem, however, that Ricardo had a firm grasp on the structure of his own argument.

The second and final danger that Ricardo perceived as arising from dependence was that the exporting countries who supplied Britain would periodically experience poor harvests, leading them to withhold supply in preference for the welfare of their own citizens. The risk, again, was famine in Britain. Ricardo's response was based on further probabilistic reasoning derived from his account of inter-European markets. He predicted that if Britain were to permit free trade, then the supply of European corn would expand as nations that had never before exported to Britain began to do so in earnest. Such an expanded source of

---

[115] Ricardo, 'An Essay on the Influence of a low Price of Corn on the Profits of Stock', 28.
[116] Ibid., 29.
[117] Ibid., 29–30.

supply would mitigate the possibility for bad seasons to affect Britain in the way that Malthus's argument required. Furthermore, the price of corn was sensitive to even moderate shortfalls in supply, implying that high prices would engage the self-interest of exporting nations as their corn could exchange for greater quantities of Britain's manufactured goods. Finally, poor seasons were never universal thanks to God's ordering of the world in which scarcity in one nation was offset by plenty in another. As Ricardo wrote, 'Providence has bountifully secured us from the frequent recurrence of dearths'.[118] The effect of these arguments was to reduce the risk associated with dependence on foreign supply. Once again, what should be emphasized is that this minimizing of risk was dependent on a rational-providential account of international trade, one that stood in competition with the tradition of making international relations intelligible in terms of interest analysis and 'jealousy of trade'.[119] In consequence, although Ricardo acknowledged the existence of danger surrounding the nation's ability to guarantee a food supply, he was not a thinker committed to prudence as the master political virtue because he was instead committed to rational progress, for which free trade was a driving force.

Ricardo next turned to consider the justice arguments that had been raised by Malthus, targeting Malthus's focus on the loss of agricultural capital that would be caused by free trade. The basic premise of Ricardo's response was that whatever losses might be suffered by the holders of agricultural capital, it would nevertheless be the case that 'the public would gain many times the amount of their losses'.[120] Still, Ricardo was prepared to allow that such persons should be protected against these losses.

> [I]t might be just to lay restrictive duties on importation for three or four years, and to declare that, after that period, the trade in corn should be free, and that imported corn should be subject to no other duty than such as we might find it expedient to impose on corn of our own growth.[121]

In this passage, Ricardo addressed the same 'humanity' exception that was registered by Smith, Parnell, and Torrens, replacing 'humanity' with the adjective 'just'. At this point Smith had marshalled the weight of the natural law tradition, and this points to an important aspect of Ricardo's intellectual formation: he entered this intellectual milieu from the outside, as it were, and not through a

---

[118] Ibid., 31.
[119] Though note that Sergio Cremaschi has thrown doubt on Ricardo's subscription to providence as an ordering force in the world: Cremaschi, 'Theological Themes in Ricardo's Papers and Correspondence', 798–9.
[120] Ricardo, 'An Essay on the Influence of a low Price of Corn on the Profits of Stock', 33.
[121] Ibid.

Scottish or English educational institution. Note further that in this same passage Ricardo also incorporated Smith's equality of taxation precept by stipulating that the duties on imported corn be limited to those borne by domestic producers.[122] Although this stricture represented Ricardo's conflation of two separate issues, it nevertheless stood as a significant modification of his position on free trade, representing the seemingly passive absorption and reproduction of existing arguments. More specifically, Smith's science was organized around the conduct of an enlightened statesman; Ricardo was attempting to discover the truth and then project its absorption by the legislature. His defence of restrictive duties because they were 'just' was thus a contextual accretion, not an example of the type of legislative judgement that defined the statesman's office, the light in which Smith's exceptions to a policy of free trade should be seen.[123] Once again, it is necessary to centre Parliament when identifying the context in which to read Ricardo's text since it is that context and its reception of Smith that makes the presence of these aspects of his text intelligible.

What of Ricardo's concern for 'the lower classes of society'?[124] Malthus argued that free trade would reduce the money price of corn, harming the interests of labour as wages were dragged down in connection with corn. Ricardo conceded that some of Malthus's claims possessed great weight, but he perceived Malthus as having failed to fully acknowledge the favourable effects that an improved distribution of capital would hold for labour. For, once capital was diverted to manufacturing, the same quantity would employ more hands and return a higher level of profit, enabling further accumulation and employment, lifting the wages of labour and improving their condition as a result. Malthus's argument regarding the manufacturing class received a similar rebuttal. Where Malthus had identified only a small proportion of this class as engaged in foreign trade and hence standing to benefit from free trade, Ricardo's identification of an inextricable link between the level of profits in agriculture and manufacturing meant that the entire class would gain from the raised level of profits.[125] A more general level of analysis was again used to respecify the circumstances of the case.

One place where Ricardo did descend into contextual detail related to Malthus's fourth class: those who received salaries and fixed incomes. Malthus had claimed that this group would benefit from free importation as the cheap

---

[122] A position repeated in *On Protection to Agriculture*, where the tithes and poor rates were named as taxes falling on corn (Ricardo, 'On Protection to Agriculture', *Works and Correspondence*, 4: 201–66, at 218–19).

[123] A case made at length in Walter, 'Adam Smith's Free Trade Casuistry'.

[124] Ricardo, 'An Essay on the Influence of a low Price of Corn on the Profits of Stock', 35.

[125] Ibid., 35–6. Note also Ricardo's discussion of class interests in *On Protection to Agriculture*: Ricardo, 'On Protection to Agriculture', 246.

corn lowered prices generally, thus increasing the real value of a fixed dividend or salary. Ricardo conceded this point but then presented it as representing a measure of compensation for the losses that this class had suffered during the war, since rising prices for corn and paper currency had eroded their wealth. This class had also suffered from the 'violation of solemn contracts', by which expression Ricardo meant Nicholas Vansittart's raids on the Sinking Fund when Minister of Finance, and Ricardo feared that more of the same was to come, in direct violation of the intentions of William Pitt.[126] This claim was an attack on the present state of Britain's national debt. It was not, therefore, an exercise in balancing principles identified by an overarching moral framework such as natural jurisprudence or natural theology, but an attempt to win the rhetorical points that could be won. Ricardo was not providing a framework in which legislators could comprehend difficult policy questions; he was providing partisan advocacy.

Having replaced Malthus's delicate class calculus with his own tendentious account, Ricardo could conclude that the only true loser from free trade would be the landlord, a creature whom Ricardo's analysis of distribution rendered in abstract terms—as the receiver of revenue created by capitalist farmers.[127] Compared to Malthus, Ricardo's arguments relied on a theoretical description of the interested parties, a providential-rationalist account of foreign markets, and an attack on a standing Minister in the name of the inviolability of contracts. It resolved the question in favour of importing corn because it was seen to advantage the nation at large, this gain being found to outweigh the dangers identified by the dependency argument. This was all brought to a head in the conclusion to the pamphlet, where Ricardo set his analysis of the public interest in opposition to the power of a class in Parliament. He wrote that good policy could hardly be achieved if 'considerations for any particular class' were 'allowed to check the progress of the wealth and population of the country' but, if this were the aim of Parliament, then not only ought the importation of corn be prohibited but improvements in farming technology should also be blocked because they also reduced the landlord's rent.[128] In other words, if landlords were to use their political power to pursue a narrow sectional interest at the expense of the nation, then they ought to do it systematically and hold back the tide of progress. In these comments we see the balancing judgement of casuistry being subordinated to a class polemic.

---

[126] Ricardo, 'An Essay on the Influence of a low Price of Corn on the Profits of Stock', 40. See [Nicholas Vansittart], Outlines of a Plan of Finance; Proposed to be Submitted to Parliament (London, 1813). Ricardo enlarged on this theme in his Funding System: Ricardo, 'Funding System', Works and Correspondence, 4: 143–200, at 159–60.

[127] Ricardo, 'An Essay on the Influence of a low Price of Corn on the Profits of Stock', 40.

[128] Ibid., 41.

Conclusion

Enough has now been said to substantiate some important claims. The first is that casuistry was the means with which the leading political economists addressed the question of free trade—by adducing circumstances that could modify the application of accepted principles. Indeed, the frequency with which these terms were used—'case', 'circumstances', 'exceptions', and 'principles'—is taken to be one of the best pieces of evidence. Malthus, for example, used 'actual state' seven times in his *Grounds of an Opinion* and 'actual circumstances' three times, while both expressions appeared in the concluding paragraph to the pamphlet.[129] Equally important is the way that these thinkers were able to express the notion that making exceptions to general rules was simply a necessary element of political judgement. Parnell, for example, wrote of the rules that Smith 'lays down for making exceptions to the general rule of a complete freedom of trade'.[130] Malthus similarly rejected 'the doctrine, that we are to pursue our general principles without ever looking to see if they are applicable to the case before us'.[131] Torrens claimed that 'every general principle, however evident its abstract truth may be, is, in its application to particular circumstances, liable to exceptions and limitations'.[132] Finally, Ricardo insisted that the 'question' could only be contested in favour of restrictions in view of 'the danger of dependence on foreign countries'.[133]

This is not to deny the obvious diversity among the styles of casuistical reasoning considered so far. Malthus's happiness calculus, for example, translated higher and lower goals of statesmanship into a common element to facilitate comparison—their contribution to human happiness. The notions of virtue and happiness were sourced from Protestant theology, but the focus on consequences was an established procedure in casuistry. In this sense, we should not call Malthus's approach 'theological utilitarianism' but rather invert the picture and wonder if utilitarianism were not an outgrowth of casuistry.[134] Torrens made no such move and instead followed Smith by treating justice and taxation as grounds for exceptions to be made by the enlightened statesman, who was imagined to be the political actor. Torrens also introduced the food supply as a further consideration, possibly indicating the influence of Malthus on the debate. Ricardo was tongue-tied on questions of the relative priority of state ends, and some possible reasons for why this was the case have been suggested in this book's Introduction. However, Ricardo was prepared to describe famines as

---

[129] Malthus, 'The Importation of Foreign Corn', 174.
[130] [Parnell], *The Substance of the Speeches of Sir H. Parnell*, 53.
[131] Malthus, 'The Importation of Foreign Corn', 158.
[132] Torrens, *An Essay on the External Corn Trade* (1815), 97.
[133] Ricardo, 'An Essay on the Influence of a low Price of Corn on the Profits of Stock', 26.
[134] Condren, *Argument and Authority in Early Modern England*, 184.

causing 'evil', and this might represent his attempt to weigh disparate phenomena in the scales of happiness and misery, analogous to Malthus's manner of proceeding. Overall, though, Ricardo was distinctive because of the minimal role of probability in the structure of his argument. His faith in markets was seemingly underwritten by his rationalist-Unitarian commitments. In summary, while the casuistry of each thinker was influenced by a broader set of assumptions and beliefs, intellectual inheritance, and contextual factors, we must still register the distance between their manner of pondering free trade and our own.

This, it is hopefully clear, reverses the standard account of this period as one in which Ricardo's theoretical brilliance shone through as he began to perceive theoretical concepts in the half-light of his historical circumstances, leaving behind his peers Malthus and Torrens. Once the preoccupations of rational reconstruction are abandoned, it becomes possible to see that these early debates over free trade in Britain were conducted using a casuistry of reason of state. In this genre, Ricardo was not the star but the awkward beginner, while Malthus and Torrens displayed great skill as casuists proffering reasoning apparatuses for legislators that were able to handle the fact that statecraft required balancing multiple goals.

Another revision follows close behind. Namely, once casuistry is recognized as the form of argument, the supposed contest between free trade and protection becomes a far more nuanced affair. To see this point, consider the case of Malthus, who should not be characterized as either a free trader or a protectionist. In this respect, Samuel Hollander's claim that Malthus underwent 'a profound reorientation of analytical perspective' such that we can speak of his 'abandonment' of 'protectionism' reveals a presentist bias.[135] Free trade and protection are rival positions today, and we tend to think in terms of 'isms', but this was not the world of Malthus and Ricardo. Instead, Malthus was recommending a course of action in view of a calculation capable of deriving either free trade or protection as the right policy since the conclusion was taken to depend not on one's 'ism' but on the situation confronting one's nation and its interests. Hollander may be right to claim that Malthus changed his mind later in life as he observed industrial buoyancy and revised certain of his theoretical positions.[136] However, if this is so, it should hardly come as a surprise since it was shown that both the circumstances and theoretical specification of a case were crucial for arriving at a policy recommendation. In other words, casuists routinely changed their minds as the facts changed, and they did so without undergoing transformations in their mental worlds. As John Pullen suggested some decades ago, once we see what Malthus was up to, many of the accusations of inconsistency

---

[135] Hollander, 'Malthus's Abandonment of Agricultural Protectionism', 650.
[136] But it seems that Hollander's handling of evidence obliges us to suspect that he is not. See J. M. Pullen, 'Malthus on Agricultural Protection: An Alternative View', *History of Political Economy* 27/3 (1995), 517–29.

melt away.[137] Instead of a world of either/or thinking, Malthus occupied one in which it was widely accepted that, in the words of Burke, 'Political reason is a computing principle'.[138] Ricardo, however, does look like a doctrinal thinker in comparison to his peers, but from the perspective of our own doctrinal times we struggle to notice this fact.

[137] Pullen, 'Malthus on the Doctrine of Proportions and the Concept of the Optimum', 270.
[138] Burke, 'Reflections on the Revolution in France', Writings and Speeches, 112.

PART III

Introduction to Part III

The Greater Stakes of Doctrinal Contest, 1817–1820

The focus of the remaining three chapters is the doctrinal contest between Malthus and Ricardo, as found in the first and second editions of Ricardo's *Principles of Political Economy, and Taxation* (1817 and 1819), and Malthus's reply text, *Principles of Political Economy. Considered with a View to Their Practical Application* (1820). By its very nature, the inquiry must investigate fine distinctions developed within recondite argumentation. Yet it is a leading claim of this book's overall argument that these doctrinal contests hold a significance to the history of economic thought beyond their character as doctrinal contests, even if the doctrinal details are important.

Two such non-doctrinal features of the confrontation that occurred between Malthus and Ricardo are emphasized in what follows. The first is the vocabulary that both thinkers used to assess or justify a given piece of doctrinal argumentation and the values that this vocabulary invoked regarding the production of knowledge and its role in society. This requires a particular focus. Accordingly, questions such as, 'What was the content of doctrine X?' must be supplemented with a different type of question; in particular, 'What were Ricardo and Malthus trying to achieve by the articulation of doctrine X?' As we have seen, the short answer is this: to realize rival intellectual comportments as defining the role of the political economist. The rivalry here criss-crosses the issues that have been central to the argument so far, including the appropriate way to combine theory and practice, the emerging tensions between notions of counsel and science, clashing religious beliefs, and the ethical demands that the political economist was to meet.

The second feature of the Malthus–Ricardo contest to be foregrounded concerns what might be roughly called its genre. That is, the very fact that certain political economists—preeminently Ricardo—had come to think of their task as the articulation of correct doctrine is an event to be marked. For this signals a mutation in political economy's forms of argument, in comparison to authors such as David Hume and Adam Smith and certainly in comparison to the waves of literature that parliamentary debate routinely called forth. Even though the production of correct doctrine remained a minority pursuit in the period under study, it appears to have had profound consequences for the way that we write the history of political economy and economics today, since we have been writing

Before Method and Models. Ryan Walter, Oxford University Press. © Oxford University Press 2021.
DOI: 10.1093/oso/9780197603055.003.0006

doctrinal histories of one form or another ever since.[1] For this reason, doctrinal exegesis is not taken to be an end in itself in this book since the existence of doctrinal argumentation as a rival to other idioms—such as counsel and pedagogy—is a fact to be accounted for historically and not simply assumed as the natural form for economic knowledge to take.

Before turning to these issues, a few words on the texts are in order. Ricardo's *Principles* was an outgrowth of his *Essay on Profits* (1815) and shared its concern to identify the laws that governed the distribution of produce between labour, capitalists, and landholders, with a special focus on the relationship between profits and rent. The *Essay* was published in late February of 1815, coinciding with parliamentary debate over the Corn Laws, as we saw in Chapter 3. Its essential point was that restraints on the importation of foreign corn would hurt profits and production while impelling rents ever upwards. The original idea behind the text that became the *Principles* was for an expanded version of this argument, but it seems that by October of 1815 James Mill was already thinking of the work as a book. As Sraffa notes, the text was developed under the headings 'rent, profits, wages'.[2] But Ricardo foresaw that value would complicate things for both his work and his readers.

> I know I shall be soon stopped by the word price. . . . Before my readers can understand the proof I mean to offer, they must understand the theory of currency and of price.[3]

Ricardo was indeed stopped, but not for long enough. For Ricardo built on Smith's suggestion that exchange values reflected labour values only to then discover a problem once divergent capital–labour ratios were worked through the analysis. This demanded a rewrite of the manuscript to incorporate the new insights into the chapters that were already drafted, but it never happened. Worse, chapter 1 was seriously flawed. In Terry Peach's words, it was 'replete with unanswered questions, misplaced material, and internal contradictions'.[4] The issues were addressed only cosmetically in the second edition, which Ricardo essentially took one week to prepare, and it was published in February 1819.[5] In short, the composition of Ricardo's *Principles* partly explains its difficulty, and Mill's exhortation that Ricardo write for

---

[1] Starting with J. R. R. McCulloch, *A Discourse on the Rise, Progress, Peculiar Objects and Importance of Political Economy* (Edinburgh, 1824); J. R. R. McCulloch, *The Literature of Political Economy: A Classified Catalogue of Select Publications in the Different Departments of that Science, with Historical, Critical and Biographical Notices* (Edinburgh, 1845). In this latter text, see especially McCulloch's annotations in chapter 1.

[2] Sraffa, 'Introduction', *Works and Correspondence*, 1: xiii–lxii, at xiv.

[3] Ricardo, 'Ricardo to Mill', *Works and Correspondence*, 6: 347–9, at 348.

[4] Peach, *Interpreting Ricardo*, 154, and see footnote on that page.

[5] Sraffa, 'Introduction', 1: l.

'people ignorant of the subject' had little effect in making it accessible.[6] The text is better viewed as an outgrowth of an extended debate between two people who were crafting a new vocation for themselves and trying to win acceptance for it in the wider world. It was, in other words, an ambitious text despite being remarkably idiosyncratic, as we shall see.

It seems inevitable that Malthus would be drawn into debate with Ricardo in view of their friendship and intellectual rivalry. The latter probably reached its most intense moment with the publication of Malthus's own *Principles* (1820). By the time Malthus came to publish this text, he had seen the first two editions of Ricardo's text and had been practising his attacks in their personal correspondence.[7] Malthus gathered his challenges together under his titular banner: 'practical application'. Malthus further clarified the nature of his challenge in his introduction, a remarkable statement of his rival vision for political economy. In it Malthus explicitly identified two primary modes of reasoning in political economy that attached to two opposing groups, the so-called practical writers, on the one hand, and their scientific antagonists, on the other, in which latter group he and Ricardo were to be counted. The practical writers drew inferences from partial facts, and too quickly, while certain theoretical writers did not use facts at all and refused to submit 'their theories to the test of experience', a pathology for 'minds of a certain cast'; *sotto voce*, a pathology of Ricardo's mind.[8] Theory might be indispensable, but the good theorist needed to keep in mind that the whole enterprise was to serve legislators and their advisers. Malthus was consequently prepared to state his leading purpose as follows: 'to prepare the general rules of political economy for practical application, by a frequent reference to experience'.[9] Not all theorists did this, hence not all theory was safe to present to legislators. In short, Malthus's desire to realize the proper relationship between theory and practice is the key difference between their rival publications. The context for making sense of this difference in historical terms is the debate over theory that occurred in the long shadow of the French Revolution, discussed in Chapter 1.

A final feature of this clash of texts to bring to view is their structures. Ricardo's book was conceived with doctrinal ambitions—to publicly correct Adam Smith and J. B. Say and Malthus. In fact, Ricardo found time to read Smith and ponder where to insert his corrections to the doctrines that he discovered in *Wealth of Nations* while waiting to hear of the birth of his first grandchild.

---

[6] Mill, 'Mill to Ricardo', *Works and Correspondence*, 6: 337–41, at 339.

[7] Some to tremendous effect. See Peach, *Interpreting Ricardo*, 191–4. Malthus had also previewed some sections of his *Principles* to Ricardo, see Ricardo, 'Ricardo to Malthus', *Works and Correspondence*, 7: 282–5; Ricardo, 'Ricardo to Mill', *Works and Correspondence*, 7: 371–3.

[8] Malthus, 'Principles of Political Economy: Part I', 7, 10.

[9] Ibid., 16.

It is my intention to read Adam Smith once more, to take notes of all passages which very much favor, or are directly opposed to my peculiar opinions, and shall afterwards submit to you the propriety of inserting them in the proper places of my MS. In reading Adam Smith my attention may be called to other points which I may think it important to notice. . . .

I could have wished to remain at Gatcomb till the anxious time was past, but Mrs. Ricardo considers my presence as the greatest comfort to her, and she has so often told me so that I at last begin to believe her; I am therefore in quiet possession of a snug dressing room with Adam Smith and Say on my table, and pass my time with very few more interruptions that I should meet at Gatcomb.[10]

This ambition is visible in Ricardo's language throughout, and in his chapter titles, such as chapter 24, 'Doctrine of Adam Smith concerning the Rent of Land', and chapter 29 (first edition), 'Mr. Malthus's Opinions on Rent'. Even more tellingly, it is reflected in the chapter structure of Ricardo's text, and it seems that, either consciously or unconsciously, Malthus followed Ricardo's lead. This is shown in Table I.III.1.

We have, in other words, doctrinal competition as the form that Ricardo adopted for contributing to his field. Ricardo developed this template by reading Smith as if he were also producing doctrine and then correcting Smith's errors, while Malthus seems to have been drawn into this form by the need to respond to his great rival at the same time as he attempted to dispense political economy's counselling duties. Looking forward, doctrinal competition achieved the status of common sense in the twentieth century, as in, for example, monetarist and post-Keynesian positions on the money supply as being exogenous or endogenous.[11] But it was not a dominant practice in the time of Malthus and Ricardo because political economy was still tethered to its counselling duties. Nevertheless, Ricardo's focus on doctrinal truth had profound implications for how Smith's text would be read after his and Malthus's *Principles* were published for they provided resources for treating Smith as an early and flawed theorist and for it to be forgotten that Smith had conceived of political economy as a subbranch of the science of the statesman, anchored in natural law jurisprudence and his linked account of human sociability's unfolding in historical time.[12]

The texts of Malthus and Ricardo also established competition between the art of application and theoretical ingenuity as the leading goal of the science, where the latter could lead to 'discoveries' or 'novel' conclusions. Ricardo's

[10] Ricardo, 'Ricardo to Mill', *Works and Correspondence*, 7: 87–90, at 88–9.

[11] See, for example, Nicholas Kaldor's treatment of monetarism under the heading 'Elements of New Doctrine': Nicholas Kaldor, 'The New Monetarism', *Lloyds Bank Review* 97/1 (1970), 1–18, at 2–5.

[12] It is true in a superficial sense that Smith also reviewed rival systems of political economy and detected their errors, hence he used titles such as 'Of the Unreasonableness of those Restraints Even

Table I.III.1 Chapter structures for Smith, Ricardo, and Malthus

Adam Smith _Wealth of Nations_ Book I	David Ricardo _Principles_ 2nd Edition	Robert Malthus _Principles_ 1st Edition
Ch. v Of the real and nominal Price of Commodities Ch. vi Of the component Parts of the Price of Commodities	Ch. i On Value	Ch. i On the Definitions of Wealth and Productive Labour Ch. ii On the Nature and Measures of Value Ch. vi Of the Distinction between Wealth and Value
	Ch. ii On Rent	Ch. iii Of the Rent of Land
	Ch. iii On the Rent of Mines	
Ch. vii Of the natural and Market Price of Commodities	Ch. iv On Natural and Market Price	
Ch. viii Of the Wages of Labour	Ch. v On Wages	Ch. iv Of the Wages of Labour
Ch. ix Of the Profits of Stock	Ch. vi On Profits	Ch. v Of the Profits of Capital
Ch. x Of Wages and Profit in the different Employments of Labour and Stock		
Ch. xi Of the Rent of Land		
	Ch. vii On Foreign Trade	Ch. vii On the Immediate Causes of the Progress of Wealth Section viii Of the Distribution occasioned by Commerce, internal and external, considered as the Means of increasing the exchangeable Value of the whole Produce.

Note: This presentation follows Sraffa, using Ricardo's chapter progression to structure the table, setting it out in the order in which it was published in his _Principles_, then noting the equivalent chapters from Smith and Malthus.

argumentation thus threatened to be autonomous, in the sense that it produced technical doctrines that were valuable in view of their theoretical insights, not in view of their ability to lead legislators towards judicious lawmaking. This is one of the aspects of Ricardo's work that alarmed Malthus since it was clear that supervening on practical life on the basis of theory and guiding statesmen were ambitions embodied in Ricardo's text, but Ricardo had abandoned the usual mechanisms for doing so. Above all, in the *Principles*, Ricardo dispensed with the placatory rhetoric of his writings on bullion in which he attempted to use practice and experience as tests for theory. Ricardo also isolated considerations of wealth, while we have seen that in his intervention into the Corn Laws debate Ricardo allowed that security was a rival goal of government even if he did not find it to be a compelling consideration in that case. Although Malthus's table of contents shows that he allowed Ricardo to set the terms of debate to a significant degree, Malthus constantly tried to restore the art of application and practice, to account for facts, and to protest against the neglect of these precepts by Ricardo as dangerous. To summarize, the contest between Malthus and Ricardo must be recognized as doctrinal in nature, but it must also be studied with respect to the broader phenomena that this book has been concerned to recover in pursuit of historical understanding: vocabulary, theology, the ethical government of one's mind, and the multiple ends of statecraft. Attempting to do this while paying due regard to the doctrines is the aim of the chapters that follow.

Upon the Principles of the Mercantile System' (Smith, *WN*, IV.iii.a). Yet there are crucial differences to register. Above all, these errors were not simply identified in the manner of reviewing earlier articulations of doctrine from political economists and correcting errors for the present generation, as we find Ricardo presented his work. Rather, the errors of the mercantile system were traced to their imbrication with the interests and habits of a certain section of the community. That is, identifying the sources of legislative perversion was an aspect of the larger project being pursued by Smith, one that was historical and historiographical in key respects. See Knud Haakonssen, *The Science of a Legislator: The Natural Jurisprudence of David Hume and Adam Smith* (Cambridge: Cambridge University Press, 1981), 99–177.

4

Doctrinal Contest I

Value

For readers familiar with the writings of Malthus and Ricardo, the search for a standard of real value is tolerably comprehensible. For outsiders to the discipline, by contrast, the very notion is arcane. The challenge lies in coming to understand why anybody would follow Malthus and make a claim of this type: 'The difficulty is, to find a measure of real value in exchange, in contradistinction to nominal value or price'.[1] The challenge arises because today we are comfortable using price as a measure of value, and so we tend not to perceive Malthus's difficulty. Furthermore, when we do find that the general level of prices has changed through time, we are content to adjust these prices using index numbers, making it possible to speak of real and nominal prices. Some of Ricardo's contemporaries seemed to be thinking of a similar solution.[2]

Ricardo explicitly rejected this idea, however, because he had submitted to the dream of getting behind market prices to perceive the true nature of value, and he pursued this phantom until his death.[3] In his *Principles*, Ricardo made his attempt by using labour as a measure of value, at times writing as if he were dealing with the essence of value. The resulting arguments that Ricardo unfolded in the first chapter of his text stand as a classic example of how a preexisting pattern of argumentation can be raised to a higher level of abstraction and its abstractness then embraced, ignored, or resisted.[4] In the course of working through the effects of his innovation, Ricardo encountered unexpected results, most famously regarding the relationship between wage increases and price increases. Ricardo presented his discovery as a doctrinal breakthrough: 'These results are of such importance to the science of political economy, yet accord so little with some of its received doctrines'.[5] By contrast, with his eye on 'practical application', Malthus took a dim view of Ricardo's originality.[6]

---

[1] Malthus, 'Principles of Political Economy: Part II', *Works*, 6: 379.
[2] See, for example, Davies Giddy [Davies Gilbert], *A Plain Statement of the Bullion Question, in a Letter to a Friend* (London, 1811), 30.
[3] See the incomplete manuscript written in the last few weeks of his life: Ricardo 'Absolute and Exchangeable Value', *Works and Correspondence*, 4: 357–412, at 400–1.
[4] See the discussion in Pocock, *Political Thought and History*, 17–18.
[5] Ricardo, 'On the Principles of Political Economy and Taxation', *Works and Correspondence*, 1: 61.
[6] Malthus, 'Principles of Political Economy: Part II', 377.

Before Method and Models. Ryan Walter, Oxford University Press. © Oxford University Press 2021.
DOI: 10.1093/oso/9780197603055.003.0007

In fact, Malthus made Ricardo's treatment of value a defining point of their doctrinal competition and claimed that his own work continued Smith's alternative and superior approach. Malthus then took the opportunity to affirm this negative position on Ricardian value theory in his response to J. R. R. McCulloch's *Encyclopaedia* entry on political economy, in which Malthus presented value as the first principle that characterized the 'new school of political economy', declaring that the fixation on labour as the source of value represented a 'desire of simplification' that was 'inexcusable in the political economist'.[7] In short, value represented a flashpoint in the broader struggle to define political economy and the ideal conduct of the political economist.

The first step in approaching Ricardo's formidable opening chapter, 'On Value', is to understand that his essential claim represented a repurposing of some of Adam Smith's comments—that goods will exchange in a ratio determined by the quantities of labour required for their production.[8] This allowed Ricardo to assert his central claim—that profits would fall as difficulty of production in agriculture rose—without explaining how labour costs were transmuted into prices.[9] Labour theory was thus a means for incorporating the central insight of the *Essay on Profits* into the expansive new *Principles*. Furthermore, by including labour that was embodied in capital equipment, Ricardo could also use the theory to account for exchange ratios between industrial goods. In other words, 'labour' was simply standing in for difficulty of production, whether by human or machine. The fatal complication that Ricardo introduced was to notice the effect of the ratio of fixed to circulating capital. These points are first established in what follows before introducing Malthus's riposte.

Ricardo Corrects Smith

Ricardo began by treating Smith as an authority and an ally. We therefore find him quoting certain of Smith's statements in *Wealth of Nations* that concerned use value and exchange value. This pattern of quotation was not for the purpose of reconstructing Smith's meaning, however, but for invoking Smith's sanction. In particular, Ricardo used Smith to underwrite his decision to disqualify

---

[7] McCulloch's entry was republished as a standalone pamphlet in 1825 as J. R. R. McCulloch, *Outlines of Political Economy: Being a Republication of the Article Upon that Subject Contained in the Edinburgh Supplement to the Encyclopedia Britannica* (New York, 1825). Malthus, 'On Political Economy', *Works*, 7: 255–97, at 268, 270.

[8] Ricardo, 'On the Principles of Political Economy and Taxation', 13. All references are to the second edition, unless indicated otherwise.

[9] Peach, *Interpreting Ricardo*, 150.

utility as a source of value.[10] Ricardo's own account held that commodities that did not gratify humans in some way would not be exchanged, hence, utility was a precondition for value, not its source. The other claim advanced in *Wealth of Nations* that Ricardo reworked was of far greater importance than the notion of utility: the idea that quantities of labour could explain exchange ratios.

Ricardo's evidence primarily came from chapters 5 and 6 of Book I of *Wealth of Nations*, where Smith dealt with real and nominal prices and the component parts of price, respectively. Smith elaborated the essential message in the following two passages:

> Labour alone, therefore, never varying in its own value, is alone the ultimate and real standard by which the value of all commodities can at all times and places be estimated and compared. It is their real price; money is their nominal price only.[11]
>
> In that early and rude state of society . . . the proportion between the quantities of labour necessary for acquiring different objects seems to be the only circumstance which can afford any rule for exchanging them for one another. If among a nation of hunters, for example, it usually costs twice the labour to kill a beaver which it does to kill a deer, one beaver should naturally exchange for or be worth two deer.[12]

In order for us to obtain a measure of historical distance from Ricardo's reading of Smith, it is necessary to note the role that these arguments played in *Wealth of Nations*. In brief, Smith's claim was derived from his account of commercial society: as the division of labour organized society's production into increasingly specialized subtasks, individuals were faced with the necessity of selling the products of their labour in exchange for the labour of others. This was done through bartering commodities at first, but then through the use of metallic currencies. In consequence, people tended not to think in terms of labour quantity, which was merely 'an abstract notion', but in terms of currency, which 'determines the prudence or imprudence of all purchases and sales'.[13]

Since everyday life was lived using currency prices, why bother with the abstract notion of real prices? Smith's answer was that it 'may sometimes be of considerable use in practice'.[14] Smith had especially in mind specifying *reddenda* and comparing prices across time and space. The real price of labour was the

---

[10] Ricardo, 'On the Principles of Political Economy and Taxation', 11. Smith, *WN* I.iv.13. The purpose of Smith's comments was to highlight the complex set of factors underlying value, thus motivating the reader's 'patience and attention' over the next three chapters: Smith, *WN* I.iv.18.

[11] Smith, *WN* I.v.7.

[12] Ibid., I.vi.1.

[13] Ibid., I.v.5, 21.

[14] Ibid., I.v.10

quantity of necessaries and conveniences for which it would exchange, above all, corn. This is why Smith asserted that, across time, the quantity of corn given for labour would be less variable than the quantity of any other commodity and that equal quantities of corn could likewise best be estimated using labour.[15] In other words, and as we might say today, Smith was defending his choice of unit for transhistorical measurement, not attempting to define an invariable measure of value.

Smith explicitly stated as much: 'Labour, therefore . . . is the only universal, as well as the only accurate measure of value, or the only standard by which we can compare the values of different commodities at all times and at all places'.[16] Smith then added some complications. For example, from year to year, silver was likely to be more stable, and hence it stood as the preferred measure, but across centuries the price of labour in corn was best. Given the availability of sources, however, the price would normally need to be reckoned in terms of corn because it was better recorded by historians than prices of labour.[17] In typical fashion, Smith devoted the remainder of the chapter to historical details concerning the adoption of different metals as the standard in different nations, from the Romans to contemporary Britain, along with the practices of merchants and creditors in estimating payments in the face of variations in the quality of coined money.[18]

A similar point holds for Smith's discussion of the component parts of price in chapter 6, where Smith similarly used labour as the unit by which to measure the different sources of a society's annual revenue. Unlike 'rude' society, in commercial society the price of most commodities was composed of wages, profits, and rent. In consequence, the nation's annual produce was 'parcelled out among different inhabitants of the country, either as the wages of their labour, the profits of their stock, or the rent of their land'.[19] This tripartite division was used by Smith when it came to understanding the question signalled in the title of his work— why some nations progressed in wealth and why others regressed. The answer was that in poor nations the mass of the people were maintained out of the revenue of the wealthier members of the society, and this mired the nation in poverty because the process of accumulating productive labour was continually forestalled. In nations such as England, however, the people were supported by capital in the form of wages, which rendered them industrious and thriving.[20] Taking an overall view of this discussion of Smith, we can say that the notion that labour was the

---

[15] Ibid., I.v.15.
[16] Ibid., I.v.17
[17] Ibid., I.v.22.
[18] Ibid., I.v.23–41.
[19] Ibid., I.vi.17.
[20] Ibid., II.iii.7–12.

real measure of value was a means of penetrating below the confusion of national currencies and fluctuating prices when engaging in historical and analytical description of the progress of wealth. Labour was only an improvised tool for Smith.

With this account of Smith in mind, we are now in a position to answer the question: What did Ricardo do with Smith's argumentation? He first quoted selected passages from chapters 5 and 6 of *Wealth of Nations*, in which Smith described labour as 'the real price',[21] 'the first price',[22] and the basis of exchange in the 'rude state of society'.[23] Ricardo then construed these statements as constituting a 'doctrine', which he elevated to a central and yet fraught position in the science of political economy.

> That this is really the foundation of the exchangeable value of all things . . . is a doctrine of the utmost importance in political economy; for from no source do so many errors, and so much difference of opinion in that science proceed, as from the vague ideas which are attached to the word value.[24]

It turns out, however, that this was not Ricardo offering a judicious assessment of the state of the field and its conceptual problems but an *ad hoc* rationalization of his own decision to restate in more general terms his argument from the *Essay* regarding the increasing difficulty of production on the land.[25]

> If the quantity of labour realized in commodities, regulate their exchangeable value, every increase of the quantity of labour must augment the value of that commodity on which it is exercised, as every diminution must lower it.[26]

Now the difficulty of production on the land was simply a particular instance of a more general account of value.

The result of Ricardo's intervention was to elevate the labour–value relation into a governing truth for the science. From here, Ricardo could create a retrospective history in which Smith had glimpsed this truth but then prevaricated: 'Sometimes he [Smith] speaks of corn, at other times of labour, as a standard measure; not the quantity of labour bestowed . . . but the quantity which

---

[21] 'The real price of every thing, what every thing really costs to the man who wants to acquire it, is the toil and trouble of acquiring it' (Ibid., I.v.2).

[22] 'Labour was the first price, the original purchase-money that was paid for all things' (Ibid.).

[23] 'This separation too is generally carried furthest in those countries which enjoy the highest degree of industry and improvement; what is the work of one man, in a rude state of society, being generally that of several in an improved one' (Ibid., I.i.4). For Ricardo's quotation of Smith, see Ricardo, 'On the Principles of Political Economy and Taxation', 12–13.

[24] Ricardo, 'On the Principles of Political Economy and Taxation', 13.

[25] Following Peach, *Interpreting Ricardo*, 88, and, in a different way, Tribe, *Land, Labour and Economic Discourse*, 133.

[26] Ricardo, 'On the Principles of Political Economy and Taxation', 13.

it can command'.[27] By conscripting Smith's scattered comments into a flawed doctrinal statement, Ricardo could ignore the fact that Smith was really offering a defence of his unit of measurement when engaging in historical reconstruction. Of course, fidelity to Smith's text was never a part of Ricardo's purpose because his task was not historiography but doctrinal restatement in the pursuit of theoretical progress. The effect of Ricardo's history was to suggest that the divisions and errors that marred political economy in his time could be explained by Smith's inconsistency regarding the nature of value. Ricardo's rhetorical achievement was to motivate his search for an invariable standard of value.

As noted, some thinkers of the period were pursuing a rival course of inquiry by articulating notions of overall prices. That is, these writers were not pursuing the abstract idea of an invariable standard of value but searching for units of measurement that would be useful when investigating policy problems and commercial history. Ricardo, however, became fixated on his own notion, seemingly because he viewed it as essential to determining 'correct theory'.

> If any one commodity could be found, which now and at all times required precisely the same quantity of labour to produce it, that commodity would be of an unvarying value. . . . Of such a commodity we have no knowledge, and consequently are unable to fix on any standard of value. It is, however, of considerable use towards attaining a correct theory, to ascertain what the essential qualities of a standard are, that we may know the causes of the variation in the relative value of commodities, and that we may be enabled to calculate the degree in which they are likely to operate.[28]

This is a defining aspect of Ricardo's thought in this text, and it represents a turning away from studying value in relation to supply and demand, thus setting him at odds with Malthus, who would portray Ricardo and Smith as the exponents of two divergent 'systems'.[29] Ricardo's commitment to an invariable standard whose qualities could only be discerned conceptually and for the purpose of developing 'correct theory' was a wilful decision in a context of ceaseless attacks on political economy for being metaphysical and scholastic and for departing from experience. Indeed, Ricardo's decision exposed him to these very allegations.

The decision appears more remarkable in view of Ricardo's acknowledgement of the existence of different *qualities* of labour in the world. In making this concession, Ricardo relabelled Smith's notion of 'esteem' as 'estimation' and claimed that the regard in which different types of labour were held was determined by

---

[27] Ibid., 14.
[28] Ibid., 17.
[29] Malthus, 'Principles of Political Economy: Part I', 58.

the 'skill' and 'intensity' that they embodied, casually replacing Smith's notions of 'hardship' and 'ingenuity'.[30] Ricardo was attempting to extend the analysis of his *Essay on Profits*, a pamphlet intervention into parliamentary debate, into an extended treatise, but he did not choose the path of opening out these complications for study but of waving them off the page. This is why Ricardo mentioned the variable quality of labour to only then abstract away from this inconvenient fact by claiming that the market adjusted its 'estimation' of labour over generations, hence it could be ignored in his particular investigation into changes in relative values.[31] By contrast, Smith's comments represented a rationalization of wage differences using concepts drawn from his account of moral sentiments.[32]

Ricardo's reception of *Wealth of Nations* also effaced the purpose of Smith's account of society in its rude state. Ricardo presented Smith as believing that it was only in the rude state of society that exchange values were determined by labour, while in the more advanced stages of civilization, Smith supposedly claimed, profits and rent would enter as components of price. In what has become an enduring trope of rational reconstruction, Smith was taken to task for failing to answer somebody else's question: 'Adam Smith, however, has no where analyzed the effects of the accumulation of capital . . . on relative value'.[33] A fairer description would have noted that Smith used his account of capital accumulation to narrate the formation of Europe's 'retrograde order' (Book III) and to explain why the system of natural liberty would produce superior results regarding capital allocation (Books II and IV) except when higher ends of statecraft were at issue (Book V). But this was not to Ricardo's purpose.

The gap between Smith and Ricardo was also visible in Ricardo's idiosyncratic approach to capital accumulation. The nerve of Ricardo's argument was that capital was always present in the production process. It was present even in Smith's example of hunting deer and beaver in society's earliest stages because it was embodied in the weapons that hunters used. The labour contained in these weapons had a durability beyond the act of production and could therefore be thought of as stored labour, or capital. Producing this capital formed a part of the total labour needed to produce deer and beaver, and it was capable of altering the ratio in which they were exchanged.

As society exited this stage of development, Ricardo's principle continued to hold. While the movement between stages of society was generally an occasion for descriptive virtuosity for those engaged in conjectural history, Ricardo, bereft

---

[30] Ricardo, 'On the Principles of Political Economy and Taxation', 20, 22. For Smith's terms, see Smith, *WN* I.vi.3, I.x.b.2. Note Peach's perspicuous comment that Ricardo's 'remarks are most illuminating for the light they cast on his own preoccupations', Peach, *Interpreting Ricardo*, 156. A salutary reminder that ideas are not transmitted; texts are read.

[31] Ricardo, 'On the Principles of Political Economy and Taxation', 22.

[32] 'Esteem', 'hardship', and 'ingenuity' all appear extensively throughout Smith's *TMS*.

[33] Ricardo, 'On the Principles of Political Economy and Taxation', 22.

of a training in Scottish stadial history, simply wrote, 'suppose the occupations of the society extended'.[34] Ricardo's principle also held in the next stage of society, 'in which arts and commerce flourish'.[35] His example of such flourishing was stockings, which required labour at multiple stages: to cultivate the land on which cotton was grown, to build the ship that carried the cotton to its place of manufacture, to spin the cotton, to build the spinning machines, and so on. The lesson was straightforward: 'The aggregate sum of these various kinds of labour, determines the quantity of other things for which these stockings will exchange'.[36] What these comments show is that the idea of stages of society played no role in Ricardo's argument because it was simply an accretion of the argumentative context, much like his treatment of justice was seen to be in this book's previous chapter concerning the Corn Laws. His focus was different: the problem of an 'aggregate sum' of labour.

Included in this notion of aggregate labour was durable labour, or capital. Ricardo proposed a distinction between fixed and circulating capital to help capture the fact that some types of capital, such as the steam ship, would endure for long periods of time, while others, such as the wages paid to the labourer, would circulate quickly.[37] It followed that two trades might employ the same quantity of capital but differ greatly in their ratio of fixed to circulating capital. With this distinction in hand, Ricardo turned back to his hunters in early society. Ricardo supposed that his deer hunter used bows and arrows while the fisherman used a canoe and fishing tools and that both sets of implements embodied the same quantity of labour. Under such conditions, whatever quantity of deer was produced by the hunter would exchange for whatever quantity of fish was caught by the fisherman.

Before proceeding further with the exegesis of Ricardo's example, the intensely conceptual character of his analysis should be marked. For Ricardo was asserting the existence of a substance called 'value', produced by labour, that governed the exchange of goods and services. As Ricardo wrote, 'The comparative value of the fish and the game, would be entirely regulated by the quantity of labour realized in each; whatever might be the quantity of production, or however high or low general wages or profits might be'.[38] Only somebody who believed that the concept of an invariable standard was important for ascertaining 'correct theory' and who was prepared to abstract away from the different qualities of labour and from the short-term complications of markets would pursue such a chain of reasoning. Ricardo's critics did not fail to notice this abstract quality, as we will see.

Ricardo continued down this value–price track to reach the conclusion that was crucial for his theory. If labour determined value, and if prices ultimately expressed values, then wages should not affect either value or prices. To put this

---

[34] Ibid., 24.
[35] Ibid.
[36] Ibid., 25.
[37] Ibid., 52.
[38] Ibid., 26.

point another way, Ricardo homogenized labour by supposing that the differing 'estimations' of different types of labour were fixed and then used labour to homogenize what we would call input costs. As a consequence, whether a commodity was made with the labour of humans or by a machine, Ricardo could treat both identically by thinking of the machine as simply so much labour expended at an earlier date. In the beginning was labour. This was the key function of his distinction between 'circulating capital' and 'fixed capital'—it transformed steam ships, stockings, and wheat into labour, differing only by vintage and lifespan. Here was a key example of the type of intellectual conduct that Malthus would target when he wrote in his *Principles* that for 'minds of a certain cast there is nothing so captivating as simplification and generalization.'[39]

In consequence of the ectoplasmic character of labour in Ricardo's sense of the term, it did not matter if it came from human labour or from a machine: the output of 100 units of labour must exchange for the output of 100 units of labour. Ricardo demonstrated the correctness of his conclusion with the following numerical example, in which a fisherman and a hunter used identical quantities of fixed and circulating capital to produce 20 salmon and 10 deer per day, respectively. The result was that the 'natural price' of 2 salmon would be 1 deer.[40]

Fisherman
Canoe (£100) that lasts 10 years
  + 10% profits = £16.27
  (£16.27 as an annual annuity payment for 10 yrs = £100 when rates are 10%)

Employs 10 men for total costs of £100 per annum
  + 10% profits = £110

  Annual revenue: £126.27 (£110 + £16.27)

  Produces 20 salmon per day

Hunter
  Weapons (£100) that last 10 years
  + 10% profits = £16.27
  (£16.27 as an annual annuity payment for 10 yrs = £100 when rates are 10%)

Employs 10 men for £100 total per annum
  + 10% profits = £110

Annual revenue: £126.27 (£110 + £16.27)

Produces 10 deer per day

---

[39] Malthus, 'Principles of Political Economy: Part I', 7.
[40] Ricardo, 'On the Principles of Political Economy and Taxation', 53.

At this point, Ricardo shifted his discussion into money prices, and here the analysis became startling. If there were a commodity that always required exactly the same quantity of labour for its production under whatever circumstances, then that commodity would act as an invariable standard that could reveal the cause of another commodity's change in value. Having already acknowledged that no such commodity existed in the real world, Ricardo simply wrote 'Suppose money to be that commodity'.[41] If the price of salmon remained constant in money, say £1, while the price of deer rose to £3, then it could be concluded safely that the change in price, or natural value, owed to the fact that more labour was now required to produce the deer. Yet as the preceding example shows, Ricardo calculated the total price needed to remunerate both the hunter and fisherman using an annuity calculation. That is, value, or prices, are not only a function of labour, but also of the discounted present value that fixed capital must receive given prevailing rates of return!

This is a remarkable combination of abstract notions of value and annuity tables, and one imagines that it is unique in the history of Western thought.[42] The awkwardness of using annuity calculations to discuss prices in the conjectured 'early stages' of society was seemingly lost on Ricardo, along with the fact that he had stripped all the analytical content from Smith's conception of the 'stages of society' that underwrote the historical jurisprudence that Smith had arranged to service the needs of statesmen.[43] 'Early society' had been a topic for conjectural history because it provided knowledge of the mechanisms of human progress. In Ricardo's hands, by contrast, the stages of society played no such role and were distinguished merely by the degree to which occupations had multiplied and capital accumulated. Putting this issue aside, the annuity calculations strained his doctrinal claims because they suggested that value was a function of an imagined labour substance *and* prevailing rates of return. Nevertheless, Ricardo claimed that he had identified the effect of capital accumulation on relative value, thereby filling the lacuna in Smith's work—the lacuna that Ricardo had fabricated by reading selected passages from *Wealth of Nations* and then treating them as articulations of value doctrine. So far, so good.

---

[41] Ibid., 54.

[42] Annuity tables were a widely used instrument and had entered into statute law. See, for example, this Act from 1812: 'An Act for Amending Two Acts Passed in the Forty Eighth and Forty Ninth Years of His Present Majesty, for Enabling the Commissioners for the Reduction of the National Debt to Grant Life Annuities', in *The Statues of the United Kingdom of Great Britain and Ireland, 52 George III. 1812* (London, 1812), 721–39, at 726–7.

[43] It was not lost on Marx: 'he [Ricardo] slips into the anachronism of allowing the primitive fisherman and hunter to calculate the value of their implements in accordance with the annuity tables used on the London Stock Exchange in 1817': Karl Marx, *A Contribution to the Critique of Political Economy*, ed., Maurice Dobb, trans. S. W. Ryazanskaya (Moscow: Progress Publishers, 1970), 60.

Ricardo's Insoluble Problem: Fixed Capital and Relative Values

Ricardo spoiled his own doctrinal triumph by exploring what would prove to be a serious weakness—that relative values *were* affected by capital accumulation. That is, the quantity of labour was not the only factor affecting value. This issue is technical in nature, and the reader is referred to chapters 4 and 5 of Terry Peach's *Interpreting Ricardo* (1993) for a detailed reconstruction. For the argument here, the key point is that Ricardo's treatment of profits as a residual that rose as wages fell and fell as wages rose led to counter-intuitive results.[44] Perhaps most striking was the claim that rising wages could produce a fall in prices. One might expect that rising wages would be passed on to consumers to some degree as higher prices, as we will see Malthus maintained. But Ricardo held that higher wages simply ate into profits.

This analysis encountered problems when confronted with different proportions of fixed and circulating capital, or equal proportions of fixed capitals that differed with respect to durability. Ricardo illustrated this effect by returning to his hunter and fisherman in early society, maintaining their equality in terms of total capital, at £200 each, but giving them divergent ratios of fixed to circulating capital. The deer hunter's bow and arrows now represented £150 of fixed capital with only £50 of circulating capital being necessary, while the reverse held for the fisherman whose fixed capital now amounted to only £50 and his circulating capital £150. According to the simple theory, because both the hunter and fisherman used the same quantity of labour, their output should sell for the same revenue. But Ricardo's calculations showed that, if profits were 10 per cent, then the value of the fisherman's fixed capital would be heavily discounted, and his output would sell for less than half the price of the hunter's.[45] Ratios of fixed to circulating capital mattered.

Ricardo then confronted a further complication. When wages rose, the effects on the hunter and fisherman would be disproportionate. A greater proportion of the fisherman's total input costs were bound up in wages, while the hunter's fixed capital had been produced at a previous point in time and so its 'value' related not to wages but to the interest rate that capital attracted. Ricardo conceded that doctrinal modification was required.

> It appears then that the division of capital into different proportions of fixed and circulating capital, employed in different trades, introduces a considerable modification to the rule, which is of universal application in the early stages of

---

[44] Ricardo, 'On the Principles of Political Economy and Taxation', 53–4.
[45] Ibid., 57.

society, namely, that commodities never vary in value, unless a greater or less quantity of labour be bestowed on their production.[46]

Ricardo drew a similar lesson regarding the durability of capital. This is the context in which we meet his famous and maligned illustration—involving a machine that would last for 100 years—that produced the incredible result that a wage rise of less than 7 per cent would see the price of machine-intensive goods fall by 68 per cent![47] Ricardo defended the results from the *British Review*'s mocking reception, writing that his reviewer had 'absurdly argued as if this supposition [of the 100 year machine] was essential to the truth of the principle'.[48] This defence is typical of Ricardo in the *Principles*: the task of the political economist is to get at true principles, not to illustrate them with cases that match practice and experience, nor to test them in the same manner, and such objections revealed only that those who made them had limited talent for constructing theory. We might interpret this response as a theorist's impatience with lesser minds.

To close this account of Ricardo's theory of value, it is worth noting that his discovery allowed him to recast the significance of the transition from early society to commercial society. Smith treated these shifts as reconfiguring the nature of public power and human sociability—inequality called forth increasingly elaborate judicial systems to manage envy and the human desire for status[49]— but in Ricardo's science early society was now interesting to the political economist for a different reason:

> before much machinery or durable fixed capital is used, the commodities produced by equal capitals will be nearly of equal value . . . but after the introduction of these expensive instruments, the commodities produced by the employment of equal capitals will be of very unequal value.[50]

Ricardo had redescribed the transition between stages of society in terms of his value theory, and the enduring lesson was that value doctrine required adjustment to capture the nature of commercial society. For Smith, by contrast, studying progress allowed the jurist to understand the nature of public power by observing its connection with forms of human sociability.[51] Furthermore, Smith's comments on the division of labour and the allocation of capital made

---

[46] Ibid., 58.
[47] Ibid., 60. This example would be excised from the third edition of *On the Principles of Political Economy, and Taxation*.
[48] Ibid., 60–1. Ricardo was responding to Anonymous, 'Article XV. Political Economy and Taxation'.
[49] See, for example, Smith, *LJ(A)* iv.6–20.
[50] Ricardo, 'On the Principles of Political Economy and Taxation', 62.
[51] See Haakonssen, *The Science of a Legislator*.

it possible to evaluate a particular trade from the point of view of the state—by asking after the quantity of productive labour that it supported.[52] Thus, it is hard to imagine a more dislocating reception context for Smith's *Wealth of Nations* than Ricardo's production of doctrinal truth concerning an invariable measure of value. But dislocation is what one must expect from a style of historical reflection that was built on selective quotation for doctrinal affirmation or correction. It is now time to see how Malthus answered Ricardo's attempt to recast political economy around the topic of value.

Malthus Responds

As shown in Table I.III.1, Malthus devoted considerable resources to responding to Ricardo's chapter 1, 'On Value'. The overall impression is one of complete rejection, beginning with what Malthus considered Ricardo's theoretical redefinition of terms at variance with their everyday use (possibly reflecting Ricardo's exposure to Thomas Belsham's precepts on this point).[53] In particular, while Malthus conceded that many writers had admitted a distinction between 'value in use' and 'value in exchange' into political economy's vocabulary, it was 'not much sanctioned by custom'.[54] Malthus's claim was that 'value' ought to be understood as arising from the activity of exchanging goods. Such a definition conveyed a clear meaning that accorded with human experience and did not force new meanings onto established terms. Malthus's first strategy was to invoke the discipline of definitional propriety to restrain the theorist's flight of fancy.

Given that value was not connected with a substance—labour—but with exchange, Malthus insisted that it was exchange that needed to form the focus for investigation. Human patterns of trade and barter were determined by the willingness and ability to exchange a given article for another that was more desired. The ratio at which any two articles were exchanged was a function of the 'relative estimation in which they are held by the parties, founded on the desire to possess, and the difficulty or facility of procuring possession'.[55] Where Ricardo had treated the desire to possess a commodity or its utility as a precondition for exchange, Malthus installed it at the heart of the exchange process via the interaction of supply and demand, where these terms were understood in conformity with their established meanings.[56]

---

[52] Smith, *WN* II.v.1–12.
[53] Sergio Cremaschi and Marcelo Dascal, 'Malthus and Ricardo on Economic Methodology', *History of Political Economy* 28/3 (1996), 475–511.
[54] Malthus, 'Principles of Political Economy: Part I', 42.
[55] Ibid., 43.
[56] Ibid., 51–7.

There was a further element in Malthus's account that was even more important than the role of individual desire. This was the way that repeated interactions between individuals formed 'average' exchange ratios, or prices, allowing rules of thumb to emerge over time. For example, a pound of venison was worth four pounds of bread, or a quart of wine, or a pound of cheese.[57] This process was easily accessible to those familiar with markets, but Malthus claimed that in the early stages of society it would be hard for such averages to emerge because they would be frustrated not only by a lack of knowledge and the infrequency of trade, but also by a lack of regular demand for all the goods to which an average might be affixed. Following both Jacques Turgot and Adam Smith, Malthus identified these inconveniences as giving rise to a medium of exchange—cattle amongst pastoral nations, cacao nuts for pre-conquest Mexico, and the precious metals in Europe.[58] 'Price' was the name given to the value of a commodity when estimated in whatever medium of exchange a society adopted, and it represented a progressive step in history by facilitating exchange and stimulating production.[59]

These money prices were of the utmost importance to merchants because they used them to estimate costs and revenues. Such 'nominal values' were of little use, however, when it came to measuring value across nations, or even through time in a single nation. What was required in such cases was some sense of 'real value in exchange', by which Malthus meant the ability to command necessaries and conveniences. In this respect, nominal values for money prices could be misleading because different nations used different currencies and because a given nation's currency was subject to variation over time. As was the case for Smith, Malthus's aim was to have a means for comparing values across time and space that would not be subject to the distortions of nominal prices. It followed that a 'correct measure of real value in exchange' would be desirable, not because knowing its properties would serve what Ricardo termed 'correct theory', but because it would make it possible to accurately compare prices and wages across time and space while investigating the 'nature and causes of the wealth of nations'.[60] (In these comments Malthus was not only rejecting Ricardo's notion of real value but also the very purpose for which it had been crafted.) The reality, however, was that no such commodity could possibly exist because all articles were subject to change. The implication was that an approximation would have to suffice. What was needed was some estimate of the 'power of commanding the necessaries and conveniences of life, including labour'.[61] Malthus

[57] Ibid., 43.
[58] Ibid., 43–5. Malthus was referencing A. R. J. Turgot, *Réfléxions sur la Formation et la Distribution des Richesses* (Paris, 1788); Smith, *WN* I.iv.
[59] Malthus, 'Principles of Political Economy: Part I', 46.
[60] Malthus, 'Principles of Political Economy: Part II', 364–5.
[61] Ibid., 365.

was not conceiving of an essential labour substance, abstracted from differences in labour quality and capable of explaining exchange ratios, but instead some measure that would permit the political economist to make comparisons in the course of their studies.

Malthus could thus reject Ricardo's definition of real value not only because it represented a failure to adhere to the relevant protocols for using technical terms—namely, following common usage—but because it was also less useful than the terms that were already available.

> We are not however justified, on this account, in giving a different definition of real value in exchange, if the definition already adopted be at once the most usual and the most useful. We have the power indeed arbitrarily to call the labour which has been employed upon a commodity its real value; but in so doing we use words in a different sense from that in which they are customarily used; we confound at once the very important distinction between *cost* and *value*; and render it almost impossible to explain, with clearness, the main stimulus to the production of wealth, which, in fact, depends upon this distinction.
>
> The right of making definitions must evidently be limited by their propriety, and their use in the science to which they are applied.[62]

Malthus was not being terribly fair when accusing Ricardo of conflating cost and value, given what has been said earlier about Ricardo's analysis. Indeed, Malthus might be accused of polemical intent by having embellished the image of Ricardo as a mad theorist whose pseudo-insights were merely a product of his having lost control of his faculties. (This point is returned to at the close of this chapter.) Still, with whatever justice or injustice, Malthus had separated Ricardo's usage from accepted meaning.

Malthus then severed Ricardo's connection with Smith. For Malthus closed his discussion on this point by insisting on the judiciousness of his own definitions, a claim that he supported by noting that they were essentially the definitions of Smith and 'properly belong to his system', with Smith's inconsistencies on this point needing to be seen merely 'in the light of inadvertences'.[63] In other words, Malthus was using Smith as an authority to isolate Ricardo's self-avowed novelty, which he had treated as a product of neglecting the precepts of sound thinking. In summary, Malthus attacked Ricardo's thought with a mix of doctrinal correction, Smith invocation, and ethics-talk: talk of method and models was absent.

Malthus continued his attack by targeting Ricardo's central claim—that a commodity's cost of production was capable of explaining its exchange value.

---

[62] Ibid., 364–5.
[63] Ibid., 365.

Malthus's first step was to assert that the relation between supply and demand was constantly operating to determine the actual prices at which goods sold. This meant that, *pace* Smith, both market and natural prices were determined by the willingness and ability of buyers and sellers to exchange. The cost of production was merely an ingredient.[64] Malthus insisted that this claim was borne out not merely in 'imaginary cases'—note the negative redescription of Ricardo's theoretical virtuosity—but in 'actual experience'.[65] By 'experience' Malthus was referring to three examples. First, the perennially low pay of curates, which owed to the fact that they were permanently in excess supply. Second, the operation of the poor rates to lower the wages of labour because the real costs of labour were subsidized by the parish. Third, Ricardo's own example of Bank of England paper, which was depreciated because it had been issued to excess.[66] There was no escaping the empire of supply and demand.

As we have seen, however, Ricardo's rival system was premised on just such an escape, and it was achieved in a pristine moment at the beginning of society's history when production was so simple that ratios of labour determined the ratios in which goods would be traded without complication and exception. Yet Malthus's analysis of supply and demand reached back even here to contest Ricardo's claims: What if, Malthus asked, objects were found by accident? Or what if the labour employed on objects was completely unknown? It would make no difference, Malthus insisted, for they would be traded based on supply and demand and thus find their price without difficulty.[67] According to Malthus, this was the first flaw in Ricardo's theory.[68]

Another flaw had been noted by Ricardo himself: the 'quickness' with which capital received its profits varied and always affected price. This was, in other words, a factor completely unrelated to the quantity of labour embodied in a commodity.[69] Furthermore, the ability for a 'savage' to plan ahead, to provide a store of subsistence for a long period of time during which a rare tool, such as a canoe, would be constructed, would require great foresight and the postponement of present enjoyment for future benefits. These were 'rare qualities in the savage'.[70] Malthus's point was that the rarity of these qualities in his imagined 'savage' would ensure a limited supply and that *this* would raise the price, not the

---

[64] Malthus, 'Principles of Political Economy: Part I', 58–69.
[65] Ibid., 60.
[66] Ibid., 60–1.
[67] Malthus, 'Principles of Political Economy: Part II', 367.
[68] It is perhaps better seen as a limitation since Ricardo had restricted the class of objects to which his analysis would apply as those that were reproduced under competitive conditions. Peach, *Interpreting Ricardo*, 155.
[69] Malthus, 'Principles of Political Economy: Part I', 71.
[70] Ibid., 72.

quantity of labour. A yet further weakness in Ricardo's theory was the problem of diverging ratios of fixed capital, which we have seen exercised Ricardo, too. The critical undertow of Malthus's discussion was that even in early society the Ricardian theory would not work.[71]

Malthus then turned from early society to intervene in Ricardo's discussion of the 'curious effect'—by which a rise in wages could produce, counterintuitively, a fall in price. Malthus noted that Ricardo's presentation suffered from 'a very paradoxical air',[72] which had been a focus for his negative reviewers. This appearance could be removed if the proposition were stated in a clearer manner: what Ricardo really meant was that prices would decline after a fall in profits.[73] Malthus then drew attention to the class of commodities whose prices would rise with wages because the increased costs were passed on to consumers in the form of higher prices. That is, Malthus was arguing that where the share of fixed capital was either small or zero because it was tied up in daily wages, the rise in wages would be passed on or the production of such commodities would have to cease. It followed that Ricardo was wrong to break the link between rising wages and rising prices.[74]

This was the strongest challenge possible in the genre that Ricardo was pioneering: doctrinal refutation. Yet Malthus went further by showing that there would be some commodities where prices increased, some where they fell, and that there would also be a small class of commodities where prices stayed the same. This got to the heart of Ricardo's theory because this last class of commodities where prices did not change was actually Ricardo's invariable standard. But this class, Malthus insisted, must form 'little more than a line', amounting to an unacceptably 'peculiar case' to justify such an important doctrine.[75] More fatally for Ricardo, it made no difference which 'case' of commodity production—which combination of fixed and circulating capital—was chosen to illustrate the invariable standard. For the fact was that the world of commodities was characterized by utter diversity regarding ratios of fixed to circulating capital and frequency of returns, which meant that any one set of conditions, or 'case', would only ever represent just that: an unremarkable specimen from a multitude. Malthus put the point in the following way:

---

[71] Ibid., 72–3.

[72] Ibid., 74.

[73] This, it should be clear, represented a restatement of Ricardo's argument, as Malthus was attempting to detach Ricardo's treatment of wages and profits (as standing in a zero-sum relation) from his claim about profits and prices.

[74] Malthus, 'Principles of Political Economy: Part I', 75.

[75] Ibid., 76; Malthus, 'Principles of Political Economy: Part II', 367.

wherever the line may be placed, it can embrace but a very small class of objects; and upon a rise in the price of labour, all the rest will either fall or rise in price, although exactly the same quantity of labour continues to be employed upon them.[76]

Ricardo later acknowledged that Malthus was right.[77] The effect of this for Ricardo's system was disastrous, and Malthus lingered over the victory, posing and answering his own question:

> What then becomes of the doctrine that the exchangeable value of commodities is proportioned to the labour which has been employed upon them? Instead of their remaining of the same value while the same quantity of labour is employed upon them, it appears that, from well-known causes of constant and universal operation, the prices of all commodities vary when the *price* of labour varies, with very few exceptions.[78]

There was a final nail to be driven in. Malthus enumerated still further causes—beyond ratios of fixed–circulating capital and the timing of profits—that affected exchangeable value and operated independently of the quantity of labour. Namely, imports, taxation, and rent. It was simply the case that the world of production was too varied to be reduced to labour. However 'curious and desirable' a knowledge of relative quantities might be thought, it was simply the fact that a perfect standard was 'unattainable'.[79] Rather like the rejection of imaginary utopias in regards to political organization, Malthus was rejecting the pursuit of a perfect theoretical standard as a defensible activity. Ricardo's temper was different, and he would remain fixated on an invariable standard, working on it in the final weeks of his life.[80]

Conclusion

It is hopefully clear that Malthus's rejection of Ricardo's value theory only concerned its doctrinal aspects in part. For what was primarily at issue was Ricardo's mode of argument and the motivations that underlay it. This is clearly visible in the first step of Malthus's response—the attempt to undermine Ricardo's groundwork by asserting that it violated the protocols of definitional propriety.

---

[76] Malthus, 'Principles of Political Economy: Part I', 76; 'Principles of Political Economy: Part II', 367.

[77] See Peach, *Interpreting Ricardo*, 202–5.

[78] Malthus, 'Principles of Political Economy: Part I', 76; 'Principles of Political Economy: Part II', 367.

[79] Malthus, 'Principles of Political Economy: Part II', 370, 379.

[80] Sraffa, 'Note on "Absolute Value and Exchangeable Value"', *Works and Correspondence*, 4: 358–60, at 358.

It should be noted that this was not merely a cudgel invented by Malthus, but an aspect of the general intellectual culture, as we have seen. Malthus would go on to underline the importance of this aspect of political economy in his teaching text, *Definitions in Political Economy* (1827), with the first chapter titled 'Rules for the Definition and Application of Terms in Political Economy'.[81] In the chapter that assessed Ricardo's performance on this score, Malthus found that his friend had been 'very far from cautious in the definition and application of his terms', compromising the consistency of his argument not just in the chapter on value but across the *Principles* as a whole.[82]

The second thrust of Malthus's attack that we have been examining concerned the very idea of an invariable standard and the 'paradoxical' results that Ricardo had produced with its assistance. It seems that at this point Malthus was building on the image of Ricardo as a confused reasoner who had lost control of his mind because he had submitted to the seductions of theory and system. We have seen that this image of Ricardo had been propagated by Bosanquet and other of Ricardo's critics in relation to the Bullion Controversy. Yet this caricature had also circulated in the most critical reviews of Ricardo's *Principles*. The first edition, for example, had been considered in the *British Review* in 1817, by a writer who was evidently sympathetic to political economy and prepared to acknowledge Ricardo's success in his earlier writings. Ricardo's *Principles*, however, was described as containing 'more of extravagant paradox and learned absurdity than we have encountered in any similar publication'.[83] The key failing was traced to Ricardo's intellectual capture by his own theory and his insouciance towards reality.

> His reasoning, generally speaking, is seldom found to respect the actual state of things as they appear to the observation of ordinary men who have no theory to maintain, but most commonly turns on a collection of hypothetical cases springing out of his own imagination, and accommodated to his own particular views.[84]

Ricardo appeared to have 'constructed the model of a political system after his own imagination, to have set it up before his eyes in the solitude of his study', in which solitude Ricardo had been 'led away by the deceitfulness of his theoretical notions'.[85] The reviewer traced these pathologies to Ricardo's failure to impose the necessary intellectual disciplines on himself. Above all, Ricardo's argument

---

[81] Malthus, 'Definitions in Political Economy', *Works*, 8: 1–120, at 5.
[82] Ibid., 21.
[83] Anonymous, 'Article XV. Political Economy and Taxation', 309.
[84] Ibid.
[85] Ibid., 310, 318.

was ungrounded in 'statistical facts' or 'experience', and he had 'fallen diseased into that condition of the speculative faculties, in which men will not condescend to look at any truth'.[86] Ricardo stood as sorry evidence of 'how ready men are, in certain circumstances, to sacrifice their good sense to the spirit of theory'.[87]

A similar assessment was reached by the anonymous reviewer for the *British Critic*. In relation to Ricardo's 'curious effect' material, the critic wrote that he was tempted to 'whisper into the ear of this wonder-working economist, "Pray, Sir, raise the wages a per cent. or two more, and then we shall get the goods for nothing"'.[88] Ricardo's 'love of theory' was adduced as the source of Ricardo's delusion, allowing him to announce such a ridiculous claim 'in the gravest manner possible, and with the full self complacency of a man who feels that he is striking out lights for the good of society'.[89] Ricardo's decision to follow the implications of his labour theory so deeply and to air his discoveries had exposed him to the charge of theoretical enthusiasm.

By contrast, an anonymous reviewer of Malthus's *Principles* for the *British Critic* noted the judicious way in which Malthus combined fact and theory, in contradistinction to Ricardo's argumentation. The critic wrote that 'it is the characteristic weakness of Mr. Ricardo, to lay greater stress upon theoretical assumptions, than upon all the facts and experience which have been collected by past generations'.[90] Their summary judgement of Ricardo was that while he displayed ingenuity, the 'absurdity' of his claims was patent and derived from his 'love of paradox and mysticism, his affectation of novelty, and his abuse of words'.[91] In relation to this last failing, another reviewer wrote that 'Mr. Ricardo perplexes his reader and bewilders himself, by using old words in a new sense'.[92] Ricardo's mysticism was illustrated by referring to his 'hundred year machine' that established the paradox of falling prices emerging from rising wages. Although the author conceded that Ricardo was circling an important truth in this discussion regarding the link between prices and profits, he complained that it had been concealed by ambiguous language and impossible hypotheses.[93] These reviews show that Malthus was using a shared idiom to repeat a standing allegation

---

[86] Ibid., 312, 314, 319.

[87] Ibid., 320.

[88] Anonymous, 'Review of *Des Principes de L'Economie Politique et de L'Impôt*', 136. This article was initially printed in *The British Critic*, but references are to the reprint in Terry Peach's *David Ricardo: Critical Responses*, vol. 1, 130–44, at 136.

[89] Ibid., 138–9.

[90] Anonymous, 'Review of *Principles of Political Economy*, Part II', *The British Critic* 14 (September 1820), 275–93. Reprinted in *David Ricardo: Critical Responses*, vol. 1, 193–208, at 198.

[91] Ibid., 208.

[92] Anonymous, 'Review of *Principles of Political Economy*, Part I', *The British Critic* 14 (August 1820), 117–38. Reprinted in *David Ricardo: Critical Responses*, vol. 1, 173–92, at 180. All references are to the reprint.

[93] Ibid. 175–6.

against Ricardo: the idiom was ethics-talk, and the allegation was theoretical enthusiasm.

How did Ricardo respond? Ricardo mentioned the article in the *British Review* in letters to Hutches Trower and Malthus towards the end of 1817, writing that 'in every page I am charged with ignorance and absurdity', but the reviewer had made his claims 'in an ungentmanly [sic] way'.[94] Along with this slighting of his antagonist's ethos, Ricardo described the reviewer's reasoning as shallow.[95] This response was obviously harder to maintain in relation to Malthus, a friend and a critic who was able to follow Ricardo's reasoning perfectly well.

In determining how Ricardo responded to Malthus, we are invaluably served by the notes that Ricardo took on Malthus's *Principles* in 1820, in which he commented on his disagreements with Malthus, noting both the page and the first few words of the relevant passage. In other words, it has been possible to determine the particular passages in Malthus's text to which a given section of Ricardo's notes relate. Ricardo seems to have prepared them with publication in mind as a serious possibility, perhaps as an appendix to the third edition of his *Principles*, but he was ultimately dissuaded against publication in any form by friends (Mill, McCulloch, and Trower). Yet it is important to note that some of the material from the notes went into the third edition of the *Principles* (1821), and that Ricardo described his mode of composition as one of writing down whatever came to mind.[96] Given these facts, the *Notes* will be treated in what follows as providing insight into when Ricardo thought that he had the upper hand over Malthus and when and how he defended his own work.

Regarding the issue of *how* Ricardo rebutted Malthus, we find in the *Notes* that he directed little in the way of philosophical firepower at Malthus's text and that Ricardo struggled to articulate a rival set of disciplines or intellectual values that might have justified his mode of argument in the *Principles*. An indicative example is Ricardo's response to the passage from Malthus quoted earlier, in which Malthus asked the question, 'What then becomes of the doctrine, that the exchangeable value of commodities is proportioned to the labour which has been employed upon them?' As we saw, Malthus's answer was that Ricardo's doctrine was extremely limited in applicability compared to the existing Smithian-Malthusian account. Ricardo's reply amounted to little more than a plea for intellectual tolerance.

---

[94] Ricardo, 'Ricardo to Trower', *Works and Correspondence,* 7: 218–21, at 219.

[95] For further discussion of Ricardo's response to this review, see Ryan Walter, 'The Enthusiasm of David Ricardo', *Modern Intellectual History* 15/2 (2018), 381–409, at 405–6.

[96] Sraffa, 'Introduction', *Works and Correspondence,* 2: vii–xviii, at ix–xi.

The principles of political Economy cannot be explained by the changes which take place in nominal price. Every one who attempts to explain those principles should adopt the best measure of real value that he can obtain, for that purpose.

Mr. M. has adopted one which he thinks the best, and to the use of that he should have confined himself.[97]

Equally revealing is Ricardo's response to those passages in Malthus's second chapter, on measures of value, where Malthus set out to show that no suppositions could be made regarding the production of precious metals that would fit them to measure quantities of labour realized in the mass of commodities.[98] A certain annoyance on Ricardo's part is detectable.

It was never contended that gold under the present circumstances was a good measure of value, it was only hypothetically, and for the purpose of illustrating a principle, supposed that all the known causes of the variability of gold, were removed. . . . Am I answered by being told that gold is variable, and that I have omitted to mention some of the causes of its variation?[99]

Putting the two responses together, we have Ricardo insisting on his right to be left alone to choose his own measure of value, and Ricardo complaining that his hypothetical illustrations ought to be acknowledged as such. What was missing was a positive defence of his mode of argument, one that met the twin accusations of theoretical enthusiasm and inapplicability to the real world. A defence, in other words, of theory as a vocation, along the lines of Ricardo's claims mentioned earlier regarding the importance of attaining 'correct theory'.[100] The absence of such a defence points to the overall argument of this book: theory of this type had not yet won a place for itself in the world. That it has such a place in our world has made it easy to treat Ricardo as familiar in retrospective reconstructions, but in doing so what is lost is the sustained nature and extent of the opposition that met Ricardo's work in his own time.

---

[97] Ricardo, 'Notes on Malthus's *Principles of Political Economy*', *Works and Correspondence*, 2: 67.
[98] Malthus, 'Principles of Political Economy: Part II', 371–5.
[99] Ricardo, 'Notes on Malthus's *Principles of Political Economy*', 83.
[100] Ricardo, 'On the Principles of Political Economy and Taxation', 17.

5

Doctrinal Contest II

Rent

In the second chapter of his *Principles*, 'On Rent', Ricardo continued his revisionist march through the doctrines of political economy by presuming to correct the errors of his predecessors. Once again, Smith's *Wealth of Nations* was subjected to rough handling, and, again, Ricardo departed from Smith's historical and institutional treatment in favour of theoretical virtuosity. For Ricardo, this meant focusing on the question of whether or not rent affected the relative values of commodities. If rent did enter into price, then a modification of Ricardo's value doctrine would have been required. In other words, while Ricardo could fairly characterize his investigations as concerning 'the nature of rent, and the laws by which its rise or fall is regulated', it was also the case that he was proceeding down this path in pursuit of value.[1] Given that Ricardo's approach to value was likely a unique event in the history of Western thought, whomever he measured by this standard would have been found deficient. It is not, therefore, surprising that Ricardo found Smith's analysis to be inferior to his own. The key assessment came in chapter 24, 'Doctrine of Adam Smith concerning the Rent of Land', where Ricardo chastised Smith for treating rent as a component part of price.

Malthus's account of rent fared little better, with Malthus elevated to titular significance in the same manner as Smith in chapter 31 of the second edition of the *Principles*, 'Mr. Malthus's Opinions on Rent'. Bringing to view Ricardo's corrections of Smith and Malthus on rent doctrine is the first step in what follows. The chapter then turns to consider Malthus's response. One imagines that being named in a chapter title would have been sufficient provocation for Malthus to respond. But the nature of Malthus's response permits a second stimulus to also be conjectured; namely, Ricardo's hostile portrayal of landlords as passive in the process of wealth creation. For Malthus's counter to Ricardo focused on reversing two of Ricardo's conclusions: the supposed inadequacy of Smith and the status of rent as a national burden.

---

[1] Ricardo, 'Principles of Political Economy and Taxation', 67.

Before Method and Models. Ryan Walter, Oxford University Press. © Oxford University Press 2021.
DOI: 10.1093/oso/9780197603055.003.0008

The discussion that follows brings these doctrinal clashes to view. Yet it also foregrounds the fact that a key feature of Malthus's account was that he drew on the resources of natural theology to portray rent as a dispensation from God. Examining this characteristic of Malthus's argument allows us to see that political economy's theological content and its relationship to the Anglican state was also at issue in the Malthus–Ricardo contest. Malthus did not, however, present his claims as superior to Ricardo's simply because they were theologically correct but because they represented good theorizing. In this respect, Malthus sought to expose the inadequacies of Ricardo's reasoning by showing that he had failed to submit to the disciplines that secured theoretical inquiry from its inherent risks. Foremost amongst these disciplines was the need to apply theory in the appropriate manner, whereby both the facts of the real world and the limitations of theory were kept in view as a means for preventing the theorist from ascending to dangerous heights of speculation. Malthus's assessment of Ricardo as failing these ethical challenges thus stands as another example of how their doctrinal disputes were simultaneously disputes over the ethico-intellectual office of the political economist.

Ricardo Corrects Smith

Smith had isolated agriculture as special by using the ornate notion that 'nature labours along with man' and 'her labour costs no expence'.[2] Accordingly, rent arose as a surplus payment made possible by the land's fecundity. In manufacturing, by contrast, nature did not labour, all was man, and no rent was afforded in consequence. But, awkwardly, Smith had also discussed rent as a monopoly payment, in Book I, that the landlord extracted from the farmer.[3] The instability in Smith's argument was not as important as his claim that agriculture was special owing to nature's free labour, since it was this claim that allowed Smith to identify the natural path to opulence for all nations. Namely, for capital to first be concentrated in agriculture where the greatest quantity of productive labour was supported. This drove the central argument of Book III of *Wealth of Nations*: Europe had followed a 'retrograde' path in which wealth accumulated in the towns, not the country, because of the institutional peculiarities of post-Roman Europe. This paved the way for Smith's account of the 'Mercantile System' in Book IV, where the endless restrictions and privileges that the merchant class had managed to extract from the legislature continued to draw capital to overseas trade. By doing so, the merchants were frustrating a process that would otherwise have

---

[2] Smith, *WN* II.v.12.
[3] Smith, *WN* I.xi.a.1, 6.

appeared providential in its ability to naturally favour agriculture, the special sector.

Ricardo also rendered agriculture as special, but in the opposite way to Smith. Ricardo did so by creating an analogy between nature and machinery: in industrial production all the machines were equal, but in agriculture the machines were land, and lands differed in quality. Because of this variety in nature's machines there was variety in the profitability accruing to agricultural capital, and the variety was equalized by the extraction of rent.[4] That is, uniform profits were taken to be an organizing principle of economic life, and, in Ricardo's work, the role of equalizer fell to landlords who absorbed differential profits as rent, leaving all capitalist farmers with the same rate of profits. Ricardo arrived at this conclusion after developing an intricate set of arguments, and along the way he ascribed a doctrinal position on rent to Smith for the purpose of then rejecting it.

Ricardo's first step was to define rent in a technical sense. While it was the case that in 'popular language' rent was used to refer to the annual payments that a farmer made to their landlord for the use of their land, this was hardly satisfactory from the point of view of a theory of distribution between capitalists, landlords, and workers.[5] For the payments that were denoted by the common meaning of the term were an amalgam of phenomena that were subject to distinct laws of commercial life. As Ricardo wrote: 'the laws which regulate the progress of rent, are widely different from those which regulate the progress of profits'.[6] Rent, in the sense in which Ricardo wished to use the term, was the payment made for using the fecund properties of the earth. In terms of the preceding analogy, rent was the price for renting nature's machines, paid to whoever enjoyed their possession.

To make this point, Ricardo imagined two farms. One farm bore improvements carried out by the landlord—such as buildings and manuring—and the other did not. The rent paid on both farms would not be equal even if the land on both were of the same quality since the payments made by the tenant on the improved farm would also include compensation for the landlord's capital that was tied up in the buildings and soil improvements. The payments made by the farmer on the improved farm thus included both rent and interest, and it was a conflation to refer to both together as rent. With this point made, Ricardo was prepared to set out his definition of rent.

---

[4] Ricardo also imagined variety in profitability in relation to increments of capital being applied to the same unit of land, that is, the so-called *intensive case*. Ricardo, 'On the Principles of Political Economy and Taxation', 71–2. The idea of units of land that differed in quality, however, formed his focus.

[5] Ibid., 67.

[6] Ibid., 68.

In the future pages of this work, then, whenever I speak of the rent of land,
I wish to be understood as speaking of that compensation, which is paid to the
owner of land for the use of its original and indestructible powers.[7]

Ricardo's definition was unstable because it sometimes required that nature's
'powers' were 'original' and sometimes not.[8] For the argument here, however, the
issue of the stability of Ricardo's definition is less important than the fact that
it was an abstract definition that ran counter to the word's everyday meaning.
Such theoretical definition was required to facilitate the discovery of general
laws that were otherwise concealed when the theorist remained at the level of
everyday language.[9] Smith, for example, struggled to discover such laws, according to Ricardo, because he sometimes used rent in the everyday sense and
at other times in the technical sense. This fact was supposedly revealed in Smith's
treatment of the rent of forests and mines.[10] Smith, in other words, only glimpsed
the theoretical insights necessary to the study of rent. As we have seen in Part I,
this tactic of redescription was commonly employed by 'theorists' against their
practical enemies, with Dugald Stewart going to elaborate lengths to characterize
the 'vulgar' mind as untheoretical. That Ricardo was prepared to describe Smith
as only partially escaping a quotidian understanding of the topic—when Smith
had been regarded in his own time as rising dangerously above practice on the
wings of theory—is a sign of the degree of theoretical virtuosity at which Ricardo
aimed and that we are examining a moment in which a writer was attempting to
move a preexisting vocabulary onto a higher level of abstraction.

The second demotion to which Ricardo subjected Smith was even more severe. It relied on a hypothetical account of 'progress', in much the same manner
that we encountered in relation to Ricardo's *Essay on Profits* (1815) in Chapter 3.[11]
In this same vein, Ricardo began his account by imagining 'the first settling of a
country', in which fertile land was so abundant as to be freely available.[12] Under
such conditions, no rent was paid because all people could own nature's best machines. This situation changed because of the 'progress of society'.[13] By this shorthand Ricardo did not mean the usual processes premised by Scottish conjectural
history: the expansion of the division of labour, the discovery of new markets,
or the thickening of social interactions between sympathetic subjects. Instead,

---

[7] Ibid., 68–9.

[8] Ibid., 69 at n1.

[9] See the discussion of Malthus's and Ricardo's rival approaches to definition in Cremaschi and
Dascal, 'Malthus and Ricardo on Economic Methodology', 489–90.

[10] Ricardo, 'On the Principles of Political Economy and Taxation', 67–8. For the passage of Smith
that Ricardo referred to, see Smith, *WN* I.xi.c.5.

[11] Ricardo, 'An Essay on the Influence of a Low Price of Corn on the Profits of Stock', 10–12.

[12] Ricardo, 'On the Principles of Political Economy and Taxation', 69.

[13] Ibid., 70.

Ricardo had the comparatively restricted notion of population growth that saw second-rate land brought under cultivation to meet the demand for food. Hence, we are asked to 'suppose land—No. 1, 2, 3,—to yield, with an equal employment of capital and labour, a net produce of 100, 90, and 80 quarters of corn'.[14] Ricardo held that, if capital employed by farmers in agriculture were to receive the same rate of profit, then the differences in produce must be appropriated by landlords as rent. That is, the landlord of land No. 1 must extract 20 quarters of produce from their tenant and the landlord of land No. 2 must extract 10 quarters if all farmers were to receive the same rate of profits, as determined by land No. 3, the last unit of land to be cultivated. Rent, in other words, varied depending on the quality of nature's machines, while the condition of farmers was equalized through the uniform rate of return to capital. The land's variability created rent, while capital's homogenizing forces acted to level profits.

At this point we see Ricardo's account of value intersecting with his theory of rent. Ricardo asserted that the exchangeable value of a commodity such as corn—produced by machines of varying quality—was set by the greatest quantity of labour required per unit of output.[15] In Ricardo's example just given, this was the quantity of labour used to produce the crop on land No. 3. The crucial effect of this analysis was to separate the high price of corn from the existence of rent. Acknowledging that he was at one with Malthus on this point, Ricardo was able to write that 'Corn is not high because a rent is paid, but a rent is paid because corn is high'.[16] It was immaterial whether or not rent was collected by gentleman landlords because the price of corn would be the same regardless: once a nation had to engage nature's poorer machines, its food would become costly, and in this respect it mattered not at all who benefited from owning the better machines.

On the surface, Ricardo's account legitimized the landlord's rent since these payments did not determine the high price of corn but were merely the result of a fact of the world: land was both limited in quantity and variable in quality. It was this analysis, however, that enabled Ricardo to attack the Corn Laws with such power because it showed that these laws protected the landed interest by obliging Britain to feed itself from poor lands. Far better, according to Ricardo, to let other nations feed Britain with food produced on the best machines that nature could furnish, while Britain paid for this food with manufactured goods produced on the best machines that human ingenuity could furnish. In this way, all the world would gain in wealth. (As we saw, Malthus objected to this analysis in his essays of 1814 and 1815 by insisting that national happiness was composed of more elements than wealth and that, among these elements, security ought to

[14] Ibid.
[15] Ibid., 72–4.
[16] Ibid., 74.

be valued above wealth.) With this account in hand, Ricardo proceeded to de-molish one of the central struts of Smith's system: the superiority of agriculture to all other sectors.

Ricardo glossed Smith's line of argument in dismissive terms, writing that 'Nothing is more common than to hear of the advantages which the land pos-sesses over every other source of useful produce, on account of the surplus which it yields in the form of rent'.[17] The truth was, according to Ricardo, quite the op-posite. The nerve of his argument was this: land contrasted with nature's other agents that aided manufacturing production because it was finite and variable in quality. By contrast, such natural agents as the air and the elasticity of steam were unlimited in supply and constant in their quality. From here, Ricardo could mock the pre-theoretical idea that agriculture was preeminent simply because it paid rent. On this logic, Ricardo claimed, it would also be desirable that 'every year, the machinery newly constructed should be less efficient than the old' since that would similarly create a rent for those possessing the older, more efficient machines.[18] The earlier treatment of rent had the matter upside down.

From this position, Ricardo could explicitly correct Smith on the nature of rent. In a long footnote, Ricardo quoted the relevant passages from Book II of *Wealth of Nations* in which Smith wrote that 'nature labours along with man', in contrast to manufacturing, where 'nature does nothing; man does all'.[19] In these passages Smith was using his notion of productive labour to distinguish between different employments of capital from the point of view of a nation that valued wealth creation. This exercise yielded a hierarchy of capital employ-ments that allowed Smith to dispute the arguments of the so-called agricultural or Physiocratic and mercantile systems. Where the Physiocratic system insisted that manufactures were sterile, Smith was able to show that, in fact, this use of capital was the second most beneficial to the community; where the mercan-tile system held that overseas trade deserved the greatest encouragement, Smith could show that it did not because it employed the smallest quantities of pro-ductive labour. Ricardo targeted both claims and, in consequence, was able to dismantle Smith's entire edifice.

The first step was to show that Smith's privileging of agriculture was based on an error. Namely, rent was not paid because nature laboured for free, but be-cause nature extracted an increasingly high price for its work as a nation grew in population. In making these statements, Ricardo was rephrasing his claim that rent arose to equalize profits as society began to call on land of varying quality. He thus wrote, 'In proportion as she [nature] becomes niggardly in her gifts, she

---

[17] Ibid., 75.
[18] Ibid.
[19] Smith, *WN* II.v.12.

exacts a greater price for her work.[20] Smith's claim that in manufacturing nature contributed nothing was also wrong: the elasticity of steam, the role of heat in softening metals, and the nature of wind and water were all examples of nature's role in manufacturing. Ricardo construed these examples as clear evidence that there was not 'a manufacture which can be mentioned, in which nature does not give her assistance to man, and give it too, generously and gratuitously'.[21] Ricardo was explicitly targeting and overturning Smith's central claim regarding the nature of rent and the privileged role of agriculture in producing national wealth, even to the extent of translating his own arguments into Smith's anthropomorphic image of nature as a productive labourer.

Ricardo underlined his supersession of Smith on this point by quoting a lengthy passage from Buchanan's edition of *Wealth of Nations* in which Buchanan presumed to correct Smith's treatment of agriculture. The effect was to suggest that, whether one learned it from reading a modern edition of Smith or from reading Ricardo, one ought to know that rent was the result and not the cause of a high price of corn. In Ricardo's presentation, Smith's errors on the principle of rent seriously compromised his credentials as a political economist because of the topic's central place in the science. As Ricardo wrote, 'clearly understanding this principle is, I am persuaded, of the utmost importance to the science of political economy'.[22] Here is one of the reasons for why Smith's 'invisible hand' withered so quickly in the nineteenth century: the root argumentation had been identified as erroneous doctrine and then destroyed.[23]

Ricardo's doctrinal correction of Smith was continued in chapter 24, 'Doctrine of Adam Smith Concerning the Rent of Land'. Ricardo's title was as telling as his opening move. He quoted a passage from Smith's Book I, in which Smith ostensibly approached the correct doctrine on rent, and Ricardo wrote that 'This passage would naturally lead the reader to conclude that its author could not have mistaken the nature of rent'.[24] Alas, Smith had demonstrated that the contrary was indeed the case in subsequent passages. Smith could not have correctly understood rent's nature, Ricardo insisted, because he did not

---

[20] Ricardo, 'On the Principles of Political Economy and Taxation', 76 at asterisked note.
[21] Ibid.
[22] Ibid., 77 at asterisked note.
[23] The other reason is that Smith only used the phrase 'invisible hand' to indicate a providential organization of some aspect of life. Hence, for example, Malthus made the same point regarding the alignment of private and public interests (Malthus, 'High Price of Provisions', 9). The 'invisible hand' was not a theory of free markets but a rhetorical flourish that had purchase in a Christian nation; it is impossible that Smith thought it had operated or was operating because 'Europe's retrograde order' and then the 'mercantile system' distorted the allocation of capital. This is overlooked by those who favour a providential reading, see, for example, Peter Harrison, 'Adam Smith and the History of the Invisible Hand', *Journal of the History of Ideas* 72/1 (2011), 29–49. An invaluable corrective is Terry Peach, 'Adam Smith's "Optimistic Deism", the Invisible Hand of Providence, and the Unhappiness of Nations', *History of Political Economy* 46/1 (2014), 55–83.
[24] Ricardo, 'On the Principles of Political Economy and Taxation', 327. Smith, *WN* I.xi.a.6.

grasp the fact that rent did not form a component of the price of corn. Of course, in Ricardo's analysis, the price of corn was set by the conditions of production on the unit of land that yielded no rent.[25] Smith, however, had held that food was special because of the constant nature of the demand for food (since food enabled population growth and so ensured its own demand). Given such constant demand, Smith held that land would always provide enough produce to support the labourers who tilled the land and to provide profits, with a residual that could be claimed as rent. Smith's leading 'proof' (Ricardo's word) for this argument was that even the moors in Norway and Scotland afforded a rent for the landlord.[26]

It is instructive to consider the way that Ricardo dispatched Smith's reference to these rent-yielding moors. For Ricardo referred to the fact that in America there existed lands paying no rent but yielding produce sufficient to cover expenses and the usual level of profits. Despite possessing this counter-datum, however, Ricardo asserted that the matter could not be resolved with a 'fact' of this type, insisting on the need for theoretical argument to decide the issue. Namely, that the price of corn needed to be sufficient to return the usual rate of profits to the farmer on the marginal unit of land, or it would not be cultivated. This theoretical 'fact' decided the matter.

> If the comprehensive mind of Adam Smith had been directed to this fact, he would not have maintained that rent forms one of the component parts of the price of raw produce; for price is every where regulated by the return obtained by this last portion of capital, for which no rent whatever is paid.[27]

Notice how this is a different style of disputation to what Ricardo produced in relation to the Bullion Controversy, where he did seem to evince an openness to what we would call empirical phenomena. By contrast, the mode of argument here is theoretical refutation: the 'proofs' are arguments about relations between categories that are defined by theoretical argument, producing a circularity that is impregnable by the outside world of moors and Americas.

Ricardo continued his engagement with Smith's rent doctrine by examining the rent of mines, the topic on which Ricardo considered Smith to have glimpsed but not grasped the correct analysis. Given that Smith treated agriculture as special because food created its own demand and thereby ensured that land would always pay rent, the laws regulating the rent of mines would need to be different on Smith's account since gold and silver were not sources of food. In Ricardo's

---

[25] Ricardo, 'On the Principles of Political Economy and Taxation', 329.
[26] Ibid., 328. For the relevant section in Smith, see Smith, *WN* I.xi.b.1–3.
[27] Ricardo, 'On the Principles of Political Economy and Taxation', 329.

eyes, this was the source of Smith's error since Ricardo did not distinguish between those sectors that provided a nation with its subsistence and those that did not. The Ricardian account instead posited natural resources of variable rates of fertility. Ironically, this was the exact treatment that Smith gave to mines, stipulating that whether or not a mine paid rent was determined by its 'fertility' and the convenience of its location.[28] Ricardo wrote approvingly that 'The whole principle of rent is here admirably and perspicuously explained'.[29] Overall, however, Smith was no master of the doctrine, and so it was left to Ricardo distinguish between error and insight in Smith's work.

With these points in hand, Ricardo considered the politically explosive issue of the landlord's interests in relation to the nation's interests.[30] He did so by underlining yet another error in Smith, this time regarding the proportion that the landlord's share of produce bore to the nation's total produce. Smith's essential claim was that as the quantity of land under cultivation fell, the share that went to the landlord increased. In fact, the reverse was true owing to the inverse relationship between profits and rent.[31] Here the core of Ricardo's account was on display: scarcity of land obliged the community to resort to low-quality land that drove up the cost of producing food for workers, which slowed the process of capital accumulation, but, all the while, those who possessed the more fertile grades of land reaped increasing gains. As Ricardo wrote, 'All classes, therefore, except the landlords, will be injured . . . the loss is wholly on one side, and the gain wholly on the other'.[32] Smith compounded his error later in his work, in Book IV, by failing to see that a high value of corn in terms of other goods was the crucial effect of the Corn Laws. High prices for corn were one thing, but it was a different matter when the *value* of corn rose because of its increasing difficulty of production. Not perceiving this fact, Smith concluded that 'the interest of the landlord is not opposed to that of the rest of the community'.[33] In truth, Ricardo declared, it was.

The question of how to construe the landlord's interest in relation to the community's interests illustrates how high the stakes of doctrinal contest could rise. Far more than a means for point scoring between leisured men, political economy was a science of society and legislation, and Ricardo was claiming that Smith's lack of theoretical sophistication had compromised his political counsel regarding landlords. For only with the correct doctrinal knowledge of

---

[28] Smith, *WN* I.xi.c.10; Ricardo quoting *WN* I.xi.c.10–14.

[29] Ricardo, 'On the Principles of Political Economy and Taxation', 330. Not the whole principle, however, as Ricardo then found that Smith had erred in his claim that it was the most fertile mine that set the price for all mines (Ricardo, 'On the Principles of Political Economy and Taxation', 331–2).

[30] This discussion was significantly enlarged in the third edition (Ibid., 334–5).

[31] Ibid., 333–4, regarding Smith, *WN* I.xi.

[32] Ricardo, 'On the Principles of Political Economy and Taxation', 336.

[33] Ibid.

rent could the social costs of the Corn Laws be perceived, just as Ricardo had argued in his *Essay on Profits*. It is worth noting that this is exactly the type of analysis that Burke had feared: a rationalism that was irreverent towards established interests. In this case, the established interest was an aristocracy that Burke had treated in sacralizing terms.[34] Of course, from the point of view of Ricardo, Burke's analysis might be either an instance of the anti-rationalist fallacies that held back the tide of change, as Bentham would shortly diagnose in his *Book of Fallacies* (1824), or it was simply pre-theoretical. In the latter aspect, insulating the aristocracy from rational legislation was rather like allowing the Bank of England to continue to run on instinct: the national interest would be sacrificed to superstition. We might say that a middle point between superstition and reason was held by Smith's statesman, whose virtues were not exhausted by rationality because they also included extra-rational prudence.[35] But Ricardo would have struggled to understand prudence in Smith's terms because Ricardo's doctrinal claims were not addressed to a legislator who would then dispense them by mobilizing political virtues; instead, Ricardo's truths were to unfold through the world's rational progress. This was also a source of tension between Ricardo and Malthus.

Ricardo Corrects Malthus

Having established the core of Ricardo's doctrine on rent and the manner in which he dispatched Smith's rival account, we are now in a position to observe the treatment that Ricardo gave to Malthus. The key statement comes from chapter 31 of the second edition of the *Principles*, 'Mr. Malthus's Opinions on Rent'. Ricardo motivated this additional chapter on rent by noticing Malthus's reputation.

> I consider myself bound to notice some opinions on the subject, which appear to me erroneous, and which are the more important, as they are found in the writings of one, to whom, of all men of the present day, some branches of economical science are the most indebted . . . yet he appears to me to have fallen into some errors, which his authority makes it the more necessary, whilst his characteristic candour renders it less unpleasing to notice.[36]

---

[34] See Donald Winch's discussion of Smith and Burke on the landed aristocracy: Winch, *Riches and Poverty*, 175–85.

[35] See *WN* Iv.v.b.53 and *TMS* VI.ii.2.16.

[36] Ricardo, 'On the Principles of Political Economy and Taxation', 398.

Ricardo began the task of weeding out his friend's errors by examining the notion that rent represented the creation of wealth.[37] Ricardo was precluded from acceding to this conclusion because of the different way in which he conceived of wealth and value. On the one hand, wealth referred to a society's necessaries and conveniences—to that fund of wealth from which it could 'maintain fleets and armies', exactly Smith's phrase.[38] Value, on the other hand, related to difficulty of production, as detailed in the previous chapter.

Ricardo worked through Malthus's list of reasons why the price of corn was higher than the cost of bringing it to market: the fecundity of the earth, that foodstuffs were peculiar because they create their own demand, and the scarcity of fertile land. According to Ricardo, what this argumentation revealed was Malthus's incomplete understanding of the principle of rent. We have already seen that Ricardo had reversed the claim regarding the earth's supposed fecundity in his engagement with Smith. It was simply the case that rent arose because of the existence of variable rates of profitability. The trouble with Malthus's presentation, according to Ricardo, was that it averred the role of the 'absolute' fertility of the land when rent was proportioned to 'relative fertility'.[39] Ricardo then turned to Malthus's distinction between the laws regulating the rent of mines, on the one hand, and the rent of land that yielded the necessaries of life, on the other, finding that 'This distinction does not appear to me to be well founded'.[40] Ricardo also sought to expose inconsistencies between Malthus's texts, quoting from Malthus's *Observations* to argue against his *Inquiry into Rent*.[41] To this point, however, Ricardo was only skirmishing, for his real attack was on Malthus's claim that food was special because it created its own demand. In a master stroke, Ricardo struck Malthus with his own weapon by using population theory to claim that food did not call forth increased population; capital played that role, via the demand for labour.[42]

Ricardo's other major riposte to Malthus concerned the distributional implications of the price of corn. Dense intersections arose at this point between correct

[37] Malthus had made this claim in his *Inquiry into Rent*. Malthus, 'The Nature and Progress of Rent', 116–8. There Malthus surveyed noteworthy writers and similarly presumed to identify their errors, including Adam Smith, David Buchanan, J. B. Say, and J. C. S. L. Sismondi.

[38] Ricardo, 'On the Principles of Political Economy and Taxation', 400. Smith, *WN* Iv.i.4.

[39] Ricardo, 'On the Principles of Political Economy and Taxation', 403–4. In the third edition of the *Principles*, Ricardo added a footnote that acknowledged that Malthus had claimed to have been misunderstood by Ricardo on this point (Malthus, 'Principles of Political Economy: Part I', 122 at n15); Ricardo quoted Malthus again to show that this seemed to be the only possible interpretation that Malthus's words would bear, but discharged Malthus of responsibility in order to combat the claim and not its author (Ricardo, 'On the Principles of Political Economy and Taxation', 404 at asterisked note).

[40] Ricardo, 'On the Principles of Political Economy and Taxation', 405. A point noticed by Malthus (Malthus, 'Principles of Political Economy: Part I', 119).

[41] Ricardo, 'On the Principles of Political Economy and Taxation', 408–10, 414.

[42] Ibid., 406–7.

doctrine and the science of legislation. Ricardo began by citing with approval Malthus's claim in his *Inquiry into Rent* that the essential cause of a high price of corn was its cost of production.[43] Yet Malthus's error, according to Ricardo, was to have maintained that a fall in the money price of corn would be reflected in all commodities.[44] In making this claim in his *Grounds*, Malthus had been focusing on the effects of what we would call deflation for the holders of government debt. That is, as prices in general fell, the fixed payments made to debt holders would rise in value. It would represent a handsome profit but one funded by the rest of society—by labour, and by landlords.[45] In other words, Malthus was indicating the political complexities that commercial change could cause.

According to Ricardo, there were two problems with Malthus's argument. The first was that the logic was broken. If stockholders benefited when the price of corn fell, then that fact lent no support for making corn dear. It should be noted that here Ricardo was misconstruing Malthus's argument, since Malthus's point was that a piece of legislation that lowered the price of corn would only benefit one class; Malthus was not assessing the proposition that corn should bear a high price. Ricardo was on firmer ground when he asserted that if it truly were the case that stockholders benefited to a degree that was unjust, then the legislature could always 'devise a remedy'.[46] Once again, the weakness of this aspect of Ricardo's thinking was noticeable since he simply did not possess a framework for conceiving of governmental action in remedial mode or for weighing the merits of alternative actions.

The second problem that Ricardo identified in Malthus's argument was that the general deflation that followed a fall in the price of corn would not be as great as Malthus supposed and neither would be the tax implications. Ricardo's prediction was that, were cheap corn to be imported from abroad, the prices of other goods would only be affected to the extent that corn entered into the 'real value, or cost of production' of these other goods.[47] Making this reply to Malthus was crucial for Ricardo's case because it meant that the loss to landholders would represent the primary harm to arise from importing corn. Furthermore, the harm would be offset by gains flowing to the truly productive agents, 'capitalists', since the wages that capitalists paid would be lowered, leaving a larger residual to be taken as profits.[48] What can we make of these claims in relation to Ricardo's earlier performances? As with Ricardo's account of the winners and losers to emerge from abolishing the Corn Laws, but unlike his argument in the

---

[43] Ibid., 417. See Malthus, 'The Nature and Progress of Rent', 135.
[44] Ricardo, 'On the Principles of Political Economy and Taxation', 419.
[45] Malthus, 'The Nature and Progress of Rent', 169.
[46] Ricardo, 'On the Principles of Political Economy and Taxation', 425.
[47] Ibid., 417.
[48] Ibid., 420–5.

Bullion Controversy, Ricardo simply deployed his own concepts and doctrines without adducing relevant evidence, such as corn prices and the quantities that were likely to be imported. Instead, theory was being crafted as an autonomous form of proof with the force to direct legislation.

Ricardo brought his argument to a head by quoting Malthus's endorsement of Smith's treatment of agriculture as special, then overturned this claim by combining his own doctrines on rent and value. In short, if Smith's claim that agriculture was special were true, then it was only true in the sense that the non-uniformity of agricultural machines, or land, gave rise to value.[49] But value was not the thing that mattered to a nation: wealth mattered. And, by creating value through the variability of its machines, agriculture acted as a break on all commerce by raising the cost of food and wages, depressing profits until the capitalist would refuse to invest in agriculture. Ricardo had thus shown that Smith's central premise—that agriculture represented the natural and ideal first step to national wealth—was false. Ricardo had also battered Smith's reputation in the process, for the Scottish Professor emerged as having misunderstood rent and mistaken nature's niggardly character for generosity. Malthus, as an avowed follower of Smith, defender of landlords, and named antagonist in Ricardo's chapter, had his work cut out for him in forming a reply.

Malthus Responds

In view of what has been said, it appears that Malthus's chapter on rent needed to meet two strategic goals. In the first place, Ricardo's rent doctrine needed to be opposed since it portrayed rent as a by-product of progress that was unnaturally raised by protection to the benefit of the landed interest. Given his commitment to viewing the 'country' interest as playing a special constitutional role in the nation and his defence of the landed interest in Inquiry into Rent, Malthus could hardly have allowed this claim to stand uncontested. In the second place, Ricardo's disparagement of Malthus's work in chapter 31, 'Mr. Malthus's Opinions on Rent', naturally relied on the Ricardian account of rent. If Malthus were able to establish a rival treatment of rent, then he would have the basis for repelling Ricardo on both fronts. Malthus duly produced such an alternative account. In it, he naturalized rent as a gift from God and as a normal and beneficial outcome of material progress. As the key moves of this account are set out in what follows, it will also become clear that Malthus adopted the same tactic that he used in his Inquiry into Rent: to articulate an abstract definition of rent and then use it to indict earlier attempts to examine the issue.[50] We have just seen that this was

---

[49] Ibid., 429.
[50] Malthus, 'The Nature and Progress of Rent', 115–16.

also the way in which Ricardo had proceeded in both his *Essay on Profits* and in his *Principles*. It therefore seems that political economy was developing a style of intellectual conduct in which theoretical definitions played a central role, and, in consequence, protocols on good and bad definitions again featured as a *topos* of debate.

In this respect, Malthus possessed an advantage because he could often claim to be deploying definitions that adhered to common usage, as seen in the previous chapter. In addition, the tendency for theorists to produce their own definitions of terms in opposition to common usage was seen in Chapter 1 to represent a favourite point of attack for their enemies.[51] Malthus was able to draw these existing resources to his side, and, in general, he appears to have been better skilled at articulating protocols for the use of terms. It is likely that the resources that might have aided Ricardo in defending his flair for new definitions—the philosophy of mind that he read under Mill's tutelage, including Stewart and Locke—only became objects of focus late in 1817, after the publication of the *Principles* in April that year.[52] And his aptitude as a student is an open question: as Ricardo wrote to Mill in correspondence regarding Berkeley, Stewart, Hume, Locke, and Reid, 'I suspect that I do not understand the language that is applied to the operations of the mind'.[53] Equally revealing is Ricardo's response to Hutches Trower's request that he make a 'greater point of *defining accurately* and *rigidly*, the *terms employed*', perhaps in an opening chapter of the next edition of the *Principles*.[54] Ricardo wrote in reply that such a chapter 'would be of great use, but it requires a degree of precision and accuracy beyond what I could furnish'.[55] Malthus may have been aware of Ricardo's weakness here; whether or not he was, he certainly made the issue of definitions a major feature of his complaints in personal correspondence and his attacks in public on Ricardo's intellectual conduct.[56]

How did Malthus define rent? It was the surplus that remained after costs of production and ordinary agricultural profits were paid. The list of those who had failed to grasp rent correctly included Quesnay and his school of Economists, Jean-Baptiste Say, Smith, and 'modern writers', Ricardo included.[57] The problem that all of these writers shared, according to Malthus, was the tendency to assimilate rent to a monopoly payment, even Smith, despite some moments of insight.

---

[51] Recall the passage from Burke quoted earlier, in Chapter 1, in which Burke noted the rage for redefinition in metaphysics, while 'prudence is cautious how she defines', supra, p.39.

[52] Mill, 'Mill to Ricardo', *Works and Correspondence*, 7: 194–9, at 197.

[53] Ricardo, 'Ricardo to Mill', *Works and Correspondence*, 7: 227–9; at 229.

[54] Hutches Trower, 'Trower to Ricardo', *Works and Correspondence*, 7: 255–8, at 256.

[55] Ricardo, 'Ricardo to Trower', *Works and Correspondence*, 7: 258–61, at 259. In relation to his *Principles*, Ricardo's self-assessment is fair.

[56] See, in particular, Malthus, 'Malthus to Ricardo', *Works and Correspondence*, 6: 40–2; Malthus, 'Malthus to Ricardo', *Works and Correspondence*, 6: 61–3; Malthus, 'Malthus to Ricardo', *Works and Correspondence*, 7: 213–5.

[57] Malthus, 'Principles of Political Economy: Part I', 110–11.

Thus it emerges that Malthus, too, was susceptible to producing retrospective, *ad hoc* doctrinal history. In other words, in these doctrinal clashes between Malthus and Ricardo we are witnessing the birth of rational reconstruction as the primary mode of narrating the history of economic thought.

Returning to rent, Malthus acknowledged the finite supply of land, but he insisted that the soil's fecundity was the more important fact because it meant that the land's produce could support more labourers than were needed to bring that produce to market. Malthus referred to this as the earth's '*power*', standing as a 'gift of nature to man', to which the rent of any given piece of land would be proportioned.[58] The other reason why agricultural produce bore a surplus price was closely related and drew on Malthus's population principle: food created its own demand by allowing population to expand. As Malthus put the point, the land produced 'the means by which, and by which alone, an increase of people may be brought into being and supported'.[59] Malthus's counter-account of rent turned on this claim. It will be recalled that the key to Ricardo's argument was that the laws governing the rent of mines were identical to those governing the rent of land because mines possessed the same nature as land: they varied in quality and were of limited supply.[60] In contradistinction, and like Smith, Malthus held that land was 'fundamentally different from every other kind of machine known to man' because humanity depended on food for its existence, not on gold and silver.[61] With these claims in place, Malthus could rebut Ricardo's analysis.

Ricardo's argument was that rents rose as the fertility of the marginal unit of land fell. Ricardo could therefore postulate that if the fertility of land in general were to fall, then providing the same quantity of food would require that lands of lower fertility were drawn into cultivation, thus pushing up rents.[62] By contrast, Malthus's argument premised that rent was a sign of fertility; hence a general fall in the earth's fecundity would reduce rent as the wealth and population formerly supported by the earth's 'power' was destroyed. The gold and silver produced by the world's mines, however, played no such role in supporting wealth and population; hence the rent of mines was determined by the degree of monopoly, not by the earth's 'power', as it was in agriculture. Turning to one of his preferred idioms, Malthus claimed that, in failing to distinguish between mines and land, Ricardo had failed to observe God's ordering of the world. Malthus claimed his victory in the form of a rhetorical question: 'Is it not . . . a clear indication of

---

[58] Ibid., 113–4.
[59] Ibid., 115.
[60] Ricardo, 'On the Principles of Political Economy and Taxation', 85–7.
[61] Malthus, 'Principles of Political Economy: Part I', 115.
[62] Ricardo, 'On the Principles of Political Economy and Taxation', 412. Referenced by Malthus at Malthus, 'Principles of Political Economy: Part I', 116.

a most inestimable quality in the soil, which God has bestowed on man—the quality of being able to maintain more persons than are necessary to work it?'[63] This was the first step in Malthus's strategy to draw on the resources of natural theology to underwrite his account of rent.

The second step was to identify the fertility of the land as the original source of the surplus that made human progress possible. Malthus took this step by developing a speculative history that illustrated the functioning of his three causes of rent. This history premised that the first settling of a new colony would see the knowledge and capital of an old society applied to those lands of the highest fertility, which would yield high profits and high wages simultaneously, but no rent, since the land was freely available.[64] A mechanism soon began, however, as population growth (called forth by the population-supporting nature of agricultural produce) expanded the supply of labour, putting downward pressure on wages, while the accumulation of capital brought second-rate land under cultivation, putting downward pressure on profits. These two factors would raise the exchangeable value of food above its cost of production, giving rise to rent for those who held title to the land's 'power'.[65] Rent was simply a side effect of progress, and here Malthus could reverse Ricardo's barbs in the *Essay on Profits* and *Principles* about the desirability of progress.[66] If the very existence of rent were so odious, Malthus countered, then it would be better that 'a country which might maintain well ten millions of inhabitants ought to be kept down to a million'.[67] He continued:

> The transfer from profits and wages, and such a price of produce as yields rent, which have been objected to as injurious, and as depriving the consumer of what it gives to the landlord, are absolutely necessary in order to obtain any considerable addition to the wealth and revenue of the first settlers in a new country; and are the natural and unavoidable consequences of that increase of capital and population for which nature has provided in the propensities of the human race[68]

---

[63] Ibid., 119. (The passage is mistranscribed in *Works*.)

[64] Malthus was not insensible to the actual processes of colonization: Alison Bashford and Joyce E. Chaplin, *The New Worlds of Thomas Robert Malthus: Rereading the Principle of Population* (Princeton, NJ: Princeton University Press, 2016), 115, 203–5, 234.

[65] Malthus, 'Principles of Political Economy: Part I', 121.

[66] Malthus quoted Ricardo's *reductio ad absurdum* attack on rent: 'If the surplus produce which the land affords in the form of rent be an advantage, it is desirable that every year the machinery newly constructed should be less efficient than the old, as that would undoubtedly give a greater exchangeable value to the goods manufactured, not only by that machinery, but by all the other machinery in the kingdom; and a rent would be paid to all those who possessed the most productive machinery' Ibid., 169, imperfectly quoting Ricardo, 'On the Principles of Political Economy and Taxation', 75–6.

[67] Malthus, 'Principles of Political Economy: Part I', 122.

[68] Ibid., 122–3.

The reference to humanity's 'propensities' should be taken to refer to the premises of Malthus's *Essay* (1798): humans need food to survive, and the passion between the sexes is not susceptible to amelioration. Malthus's injunction in his *Essay* was that these aspects of human life represented 'fixed laws of our nature', and theorists were not to suppose that they would change without 'an immediate act of power in that Being who first arranged the system of the universe'.[69] This was a clever move: Malthus was exploiting the status of his principle of population, ordained by God in the Malthusian version, and endorsed in one version or another by the majority of political economists, including Ricardo.[70] With rent so naturalized, Malthus could afford to concede that governments ought to avoid the 'premature formation' of rent via monopolies, most spectacularly seen in the 'great eastern monarchies' of the Indian and Chinese nations where the sovereign was considered the owner of the soil.[71] Rent would come naturally, and its unnatural creation by governmental incompetence was undesirable.[72]

The third and final step in Malthus's theological riposte to Ricardo's doctrine on rent was to set out the correct manner by which one could identify the gifts of providence. As we have seen, Malthus's defence of rent built from the premise that the land's fecundity was a gift from God. This represented a variation on an old theme for political economy, one on which Smith had also improvised in his pseudo-providential account of capital in *Wealth of Nations*. Given that it was a natural preference to have one's capital under view, merchants operating under a system of liberty would prefer to invest their capital in agriculture, thereby aligning their interests with those of the community, as if guided by an 'invisible hand'—the hand of God's providence operating through general laws. As we have seen, of course, Smith's argument was that Europe's past had been retrograde, owing to the contingencies of its post-Roman history, as was its present, owing to the distortions of the mercantile system.[73] Smith, in other words, had drawn on the rhetoric of providence for descriptive purposes. In Malthus, by contrast, we are dealing with a providential argument: agricultural surplus represented 'a bountiful gift of providence'.[74]

A rival account to this sacralizing treatment of land was at the heart of Ricardo's work, and Malthus quoted the very passage in which Ricardo contrasted the constancy of the 'elasticity of steam' with nature's niggardliness.[75] In allowing himself to discourse on nature's usefulness to the human race, Ricardo had entered Malthus's home territory of natural theology, where the task was to

---

[69] Malthus, 'An Essay on the Principle of Population (1798)', 8.
[70] For this, see Walter, 'Malthus's Principle of Population in Britain: Restatement and Antiquation'.
[71] Malthus, 'Principles of Political Economy: Part I', 124.
[72] Ibid., 127–43.
[73] Smith, *WN* Books III and IV, respectively.
[74] Malthus, 'Principles of Political Economy: Part I', 168.
[75] Ibid.

investigate the nature of God with reference to human nature and the natural world. Moreover, it was a terrain of which Malthus was a master by training and by his virtuoso performances in the various editions of the *Essay*. It was to these arguments that Malthus turned in his reply to Ricardo.

Malthus began by setting down the central precept of the genre: a gift of providence could be identified by estimating its value in relation to 'the laws and constitution of our nature, and of the world in which we live'.[76] Would limitless food since the beginning of the Christian era represent such a gift? To answer the question, Malthus adduced the leading law of the human constitution: the power of population that, when unchecked, saw population double every twenty-five years or less. It followed that limitless food would have produced extreme overpopulation, reaching even beyond 'all the planets of our solar system'.[77] In consequence, so long as human nature maintained its current constitution, it was absolutely essential that some limit on the food supply existed. By contrast, human nature called forth no such limit on the elasticity of steam. Ricardo had, in other words, failed to develop his natural theology using the appropriate protocols for that form of reasoning, and this had prevented him from noticing that an unlimited food supply would represent a curse on humanity, inconsistent with a loving God. Malthus drew out the lesson for Ricardo.

> A benevolent Creator then, knowing the wants and necessities of his creatures, under the laws to which he had subjected them, could not, in mercy, have furnished the whole of the necessaries of life in the same plenty as air and water....
> But if it be granted, as it must be, that a limitation in the power of producing food is obviously necessary to man confined to a limited space, then the value of the actual quantity of land which he has received, depends upon the small quantity of labour necessary to work it, compared with the number of persons which it will support; or, in other words, upon that specific surplus so much underrated by Mr Ricardo, which by the laws of nature terminates in rent.[78]

Ricardo had rejected natural theology as an explicit source of knowledge for political economy, but in this passage he was exposed to its full force, in particular, its ability to act as a type of theoretical check on hasty philosophy, a version of the move that Malthus had made in the first and subsequent editions of his *Essay* against Condorcet and Godwin, enthusiasts both.

Malthus closed his defence of rent by suggesting that it be thought of as a measure of the relief that providence had granted man from labour.[79] That is,

[76] Ibid., 169.
[77] Ibid.
[78] Ibid., 169–70.
[79] Ibid., 170.

given that rent primarily arose from the ability of the land to support more la-bourers than were needed for its cultivation, thus freeing workers to produce manufactures and luxuries, the size of a nation's total rent revenue was an indi-cation of its capacity for material refinement. The implication was that small rent suggested small progress, a conclusion underwritten by a knowledge of God's intentions, as divined by Malthus in the correct manner. Theology was a leading element of Malthus's thought, and Ricardo had gambled unsuccessfully when he decided to use it himself.

There is a final aspect of Malthus's rival treatment of rent to notice. It con-cerned the complexities by which landlords adjusted their rents, a topic wholly elided by Ricardo, who simply assumed a straightforward mechanism in the interests of elucidating the relationship between rent and profits. For Malthus, by contrast, the intricacies or 'frictions' were an important object of analysis.[80] He developed his examination by noticing two errors that could harm land-lords when it came to re-letting their lands. The first was to choose the highest bidder, regardless of whether or not the farmer had sufficient capital to improve the land and cultivate it in the ideal manner.[81] The second and more important error to which landlords were exposed was to perceive a temporary rise in the price of agricultural produce as a permanent rise, raising rents in reliance on this observation. This created undesirable consequences for the landlord and for society. For the landlord, it meant that when prices returned to their natural levels their tenants would fail financially, leaving the lands in ruin. For society, the issue was that tenant farmers needed these short periods in which prices rose but rents remained constant because it was during these phases that cap-ital could be accumulated and invested in land in the form of improvements. In other words, the imperfections of markets created the basis for future pros-perity, and imperfections ought not, in consequence, be excluded from the theorist's sight.[82]

If the foregoing will suffice as an account of Malthus's rival theory of rent, then it is now time to examine the tactics and vocabulary with which he described and impeached Ricardo's claims. In particular, Malthus focused on Ricardo's presentation of rent as a phenomenon that arose from the land's varying quality. Instead, Ricardo should have isolated the land's special role in human life; rent was natural in Malthus's schema. Even if the land of a nation were all of the same quality, *progress* would still call forth high rent as the population grew and capital accumulated. Ricardo's mistake was to have drawn 'too large an inference from

[80] See J. M. Pullen, 'Malthus on Causality', *The European Journal of the History of Economic Thought* 23/3 (2016), 349–77; Cremaschi and Dascal, 'Malthus and Ricardo on Economic Methodology', 478.
[81] Malthus, 'Principles of Political Economy: Part I', 155.
[82] Ibid., 155–7.

the theory of rent'.[83] This was an instance of the tendency for some theorists to reason hastily.

Ricardo had inferred another erroneous conclusion that was of even greater importance when he claimed that it was the last unit of land taken into cultivation that set the rate of profits for all cultivation. In Ricardo's example, if lands number 1, 2, 3 were under cultivation, then it was land No. 3 that paid no rent. Ricardo had 'inferred' from his theory that when the process was reversed, and land No. 3 was thrown out of cultivation, profits also retraced their steps, rising to the level set by No. 2, which would become the unit of land that yielded no rent. The trouble with this account, according to Malthus, was that the 'premises' did not match with life in the civilized world, where land always paid rent, as per Smith, even after a diminution in a nation's wealth.[84] Capital might fall to zero, but rent would not, since land could always draw a moderate rent by acting as pasturage.

The ultimate stakes of this dispute were high for Malthus because of its connection to the politically combustible issue of the interests of landlords with respect to society in general. We have seen that, in Ricardo's account, landlords were opposed to the importation of corn because it caused the withdrawal of capital from the land, which destroyed large portions of rent instead of simply reducing them, as in Malthus's account. This difference allowed Malthus to respecify the role of the landlord's interests, seen in his subtitle, 'On the Strict and Necessary Connection of the Interests of the Landlord and of the State in a Country Which Supports its Own Population'.[85] The essence of Malthus's position was that, since rent arose from the growth of capital and population, when landlords wished for rents to grow they were merely wishing for progress, hardly an indictable offence and perfectly compatible with society's general interest.

According to Malthus, Ricardo was only led to take an opposing position because of the peculiar manner in which he understood rent, where rent increased not with progress but with the need to turn to nature's inferior machines, increasing the difficulty of production. Malthus assessed this view, however, to be neither 'just' nor 'true'.[86] Why was it neither just nor true? It turns out that what

---

[83] Ibid., 146. Malthus might be seen as having misrepresented Ricardo by turning his use of a didactic device into a claim about the world. For Ricardo was able to account for Malthus's criticisms in his *Notes* by pointing to his intensive case: the 'employment of an additional capital on the old land, without as large a return'. Ricardo, 'Notes on Malthus's *Principles of Political Economy*', *Works and Correspondence*, 2: 170.

[84] Malthus, 'Principles of Political Economy: Part I', 147. Note also Malthus's discussion of this issue in the preceding chapter on value, where he wrote that 'To say that the prices of wool, leather, flax, and timber are determined by the cost of their production on the land which pays no rent, is to refer to a criterion which it is impossible to find. I believe it may be safely asserted that there is no portion of wool, leather, flax, and timber produced in this country which comes from land that can be so described' (Malthus, 'Principles of Political Economy: Part II', 369).

[85] Malthus, 'Principles of Political Economy: Part I', 158.

[86] Ibid.

Malthus was taking issue with was Ricardo's use of the 'doctrine of the gradations of soils' for the purpose of 'drawing practical conclusions', in this case, identifying landlords as possessing a distinct interest from the state and the people, and doing so without following the precept that 'great care should be taken to apply it [the doctrine] correctly'.[87] Malthus simply held that it was preposterous to talk of what would happen if there were a great improvement in agricultural technology overnight. On Ricardo's terms, such an event would have allowed capital to be drawn off the least fertile unit of land, allowing the society to retrace its steps from land No. 3 to land No. 2. The key point for Ricardo was that rents would fall. It was on the basis of this argument that Ricardo had claimed that landlord interests were served by agricultural production continuing on poor lands. What was so concerning to Malthus in this way of thinking was its neglect of the art of drawing practical conclusions.

The particular conclusion that worried Malthus was Ricardo's divisive finding that the most influential class in society possessed a distinct interest that harmed the whole. As Malthus wrote, it was simply impermissible to *'dwell upon*, and draw general inferences from suppositions which never can take place'.[88] In this case, the impossible supposition was sudden improvement in agricultural practices, which helped Ricardo to isolate the landed interest. Instead of averting to such 'suppositions', Malthus insisted, it was necessary to bind theory to the world as it was known to exist by experience because that was the world where practical conclusions would be put to work.

> What we want to know is, whether, living as we do in a limited world, and in countries and districts still more limited, and under such physical laws relating to the produce of the soil and the increase of population as are found by experience to prevail, the interests of the landlord are generally opposed to those of the society. And in this view of the subject, the question may be settled by an appeal to the most incontrovertible principles confirmed by the most glaring facts.[89]

Malthus had in mind two 'glaring facts', and they both undermined Ricardo's account. The first was that Ricardo's 'fanciful suppositions' of drastic improvements in agriculture had never been found in 'practice'; indeed, there was likely to have never been 'a single instance in the history of Europe'.[90] The second fact that invalidated Ricardo's position was that improvements operated gradually, enabling the power of population to exert itself, prompting farmers to extend

---

[87] These comments are taken from the second edition (Ibid., 149).
[88] Ibid., 159.
[89] Ibid.
[90] Ibid.

cultivation. As we have seen, Malthus went to considerable efforts to convey something of the complexity of these processes. These efforts included his discussion of the formation of rent over time in the face of complex wage-population-profit dynamics and his account of the lease-setting process and the errors to which landlords were susceptible. And this discussion was, of course, housed by Malthus's overarching narrative that naturalized and legitimized rent as a natural sign of progress. Ricardo was led to the opposite view, according to Malthus, because he had failed to apply the necessary disciplines to his reasoning. Above all, Ricardo had failed to tether his theory to the leading facts of the matter as disclosed by experience. Instead of submitting to this procedure, Ricardo had analysed rent by simply imagining a society that possessed lands 1, 2, 3, each of successively poorer quality. As the quality of land fell, prices rose. But this was merely a 'simple and confined view of the progress of rent', one that departed from facts, such that 'any general inferences from it must be utterly inapplicable to practice'.[91] Failing to test theory with practice and experience was dangerous, and Ricardo had not paused despite both his neglect of this discipline and the drastic implications that his theory held for the nation's political harmony. Even for someone committed to theory, as Malthus was, Ricardo the theorist appeared to be a danger to his society.

Conclusion

In these replies to Ricardo, Malthus was articulating a version of some standard criticisms of the theorist's ill-governed mind that we encountered in Chapter 1 and Chapter 2. Correspondingly, Malthus used language with which we have now become familiar, such as the opposition between fancy and supposition, on the one hand, and practice and experience, on the other. Malthus used this language to portray Ricardo as ignoring the complex mechanisms surrounding rent that were actually in play in a nation at any given point in time, meaning that Ricardo's science was recklessly simplifying and speculative. When this science presumed to offer itself as a basis for lawmaking, the stakes became serious. The danger was heightened by the fact that Ricardo tended to present his policy recommendations in such confrontational terms. This aspect of Ricardo's thought had led one anonymous reviewer, writing for *Blackwood's Edinburgh Magazine* in 1818, to underline how Ricardo's theoretical error had produced an account of society that portrayed one class of men to be the 'enemies' of all others.[92] Ricardo

---

[91] Ibid., 163.
[92] Anonymous, 'Ricardo and the Edinburgh Review', *Blackwood's Edinburgh Magazine* 4/19 (1818), 58–62. Reprinted in *David Ricardo: Critical Responses*, vol. 1, 99–107, at 99.

was not helped by the fact that this incendiary doctrine was propagated as truth for the public to absorb, as against a species of counsel addressed to the figure of the statesman whose moral *persona* might contain its implications by dousing them with prudence or allied virtues, as found in Smith. Moreover, Ricardo's anonymous reviewer considered all of this in the context of a tense historical moment and wondered if the public mind might not lurch into levelling: how else to permanently rid society of its landlord enemies unless the '*whole mass of the people should assume the whole mass of the land, and cultivate it, for the mutual benefit, by Committees*'?[93]

In short, and from the point of view of his critics, the trouble with Ricardo was not limited to the erroneous content of his doctrines. Certainly that was an issue, but even errors could aid science over a long horizon, as Malthus's account of Smith revealed. Rather, the real trouble with Ricardo was his intellectual recklessness. This was not a critique of Ricardo's method. It was alarm at Ricardo's theoretical enthusiasm, a failing that made it possible to link him with the destructive forces that had ruined France. For his part, Ricardo understood himself to be not simply producing science but to be exposing harmful connections between interests and legislation. First the Bank of England and paper money, and now landlords and protection. As we saw in his rejection of the Burkean idea that citizens ought to be grateful for whatever benefits happened to have been secured to their nation through custom, Ricardo took truth, not political prudence, for his lodestar. Doctrines and political sensibilities were tightly intertwined because the former were not articulated independently of the latter.

[93] Ibid., 100.

6

Doctrinal Contest III

Profits

This chapter closes the study of the doctrinal contest between Malthus and Ricardo by examining their conflicting accounts of profits. The essentials of the argument that Ricardo set out in chapter 6 of the *Principles*, 'On Profits', were already present in his *Essay on Profits* (1815), and he maintained this view of profits throughout his subsequent writings.[1] The vital claim was that if a nation were obliged to provide its own corn by drawing on progressively inferior lands or by increasing the intensity of farming on lands already under cultivation, then the price of corn would rise. Given the status of corn as a key component of natural wages—of the wages necessary for a worker to maintain his family in the manner acquired by 'habit'—this would represent a standing threat to profitability and, in turn, national progress.[2] This was the crux of Ricardo's attack on protection to agriculture that we encountered in Chapter 3.

As with other key aspects of the *Principles*, Ricardo developed his theory by reading Smith as if he were setting out Ricardian doctrine with limited acuity, which provided the occasion for Ricardo to rehearse corrections of Smith. Perhaps the most noteworthy aspect of Ricardo's strictures is the way that the remaining infrastructure of Smith's 'invisible hand' argument was destroyed. The fact that Malthus's defence of Smith did not include a restoration of these aspects seems to have sealed the fate of Smith's ornate argument concerning nature's *gratis* labour. What Malthus did preserve from Smith, however, in his chapter, 'Of the Profits of Capital', was an analysis of supply and demand. According to Malthus, the outstanding failure of Ricardo's new theory of profits was its disqualification from the analysis of those factors that Smith had underlined: the supply and demand of capital in relation to the supply and demand of labour.

---

[1] Peach, *Interpreting Ricardo*, 88–103.

[2] Ricardo, 'On the Principles of Political Economy and Taxation', 93. It was this aspect of Ricardo's theory that made it possible to treat him as a pessimistic thinker, perhaps most famously (and tendentiously) by Michel Foucault. Ricardo was positioned as a pessimist regarding the material future (a steady-state of low profits) in contrast to Marx the optimist (plenty from communism); Michel Foucault, *Order of Things* (London: Routledge, 2002), 284–5. Since he treated Ricardo as protruding out of the strata of Western reason, Foucault did not notice the actual context—a British parliamentary debate over the Corn Laws—and neither did he notice that Ricardo the Unitarian was sanguine about the future, since these facts are too fine-grained to be preserved by Foucault's 'archaeology'.

Before Method and Models. Ryan Walter, Oxford University Press. © Oxford University Press 2021.
DOI: 10.1093/oso/9780197603055.003.0009

As we will see, Malthus may not have been entirely honest in his presentation of Ricardo's arguments on this point. Whatever the case, Malthus's key move was to identify a startling divergence between Ricardo's theory and the world as it really was, or what Malthus repeatedly referred to as 'the actual state of things'.[3] Correspondingly, Malthus's rhetoric was focused on presenting the test of science as the ability to account for the observed facts, and his conduct seemed to match his combative talk since Malthus provided these facts by turning to historico-factual accounts of Britain's commercial life.

As these details suggest, the debate over the correct theory of profits appears to have replayed the earlier struggle in the Corn Laws debate. One key difference in this encounter, however, was that the facts were not being used to aid in the resolution of a policy question before Parliament but to establish correct doctrine. A further difference was that Malthus attacked Ricardo because his theory postulated long-term dynamics that, Malthus claimed to have shown, could be overwhelmed by short-term factors. In this way, Malthus was building on his criticisms of Ricardo's theory of rent, thereby developing a sustained account of Ricardo's intellectual conduct as deficient. In opposition, Ricardo privileged the theoretical identification of a principle using hypothetical numerical illustrations and repeated his defence that his numbers only exemplified: 'I have been desirous only to elucidate the principle'.[4] Thus, Ricardo's virtuoso elucidation of principles will emerge in what follows as contesting with Malthus's purported attempt to account for the facts of the world as disclosed by experience. If we view the issue with the benefit of hindsight, then it seems that Malthus was unable to vanquish his rival despite having tremendous intellectual and rhetorical resources at his disposal. As a result, the campaign to secure the standing of theoretical labour as an end in itself continued throughout the nineteenth century. Setting out the shape of the clash between Malthus and Ricardo begins with the latter's corrections of Smith.

Ricardo Corrects Smith

Ricardo began his chapter, 'On Profits', by acknowledging the veracity of Smith's argument that profits varied between employments of capital based on factors inherent to the occupation.[5] This was the idea that a capitalist would take into account factors beyond pecuniary return. As Ricardo expressed this point,

---

[3] Malthus, 'Principles of Political Economy: Part I', 228.

[4] Ricardo, 'On the Principles of Political Economy and Taxation', 121.

[5] In chapter 10 of Book I, Smith had enumerated five circumstances that affected the agreeableness of an occupation, treating them as partially explaining differences in rates of profit. See Smith, WN, I.x.b.4, 10, 16, 20, 33.

A capitalist . . . will naturally take into consideration all the advantages which one occupation possesses over another. He may therefore be willing to forego a part of his money profit, in consideration of the security, cleanliness, ease, or any other real or fancied advantage which one employment may possess over another[6]

In this passage, Ricardo was sifting the remnants of Smith's analysis. For Smith had given a key role to the attractions of investing capital in agriculture—security and the charms of country life—in drawing capital that would otherwise find its way to manufacturing or trade, and it was this concatenation that allowed Smith to project the harmony of private and public interests under a system of natural liberty. As seen in the previous chapter, however, Ricardo had destroyed Smith's account of agriculture as a superior trade. In consequence, the Ricardian system had no need to conjure the security and charms of country life to guarantee that capitalists would naturally prefer to direct their capital to agriculture. Ricardo nevertheless recycled this aspect of Smith's argumentation, presumably because he wrote his *Principles* by working through *Wealth of Nations*, and found that these claims regarding the non-pecuniary advantages of some trades over others were unobjectionable. Once again, close inspection reveals contextual accretions on Ricardo's work.

It should be marked, however, that the role of these natural inclinations and disinclinations towards certain professions was now greatly reduced—no longer revealing some aspect of human character, or the pernicious influence of European policy over the centuries, or the desirability of a system of liberty. Instead, in the *Principles* these non-profit factors were simply noted and then assumed to 'probably continue permanently with that relative difference',[7] never to play a role in the argument. All this is to be expected, of course, since Ricardo's was not a work of police science in the key of natural law, and his concern instead was to address a narrow topic, 'the cause of the permanent variations in the rate of profit'.[8] To this point, Smith was not so much being corrected for doctrinal errors as he was being picked over. Ricardo's explicit correction of Smith in doctrinal terms would come in relation to capital and profit. Before turning to this theme, it is first necessary to describe the way that Ricardo studied his 'permanent variations in the rate of profit' by imagining adjustments in quantities.

Ricardo's initial premise was that the difficulty of agricultural production was increasing due to inferior grades of land being brought under cultivation. The discursive presentation of numbers and implicit calculations in Ricardo's *Principles*

Table 6.1 Ricardo's calculations of price and rent

Land	Quantity of Labour in men (Men in Land 1 terms)	Output in quarters of wheat	Price (£ s d)	% pp rise (on £4)	Farmer's revenue (£)	Rent on Land 1 in quarters of wheat
1	10	180	4	N/A	720	0
2	10 (9.44)	170	4 4 8	6	720	10
3	10 (8.88)	160	4 10	12.5	720	20
4	10 (8.33)	150	4 16	20	720	30

has been converted into table form (Table 6.1).[9] Ricardo did two things in these calculations. First, he imagined a piece of land (Land 1) that bore a certain ratio between input (in terms of labour) and output (in terms of wheat). Thus, on Land 1, the labour of 10 men produced 180 quarters of wheat, or 18 quarters per man. This brought the question down to a matter of quantities. Ricardo then imagined successive units of land where, owing to diminished fertility, output fell (Land 2, 3, 4). This meant that these lands bore lower labour–output ratios. Thus, on Land 2, the same 10 men would only produce 170 quarters of wheat, which was equivalent to what 9.44 men would have produced on the superior land, Land 1. Second, Ricardo calculated the price increases that would be necessary to guarantee that the farmers on the less fertile lands received the same revenue as the farmer on Land 1. For example, Land 4 had only 150 quarters of wheat to sell, and they would need to be sold for £4 16s in order to receive the same £720 in revenue that the farmer of Land 1 received. This allowed Ricardo to illustrate his claim that the physical output from the final portion of land set the price for the entire industry—selling 150 quarters of wheat for £4 16s per quarter. But, it might be asked, if the farmer of Land 1 also received £4 16s per quarter on their more fertile land, then would not their revenue be higher? It would not. The difference of 30 quarters would be paid as rent, the amount needed to bring the farmer on Land 1 into equality with the farmer on Land 4. The example revealed rent to be the great leveller for farmers and the great windfall for landowners.

This was the first step in Ricardo's treatment of profits. To examine the next step, it is first necessary to backtrack briefly, to chapter 5, 'On Wages', and note the treatment of wages that Ricardo had presented earlier in his text. For Ricardo imported arguments and calculations in this chapter into his discussion of profits in chapter 6. Ricardo opened his account of wages by defining labour's natural

---

[9] Drawn from Ibid., 83, 112–13.

price as the bundle of food and goods necessary for labourers 'to subsist and to perpetuate their race, without either increase or diminution', as determined by 'habit'.[10] That is, these were the wages that a labourer would require to maintain a family consisting of two parents and two children. This is an unusual piece of argumentation to contemporary eyes because we tend to think of wages as being above or below the poverty line, which we do not define with reference to the ability of a 'race' of workers to reproduce itself but, instead, with reference to the needs of a single human or household. In Ricardo's time the strangeness of his claim did not derive from the idea of a 'race' because that represented an adaptation of Malthus's arguments and language regarding population.[11] Ricardo was novel, however, in defining his natural wage with reference to a steady population and without reference to the demand for labour. His definition isolated what Malthus would redescribe as 'the cost of producing labour'.[12] Ricardo's decision made perfect sense in view of his focus on the increasing difficulty of food production, which continuously raised the natural price of labour. These increments could be offset by improvements in agricultural technology and by new sources of food from other nations, as when prohibitions on importing wheat were lifted.[13]

Ricardo next distinguished this natural price for labour from its market price, which was the price actually paid for labour at a given point in time. His essential idea was that when the demand for labour was high, wages would also be high, above the natural price, which implied that the 'race' of labourers would reproduce itself beyond the stationary rate. Or, when the mechanism acted in reverse, population grew and the supply of labour increased, which depressed wages back towards the natural price or even below it for a period of time. This process more or less determined the 'general condition' of the labouring class, oscillating between 'flourishing' and 'wretched'.[14] Here, too, we can register an adaptation of Malthus's analysis.

---

[10] Ibid., 93.

[11] Malthus also spoke of workers as a 'race'. The following statement is found in all editions of the *Essay on the Principle of Population*: 'In every country, the population of which is not absolutely decreasing, the food must be necessarily sufficient to support, and to continue, the race of labourers'; Malthus, 'An Essay on the Principle of Population (1798)', 50, and Malthus, 'An Essay on the Principle of Population (1826): Part I', 314. Note that Ricardo also referred to the 'race of Political Economists' (Ricardo, 'Ricardo to Trower', *Works and Correspondence*, 8: 332–5, at 333). That is, 'race' was being used to refer to a group.

[12] Malthus, 'Principles of Political Economy: Part II', 383.

[13] Ricardo, 'On the Principles of Political Economy and Taxation', 93. Wages could also be reduced by 'progress', more specifically, an improved distribution of labour, and superior manufacturing technology and skill, when these developments lowered the cost of those manufactured goods that formed a part of labour's wage goods. Ibid., 94.

[14] Ibid., 94, 102. This has been a point of doctrinal dispute in the secondary literature: see Peach, *Interpreting Ricardo*, 104–11.

Ricardo then complicated his process by introducing a distinction between the value and quantity of capital. Capital was the portion of a nation's wealth that set labour to work, consisting of food, clothing, necessaries, raw materials, tools, and machinery. As we would expect, Ricardo held that the value of this capital was determined by the quantity of labour involved in its production. Ricardo developed two scenarios to illustrate the importance of distinguishing between the value and quantity of capital. In the first scenario, capital increased in quantity and value, as when more food was produced but with more labour required per unit. In the second scenario, capital increased without its value increasing, as when more food was produced with the same quantity of labour per unit. In both scenarios, the wages of labour rose because there was greater demand for it.

Only in the first case, however, did the natural price of labour also rise—because the value of food had increased, and food was a component of the bundle of wage goods.[15] Under the second scenario, the situation of the labourer was little improved because the increase in their wages was largely absorbed by the increase in their food bill. Ricardo was thus able to state the following conclusion: wages rose or fell in response to the supply and demand for labour and in response to the price of commodities in the labourer's wage bundle, as defined by the habits existing in the time and place.[16] The thrust of Ricardo's analysis was that the accumulation of capital was the key factor in the short term, while population growth operated over a longer time scale.[17]

With this account in hand, we can now return to chapter 6, 'On Profits'. Ricardo imagined a hypothetical worker, who needed 3 quarters of wheat to support himself and his family, and who was paid £24 when the price of wheat was £4 per quarter. This implied that the worker was paid the equivalent of 6 quarters of wheat, with 3 quarters, or £12, to be used for purchasing other commodities. Ricardo then introduced his central dynamic: in response to an increased demand for food, the society expanded food production, raising the cost of wheat to £4 4s 8d. This implied that, in order for the labourer to still acquire 3 quarters of wheat, wages would need to rise to £24 14s, the other expenses not changing in price. This new wage of £24 14s was, however, only the equivalent of 5.83 quarters of wheat. In short, Ricardo posited that the worker's corn wage would fall even as their money wage rose. Ricardo conveyed this deterioration in the worker's condition by setting out the following table (Table 6.2).

With these calculations given, we can now turn to examine how Ricardo used them in his chapter on profits. His question was how a constant revenue for the farmer of £720 would be distributed between labourers and farmers.

---

[15] Ricardo, 'On the Principles of Political Economy and Taxation', 95.
[16] Ibid., 97.
[17] Ibid., 98, 101.

Table 6.2 Ricardo's illustration of rising money wages and falling corn wages

Price of Wheat (£ s d)	Money Wages (£ s d)	Corn Wages (in quarters of wheat)
4 4 8	24 14	5.83
4 10	25 10	5.66
4 16	26 8	5.50
5 2 10	27 8 6	5.33

Table 6.3 The division of revenue between farmers and labourers as the price of wheat rises

Price of Wheat (£ s d)	Labour's Share (of £720) (£ s d)	Farmer's Share (of £720) (£ s d)	Farmer's Profits %
4 4s 8d	247	473	15.7
4 10s	255	465	15.5
4 16s	264	456	14.8

As Table 6.3 shows, Ricardo's answer was that the revenue would be shared in a ratio that would shift because of the rising costs of paying to labour money wages that were linked to the price of 3 quarters of wheat. In consequence, the farmer's rate of profits would fall.[18] The lesson that Ricardo drew from these examples was the same as always.[19]

> The natural tendency of profits then is to fall; for, in the progress of society and wealth, the additional quantity of food required is obtained by the sacrifice of more and more labour. This tendency, this gravitation as it were of profits, is happily checked at repeated intervals by the improvements in machinery, connected with the production of necessaries, as well as by discoveries in the

[18] Table 6.3 combines and truncates two of Ricardo's tables: Ricardo, 'On the Principles of Political Economy and Taxation', 116–17. For a more detailed treatment, see Peach, *Interpreting Ricardo*, 92–94.

[19] A technical wrinkle has been omitted here for the sake of simplicity, that Ricardo was thinking of labour's wages in terms of a bundle of goods consumed by labour (Ricardo, 'On the Principles of Political Economy and Taxation', 103). He was therefore sensitive to the allegation that he had 'taken it for granted, that money wages would rise with a rise in the price of raw produce' (Ricardo, 'On the Principles of Political Economy and Taxation', 118). Ricardo held that eventually this mechanism would operate: a rise in the price of necessaries would raise wages, causing profits to fall.

science of agriculture which enable us to relinquish a portion of labour before required, and therefore to lower the price of the prime necessary of the labourer. The rise in the price of necessaries and in the wages of labour is however
limited; for as soon as wages should be equal . . . to £720, the whole receipts of
the farmer, there must be an end of accumulation; for no capital can then yield
any profit.[20]

How did Ricardo justify choosing these numbers and making these simplifica-
tions? Towards the end of the chapter he offered an explicit rationalization.

In all these calculations I have been desirous only to elucidate the principle, and
it is scarcely necessary to observe, that my whole basis is assumed at random,
and merely for the purpose of exemplification. The results though different in
degree, would have been the same in principle, however accurately I might have
set out in stating the difference in the number of labourers necessary to obtain the successive quantities of corn required by an increasing population, the
quantity consumed by the labourer's family, &c. &c. My object has been to simplify the subject.[21]

To prepare the discussion of Malthus's response to this aspect of Ricardo's
account, what should be noted in these comments is the style of intellectual conduct that was being justified. It is simply taken for granted that the key task is to
'elucidate' principles that are grounded only in the exercise of doctrinal correction and argumentation. Or, in other words, Ricardo had come to discourse on
profits using concepts such as 'labour', 'improvement in machinery', 'progress',
and so on, and he assumed that correct theory could be produced with these
concepts and without any checks from 'practice'. In fact, Ricardo would explicitly
reject such an idea, writing to Malthus that 'It is no answer to my theory to say
that "it is scarcely possible that all my calculations should not be necessarily and
fundamentally erroneous", for that I do not deny'.[22] Malthus, as we will see, took
for granted that it was an answer, and a powerful one.

With this infrastructure now exposed to view, it is time to turn to chapter 21,
'Effects of Accumulation on Profits and Interest', where we find Ricardo using his
account of profits to correct Smith's arguments in *Wealth of Nations*. Once again,
the crucial reception dynamic to note is Ricardo's construal of Smith as having
articulated doctrines that were susceptible to correction using Ricardo's own
style of argumentation. This reading strategy licensed the selection of statements

---

[20] Ibid., 120.
[21] Ibid., 121–2.
[22] Ricardo, 'Ricardo to Malthus', *Works and Correspondence*, 8: 128–31, at 130.

from *Wealth of Nations* regardless of the overall purpose and pattern of Smith's text. Ricardo began by quoting passages from chapter 9 of *Wealth of Nations*, 'Of the Profits of Stock', where Smith argued that the accumulation of capital, by creating competition amongst capitalists, would lower the rate of profit. In this context, Smith had pointed to Holland as an example of a nation so well advanced along the path to prosperity that its profits had been forced low while its wages were high.[23] In making these claims, Smith had contravened two doctrines at the heart of Ricardo's mature writings.[24]

The first of these doctrines was that 'demand is only limited by production', in support of which Ricardo invoked J. B. Say as an authority.[25] The implicit suggestion in Smith's argument was that a capitalist might enter the production of some good unaware that by doing so they would sink the average level of profits. Ricardo found this claim to be implausible. He wrote that 'It is not to be supposed that he [the capitalist] should, for any length of time, be ill-informed of the commodities which he can most advantageously produce'.[26] The second and closely related doctrine that Smith had violated was that permanent falls in the rate of profit were only a function of the rising cost of the necessaries of labour. This was seen in Smith's treatment of Holland, to which Ricardo offered a counter-characterization: yes, it was true that interest rates and profits were low in Holland while wages were high, but these facts could be explained with reference to the necessity to import corn and by the heavy taxation of labour's necessaries.[27]

[23] Ricardo, 'On the Principles of Political Economy and Taxation', 289–90, quoting Smith, *WN* I.ix.2, 10. The guiding premise for Smith's discussion of profits was that, as with wages, observing the average level at any given point in time was difficult because of its constant fluctuation. Even a person carrying on a single trade would not, we are told, have a sure idea of their annual profit. In consequence, Smith's discussion proceeded by tracking two rules of thumb. The first was that interest rates were a fair proxy for profit levels. Holland, for example, was an extremely wealthy nation on a per capita basis, with a large pool of accumulated capital that had raised wages and driven down both interest and profit rates to 2–3 per cent as a natural consequence of prosperity (Smith, *WN* I.ix.10). Smith's second rule of thumb related to what we would call development, and it held that more advanced nations would have large quantities of capital that bore low rates of return owing to the intensity of competition (Smith, *WN* I.ix.13). There was a third theme that Smith developed in his chapter on profits, the relationship between wages and profits. This was also conducted in a developmental key: in rich societies where capital was plentiful, labour would be in steady demand. And the demand for labour depended on the quantity of capital, not on the rate of profit (Smith, *WN* I.ix.11). By contrast, in poor nations the paucity of capital represented a paucity of funds for maintaining labour, and this weak demand was reflected in wages. Once again, where capital was scarce, profits were high, in part because wages were low. Thus did Holland appear as one of the most advanced nations in Europe, where profits were the lowest of any nation while wages were some of the highest (Smith, *WN* I.ix.10, 13).

[24] Note that Ricardo seems to have agreed with Smith earlier in his career regarding the so-called 'competition of capitals thesis': Peach, *Interpreting Ricardo*, 40–9, 131–43.

[25] Ricardo, 'On the Principles of Political Economy and Taxation', 290. But his source may have been James Mill, see Peach, *Interpreting Ricardo*, 47, 65.

[26] Ricardo, 'On the Principles of Political Economy and Taxation', 290.

[27] Ibid., 290 at asterisked note.

With these two errors identified and corrected, Ricardo then produced further quotations from Smith as yet more evidence of heresy.[28] The passages selected are telling: they make it clear that Ricardo did not come to terms with Smith's central argument regarding the existence of a hierarchy of capital employments that could be identified by inspecting the quantities of productive labour that each employment supported. Indeed, Ricardo even quoted from chapter 5 of Book II, where Smith described agriculture as special because nature laboured for free. Having ignored the structure of Smith's arguments, Ricardo was free to use his own conceptions to weigh Smith's errors against his insights. Ricardo found that, on balance, Smith's true commitments laid with correct doctrine: 'this opinion of Adam Smith is at variance with all his general doctrines on this subject'.[29] Above all, Ricardo judged that Smith did not truly believe that capital moved mechanically through a series of employments—running from agriculture to the carrying trade—but merely responded to individual advantage. This is a perfect example of the tendency for doctrinal readings to make a mess of texts since Smith had identified a *natural* progression and then described why it had not been followed over two entire books.[30] Ricardo was simply unattuned to the overall argument of *Wealth of Nations* because he was reading it for signs that Smith agreed with or diverged from his own, newly minted doctrines.

From here Ricardo used some of Smith's statements as an opportunity to restate correct doctrine.

> It follows then from these admissions that there is no limit to demand—no limit to the employment of capital while it yields any profit, and that however abundant capital may become, there is no other adequate reason for a fall of profit but a rise of wages, and . . . the only adequate and permanent cause for the rise of wages is the increasing difficulty of providing food and necessaries for the increasing number of workmen.[31]

This is a noteworthy moment in the history of economic thought. For in these passages Ricardo completed the destruction of Smith's mechanism—which was so harmonious that Smith likened it to the invisible hand of God's providential design—and demoted Smith to having imperfectly perceived Ricardian doctrine on profits. The idea that Smith's invisible hand was the free market, and that this idea captured and held the high analytical ground in political economy, is a myth. Rather, Ricardo built his book out of Smith's *Wealth of Nations*, in the process substituting Smith's deep account of the motives for accumulating

---

[28] Ibid., 293–4, quoting Smith, *WN* I.xi.c.7, I.xi.p.4, II.v.35, II.v.36.
[29] Ricardo, 'On the Principles of Political Economy and Taxation', 295.
[30] Smith, *WN*, Books III and IV.
[31] Ricardo, 'On the Principles of Political Economy and Taxation', 296.

capital—the *Theory of Moral Sentiments* consists of more than forty chapters—with an abstraction called the 'motive for accumulation'. On this abstraction Ricardo could only elaborate in the most banal terms, as when he wrote that 'for no one accumulates but with a view to make his accumulation productive', and, in relation to risk, 'Their motive for accumulation will diminish with every diminution of profit, and will cease altogether when their profits are so low as not to afford them an adequate compensation for their trouble, and the risk'.[32] As we might say today, a thick description of human action had become thin. For his part, Malthus restored something of the depth of Smith's account of human motives by drawing on theology. But the flourish that the invisible hand brought to Smith's treatise of conjectural history and police found no place in Malthus's grimmer outlook because this natural felicity had been replaced with the old contest between virtue and vice.

Malthus Responds

As shown in the Introduction to Part III, Malthus mirrored Ricardo's text by placing his chapter on profits after his chapter on wages. Hence, as with Ricardo, Malthus's treatment of wages in chapter 4, 'On the Wages of Labour', must first be considered before turning to his discussion of profits in chapter 5, 'Of the Profits of Capital'. It will be seen that the nerve of Malthus's argument against Ricardo's 'new theory of profits' was that Ricardo's crude treatment of wages had created errors in his account of profits.[33] In other words, Malthus had once again identified the desire for simplification and its mental pleasures as a pathology in Ricardo's thought.

Central to Malthus's chapter on wages was his rejection of Ricardo's analysis of the natural wage. This analysis treated the natural wage as the bundle of goods necessary for the race of labourers to maintain their numbers given the habits of time and place. Malthus's tactic was to show that this wage bundle only affected the supply of labour and only over the long term. Thus, what Ricardo considered the heart of the question was redescribed by Malthus as the 'cost of producing labour' and then demoted to being merely a cost that 'only influences wages as it regulates the supply of labour'.[34] In other words, the natural wage was merely one factor amongst others that affected the supply of labour. Ricardo's framework was, in consequence, neither complete nor accurate. It followed that a better analysis would require a new definition of the natural wage. Above all, the

---

[32] Ibid., 122.
[33] Malthus, 'Principles of Political Economy: Part II', 391.
[34] Ibid., 383.

new definition would need to allow the political economist to incorporate the natural wage into a more general analysis of supply and demand. The issue of wages thus represents a moment in the broader clash between the rival analyses of Malthus and Ricardo: supply and demand versus value and costs of production. As Malthus wrote, 'The principle of demand and supply is the paramount regulator of the prices of labour as well as of commodities, not only temporarily but permanently'.[35] Where Ricardo had tried to pierce the noise of prices and quantities, Malthus insisted that the political economist simply had to submit to its symphony.

This precept explains why Malthus rejected Ricardo's claim that the natural wage exerted a gravitational pull on the market wage via population adjustments—Ricardo's 'flourishing' and 'wretched' conditions for the race of labourers.[36] Malthus treated Ricardo's natural wage as a curiously 'unnatural price' because it would only arise in a steady state—in some future condition where neither domestic nor foreign agricultural production could be increased, bringing the drama of material life to a resolution.[37] Until that time, Malthus insisted, wages would be buffeted by the interaction of the supply and demand for labour. Malthus then unfolded the population–wage dynamics at the heart of his analysis of population, which included the subtle interactions between habits and wages and the mediating influence of virtue and government. Above all, Malthus underlined that happiness for the masses hinged on the ability 'to reason from the past to the future' and to forsake 'present gratification' for fear of privation in the future.[38] Malthus's possession of a moral anthropology comparable to Smith's analysis of manners and historical change was on full display in these sections, while Ricardo's categories provided scant resources for describing habits and manners.[39]

Malthus then demonstrated the dexterity of his analysis by investigating the effects of a fall in the value of money on the demand for labour, developing a history of prices over 500 years using sources such as Young's *Annals of Agriculture* (1812) and Eden's *State of the Poor* (1797).[40] It was a masterful deployment of selective evidence to set his categories in motion on a historical stage and showcase their analytical power. The analysis culminated with an attack on Ricardo's natural wage, or the cost in labour of producing labour's wage, which was said

[35] Ibid.

[36] Ricardo, 'On the Principles of Political Economy and Taxation', 94.

[37] Malthus, 'Principles of Political Economy: Part I', 181.

[38] Ibid., 184.

[39] Note further the complex linkage that Malthus described between civil liberty and prudential habits among the lower classes (Ibid., 184).

[40] Ibid., 195–211, citing Arthur Young, *Annals of Agriculture* 46/270 (1812); and Sir Francis Morton Eden, *State of the Poor, or an History of the Labouring Classes in England, from the Conquest to the Present Period*, 3 vols. (London, 1797).

to be incapable of elucidating the history of the nation in the way that Malthus had just demonstrated. The reason was that, where Malthus's analysis took in the supply and demand of labour, Ricardo's account only examined the supply of labour, which operated over sixteen to eighteen years, while the additional forces identified by Malthus's analysis could not only overwhelm that influence, but do so many times, and reverse direction, all in the same period.[41]

The root cause of this weakness in Ricardo's theory, according to Malthus, was that it disqualified from analysis the factors that Smith had underlined: the supply and demand of capital in relation to the supply and demand of labour. The consequence was a divergence between Ricardo's theory and the world as it really was, or what Malthus again referred to as 'the actual state of things'.[42] This language is symptomatic of the larger process that we are narrating—of how a discourse that was used to resolve policy cases such as the Corn Laws was being reworked at a higher level of abstraction by Ricardo, and how another user of this discourse was attempting to resist its modification in this way. As we will see, Malthus pursued this goal by treating Ricardo's omission of key causes of profitability as a 'theoretical' failure, one paired with his inability to account for the leading 'facts' emerging from the past century of Britain's commercial life. Malthus might be said to have adopted a tethering strategy in which the theorist's ability to account for salient facts in the real world is the privileged skill, in contrast to Ricardo's desire to elucidate principles unrestrained by the question of their applicability. We can think of Malthus as deploying this strategy through a series of linked criticisms of Ricardo's work before demonstrating his own ability to produce good theory.

Malthus's first step was to allege that Ricardo's focus on the cost of producing wage goods excluded crucial phenomena from the science of political economy. As we have now come to expect, Malthus began this task with a definition: the rate of profits was the proportion between the value of the advances that a capitalist was obliged to make to produce a good, on the one hand, and the value of the returns that were received after its sale at market, on the other.[43] Accordingly, the rate of profits was high when the value of returns greatly exceeded the value of costs, and profits fell as the excess of returns over costs became small. Keeping this point in mind would direct the political economist's attention to the circumstances that determined the value of costs and revenue. And the most important factor affecting costs was the wages paid to labour.

Wages were, in turn, determined by two factors. The first was the factor that Ricardo had fixed his attention upon: the difficulty of producing foodstuffs on

---

41 Malthus, 'Principles of Political Economy: Part II', 384, 385.
42 Malthus, 'Principles of Political Economy: Part I', 228.
43 Malthus, 'Principles of Political Economy: Part II', 385.

the land. Yet the second factor was what Ricardo had detected as corrupting Smith's analysis: the demand for labour in relation to the supply of labour. This second factor, according to Ricardo, needed to be disqualified from analysis on the grounds that it was merely a short-term issue. In opposition to this narrative, Malthus insisted that no single factor could account for all of the variation that was observed in profits. Furthermore, he laid it down as a precept that it was the task of the political economist to be watchful for other additional factors that would complicate the phenomena under study.

> Each of these causes is alone sufficient to occasion all the variations of which profits are susceptible. If one of them only acted, its operation would be simple. It is the combination of the two, and of others in addition to them, sometimes acting in conjunction and sometimes in opposition, which occasions in the progress of society those varied phenomena which it is not always easy to explain.[44]

Once again, the political economist was being shaped by Malthus as someone who refused the temptation to simplify, a restraint on theoretical virtuosity of the type that Ricardo pursued.

At this point, Malthus attempted to expose the faultiness of Ricardo's theory. He traced the effects on profits of expanding agricultural production given fixed wages in corn and using Ricardo's framework. Under such circumstances, it was obvious that profits in agriculture would be in proportion to the fertility of the last land taken into cultivation. In other words, Ricardo's conclusion held. The conclusion was, however, inadmissible because of the 'supposition' of constant corn wages—the 3 quarters per labourer discussed earlier—which was 'not only contrary to the actual state of things, but involves a contradiction'.[45] The contradiction arose because Ricardo's theory did not explain how the increase in population that obliged the society to have recourse to lower quality land could be possible. If corn wages of 3 quarters of wheat per labourer were compatible with a steady population, then no increase in population would occur. Conversely, if 3 quarters of wheat were compatible with an increase in population, then this implied a continual increase of population—exactly the fallacy that Malthus's *Essay* was intended to expose.

More plainly, Malthus's complaint was that Ricardo had assumed away the very stuff of analysis: the interaction of the real price of labour with the supply and demand of capital, revenue, and food. From an illegitimate drive to simplify, Ricardo had ejected from view the phenomena that Malthus and Smith had placed at the centre of their analyses. Malthus continued his attack on Ricardo

[44] Ibid.
[45] Malthus, 'Principles of Political Economy: Part I', 220.

along this line by elevating the importance of supply and demand over declining fertility on the land. He did this by emphasizing the diverging timescales over which each factor operated: the supply of labour adjusted with relative slowness, with sixteen to eighteen years required for the next generation to enter the market. The supply of capital, by contrast, adjusted rapidly. The result was that capital and population did not march in time, hence changes in capital could influence the rate of profits to any degree for up to sixteen years before offsetting changes in population could operate.[46]

What of the centrepiece of Ricardo's theory—the need to resort to less fertile lands as society progressed? Malthus acknowledged that this process operated, but demoted it in practical importance to a background factor that could be set to the side for most analytical purposes. It was simply impossible 'to attempt to estimate the rate of profits in any country by a reference to this cause alone, for ten, twenty, or even fifty years together', and attempting to do so would lead to 'the greatest practical errors': the fault of Ricardo's theory was 'the utter inadequacy of this single cause to account for existing phenomena'.[47]

Malthus pursued this line of argument by comparing his ability to explain diverging rates of profit in Poland and America with Ricardo's inability to account for this variation. The facts of the comparison were given as follows. The last piece of land brought under cultivation in Poland was less fertile than the last land cultivated in America, and wages were nearly half of what they were in America. Ricardo's theory would have construed the low fertility and high wages as forces that repressed profits, yet profits in Poland were higher than they were in America. The reason, Malthus insisted, was the scarcity of capital in Poland. In America, capital was plentiful relative to the supply of labour, a circumstance that could keep wages high in that nation for another hundred years. The lesson was that the political economist was obliged to apportion 'adequate weight to the principle of demand and supply, or competition, in every explanation of the circumstances which determine profits'.[48] In most cases, Malthus asserted, the adequate weight that needed to be given to supply and demand was far greater than that belonging to the barely perceptible operation of declining fertility on the land. This was a tremendous attack on Ricardo: his central principle was being portrayed as irrelevant to understanding the real world in historical time. Ricardian theorists, it seemed, only dealt with theoretical time.

The fact that three further factors also influenced the rate of profits only reinforced this conclusion, at least in Malthus's mind. These factors were improvements in agricultural technology, changes in the productivity of labour, and

---

[46] Ibid., 226.
[47] Malthus, 'Principles of Political Economy: Part II', 386–7.
[48] Malthus, 'Principles of Political Economy: Part I', 227.

changes in the value of raw produce. All three forces tended to offset the effect of declining fertility on the land. In consequence, Malthus could claim that 'in the actual state of the world' declining fertility was frequently 'counteracted and overcome' by these other causes.[49] In these comments Malthus was not only attempting to invalidate one of Ricardo's core doctrines but the performance by which Ricardo had produced it, too. Malthus was instructing the political economist to mind a variety of factors and refrain from focusing on one alone and to look for the combined effects of all factors together as a practical question to be investigated with relevant types of evidence. Judged by this standard, Ricardo had not only failed but stood as an example of an intellectual pathology that we have seen was of great concern in this period: the neglect of experience.

> [T]he conclusion drawn by Mr Ricardo must necessarily contradict experience; not slightly, and for short periods . . . but obviously and broadly, and for periods of such extent, that to overlook them, would not be merely like overlooking the resistance of the air in a falling body, but like overlooking the change of direction given to a ball by a second impulse acting at a different angle from the first.[50]

In other words, Ricardo was failing in a basic task of the science—to explain observed phenomena—because he was developing his theories without ensuring that his 'premises' agreed with reality.[51] Here the attempt to portray Ricardo as untethered to the facts of the world made perfect sense given the context of widespread anxiety regarding theories that could be used to reshape political life but held no warrant beyond the passions of the theorists who purveyed them.

Whatever its strategic astuteness, Malthus's presentation of the issue was jaundiced since Ricardo had allowed the influence of Malthus's offsetting factors: it was just that Ricardo then set them to the side to isolate the role of the rising cost of food. In consequence, Malthus's claim that Ricardo's arguments were 'theoretically' untenable because the set of factors was incomplete is unreliable. Instead, it is better to see that Malthus was objecting to Ricardo's preference to elucidate principles in isolation using hypothetical and abstract argumentation that was not subjected to the test of practice and experience. Malthus's ambition was evidently to best Ricardo theoretically and practically. Having won the first contest, at least to his own satisfaction, Malthus proceeded to surpass Ricardo 'practically' by testing Ricardo's and his own theories against British experience since

---

[49] Malthus, 'Principles of Political Economy: Part II', 388.

[50] Ibid., 387.

[51] Ibid. Recall Stewart's similar discussion of premises and hypotheses in Chapter 1 of this book, pp. 53–6. This comment is not intended to suggest a line of descent from Stewart to Malthus, but to identify a shared vocabulary.

the early eighteenth century.[52] As with Malthus's essays on the Corn Laws, this meant turning to contemporaries working in the rival genre of political arithmetic for a supply of facts.[53]

It is instructive to note the sources that Malthus used. One was *An Estimate of the Comparative Strength of Great-Britain* (1786), by George Chalmers.[54] As the title suggests, Chalmers was operating with an older understanding of state strength, and he took it for granted that strength was a function of population.[55] This was precisely the terrain that Malthus had turned upside down in his *Essay* by framing the issue in terms of virtue, vice, and the natural limits to population, not strength, wealth, and unlimited expansion. It is therefore no surprise to find that Chalmers used the vocabulary common to those who collected facts: his target was those 'theorists' who were driven by 'delusive speculation' and the 'zeal of paradox', and he treated his numerical estimates as '*the best evidence which the nature of the case admits*', rejecting 'mathematic demonstration' as unattainable.[56] In other words, Chalmers can be placed with the 'practical' writers whom Malthus had identified in his Introduction.[57] A similar point can be made regarding Malthus's other source at this point of his argument, Arthur Young's *Annals of Agriculture* (1784–1815). Young prefaced his researches self-deprecatingly, writing that 'my first business has been to collect facts', while 'to reason upon them, is an employment for those who move in a superior sphere, and whose minds are more accustomed to political disquisitions'.[58] Young was prepared, however, to lament the manner in which discussion of the Bullion Controversy and the Corn Laws had been carried on: 'theories of political economy were so generally introduced, without a clear statement of those facts from which alone any sound theory can be drawn', rendering these theories 'utterly unworthy of attention'.[59] In other words, Malthus's sources were produced in opposition to theory of the very type that he produced.

Despite this awkward circumstance, Malthus was capable of using the facts of Chalmers and Young to adjudicate between his theory and Ricardo's by

---

[52] Malthus, 'Principles of Political Economy: Part II', 388.

[53] Malthus, 'Principles of Political Economy: Part I', 230. Malthus's sources were George Chalmers, *An Estimate of the Comparative Strength of Great-Britain* (London, 1786); Young, 'An Enquiry into the Progressive Value of Money', 96–7; and Arthur Young, 'An Enquiry into the Rise of Prices in Europe', *Annals of Agriculture* 46/271 (1815), 215.

[54] Incorrectly given in *Works* as 'W. Chalmers', and '1788'. The 1786 edition has been used here.

[55] For this older conception, see Walter, 'Adam Smith's Free Trade Casuistry', 63–8.

[56] Chalmers, *An Estimate of the Comparative Strength of Great-Britain*, v, x, emphasis added. Chalmers first published his *Estimate* in 1782, and his original target was Richard Price's pessimism regarding Britain's power and wealth: John E. Crowley, 'Neo-Mercantilism and *The Wealth of Nations*: British Commercial Policy after the American Revolution', *Historical Journal* 33/2 (1990), 339–60, at 343.

[57] Malthus, 'Principles of Political Economy: Part I', 7.

[58] Young, 'An Enquiry into the Progressive Value of Money', v.

[59] Young, 'An Enquiry into the Rise of Prices in Europe', 144–5.

deploying one of the theorist's defining skills: the ability to correctly interpret facts in relation to the multiple causal forces at play, thus rendering them fit for testing theories.[60] From the particulars presented in these accounts, Malthus discovered a twenty-year period around the turn of the nineteenth century during which interest rates had risen to 5 per cent, well beyond their range of 3 to 3.5 per cent before and after this interregnum.[61] During this special period, according to Malthus, a great quantity of capital had been accumulated and new lands brought under cultivation. This was a tremendous find for Malthus: not only had interest rates moved in the opposite direction to what Ricardo's theory would have foretold (on Malthus's reading), but they then reversed their course, implying the operation of short- and medium-term factors. The implication for Ricardo's theory was plain: 'The facts, which are incontrovertible, not only cannot be accounted for upon this theory, but . . . they ought to be directly the reverse of what they are found to be in reality'.[62] Indeed, Malthus underlined the decisiveness of this test for Ricardo's theory, writing that

> the facts must be accounted for, as they are so broad and glaring, and others of the same kind are in reality of such frequent recurrence, that I cannot but consider them as at once decisive against any theory of profits which is inconsistent with them.[63]

Having shown that Ricardo's theory was incapable of meeting the test of experience, Malthus then turned to demonstrate that his own account could accommodate the facts perfectly well. In short, improvements in agriculture, greater exertion from labour following the introduction of piece-work and the entry of women and children into the labour force, and a rise in the money price of corn all combined during this period (c. 1793–1813). The result was a fall in the corn wages simultaneous with an increase in the money price of the farmer's produce. The joint effect of these factors more than offset the land's declining fertility. This was why profits rose.[64] Indeed, Malthus ventured, the last piece of land taken into cultivation in 1813 was more profitable than the last piece in 1727, a fact that his arguments were able to 'account for . . . theoretically'.[65] Despite being in operation for close to 100 years, Ricardo's prized principle had been overturned by those causes that he had excluded from study and which Malthus had shown

---

[60] Recall Ricardo's preparation of what we would call data in his bullion writings, discussed in Chapter 2 of this book.

[61] Malthus, 'Principles of Political Economy: Part I', 230–1.

[62] Ibid., 231.

[63] Ibid., 232.

[64] Ibid., 232; Malthus, 'Principles of Political Economy: Part II', 388–9.

[65] Malthus, 'Principles of Political Economy: Part II', 389.

were the factors upon which 'the rate of profits will practically depend'.[66] Note the way that Malthus was again laying claim to both theory and practice: he was not only purporting to outdo Ricardo in his ability to account for the observed facts, but to be a superior theorist because he could cognize the full set of causal factors working in combination. Malthus did not surrender the theoretical high ground, whatever today's textbooks may say, but claimed it, along with the ability to meet the test of experience.

Conclusion

We can imagine that Malthus's challenge put pressure on Ricardo to respond, and two strategies seem most obvious. One was to specify a type of theoretical virtuosity different from what Malthus had claimed for himself and at which Ricardo surpassed Malthus. The other strategy was to deny the justness of Malthus's account. If we turn to Ricardo's *Notes*, then we find only minimal evidence of the first strategy being adopted, primarily in Ricardo's muted comments on the nature of theoretical competence. Ricardo did not respond to the full-frontal assault quoted earlier—that 'the facts must be accounted for'—but he did reply to Malthus's attack that began 'to attempt to estimate the rate of profits in any country by reference to this cause alone . . '. Ricardo did so in his commentary by insisting that he also subscribed to two causes: difficulty of production on the land, and supply and demand. But Ricardo claimed that he had 'endeavored to shew that they might be classed under one head', by which he meant that both effects would manifest themselves in the wages paid to labour.[67] This was an implicit claim regarding the value of theoretical simplification, but Ricardo can hardly be said to have given it forceful expression.

As for the other strategy—the fairness of Malthus's account—Ricardo is found complaining of Malthus's presentation. Ricardo wrote, for example, 'we mean, and he knows we mean, the same thing'.[68] Ricardo also protested his treatment in Malthus's purported demonstration that agricultural profits had risen, the point at which Malthus had relied on Young's tables. Ricardo was emphatic that he had never denied the role of labour efficiency in determining profitability, writing of Malthus's claim, 'This is disingenuous'.[69] Ricardo paraphrased Malthus's charge as amounting to the assertion that 'My principles are right . . . but I have not weighed the force of each with sufficient nicety', and he then listed the pages of his book where he might point for evidence that he had, in fact, weighed them

---

[66] Malthus, 'Principles of Political Economy: Part I', 233.
[67] Ricardo, 'Notes on Malthus's *Principles of Political Economy*', 264, and see also 252, 279.
[68] Ibid., 264.
[69] Ibid., 276.

in the required manner.[70] Ricardo also identified some moments of doctrinal coincidence between his theory and Malthus's that only appeared divergent due to their manner of expression, along with Malthus's refusal to apprehend value in relation to quantities.[71] In summary, Ricardo leaned heavily on the idea of having been misrepresented and misread and looked for doctrinal convergence between himself and Malthus below the level of written expression.

For this book's overall argument, the point to underline is that Ricardo refused to avow a rival mode for conducting political economy even as he also refused to be indicted on the basis of Malthus's strictures for good political economy. The crucial piece of context to bring forward when making sense of this fact is that Ricardo was in a rhetorical no-man's land. For Malthus's insistence on submitting theory to the test of experience as disclosed by political arithmetic was awfully difficult to countermand given the charges to which Ricardo had been subjected by critics generally. Equally difficult to deny was Malthus's emphasis on the ability to construe facts in terms of multiple causal factors operating on different time scales. In such a situation, we might guess that "staying schtum" on the purpose of theory was indeed the best strategic choice available to Ricardo. The alternative strategy of avowing a type of intellectual conduct that was so theoretical that it was above being judged by facts—even facts prepared by a theorist such as Malthus—would likely have been a losing ploy given the context. (It is easier today.) Equally difficult for Ricardo to sell would have been to insist on handling distinct causes separately and ignoring their interaction, since we saw earlier how Malthus cleverly invoked Newtonian mechanics to say that Ricardo's approach was 'like overlooking the change of direction given to a ball by a second impulse acting at a different angle from the first'. Far better, then, to do as Ricardo actually did and not pick up the gauntlet but claim that it need not have been thrown down in the first place.

In short, even if we assume that Ricardo's strategy was the wisest possible, it was still the case that his *Notes* hardly offered the resources for a powerful defence. He simply left implicit the idea that originality and 'correct theory' were the overriding aims of political economy. By contrast, when on the front foot in his *Principles*, Ricardo had emphasized the discovery of new principles and the doctrinal correction of his forebears as his leading contributions to the science. Faced with Malthus's rejection of the reasoning that was needed to achieve such novelty, Ricardo had little to say in reply. In Ricardo's time, theoretical virtuosity was not a self-justifying activity. This points to the overall implications of this book, to which attention now turns.

---

[70] Ibid., 268.
[71] Ibid., 266–7.

Conclusion

A New Past

I may be so foolishly partial to my own doctrine, that I may be blind
to its absurdity. I know the strong disposition of every man to de-
ceive himself in his eagerness to prove a favourite theory, yet I cannot
help viewing this question as a truth which admits of demonstration
and I am full of wonder that it should admit of a doubt.

—David Ricardo[1]

It will help to clarify the overall argument of this book by considering the conception of the history of economic thought that it is attempting to overturn. This
dominant conception can be described in terms of three characteristics. First, it
asserts the existence of grand phases of thought, with the key unities in Britain
being 'mercantilism' and 'classical political economy'. 'Mercantilism' was supposedly brought to an end by Adam Smith's exposé of that system's theoretical
flaws, and this breakthrough opened the way for Malthus and Ricardo to build
on Smith's analysis. They did so, but with diverging methods, with Malthus the
great empirical, inductive thinker, while Ricardo was the precociously abstract,
deductive thinker. Despite these differences between Malthus and Ricardo, and
between both of them and Smith, the unity of the category 'classical political
economy' is assumed to remain intact. At the extreme, this unity is explicated
in terms of a model that expresses the thought of all three figures, the so-called
canonical model that stands as an analytic statement of the core of the period's
thought. In this dynamic model of equilibrium, production is a function of
land, labour, and capital, with a long-run equilibrium emerging when the fact of
diminishing returns in agriculture reduces wages and profits to their minimum
levels.[2] First characteristic: the creation of analytico-temporal unities, such as
'classical political economy'.

---

[1] Ricardo, 'Ricardo to Malthus', *Works and Correspondence*, 7: 250–2, at 251.
[2] Samuelson, 'The Canonical Classical Model of Political Economy'.

Before Method and Models. Ryan Walter, Oxford University Press. © Oxford University Press 2021.
DOI: 10.1093/oso/9780197603055.003.0010

The second characteristic is a willingness to translate the language found in historical texts into today's vocabulary. It should be acknowledged that the type of anachronism that is caused by translation is something of a 'wicked problem' for historians, and the extent of the difficulties is still being discovered.[3] In short, because intellectual history will usually deal with 'language-entangled facts' and must describe these facts with language, even the best efforts to avoid anachronism may amount to little more than 'historiographical damage control'.[4] Despite this challenge, the relevant feature of so much of the existing historiography is not the greater or lesser degree of success in avoiding translation but the assumption that translation is a valid operation for the historian to perform. Indicative here is Roy Ruffin's unintentional paradox when dealing with Ricardo: 'It is important to begin with a modern statement of Ricardo's law of comparative advantage to fully appreciate Ricardo's own statement'.[5] And the issue of translation relates to reading as much as to writing. This claim from George Stigler is illustrative: 'At no point in this discussion of how to read scientific works has the word "past" been used: the correct way to read Adam Smith is the correct way to read the forthcoming issues of a professional journal'.[6] (One wonders if Stigler would have read Portuguese as if it were really English.)

The third and final characteristic of so much of the existing treatment of Malthus and Ricardo that this book is contesting is the presumption to judge a piece of past thought from a contemporary point of view. This requires that the historian first translates a text into today's vocabulary, usually on the assumption that the text contains 'economic analysis'. Once the translation is completed, the economist-historian can rely on the twin advantages of hindsight and superior technique to detect scientific progress. That is, there is presumed to be a silent mover behind the history of economic discourse, something like economic reason, the latest moment of which the historian inherits and so stands above their predecessors.[7] This approach yields such judgements as Giancarlo de Vivo's claim that Ricardo's *Essay on Profits* (1815) took the debate over the Corn Laws onto a 'higher, analytical plane' while the arguments of the protectionist Henry Parnell are 'not really worth discussing'.[8] This approach also produces endless debates over precedence for the 'discovery' of 'laws', such as comparative advantage,

---

[3] See, for example, Conal Condren, 'The History of Political Thought as Secular Genealogy: The Case of Liberty in Early Modern England', *Intellectual History Review* 27/1 (2017), 115–33.

[4] Conal Condren, 'Political Theory and the Problem of Anachronism', in Andrew Vincent, ed., *Political Theory: Tradition and Diversity* (Cambridge: Cambridge University Press, 1997), 45–66, at 53.

[5] Ruffin, 'David Ricardo's Discovery of Comparative Advantage', 729.

[6] Stigler, 'Does Economics Have a Useful Past?', 221.

[7] Joseph Schumpeter treats progress in economics as analogous to the progress that dentistry has made in the extraction of teeth: Schumpeter, *History of Economic Analysis*, 39.

[8] Giancarlo de Vivo, 'David Ricardo's *An Essay on the Effects of a Low Price of Corn on the Profits of Stock*', *History of Economics Review* 62/1 (2015), 76–97, at 76, 79.

whether in Robert Torrens or Ricardo. In the most recent addition to this particular debate, a 'model' is found subsisting beneath the texts of Torrens, which is then used to undermine his 'alleged anticipation of the comparative advantage theory'.[9] Here historiography proceeds by using one retrospective projection to make assessments about another.[10]

The chapters of this book have contributed to a counter-account of the history of political economy, and it is worth sketching the leading features of the overall image that they are intended to produce. Of paramount importance was to establish a historical vocabulary that could act as a rival starting point to the unhistorical vocabulary of method, model, classical political economy, and related terms. The source for this rival vocabulary was the debate in 1790s Britain regarding the relationship between theory, on the one hand, and political practice and experience, on the other. In this period of British life, it was thought that revolutionary zeal of the type that had destroyed France was caused by enthusiasm and that theory might lead to enthusiasm, or represent a form of enthusiasm disguised as science. This explains the period's synonyms for enthusiasm—'love of theory', 'spirit of system', 'spirit of theory', and Ricardo's periphrasis on display in the epigraph to this chapter. Bringing this vocabulary to view in Chapter 1 made it possible to test in subsequent chapters whether or not it was used in relation to political economy, in particular, in the Bullion Controversy, in the Corn Laws debate, and by Malthus and Ricardo in their doctrinal contests.

To be plain, establishing this alternative vocabulary was important for the book's central argument because it is not simply a matter of different words having been used to convey the same ideas that we have today. Instead, this vocabulary revealed that writers in this period had different ideas to our own. The most fascinating—or simply the most alien—feature of this vocabulary was that it led one to understand good and bad thinking as primarily a function of good and bad ethical self-government; before method and models there was ethics-talk. Theory, for example, could be bad when it was done from what Smith called the 'spirit of system' because the theorist allowed the pleasure of building a theoretical system to blind them to the limits and proper purposes of speculation. Today, by contrast, economists are likely to assess a piece of economics as good or bad in view of method and in view of the properties of the model that is produced, whether in terms of predictive power, or realism, or its micro-foundations, or whatever. And, of course, we have no standing suspicion against theory in political life, perhaps, in part, because 'enthusiasm' has become

---

[9] Michael Gaul, 'Robert Torrens' Model of Trade and Growth: Genesis and Implications for the Discovery of Comparative Advantage', *The European Journal of the History of Economic Thought* 28/2 (2021), 201–228, at 215.

[10] For the evidence in relation to Ricardo, see Pullen, 'Did Ricardo Really Have a Law of Comparative Advantage?'

a commendatory term, depriving us of what had been the most powerful word for registering unease about theory in politics, while 'ideology' is now assumed to be ubiquitous and inescapable.

Evidence was adduced in Chapter 2 that this vocabulary was, indeed, used by political economists and their critics in the Bullion Controversy and that talk of method and models was absent. This is taken to be a decisive blow against the endless rational reconstructions of monetary theory in this period and against the overarching narrative of classical political economy as coming into being after Smith and representing a style of macroeconomics analogous to our own. If such accounts are unhistorical, then the question must be asked: If Malthus, Ricardo, and the other participants in the debate were not doing macroeconomics or classical political economy, then what were they doing? And if they did not have methods, then how did they produce their arguments?

The short answer to the first question—What were these thinkers doing?—is that they were participating in Britain's culture of public debate that centred on Parliament's deliberations. In this regard, it was shown that the Bank of England was an old target for political polemic, and, in the earliest stage of debate, the attacks on the Bank and paper money were heard in an idiom that can be traced back to at least the sixteenth century. Moreover, the contours of the debate were shaped by two parliamentary documents—the 1804 *Report* and the 1810 *Report*—while Ricardo's first contributions were in newspapers, then in pamphlets addressed to the legislature, with Malthus contributing by reviewing these and other texts. More plainly, the texts of Malthus and Ricardo were only possible because of the British tradition of debating legislation inside and outside of Parliament. To appreciate this point, one can glance sideways to the German states, where there was no equivalent institution to Parliament and no equivalent culture of public debate. As a result, instead of reviewing and pamphleteering of the type done by Malthus and Ricardo, one finds a completely different pattern of thought and a completely different set of texts—the treatises of Cameralism being produced by professors in the form of textbooks for future administrators. We can surmise that Ricardo of the London Stock Exchange would not have written in that context.[11] By centring Parliament in this way, the alternative account offered here is intended to answer the recent call for intellectual historians to tend to institutions.[12] More importantly, Parliament provides an alternative ur-context for studying the history of economic thought in Britain, replacing the more familiar but imaginary context of a 'classical political economy'.

---

[11] Keith Tribe, *Governing Economy: The Reformation of German Economic Discourse, 1750–1840* (Cambridge: Cambridge University Press, 1988).

[12] Max Skjönsberg, 'The History of Political Thought and Parliamentary History in the Eighteenth and Nineteenth Centuries', *The Historical Journal* 64/2 (2021), 501–13, 1–13, at 503–4.

This first answer provides part of the answer to the second question: How did these thinkers produce their texts? They did so by reproducing and modifying the genres and conventions that were active in the argumentative contexts into which they intervened. In the case of Ricardo, for example, he entered the Bullion Controversy at a point when it had come to be conducted in relation to a preexisting debate regarding political society and the status of theory, and in this context the vocabulary recovered in Chapter 1 played a decisive role. Far from possessing his own vocabulary because he was a political economist, Ricardo re-purposed existing terms of debate. And, because of the side of the debate that he took, Ricardo held a strategic advantage by presenting himself as better able to account for the nation's practice and experience with paper money. It is simply not possible to derive these facts by endowing Ricardo with a method that exists independently of the contests in which he engaged, and, since neither he nor his friends and enemies tended to use the term 'method' in the sense of an epis-temology, or to *think* in terms of a general epistemological position such as 'em-piricism', there is no good reason for the historian of economic thought to use it in relation to Ricardo. In short, in the place of notions of method, a genuinely historical approach to past thinking will reconstruct contexts and then read texts in relation to them, noting rhetorical and argumentative choices without pre-suming that they answer to a global method.

Much the same answer can be given when it comes to understanding those texts of Malthus and Ricardo that engaged the Corn Laws, as studied in Chapter 3. On the standard view, this episode has been examined as a moment of conceptual triumph as Malthus, Ricardo, and Torrens clambered towards the concepts of diminishing returns and comparative advantage. This treatment re-lies on the presumption that developing economic concepts was a vocation in the early nineteenth century; in short, that 'classical political economy' is the context in which to read the texts of Malthus, Ricardo, and Torrens. Once again, how-ever, the historical context that was recovered in Chapter 3 was parliamentary debate.

Read in that context, the debate was shown to have already been under way by the time Malthus and Ricardo wrote and to be structured by the presupposition that there was more to statecraft than maximizing wealth, with goals such as hap-piness and security standing above others. In this setting, the political economist was expected to behave like a counsellor who could ascertain those cases where national wealth ought to be subordinated to higher goals. So clarified, it emerged that free trade was not an ideology or a doctrine but a strategic recommendation that a casuist of state would sometimes make, and sometimes not, depending on the circumstances. Ricardo was different because he *had* been developing his analysis of profits independently of the needs and expectations of counsel and *did* tend to think of free trade as a doctrine. This fact explains Mackintosh's reception of Ricardo's text as unhelpful for parliamentary reasoning and the awkwardness of the *Essay on Profits* (1815) when it shifted to counsel mode, which Ricardo was evidently constrained to adopt despite his lack of facility with casuistical reasoning. Of course, Ricardo's maladroitness may have owed to his intellectual resistance to the genre: if free trade were an instrument of progress, then exceptions to free trade were really exceptions to progress. Far from being a theoretical genius ahead of his time who lifted the debate onto de Vivo's 'higher plane', Ricardo emerges as uncomfortable in the genre in which he wrote and unattuned to the needs of the institution that it was expected to serve.

The thrust of Part II of the book is, in consequence, that most texts of political economy will need to be studied as contributions to parliamentary debate because it was this institution and culture that provided the topics and conventions that structured the discourse. By accepting this discipline, texts such as Ricardo's *Essay on Profits* can be detached from an imagined history of economic analysis and restored to their historical context. Seen in context, Ricardo was not a genius, but a player in contingent games of attack and defence, in which the pieces had been placed on the board before he arrived, and the most important pieces were vocabulary and style of argument. Argumentative context, not method, should sit at the heart of our inquiries. We have tended not to do this because we have been content to assume that these authors were participating in an autonomous discipline, 'classical political economy', and driving it forward through conceptual advances. But no such thing existed, as this label is merely a retrospective invention, and conceptual virtuosity was not a valued part of the counsellor's repertoire.

It would seem that Parliament remained political economy's centre of gravity deep into the nineteenth century. If one takes the Bullion Controversy and the Corn Laws as examples, then they were only (imperfectly) resolved by Parliament in the 1840s through the Bank Charter Act 1844 and the Importation Act 1846. The claim being made is that political economists were more commonly roused to move their pens by legislation and parliamentary debate than by a desire to refine a theory or write a treatise. If one does turn to the treatises, a minority of the period's political-economy literature, then heterogeneity is encountered. Unlike Smith's *Wealth of Nations* (1776), Ricardo's *Principles* (1817) was not underwritten by a detailed moral philosophy, contained no account of the development of commerce and political society, and served no counselling purpose. Ricardo's arguments were avowedly theoretical in nature and his goal was doctrinal truth, not its good application. Ricardo's *Principles* therefore formed a disfiguring reception context for Smith's *Wealth of Nations*; far from building on this text, Ricardo dismembered it by reworking concepts elaborated in Smith's first two books in relation to his own preoccupation with value.

It might seem, however, that a revised version of the thesis that political economy possessed an inner unity and principle of development could be sustained by pushing the moment of formation back from 1776 (and Smith's *Wealth of Nations*) to 1817 (and Ricardo's *Principles*). After all, Ricardo's text called forth Malthus's own *Principles* (1820) in reply, published in 1820. This view might even point to Part III of this book for support, where it was shown that Malthus and Ricardo did pioneer doctrinal correction as a new mode for political economy. What was also revealed in Part III, however, was that the doctrinal disputes between Malthus and Ricardo were shaped by cross-currents from theology and politics. This was seen most clearly in Malthus's correction of Ricardo for inappropriately reasoning from the earthly condition to the nature of God, the source of Ricardo's erroneous treatment of rent, and in Ricardo's supposed misunderstanding of the connection between the interests of landlords and society's interests. Moreover, the whole contest was conducted without either method or models but with the vocabulary of theory and practice. This is why the core of Malthus's rejection of Ricardo's *Principles* concerned the way that Ricardo argued, which Malthus did not characterize in terms of poor method, but in terms of a failure of ethical self-government. In summary, Malthus portrayed Ricardo's mind as ill-governed, seemingly because it was one of those 'minds of a certain cast' that derived pleasure from simplifying and generalizing, which led Ricardo to be neglectful of his duty to submit his theories to the test of experience and prepare them for application to legislation.[13] Malthus had indicted Ricardo, as had other critics of the time, by using the ideas and vocabulary uncovered in Part I—what has been termed the vocabulary of theory and practice—and in reliance on the culture of ethical self-cultivation that was pervasive in western Europe in this period.

All of this suggests that political economy had no unity; this makes it difficult to continue to believe that it had an internal principle of development. Political economy was rather a staging ground for transitory contests in which parliamentary debate intersected with the project to develop a science of politics. From the 1790s, these contests were complicated by a high-stakes debate regarding theory, practice, and reform of the state. Future research will be needed to determine if political economy ever escaped these forces and became an autonomous pursuit in something like the manner that has been assumed in traditional accounts of its history. It may be worth suggesting that the reshaping of the technical and ethical capacities of political economists by William Stanley Jevons and Alfred Marshall in the second half of the century would seem, *prima facie*, to represent continued instability. In addition, we already know that, at least in Britain, institutionalization did not represent a source of stabilization. For, in the nineteenth century,

---

[13] Malthus, 'Principles of Political Economy: Part I', 7.

there was no institutional pathway to becoming an accredited political economist analogous to the way that one could become, say, a solicitor, through five years in articles and sitting an exam, thereby producing solicitors who varied little in terms of expertise.[14] In this respect, consider how rarely political economy was taught in institutions and that, when it was, no form of expertise that was equivalent to the law emerged since the production of expertise in political economists that would be uniform across institutions was never an aim of any educational institution in the nineteenth century. Malthus, for example, taught at the East India College, which was not intended to make economists but to imbue the next generation of colonial administrators with civilized values.[15] Similarly, George Pryme mainly taught pass men at Cambridge, and no examination in the subject was required.[16] Dugald Stewart's course in political economy was an extension of his moral philosophy, lasting less than ten years, to end with his retirement in 1810.[17] Finally, the Political Economy Club was a private dining club in London, with a limited membership consisting primarily of men from commerce, and the education of these men in free trade was the Club's primary purpose.[18] For a sustained training in economic reasoning, understood as a distinct set of intellectual skills, Britons would have to wait for the Cambridge Economics Tripos that Marshall established in the early *twentieth* century.[19]

This is to look forward. The main thrust of this book, however, has been to direct attention backwards, by connecting British political economy with older debates over ethical self-government and enthusiasm. Enthusiasm was the leading source of England's troubles in the seventeenth century, culminating in the regicide of Charles I, and it was thought by contemporaries to have returned in the form of the French Revolution. In other words, the replacement conception of the history of economic thought that this book is advancing directs attention to the early modern period's debates and intellectual culture as the context for making sense of political economy in the time of Ricardo. In this setting, the key fault line was not between induction and deduction because the register was

---

[14] The exam was introduced in 1836: Richard L. Abel, 'The Decline of Professionalism?', *Modern Law Review* 49/1 (1986), 1–41, at 4–5.

[15] Keith Tribe, 'Professors Malthus and Jones: Political Economy at the East India College 1806–1858', *The European Journal of History and Economic Thought* 2/2 (1995), 327–54, at 339.

[16] Keith Tribe, 'Political Economy and the Science of Economics in Victorian Britain', in Martin Daunton, ed., *The Organisation of Knowledge in Victorian Britain* (Oxford: Oxford University Press, 2005), 115–37, at 131.

[17] Collini, Winch, and Burrow, *That Noble Science of Politics*, 37.

[18] Keith Tribe, 'Economic Societies in Great Britain and Ireland', in Massimo M. Augello and Marco E. L. Guidi, eds., *The Spread of Political Economy and the Professionalisation of Economists: Economic Societies in Europe, America and Japan in the Nineteenth Century* (London: Routledge, 2001), 32–52, at 38–40.

[19] Even then the results were modest and unappreciated by government and industry. See Keith Tribe, 'The Cambridge Economics Tripos 1903–55 and the Training of Economists', *The Manchester School* 68/2 (2000), 222–48.

not epistemology but ethics-talk, which produced tensions between theory and practice. On one side stood those who produced theory and prided themselves on the depth and power of their vision into the workings of society, scorning the merely practical men who worked with facts and knowledge drawn from their day-to-day lives. On the other side sat these mocked practical thinkers, who naturally did not perceive their own thinking as primitive but as grounded in reality and history. These practical thinkers construed their theoretical opponents, at their worst, as mad enthusiasts who would destroy society if they were allowed to reform it in the image of their fantasies. The historical distance that we need to cross to reach Malthus and Ricardo is greater than we have been accustomed to imagine.

This claim can be operationalized by suggesting two weaknesses inherent to most existing attempts to reconstruct the method of Malthus and Ricardo. The first is that such reconstructions typically gather evidence from texts produced in divergent argumentative contexts and then generate a unifying characterization by elevating some texts and suppressing others.[20] This is a dubious project given the leading implication of the two studies comprising Part II: that context holds significant explanatory power when it comes to explaining the concrete contents and arrangement of texts. This does not make unified reconstructions impossible, but it does raise the threshold for persuasive evidence. In particular, variation across argumentative contexts would need to be investigated and, if present, accounted for. The second and related weakness in reconstructing method is that developing and adhering to methodologies is something that we do today, but it was not an avowed activity in the early nineteenth century. All of this might point to a new disposition for historians to adopt: a standing suspicion that all attempts to describe a thinker's 'method'—in our sense of the word— before 1830 or so will likely produce anachronism.

It is now time to summarize the replacement account of political economy that this book has sought to advance by treating language and context as central to the history of economic thought. To do political economy in early nineteenth-century Britain was, usually, to participate in a culture of public–parliamentary debate where the topics were thrown up by party politics and the routines of Parliament. In consequence, to be qualified to pronounce on political economy in the early nineteenth century required only that one was prepared to claim to be acting for the common good and to have read Smith or other authors.[21]

---

[20] See, for example, the survey of such attempts in relation to Ricardo in John E. King, *David Ricardo* (New York: Palgrave Macmillan, 2013), 34–41.

[21] The scope was illimitable. Consider George Chalmers, whose sources included Chief Justice John Holt and who claimed, in 1811, that William Potter's 1650 text *The Key of Wealth* (London, 1650) was an ideal guide to circulation! See George Chalmers, *Considerations on Commerce, Bullion and Coin, Circulation and Exchanges; With a View to our Present Circumstances* (London, 1811), 152, 158.

A leading consequence was that political economy was spread by individuals who had tremendous freedom when it came to writing their texts. This is why political economy was constructed in an *ad hoc* and makeshift manner. That is, what we have retrospectively considered to be major theoretical statements tended to be produced as the occasion required and with second-hand intellectual materials.

To see this point, consider the following outline of the contest between Malthus and Ricardo to define political economy as studied in this book. Malthus was moved to write his *Essay* following a debate with his father, and he took aim at William Godwin's *Enquirer*.[22] Malthus's work was a success, and the expanded second edition secured his reputation and saw him appointed to the East India College. Hence, Malthus's career shifted track unexpectedly from parson to Professor of Political Economy, but he used the natural theology framework that he acquired in the former office to dispense the latter. As for Ricardo, he first encountered Smith's *Wealth of Nations* while on holiday in Bath in 1799, then read the articles on political economy appearing in the early numbers of the *Edinburgh Review*.[23] His publishing career began in the Whig newspaper *The Morning Chronicle*, in relation to what would be called the Bullion Controversy, setting out a stark vision of how prices changed, possibly based on his skill at spotting mispricing in the stock market.[24] Ricardo then published his influential *Essay on Profits*, perhaps deriving his table of distribution by mimicking contemporary reports on experimental field trials in agriculture.[25] The anti-aristocratic potential of the *Essay* attracted the attention of James Mill, who then cajoled Ricardo into expanding the piece into his *Principles of Political Economy, and Taxation*.[26] In that text, Ricardo's calculations in pursuit of a labour theory of value were dependent upon annuity calculations that he encountered in his professional life.[27] Both thinkers used materials that were ready-to-hand, sourced from disparate and often non-scientific contexts. This might prompt us to think of British political economy as an extended accident of history.

In this unstable setting, a new style of intellectual was fighting for status, the theoretical political economist. We have taken this figure for granted because it so

[22] Malthus, 'An Essay on the Principle of Population (1798)', i.
[23] Ricardo recounted the process by which he acquired his knowledge of political economy as one of being led into 'deeper consideration' through his correspondence with Malthus, resulting in 'a very consistent theory in my own mind' (Ricardo, 'Ricardo to Trower', *Works and Correspondence*, 7: 246).
[24] Terry Peach, *Interpreting Ricardo*, 142.
[25] Morgan, *The World in the Model*, chapter 2.
[26] Donald Winch, 'James Mill and David Ricardo', in Donald Winch, ed., *James Mill: Selected Economic Writings* (Edinburgh: Scottish Economic Society, 1966), 179–202, at 197–8. Note also J. C. D. Clark's suggestion that by attacking the Corn Laws Ricardo was attacking the existing social order (Clark, *English Society, 1660–1832*, 188–9). For Mill cajoling Ricardo, see especially Mill, 'Mill to Ricardo', *Works and Correspondence*, 7: 86–7, at 86.
[27] Ricardo, 'Ricardo to Mill', *Works*, 7: 82–4, at 83.

happened that their descendants in the twentieth century won tremendous prestige in our societies, achieving status for themselves in universities, government, and finance. In the beginning, however, political economists alarmed sections of British letters because of the way they reasoned, their ambitions for change, and because they might achieve those ambitions by leading Parliament to reason as they did. The effect would be to transform Parliament's work of making laws into the pursuit of theoretical systems, and the critics could not contemplate this idea without thinking fearfully of the French Revolution. Malthus and Ricardo were defending theoretical political economy in this challenging context, at the same time as they were specifying the political economist's office in incompatible ways and equipping it with rival instruments. Given such an origin, the fact that we are still unsure of the place that we want economists to have in our world seems to represent an inheritance from the world of Malthus and Ricardo. At last, a continuity.

Bibliography

Primary Sources (Note: individual titles by Burke, Malthus, Ricardo, and Smith that appear in the multivolume collections bearing their names and described in the front matter are not listed here.)

'An Act for Amending Two Acts Passed in the Forty Eighth and Forty Ninth Years of His Present Majesty, for Enabling the Commissioners for the Reduction of the National Debt to Grant Life Annuities'. In *The Statutes of the United Kingdom of Great Britain and Ireland, 52 George III. 1812* (London, 1812), 721–39.

'An Act to Regulate the Issue of Bank Notes, and for Giving to the Governor and Company of the Bank of England Certain Privileges for a Limited Period'. In W. N. Welsby and Edward Beavan, *Chitty's Collection of Statutes, with Notes Thereon*, vol. 1 (London, 1865), 214–20.

Anderson, William. *The Iniquity of Banking*, Part II (London, 1797).

Anderson, William. *A Letter to the Right Honourable Lord Althorp* (London, 1832).

Anonymous. 'Article XV. Political Economy and Taxation'. *British Review* (November 1817), 309–3.

Anonymous. *A Second Twelve-Penny Answer to a New (and Five Shillings) Edition of a Three Shillings and Six-Penny Pamphlet* (London, 1801).

Anonymous. *A Twelve-Penny Answer to a Three Shillings and Six-Penny Pamphlet* (London, 1801).

Anonymous. 'Review of *Des Principes de L'Economie Politique et de L'Impôt*'. *The British Critic* (December 1819), 561–78.

Anonymous. 'Review of *Des Principes de L'Economie Politique et de L'Impôt*'. In Terry Peach, ed. *David Ricardo: Critical Responses*, vol. 1 (London: Routledge, 2003), 130–44.

Anonymous. 'Review of *Principles of Political Economy*, Part I'. *The British Critic* 14 (August 1820), 117–38.

Anonymous. 'Review of *Principles of Political Economy*, Part I'. In Terry Peach, ed. *David Ricardo: Critical Responses*, vol. 1 (London: Routledge, 2003), 173–92.

Anonymous. 'Review of *Principles of Political Economy*, Part II'. *The British Critic* 14 (September 1820), 275–93.

Anonymous. 'Review of *Principles of Political Economy*, Part II'. In Terry Peach, ed. *David Ricardo: Critical Responses*, vol. 1 (London: Routledge, 2003), 193–208.

Anonymous. 'Ricardo and the Edinburgh Review'. *Blackwood's Edinburgh Magazine* 4/19 (1818), 58–62.

Anonymous. 'Ricardo and the Edinburgh Review'. In Terry Peach, ed. *David Ricardo: Critical Responses*, vol. 1 (London: Routledge, 2003), 99–107.

Bacon, Francis. 'Novum Organum'. In *The Works of Francis Bacon*. Eds. James Spedding, Robert Ellis, and Dean Denon Heath, vol. 1 (London: Longman & Co., 1858), 70–366.

Bacon, Francis. 'The New Organon'. In *The Works of Francis Bacon*. Eds. James Spedding, Robert Ellis, and Dean Denon Heath, vol. 4 (London: Longman & Co., 1858), 39–248.

Bacon, Francis. 'Of Innovations'. In *The Essays or Counsels, Civil and Moral of Francis Bacon*. Ed. Henry Morley (London, 1883), 113–5.

Barbon, Nicholas. *A Discourse Concerning Coining the New Money Lighter, in Answer to Mr. Lock's Considerations About Raising the Value of Money* (London, 1696).

Baring, Francis. *Observations on the Establishment of the Bank of England* (London, 1797).

Belsham, Thomas. *Elements of the Philosophy of the Human Mind, and of Moral Philosophy* (London, 1801).

Bentham, Jeremy. *Plan of Parliamentary Reform, in the Form of a Catechism, with Reasons for each Article, with an Introduction, Shewing the Necessity of Radical, and the Inadequacy of Moderate, Reform* (London, 1817).

Bentham, Jeremy. *The Book of Fallacies* (London, 1824).

Bentham, Jeremy. 'Place and Time'. In *Selected Writings: Jeremy Bentham*, Ed. Stephen G. Engelmann (New Haven: Yale University Press, 2011), 152–219.

Boase, Henry. *Guineas an Unnecessary and Expensive Encumbrance on Commerce* (London, 1802).

Bosanquet, Charles. *Practical Observations on the Report of the Bullion Committee* (London, 1810).

Boyd, Walter. *A Letter to the Right Honourable William Pitt* (London, 1801).

Boyd, Walter. *A Letter to the Right Honourable William Pitt*, second edition (London, 1801).

[Brougham, Henry]. 'Art. VIII. An Essay on the Principles of Commercial Exchanges&c'. *Edinburgh Review* 9/17 (1807), 111–36.

Burke, Edmund. *Two Letters Addressed to a Member of the Present Parliament, on the Proposals for Peace with the Regicide Directory of France* (London, 1796).

Burke, Edmund. *Writings and Speeches of Edmund Burke*. Eds. Paul Langford, L. G. Mitchell, and William B. Todd, 9 vols. (Oxford: Oxford University Press, 1981–2015).

Burke, Edmund. 'Reflections on the Revolution in France'. In *Revolutionary Writings: Reflections on the Revolution in France and the First Letter on a Regicide Peace*. Ed. Iain Hampsher-Monk (Cambridge: Cambridge University, 2014), 1–251.

Casaubon, Meric. *A Treatise Concerning Enthusiasme, As It is an Effect of Nature: but is Mistaken by Many for Either Divine Inspiration, or Diabolicall Possession, Second Edition: Revised, and Enlarged* (London, 1656).

Chalmers, George. *An Estimate of the Comparative Strength of Great Britain* (London, 1786).

Chalmers, George. *Considerations on Commerce, Bullion and Coin, Circulation and Exchanges; With a View to our Present Circumstances* (London, 1811).

Claeys, Gregory ed. *Political Writings of the 1790s*, 8 vols. (London: Pickering & Chatto, 1995).

[Combe, William]. *Brief Observations on a Late Letter Addressed to the Right Hon. W. Pitt, by W. Boyd* (London, 1801).

Davenant, Charles. 'Of the Use of Political Arithmetic, in all Considerations about the Revenues and Trade'. In *The Political and Commercial Works of that Celebrated Writer Charles D'Avenant*, Ed. Charles Whitworth, vol. 1 (London, 1771), 127–49.

Descartes, René. *Discourse on the Method. Optics, Geometry, and Meteorology*. Trans. Paul J. Olscamp, revised edition (Indianapolis: Hackett Publishing, 2001 [1637]).

Eden, Francis Morton. *State of the Poor, or an History of the Labouring Classes in England, from the Conquest to the Present Period*, 3 vols. (London, 1797).

Empson, William. 'Art. IX. – Principles of Political Economy Considered with a View to their Practical Application. By the Rev. T. R. Malthus, F. R. S. Second Edition. To which is prefixed a Memoir of the Author's Life. 8vo. London, 1836'. *Edinburgh Review* 64/130 (1837), 469–506.

First and Second Reports from the Committee of the House of Lords, Appointed to Inquire into the State of the Growth, Commerce and Consumption of Grain (London, 1814).

Fortune, Thomas. A Concise and Authentic History of the Bank of England, third edition (London, 1802).

Galilei, Galileo. 'On Motion'. In On Motion and On Mechanics. Eds. I. E. Drabkin and Stillman Drake (Madison: University of Wisconsin Press, 1960), 13–114.

Giddy, Davies [Gilbert, Davies]. A Plain Statement of the Bullion Question, in a Letter to a Friend (London, 1811).

Hales, Charles. A Correct Detail of the Finances of this Country (London, 1797).

Hobbes, Thomas. 'Leviathan'. In The Clarendon Edition of the Works of Thomas Hobbes. Ed. Noel Malcolm, vol. 4 (Oxford: Oxford University Press, 2012 [1651]).

[Horner, Francis]. 'Art. III. An Essay on the Theory of Money, and Principles of Commerce'. Edinburgh Review 10/20 (1807), 284–99.

Horner, Francis. 'Report of the Bullion Committee – Mr Horner's Resolution'. HC Deb 06 May 1811 vol. 19 cc798–818.

House of Commons Select Committee on the High Price of Gold Bullion. 'Report of the Select Committee on the High Price of Gold Bullion, 1810'. In Edwin Cannan, ed. The Paper Pound of 1797–1821: A Reprint of the Bullion Report (London: P. S. King and Son, 1919), 1–71.

Hume, David. 'Of the Populousness of Ancient Nations'. In Essays Moral, Political, and Literary. Ed. Eugene F. Miller (Indianapolis: Liberty Fund, 1987), 377–464.

Jackson, Randle. The Speech of Randle Jackson, Esq. Delivered at the General Court of the Bank of England, Held on the 20th of September, 1810, Respecting the Report of the Bullion Committee of the House of Commons (London, 1810).

Keynes, John Maynard. The Collected Writings of John Maynard Keynes. Eds. Elizabeth Johnson and Donald Moggridge, 30 vols. (Cambridge: Cambridge University Press, 1978).

King, Peter. Thoughts on the Restriction of Payments in Specie (London, 1803).

King, Peter. Thoughts on the Effects of the Bank Restrictions (London, 1804).

King, Peter. 'Bank of England Restriction Bill'. In T. C. Hansard, ed. The Parliamentary Debates from the Year 1803 to the Present Time, vol. 1 (London, 1812), 1673–6.

Macaulay, T. B. 'Mill's Essay on Government: Utilitarian Logic and Politics by T. B. Macaulay, Edinburgh Review, no. xcvii'. In Jack Lively and John Rees, eds. Utilitarian Logic and Politics: James Mill's 'Essay on Government', Macaulay's Critique and the Ensuing Debate (Oxford: Clarendon Press, 1978), 97–129.

Mackintosh, James. A Discourse on the Study of the Law of Nature and Nations (London, 1799).

Mackintosh, James. 'Vindiciae Gallicae. Defence of the French Revolution and Its English Admirers Against the Accusations of the Right Honourable Edmund Burke; Including Some Strictures on the Late Production of Mons. De Calonne'. In Vindiciae Gallicae and Other Writings on the French Revolution. Ed. Donald Winch (Indianapolis: Liberty Fund, 2006), 1–166.

Malthus, Thomas Robert. Inquiry into the Nature and Progress of Rent (London, 1815).

Malthus, Thomas Robert. 'Malthus to Ricardo'. The Works and Correspondence of David Ricardo. Ed. Piero Sraffa, vol. 6 (Cambridge: Cambridge University Press, 1951), 40–2.

Malthus, Thomas Robert. 'Malthus to Ricardo'. The Works and Correspondence of David Ricardo. Ed. Piero Sraffa, vol. 6 (Cambridge: Cambridge University Press, 1951), 61–3.

Malthus, Thomas Robert. 'Malthus to Ricardo'. *The Works and Correspondence of David Ricardo*. Ed. Piero Sraffa, vol. 6 (Cambridge: Cambridge University Press, 1951), 181–3.

Malthus, Thomas Robert. 'Malthus to Ricardo'. *The Works and Correspondence of David Ricardo*. Ed. Piero Sraffa, vol. 7 (Cambridge: Cambridge University Press, 1951), 213–5.

Malthus, Thomas Robert. *The Works of Thomas Robert Malthus*. Eds. E. A. Wrigley and David Souden, 8 vols. (London: Routledge, 1986).

Malthus, Thomas Robert. 'An Essay on Foreign Trade'. In *T. R. Malthus: The Unpublished Papers in the Collection of Kanto Gakuen University*. Ed. J. M. Pullen, vol. 2 (Cambridge: Cambridge University Press, 1997), 141–58.

Marx, Karl. *Das Kapital: Kritik der politischen Oekonomie* (Hamburg, 1867).

Marx, Karl. *Capital: A Critique of Political Economy*. Ed. Frederick Engels. Trans. from the Third German Edition, vol. 1 (Moscow: Progress Publishers, 1954).

Marx, Karl. *A Contribution to the Critique of Political Economy*, ed., Maurice Dobb, trans. S. W. Ryazanskaya (Moscow: Progress Publishers, 1970).

McCulloch, J. R. R. *A Discourse on the Rise, Progress, Peculiar Objects and Importance of Political Economy* (Edinburgh, 1824).

McCulloch, J. R. R. *Outlines of Political Economy: Being a Republication of the Article upon that Subject Contained in the Edinburgh Supplement to the Encyclopedia Britannica* (New York, 1825).

McCulloch, J. R. R. *The Literature of Political Economy: A Classified Catalogue of Select Publications in the Different Departments of that Science, with Historical, Critical and Biographical Notices* (Edinburgh, 1845).

Mill, James. 'Mill to Ricardo'. *The Works and Correspondence of David Ricardo*. Ed. Piero Sraffa, vol. 6 (Cambridge: Cambridge University Press, 1951), 337–41.

Mill, James. 'Mill to Ricardo'. *The Works and Correspondence of David Ricardo*. Ed. Piero Sraffa, vol. 7 (Cambridge: Cambridge University Press, 1951), 86–7.

Mill, James. 'Mill to Ricardo'. *The Works and Correspondence of David Ricardo*. Ed. Piero Sraffa, vol. 7 (Cambridge: Cambridge University Press, 1951), 194–9.

Mill, James. 'Mill to Ricardo'. *The Works and Correspondence of David Ricardo*. Ed. Piero Sraffa, vol. 7 (Cambridge: Cambridge University Press, 1951), 210–13.

The Moderator, no. 28 (25 August 1710).

Mushet, Robert. *An Enquiry into the Effect Produced on the National Currency and Rates of Exchange by the Bank Restriction Bill* (London, 1810).

'No. 3, Saturday, March 3, 1711'. In Donald F. Bond, ed. *The Spectator*, vol. 1 (Oxford: Oxford University Press, 1987), 14–7.

[Parnell, Henry]. *The Substance of the Speeches of Sir H. Parnell* (London, 1814).

Petty, William. *Political Arithmetick* (London, 1690).

[Playfair, William]. *European Commerce* (London, 1805).

Plowden, Francis. *A Short History of the British Empire in the Last Twenty Months* (London, 1794).

Potter, William. *The Key of Wealth* (London, 1650).

Pownall, Thomas. 'A Letter from Governor Pownall to Adam Smith'. In *The Glasgow Edition of the Works and Correspondence of Adam Smith*. Eds. E. C. Mossner and I. S. Ross, vol. 6 (Oxford: Oxford University Press, 1977), 337–76.

Price, Richard. 'A Discourse on the Love of our Country'. In *Price: Political Writings*. Ed. D. O. Thomas (Cambridge: Cambridge University Press, 1991), 176–96.

'Report from the Select Committee Appointed to Enquire into the Corn Trade of the United Kingdom, May 11 1813'. In *The Parliamentary Debates of the Year 1803 to the Present Time*, vol. 25 (London, 1813), lv–c.

Ricardo, David. *On the Principles of Political Economy, and Taxation* (London, 1817).

Ricardo, David. *The Works and Correspondence of David Ricardo*. Ed. Piero Sraffa, 11 vols. (Cambridge: Cambridge University Press, 1951).

Rose, George. *The Speech of the Right Hon. George Rose, in the House of Commons* (London, 1814).

Rose, George. 'Report of the Bullion Committee – Mr Horner's Resolution'. HC Deb 06 May 1811 vol. 19 cc798–818.

Scott, William. *Some Observations upon the Argument Drawn by Mister Huskisson on the Bullion Committee* (London, 1811).

Sinclair, John. *The History of the Public Revenue of the British Empire*, 3 vols. (London, 1785–1790).

Sinclair, John. *Letters Written to the Governor and Directors of the Bank of England* (London, 1797).

Sinclair, John. *Observations on the Report of the Bullion Committee* (London, 1810).

The Society for Bettering the Condition and Increasing the Comforts of the Poor. 'Prefatory Introduction to the Second Volume'. In *The Reports of the Society for Bettering the Condition and Increasing the Comforts of the Poor*, vol. 2, part 1 (London, 1800), 1–30.

Smith, Adam. *The Glasgow Edition of the Works and Correspondence of Adam Smith*. Eds. R. H. Campbell, D. D. Raphael, and A. S. Skinner, 6 vols. (Oxford: Oxford University Press, 1977–1987).

Southey, Robert. 'Essay V. On the State of the Poor and the Means Pursued by the Society for Bettering their Condition. 1816'. In *Essays, Moral and Political*, vol. 1 (London, 1832), 159–250.

Steuart, James. *An Inquiry into the Principles of Political Oeconomy*, 2 vols. (London, 1767).

Stewart, Dugald. *Elements of the Philosophy of the Human Mind*, 2 vols. (London and Edinburgh, 1792 and 1814).

Stewart, Dugald. 'Lectures on Political Economy'. *The Collected Works of Dugald Stewart*. Ed. William Hamilton, vols. 8 and 9 (Edinburgh: Thomas Constable and Co, 1855–1856).

Stewart, Dugald. 'Memoir of Dugald Stewart'. In *The Collected Works of Dugald Stewart*. Ed. William Hamilton, vol. 10 (Edinburgh: Thomas Constable and Co, 1858), i–cxv.

Stewart, Dugald. 'Account of the Life and Writings of Adam Smith'. In *The Glasgow Edition of the Works and Correspondence of Adam Smith*. Ed. I. S. Ross, vol. 3 (Oxford: Oxford University Press, 1980), 264–353.

Surr, T. S. *Refutation of Certain Misrepresentations Relative to the Nature and Influence of Bank Notes* (London, 1801).

'Text of the Report of 1804'. In F. W. Fetter, ed. *The Irish Pound, 1797–1826: A Reprint of the Report of the Committee of 1804 of the British House of Commons on the Condition of the Irish Currency* (London: George Allen and Unwin, 1955), 63–87.

Thornton, Henry. *An Enquiry into the Nature and Effects of the Paper Credit of Great Britain* (London, 1802).

Torrens, Robert. *An Essay on the External Corn Trade* (London, 1815).

Torrens, Robert. *An Essay on the External Corn Trade* (London, 1826).

Trower, Hutches. 'Trower to Ricardo'. In *The Works and Correspondence of David Ricardo*. Ed. Piero Sraffa, vol. 7 (Cambridge: Cambridge University Press, 1951), 255–8.

Turgot, A. R. J. *Réfléxions sur la Formation et la Distribution des Richesses* (Paris, 1788).

[Vansittart, Nicholas]. *Outlines of a Plan of Finance; Proposed to be Submitted to Parliament* (London, 1813).

Watts, Isaac. *The Improvement of the Mind, or a Supplement to the Art of Logic* (London, 1792).

Young, Arthur. 'An Enquiry into the Progressive Value of Money'. *Annals of Agriculture* 46/270 (1812).

Young, Arthur. 'An Enquiry into the Rise of Prices in Europe'. *Annals of Agriculture* 46/271 (1815).

Secondary Sources

Aaslestad, Katherine B., and Joor, Johan. 'Introduction'. In Katherine B. Aaslestad and Johan Joor, eds. *Revisiting Napoleon's Continental System: Local, Regional and European Experience* (New York: Palgrave Macmillan, 2014), 1–24.

Abel, Richard L. 'The Decline of Professionalism'? *Modern Law Review* 49/1 (1986), 1–41.

Aldrich, John. 'The Discovery of Comparative Advantage'. *Journal of the History of Economic Thought* 26/3 (2004), 379–99.

Anstey, Peter R. 'Experimental versus Speculative Natural Philosophy'. In Peter R. Anstey and John A. Schuster, eds. *The Science of Nature in the Seventeenth Century: Patterns of Change in Early Modern Natural Philosophy* (Dordrecht: Springer, 2005), 215–42.

Barker, G. F. R. 'Parnell, Henry Brooke, first Baron Congleton (1776–1842), politician'. *Oxford Dictionary of National Biography* (2004). http://www.oxforddnb.com/view/10.1093/ref:odnb/9780198614128.001.0001/odnb-9780198614128-e-21386.

Barnes, Donald Grove. *A History of the English Corn Laws: From 1660–1846* (London: George Routledge & Sons, 1930).

Bashford, Alison, and Chaplin, Joyce E. *The New Worlds of Thomas Robert Malthus: Rereading the Principle of Population* (Princeton: Princeton University Press, 2016).

Beynon, Graham. *Isaac Watts: Reason, Passion and the Revival of Religion* (London: Bloomsbury, 2016).

Blaug, Mark. 'On the Historiography of Economics'. *Journal of the History of Economic Thought* 12/1 (1990), 27–37.

Boumans, Marcel. *How Economists Model the World into Numbers* (London: Routledge, 2004).

Brewer, John. *The Sinews of Power: War, Money and the English State, 1688–1783* (Cambridge, Mass.: Harvard University Press, 1990).

Brooks, G. P. 'Isaac Watts and the Uses of a Knowledge of Astronomy: "He Taught the Art of Reasoning and the Science of the Stars"'. *Vistas in Astronomy* 36/3 (1993), 295–310.

Cannan, Edwin. 'Introduction'. In Edwin Cannan, ed. *The Paper Pound of 1797–1821: A Reprint of the Bullion Report* (London: P. S. King and Son, 1919), vii–xlix.

Carnall, Geoffrey. *Robert Southey and His Age: The Development of a Conservative Mind* (Oxford: Oxford University Press, 1960).

Carretta, Vincent. 'Combe [formerly Combes], William (1742–1823), Writer and Literary Imitator'. *Oxford Dictionary of National Biography* (2008). https://www.oxforddnb.com/view/10.1093/ref:odnb/9780198614128.001.0001/odnb-9780198614128-e-6022.

Cello, Lorenzo. 'The Legitimacy of International Interventions in Vattel's *The Law of Nations*'. *Global Intellectual History* 2/2 (2017), 105–23.

Chick, Victoria. *Macroeconomics After Keynes: A Reconsideration of the General Theory* (Cambridge, Mass.: MIT Press, 1983).

Claeys, Gregory. *The French Revolution Debate in Britain: The Origins of Modern Politics* (Basingstoke: Palgrave Macmillan Education UK, 2007).

Clapham, John. *The Bank of England: A History*, 2 vols. (Cambridge: Cambridge University Press, 1944).

Clark, J. C. D. *English Society, 1660–1832: Religion, Ideology and Politics During the Ancien Regime* (Cambridge: Cambridge University Press, 2000).

Collini, Stefan, Winch, Donald, and Burrow, John. *That Noble Science of Politics: A Study in Nineteenth-Century Intellectual History* (Cambridge: Cambridge University Press, 1983).

Condren, Conal. *The Status and Appraisal of Classic Texts* (Princeton: Princeton University Press, 1985).

Condren, Conal. *The Language of Politics in Seventeenth-Century England* (New York: Palgrave Macmillan, 1994).

Condren, Conal. 'Political Theory and the Problem of Anachronism'. In Andrew Vincent, ed. *Political Theory: Tradition and Diversity* (Cambridge: Cambridge University Press, 1997), 45–66.

Condren, Conal. *Argument and Authority in Early Modern England: The Presupposition of Oaths and Offices* (Cambridge: Cambridge University Press, 2006).

Condren, Conal. *Political Vocabularies: Word Change and the Nature of Politics* (Rochester: University of Rochester Press, 2017).

Condren, Conal. 'The History of Political Thought as Secular Genealogy: The Case of Liberty in Early Modern England'. *Intellectual History Review* 27/1 (2017), 115–33.

Connell, Philip. *Romanticism, Economics and the Question of 'Culture'* (Oxford: Oxford University Press, 2005).

Cookson, J. E. *The Friends of Peace: Anti-War Liberalism in England, 1793–1815* (Cambridge: Cambridge University Press, 1982).

Cope, S. R. *Walter Boyd: A Merchant Banker in the Age of Napoleon* (Gloucester: Alan Sutton, 1983).

Corsi, Marcella, Kregel, Jan, and D'Ippoliti, Carlo eds. *Classical Economics Today: Essays in Honor of Alessandro Roncaglia* (London: Anthem Press, 2018).

Corsi, Pietro. 'The Heritage of Dugald Stewart: Oxford Philosophy and Method of Political Economy'. *Nuncius* 2/2 (1987), 89–144.

Cremaschi, Sergio. 'Ricardo and the Utilitarians'. *The European Journal of the History of Economic Thought* 11/3 (2004), 377–403.

Cremaschi, Sergio. *Utilitarianism and Malthus' Virtue Ethics: Respectable, Virtuous and Happy* (London: Routledge, 2014).

Cremaschi, Sergio. 'Belsham, Thomas and Ricardo'. In Heinz D. Kurz and Neri Salvadori, eds. *The Elgar Companion to David Ricardo* (Cheltenham: Edward Elgar, 2015).

Cremaschi, Sergio. 'Theological Themes in Ricardo's Papers and Correspondence'. *The European Journal of the History of Economic Thought* 24/4 (2017), 784–808.

Cremaschi, Sergio, and Dascal, Marcelo. 'Malthus and Ricardo on Economic Methodology'. *History of Political Economy* 28/3 (1996), 475–511.

Crowley, John E. 'Neo-Mercantilism and *The Wealth of Nations*: British Commercial Policy after the American Revolution'. *Historical Journal* 33/2 (1990), 339–60.

Dacome, Lucia. 'Noting the Mind: Commonplace Books and the Pursuit of the Self in the Eighteenth Century'. *Journal of the History of Ideas* 65/4 (2004), 603–25.

Deane, Seamus. *The French Revolution and Enlightenment in England, 1789–1832* (Cambridge, Mass.: Harvard University Press, 1988).

Deleplace, Ghislain. *Ricardo on Money: A Reappraisal* (London: Routledge, 2017).

Dickinson, H. T. *Liberty and Property: Political Ideology in Eighteenth-Century Britain* (London: Weidenfeld and Nicolson, 1978).

Duffy, Ian P. H. 'The Discount Policy of the Bank of England During the Suspension of Cash Payments, 1797–1821'. *The Economic History Review* 35/1 (1982), 67–82.

Fetter, F. W. 'The Bullion Report Reexamined'. *The Quarterly Journal of Economics* 56/4 (1942), 655–65.

Fetter, F. W. 'The Politics of the Bullion Report'. *Economica* 26/102 (1959), 99–120.

Fetter, F. W. *Development of British Monetary Orthodoxy, 1797–1875* (Cambridge: Cambridge University Press, 1965).

Fetter, F. W. 'Introduction'. In F. W. Fetter, ed. *The Irish Pound, 1797–1826: A Reprint of the Report of the Committee of 1804 of the British House of Commons on the Condition of the Irish Currency* (London: George Allen and Unwin, 1955), 9–62.

Fontana, Biancamaria. *Rethinking the Politics of Commercial Society: The Edinburgh Review 1802–1832* (Cambridge: Cambridge University Press, 1985).

Foucault, Michel. *Order of Things* (London: Routledge, 2002).

Gallie, W. B. *Philosophy and the Historical Understanding* (London: Chatto and Windus, 1964).

Gambles, Anna. *Protection and Politics: Conservative Economic Discourse, 1815–1852* (Woodbridge: Boydell, 1999).

Gaukroger, Stephen. *The Emergence of a Scientific Culture: Science and the Shaping of Modernity 1210–1685* (Oxford: Oxford University Press, 2006).

Gaul, Michael. 'Robert Torrens' Model of Trade and Growth: Genesis and Implications for the Discovery of Comparative Advantage'. *The European Journal of the History of Economic Thought* 28/2 (2021), 201–28.

Gehrke, Christian. 'Ricardo's Discovery of Comparative Advantage Revisited: A Critique of Ruffin's Account'. *The European Journal of the History of Economic Thought* 22/5 (2015), 791–817.

Gehrke, Christian. 'British Classical Political Economy'. In Gilbert Faccarello and Heinz D. Kurz, eds. *Handbook on the History of Economic Analysis*, vol. 2 (Cheltenham: Edward Elgar Publishing, 2016), 125–49.

Ginzburg, Carlo, and Biasiori, Lucio, eds. *A Historical Approach to Casuistry: Norms and Exceptions in a Comparative Perspective* (London: Bloomsbury, 2018).

Gould, Stephen Jay. 'Piltdown Revisited'. In *The Panda's Thumb: More Reflections in Natural History* (New York: W. W. Norton and Company, 1980), 108–24.

Haakonssen, Knud. *The Science of a Legislator: The Natural Jurisprudence of David Hume and Adam Smith* (Cambridge: Cambridge University Press, 1981).

Haakonssen, Knud. *Natural Law and Moral Philosophy: From Grotius to the Scottish Enlightenment* (Cambridge: Cambridge University Press, 1996).

Haakonssen, Knud. 'The Idea of Early Modern Philosophy'. In J. B. Schneewind, ed. *Teaching New Histories of Philosophy: Proceedings of a Conference* (Princeton: University Center for Human Values, 2004), 99–121.

Harrison, Peter. 'Experimental Religion and Experimental Science in Early Modern England'. *Intellectual History Review* 21/4 (2011), 413–33.

Harrison, Peter. 'Adam Smith and the History of the Invisible Hand'. *Journal of the History of Ideas* 72/1 (2011), 29–49.

Hayek, F. A. 'Henry Thornton (1760–1815)'. In *The Collected Works of F. A. Hayek*. Eds. W. W. Bartley III and Stephen Kresge, vol. 3 (Indianapolis: Liberty Fund, 2009), 295–344.

Heyd, Michael. *'Be Sober and Reasonable': The Critique of Enthusiasm in the Seventeenth and Early Eighteenth Centuries* (Leiden: Brill, 1995).

Hilton, Boyd. *Corn, Cash, Commerce: The Economic Policies of the Tory Governments 1815–1830* (Oxford: Oxford University Press, 1977).

Hilton, Boyd. 'Peel: A Reappraisal'. *The Historical Journal* 22/3 (1979), 585–614.

Hilton, Boyd. *A Mad, Bad, and Dangerous People? England 1783–1846* (Oxford: Oxford University Press, 2006).

Hollander, Jacob H. 'The Development of the Theory of Money from Adam Smith to David Ricardo'. *The Quarterly Journal of Economics* 25/3 (1911), 429–70.

Hollander, Samuel. *The Economics of David Ricardo* (London: Heinemann, 1979).

Hollander, Samuel. 'Malthus's Abandonment of Agricultural Protectionism: A Discovery in the History of Economic Thought'. *The American Economic Review* 82/3 (1992), 650–9.

Hollander, Samuel. *The Economics of Thomas Robert Malthus* (Toronto: University of Toronto Press, 1997).

Hollander, Samuel. '"Classical Economics": A Reification Wrapped in an Anachronism'? In Evelyn L. Forget and Sandra Peart, eds. *Reflections on the Classical Canon in Economics: Essays in Honor of Samuel Hollander* (London: Routledge, 2000), 7–26.

Hont, Istvan. *Jealousy of Trade: International Competition and the Nation-State in Historical Perspective* (Cambridge, Mass.: Harvard University Press, 2005).

Hoppit, Julian. *Britain's Political Economies: Parliament and Economic Life, 1660–1800* (Cambridge: Cambridge University Press, 2017).

Horsefield, J. K. 'The Origins of the Bank Charter Act, 1844'. *Economica* 11/44 (1944), 180–9.

Hunter, Ian. *Rival Enlightenments: Civil and Metaphysical Philosophy in Early Modern Germany* (Cambridge: Cambridge University Press, 2001).

Hunter, Ian. *The Secularisation of the Confessional State: The Political Thought of Christian Thomasius* (Cambridge: Cambridge University Press, 2007).

Hunter, Ian. 'Kant and Vattel in Context: Cosmopolitan Philosophy and Diplomatic Casuistry'. *History of European Ideas* 39/4 (2013), 477–502.

Hunter, Ian. 'Religious Freedom in Early Modern Germany: Theology, Philosophy, and Legal Casuistry'. *South Atlantic Quarterly* 113/1 (2014), 37–62.

Hunter, Ian. 'The Contest over Context in Intellectual History'. *History & Theory* 58/2 (2019), 185–209.

Jacyna, L. S. *Philosophic Whigs: Medicine, Science and Citizenship in Edinburgh, 1789–1848* (London: Routledge, 1994).

Jones, Matthew L. 'Descartes's Geometry as Spiritual Exercise'. *Critical Inquiry* 28/1 (2001), 40–71.

Jonsen, Alfred R., and Toulmin, Stephen. *The Abuse of Casuistry: A History of Moral Reasoning* (Berkeley: University of California Press, 1988).

Kaldor, Nicholas. 'The New Monetarism'. *Lloyds Bank Review* 97/1 (1970), 1–18.

Kates, Steven. *Defending the History of Economic Thought* (Cheltenham: Edward Elgar, 2013).

Kates, Steven. *Classical Economic Theory and the Modern Economy* (Cheltenham: Edward Elgar, 2020).

Kearns, David, and Walter, Ryan. 'Office, Political Theory, and the Political Theorist'. *The Historical Journal* 63/2 (2020), 317–37.

Keynes, John Neville. *The Scope and Method of Political Economy* (London: Macmillan, 1891).

King, John E. *David Ricardo* (New York: Palgrave Macmillan, 2013).

Kurz, Heinz D. 'The Surplus Interpretation of the Classical Economists'. In Warren J. Samuels, Jeff E. Biddle, John B. Davis, eds. *A Companion to the History of Economic Thought* (Malden: Blackwell Publishing, 2003), 167–83.

Laslett, Peter. 'John Locke, the Great Recoinage, and the Origins of the Board of Trade: 1695–1698'. In John W. Yolton, ed. *John Locke: Problems and Perspectives. A Collection of New Essays* (Cambridge: Cambridge University Press, 1969), 137–64.

Lee, Grace Lawless. *The Story of the Bosanquets* (Canterbury: Phillimore, 1966).

Lucas, Paul. *Essays in the Margins of Blackstone's Commentaries* (unpublished PhD Thesis, Princeton University, Princeton, 1962).

Lucas, Paul. 'II. On Edmund Burke's Doctrine of Prescription; Or, an Appeal from the New to the Old Lawyers'. *The Historical Journal* 11/1 (1968), 35–63.

Mandler, Peter. 'Tories and Paupers: Christian Political Economy and the Making of the New Poor Law'. *The Historical Journal* 33/1 (1990), 81–103.

De Marchi, N. B., and Sturges, R. P. 'Malthus and Ricardo's Inductivist Critics: Four Letters to William Whewell'. *Economica* 40/160 (1973), 379–93.

Marcuzzo, Maria Cristina. 'Ghislain Deleplace, *Ricardo on Money. A Reappraisal*'. *Oeconomia* 8/1 (2018), 119–24.

Mayhew, Robert J. *Malthus: The Life and Legacies of an Untimely Prophet* (Cambridge, Mass.: Harvard University Press, 2014).

Mitchell, B. R. *British Historical Statistics* (Cambridge: Cambridge University Press, 1988).

Mitchell, L. G. *Charles James Fox* (Oxford: Oxford University Press, 1992).

Morgan, Mary. *The World in the Model: How Economists Work and Think* (Cambridge, 2012).

Moscati, Ivan. 'More Economics, Please: We're Historians of Economics'. *Journal of the History of Economic Thought* 30/1 (2008), 85–92.

Nakazawa, Nobuhiko. 'Malthus's Political Views in 1798: A "Foxite" Whig'? *History of Economics Review* 56/1 (2012), 14–28.

O'Brien, D. P. *The Classical Economists Revisited* (Princeton: Princeton University Press, 2004).

O'Flaherty, Niall. *Utilitarianism in the Age of Enlightenment: The Moral and Political Thought of William Paley* (Cambridge: University Press, 2018).

O'Gorman, Frank. *The Whig Party and the French Revolution* (New York: Macmillan, 1967).

O'Shaughnessy, Andrew J. 'Bosanquet, Charles (1769–1850), Merchant and Writer'. *Oxford Dictionary of National Biography* (2008). http://www.oxforddnb.com/view/10.1093/ref:odnb/9780198614128.001.0001/odnb-9780198614128-e-2927.

Olscamp, Paul J. 'Introduction'. In René Descartes, *Discourse on the Method. Optics, Geometry, and Meteorology*. Trans. Paul J. Olscamp, revised edition (Indianapolis: Hackett Publishing, 2001), ix–xxxvi.

Olson, Richard S. *Scottish Philosophy and British Physics, 1740–1870: A Study in the Foundations of the Victorian Scientific Style* (Princeton: Princeton University Press, 2015).

O'Neill, Daniel I. *The Burke-Wollstonecraft Debate: Savagery, Civilization, and Democracy* (University Park: Pennsylvania State University Press, 2007).

Ong, Walter J. 'Ramist Method and the Commercial Mind'. *Studies in the Renaissance* 8 (1961), 155–172.

Peach, Terry. *Interpreting Ricardo* (Cambridge: Cambridge University Press, 1993).

Peach, Terry. 'On *Interpreting Ricardo*: A Reply to Sraffians'. *Cambridge Journal of Economics* 22/5 (1998), 597–616.

Peach, Terry. 'Adam Smith's "Optimistic Deism", the Invisible Hand of Providence, and the Unhappiness of Nations'. *History of Political Economy* 46/1 (2014), 55–83.

Phillipson, Nicholas. 'The Scottish Enlightenment'. In Roy Porter and Mikuláš Teich, eds. *The Enlightenment in National Context* (Cambridge: Cambridge University Press, 1981), 19–40.

Phillipson, Nicholas. 'The Pursuit of Virtue in Scottish University Education: Dugald Stewart and Scottish Moral Philosophy in the Enlightenment'. In Nicholas Phillipson, ed. *Universities, Society, and the Future: A Conference Held on the 400th Anniversary of the University of Edinburgh* (Edinburgh: Edinburgh University Press, 1983), 82–101.

Philp, Mark. *Reforming Ideas in Britain: Politics and Language in the Shadow of the French Revolution, 1789–1815* (Cambridge: Cambridge University Press, 2014).

Pincus, Steven. *1688: The First Modern Revolution* (New Haven: Yale University Press, 2011).

Plassart, Anna. *The Scottish Enlightenment and the French Revolution* (Cambridge: Cambridge University Press, 2015).

Pocock, J. G. A. *The Ancient Constitution and the Feudal Law: English Historical Thought in the Seventeenth Century* (Cambridge: Cambridge University Press, 1957).

Pocock, J. G. A. *The Machiavellian Moment: Florentine Political Thought and the Atlantic Republican Tradition* (Princeton: Princeton University Press, 1975).

Pocock, J. G. A. *Virtue, Commerce, and History: Essays on Political Thought and History, Chiefly in the Eighteenth Century* (Cambridge: Cambridge University Press, 1985).

Pocock, J. G. A. 'Enthusiasm: The Antiself of Enlightenment'. *Huntington Library Quarterly* 60/1–2 (1997), 7–28.

Pocock, J. G. A. 'Enlightenment and Counter-Enlightenment, Revolution and Counter-Revolution; A Eurosceptical Enquiry'. *History of Political Thought* 20/1 (1999), 125–39.

Pocock, J. G. A. *Political Thought and History: Essays on Theory and Method* (Cambridge: Cambridge University Press, 2009).

Poovey, Mary. *A History of the Modern Fact: Problems of Knowledge in the Sciences of Wealth and Society* (Chicago: University of Chicago Press, 1998).

Prochaska, F. K. 'English State Trials in the 1790s: A Case Study'. *Journal of British Studies* 13/1 (1973), 63–82.

Pullen, J. M. 'Malthus on the Doctrine of Proportions and the Concept of the Optimum'. *Australian Economic Papers* 21/39 (1982), 270–85.

Pullen, J. M. 'William Anderson (fl. 1797–1832), on Banking, the Money Supply, and Public Expenditure: A Forgotten Interventionist'. *History of Political Economy* 19/3 (1987), 359–85.

Pullen, J. M. 'Malthus on Agricultural Protection: An Alternative View'. *History of Political Economy* 27/3 (1995), 517–29.

Pullen, J. M. 'Did Ricardo Really Have a Law of Comparative Advantage? A Comparison of Ricardo's Version and the Modern Version'. *History of Economics Review* 44/1 (2006), 59–75.

Pullen, J. M. 'Further Details of the Life and Financial Affairs of T. R. Malthus'. *History of Economics Review* 57/1 (2013), 16–31.

Pullen, J. M. 'Variables and Constants in the Theology of T. R. Malthus'. *History of Economics Review* 63/1 (2016), 21–32.

Pullen, J. M. 'Malthus on Causality'. *The European Journal of the History of Economic Thought* 23/3 (2016), 349–77.

Rivers, Isabel. 'Watts, Isaac (1674–1748), Independent Minister and Writer'. *Oxford Dictionary of National Biography* (2004). https://www.oxforddnb.com/view/10.1093/ref:odnb/9780198614128.001.0001/odnb-9780198614128-e-28888.

Rothschild, Emma. *Economic Sentiments: Adam Smith, Condorcet, and the Enlightenment* (Cambridge, Mass.: Harvard University Press, 2002).

Ruffin, Roy J. 'David Ricardo's Discovery of Comparative Advantage'. *History of Political Economy* 34/4 (2002), 727–48.

Samuelson, Paul A. 'The Canonical Classical Model of Political Economy'. *Journal of Economic Literature*, 16/4 (1978), 1415–34.

Schumpeter, Joseph A. *History of Economic Analysis* (Oxford: Oxford University Press, 1994 [1954]).

Sher, Richard B. *Church and University in the Scottish Enlightenment: The Moderate Literati of Edinburgh* (Edinburgh: Edinburgh University Press, 1985).

Shin, Hiroki. 'Paper Money, the Nation, and the Suspension of Cash Payments in 1797'. *The Historical Journal* 58/2 (2015), 415–42.

Skinner, Quentin. 'Meaning and Understanding in the History of Ideas'. *History and Theory* 8/1 (1969), 3–53.

Skinner, Quentin. *Visions of Politics*, 3 vols. (Cambridge: Cambridge University Press, 2002).

Skjönsberg, Max. 'The History of Political Thought and Parliamentary History in the Eighteenth and Nineteenth Centuries'. *The Historical Journal* 64/2 (2021), 501–13.

Smart, William. *Economic Annals of the Nineteenth Century, 1801–1820* (London: Macmillan and Co., 1910).

Sraffa, Piero. 'Introduction'. In *The Works and Correspondence of David Ricardo*. Ed. Piero Sraffa, vol. 1 (Cambridge: Cambridge University Press, 1951), xiii–lxii.

Sraffa, Piero. 'Introduction'. In *The Works and Correspondence of David Ricardo*. Ed. Piero Sraffa, vol. 2 (Cambridge: Cambridge University Press, 1951), vii–xviii.

Sraffa, Piero. 'Note on the Bullion Essays'. In *The Works and Correspondence of David Ricardo*. Ed. Piero Sraffa, vol. 3 (Cambridge: Cambridge University Press, 1951), 1–12.

Sraffa, Piero. 'Note on "Absolute Value and Exchangeable Value"'. In *The Works and Correspondence of David Ricardo*. Ed. Piero Sraffa, vol. 4 (Cambridge: Cambridge University Press, 1951), 358–60.

Sraffa, Piero. *Production of Commodities by Means of Commodities: Prelude to a Critique of Economic Theory* (Cambridge: Cambridge University Press, 1960).

Stigler, George J. 'Does Economics Have a Useful Past'? *History of Political Economy* 1/2 (1969), 217–30.

Tribe, Keith. *Land, Labour and Economic Discourse* (London: Routledge and Keegan Paul, 1978).

Tribe, Keith. 'Ricardian Histories'. *Economy and Society* 10/4 (1981), 451–66.

Tribe, Keith. *Governing Economy: The Reformation of German Economic Discourse, 1750–1840* (Cambridge: Cambridge University Press, 1988).

Tribe, Keith. 'Professors Malthus and Jones: Political Economy at the East India College 1806–1858'. *The European Journal of History and Economic Thought* 2/2 (1995), 327–54.

Tribe, Keith. 'The Cambridge Economics Tripos 1903–55 and the Training of Economists'. *The Manchester School* 68/2 (2000), 222–48.

Tribe, Keith. 'The Modern Fact in Theory and in Practice'. *History Workshop Journal* 52 (2001), 266–72.

Tribe, Keith. 'Economic Societies in Great Britain and Ireland'. In Massimo M. Augello and Marco E. L. Guidi, eds. *The Spread of Political Economy and the Professionalisation of Economists: Economic Societies in Europe, America and Japan in the Nineteenth Century* (London: Routledge, 2001), 32–52.

Tribe, Keith. 'Political Economy and the Science of Economics in Victorian Britain'. In Martin Daunton, ed. *The Organisation of Knowledge in Victorian Britain* (Oxford: Oxford University Press, 2005), 115–37.

Tribe, Keith. *The Economy of the Word: Language, History, and Economics* (Oxford: Oxford University Press, 2015).

Tribe, Keith. 'Donald Winch 1935–2017'. *The European Journal of the History of Economic Thought* 25/1 (2018), 196–201.

Tully, James. 'Editor's Introduction'. In James Tully, ed. *Samuel Pufendorf, On the Duty of Man and Citizen According to Natural Law* (Cambridge: Cambridge University Press, 1991), xiv–xl.

Vivo, Giancarlo de. 'David Ricardo's *An Essay on the Effects of a Low Price of Corn on the Profits of Stock*'. *History of Economics Review* 62/1 (2015), 76–97.

Walter, Ryan. 'Slingsby Bethel's Analysis of State Interests'. *History of European Ideas* 41/4 (2015), 489–506.

Walter, Ryan. 'Adam Smith's Free Trade Casuistry'. *Global Intellectual History* 1/1 (2016), 61–82.

Walter, Ryan. 'The Enthusiasm of David Ricardo'. *Modern Intellectual History* 15/2 (2018), 381–409.

Walter, Ryan. 'Defending Political Theory after Burke: Stewart's Intellectual Disciplines and the Demotion of Practice'. *Journal of the History of Ideas* 80/3 (2019), 387–408.

Walter, Ryan. 'Malthus's Principle of Population in Britain: Restatement and Antiquation'. In Gilbert Faccarello, Masashi Izumo, and Hiromi Morishita, eds. *Malthus Across Nations: The Reception of Thomas Robert Malthus in Europe, America and Japan* (Cheltenham: Edward Elgar, 2020), 18–52.

Walter, Ryan. 'Conservative Politics and Laissez Faire Economics? The Burke-Smith Problem Revisited'. *Critical Historical Studies* 7/2 (2020), 271–95.

Walter, Ryan. 'Malthus's Sacred History: Outflanking Civil History in the Late Enlightenment'. *Rethinking History* (forthcoming).

Waterman, A. M. C. *Revolution, Economics and Religion: Christian Political Economy, 1798–1833* (Cambridge: Cambridge University Press, 1991).

Waterman, A. M. C. 'Mathematical Modelling as an Exegetical Tool: Rational Reconstruction'. In Warren J. Samuels, Jeff E. Biddle, and John B. Davis, eds. *A Companion to the History of Economic Thought* (Malden: Blackwell Publishing, 2003), 553–70.

Waterman, A. M. C. *Political Economy and Christian Theology Since the Enlightenment: Essays in Intellectual History* (Basingstoke: Palgrave Macmillan, 2004).

Winch, Donald. 'James Mill and David Ricardo'. In Donald Winch, ed. *James Mill: Selected Economic Writings* (Edinburgh: Scottish Economic Society, 1966), 179–202.

Winch, Donald. *Adam Smith's Politics: An Essay in Historiographic Revision* (Cambridge: Cambridge University Press, 1978).

Winch, Donald. 'Robert Malthus: Christian Moral Scientist, Arch-Demoralizer or Implicit Secular Utilitarian'? *Utilitas* 5/2 (1993), 239–52.

Winch, Donald. *Riches and Poverty: An Intellectual History of Political Economy in Britain, 1750–1834* (Cambridge: Cambridge University Press, 1996).

Winch, Donald. 'Introduction'. In Donald Winch, ed. *Vindiciae Gallicae and Other Writings on the French Revolution* (Indianapolis: Liberty Fund, 2006), ix–xviii.

Yeo, Richard R. 'Scientific Method and the Rhetoric of Science in Britain, 1830–1917'. In John A. Schuster and Richard R. Yeo, eds. *The Politics and Rhetoric of Scientific Method: Historical Studies* (Dordrecht: D. Reidel, 1986), 259–97.

Yeo, Richard R. 'William Whewell's Philosophy of Knowledge and Its Reception'. In Menachem Fisch and Simon Schaffer, eds. *William Whewell: A Composite Portrait* (Oxford: Oxford University Press, 1991), 175–99.

Index